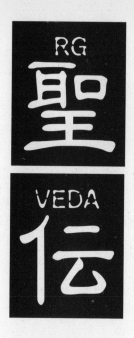

RG 聖
VEDA 伝

VOLUME 1

BY
CLAMP

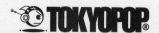

HAMBURG // LONDON // LOS ANGELES // TOKYO

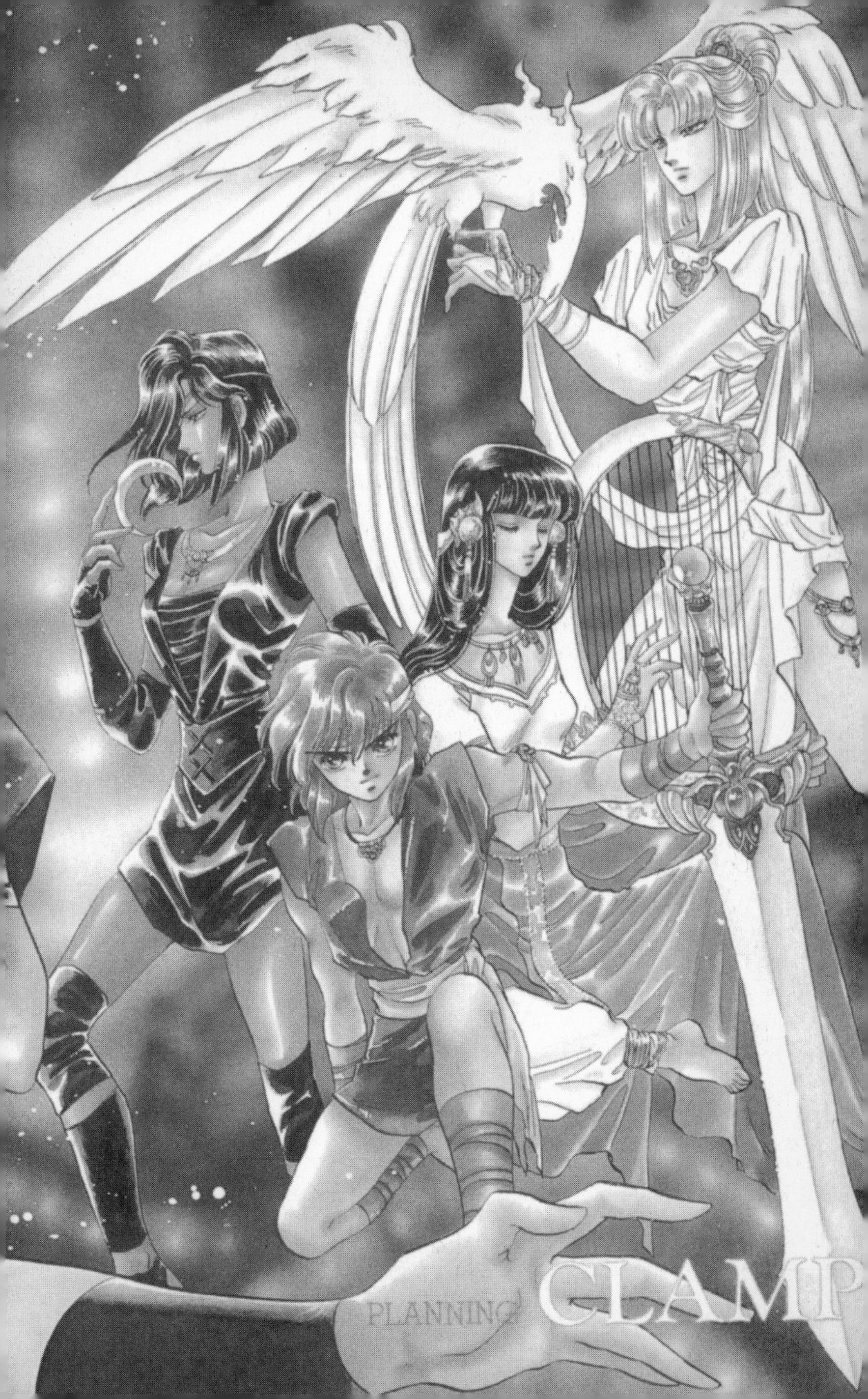
PLANNING CLAMP

R G VEDA

聖伝

第一巻

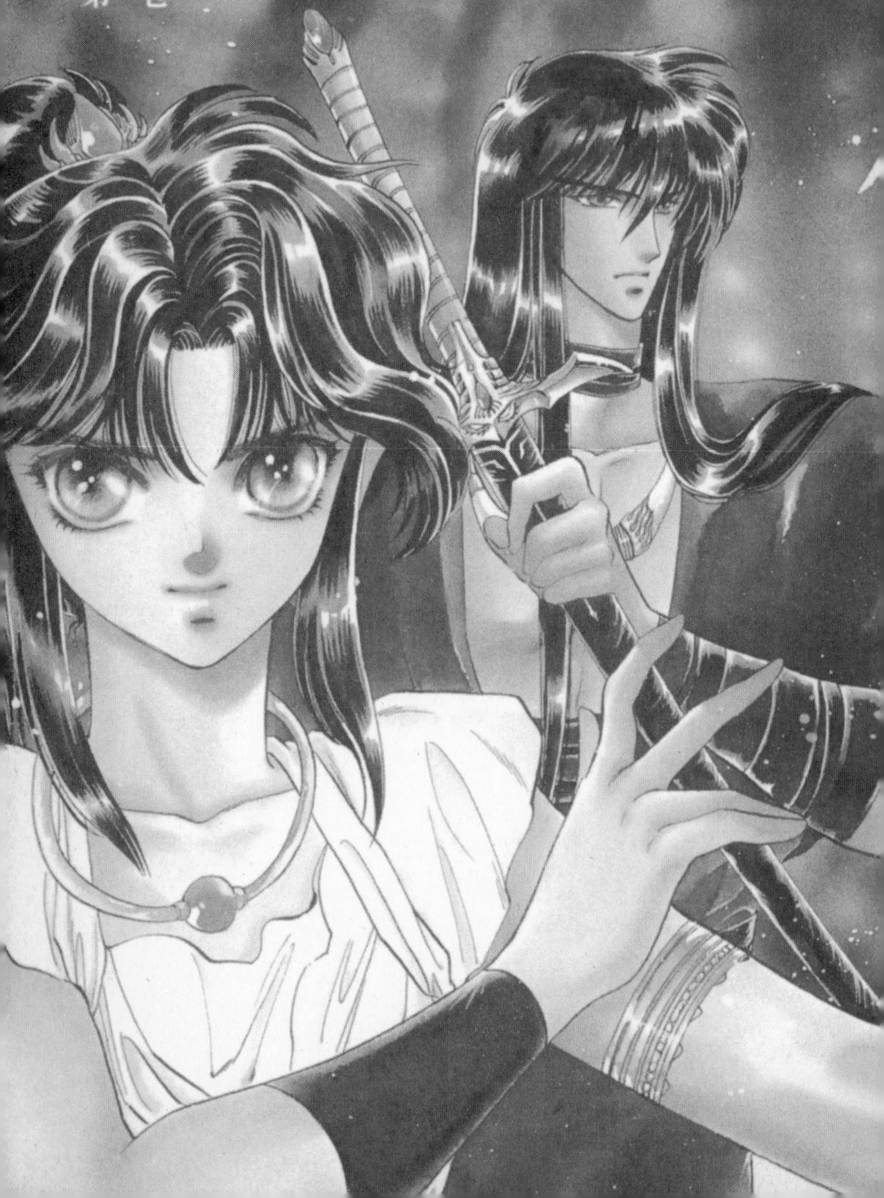

HOSHI GA NAGARERU

YOU WILL BE THE SCHISM THAT SPLITS HEAVEN.

Book Designer
大川七瀬
NANASE OHKAWA

Director
もこなあぱぱ
MOKONA APAPA

Short Comic
猫井みっく
MICK NEKOI

Art Assistants
猫井みっく
MICK NEKOI

五十嵐さつき
SATSUKI IGARASHI

CLAMP MEMBERS

Main

CLAMP MEMBERS

STORY
大川七瀬
NANASE OHKAWA

COMIC
もこなあぱぱ
MOKONA APAPA

PLANNING & PRESENTED by

CLAMP

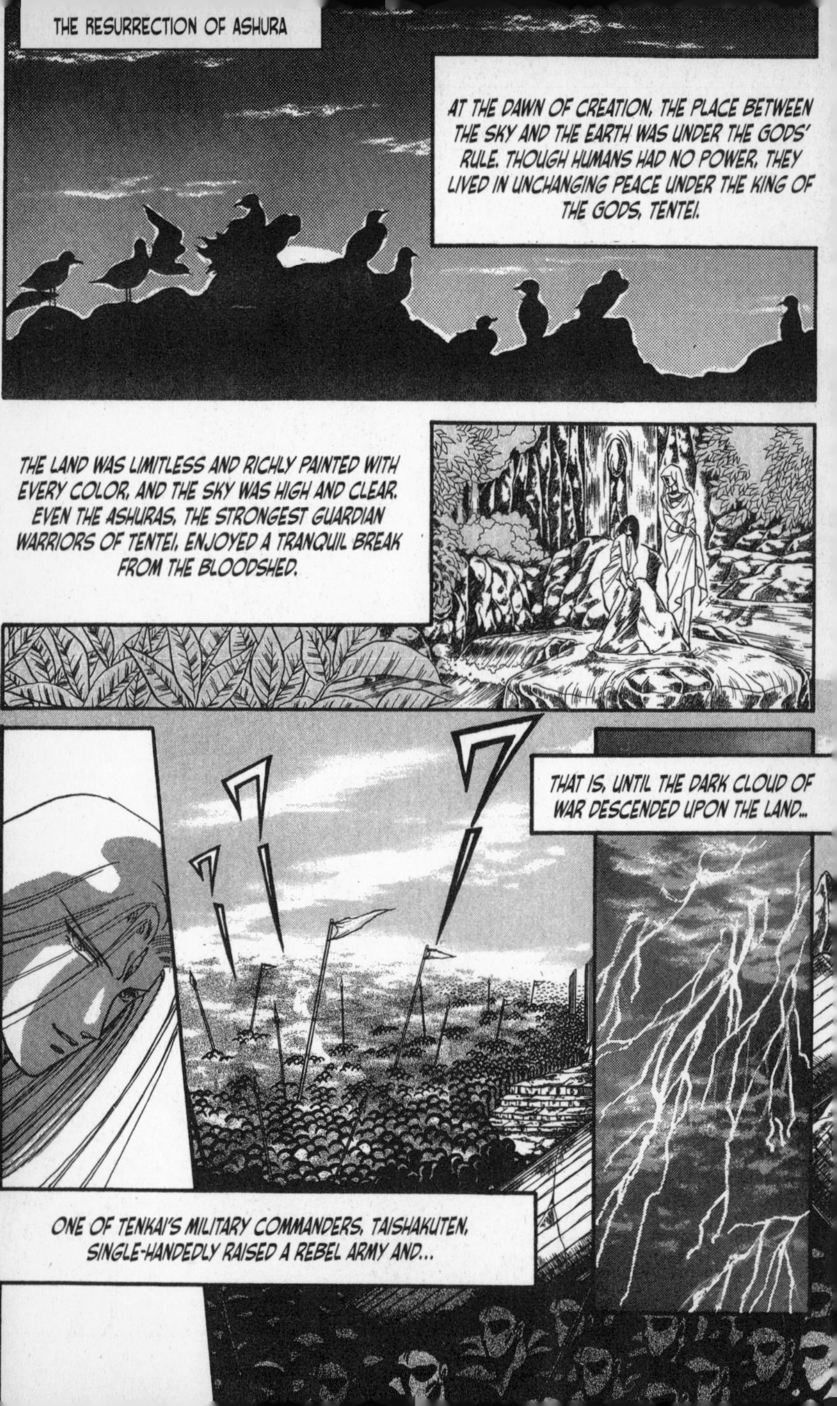
THE RESURRECTION OF ASHURA
AT THE DAWN OF CREATION, THE PLACE BETWEEN THE SKY AND THE EARTH WAS UNDER THE GODS' RULE. THOUGH HUMANS HAD NO POWER, THEY LIVED IN UNCHANGING PEACE UNDER THE KING OF THE GODS, TENTEI.
THE LAND WAS LIMITLESS AND RICHLY PAINTED WITH EVERY COLOR, AND THE SKY WAS HIGH AND CLEAR. EVEN THE ASHURAS, THE STRONGEST GUARDIAN WARRIORS OF TENTEI, ENJOYED A TRANQUIL BREAK FROM THE BLOODSHED.
THAT IS, UNTIL THE DARK CLOUD OF WAR DESCENDED UPON THE LAND...
ONE OF TENKAI'S MILITARY COMMANDERS, TAISHAKUTEN, SINGLE-HANDEDLY RAISED A REBEL ARMY AND...

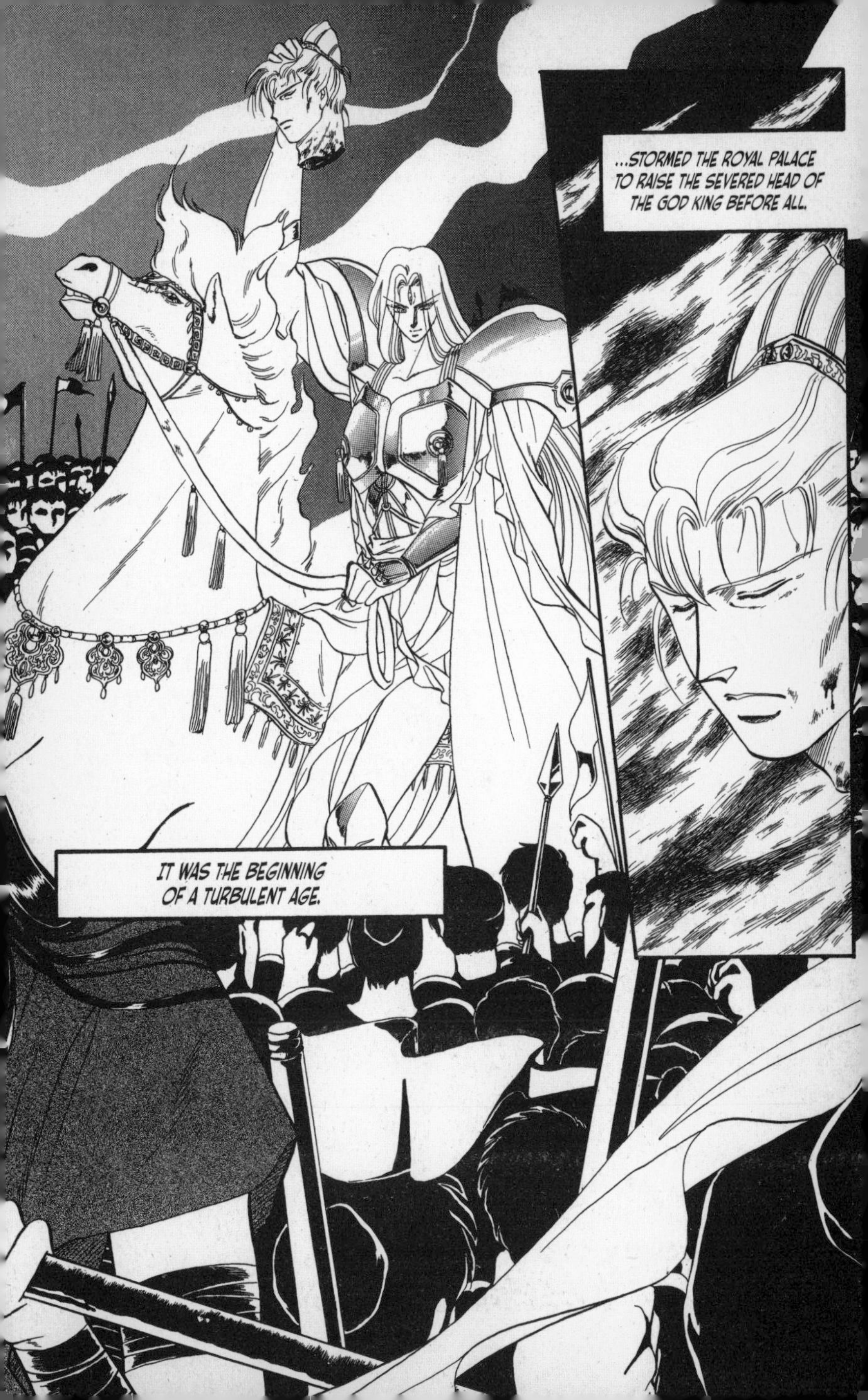
...STORMED THE ROYAL PALACE TO RAISE THE SEVERED HEAD OF THE GOD KING BEFORE ALL.
IT WAS THE BEGINNING OF A TURBULENT AGE.

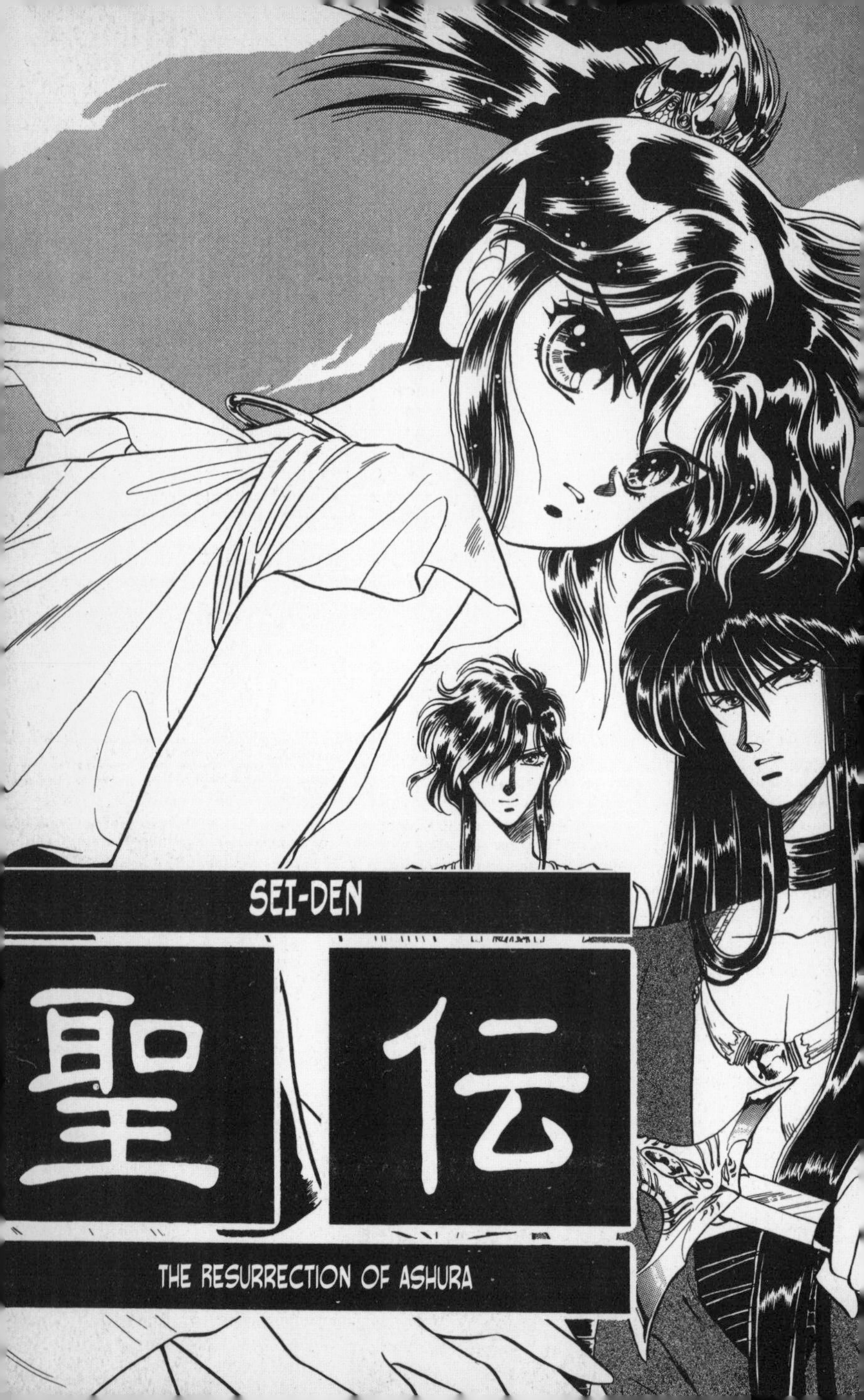
SEI-DEN
聖伝
THE RESURRECTION OF ASHURA

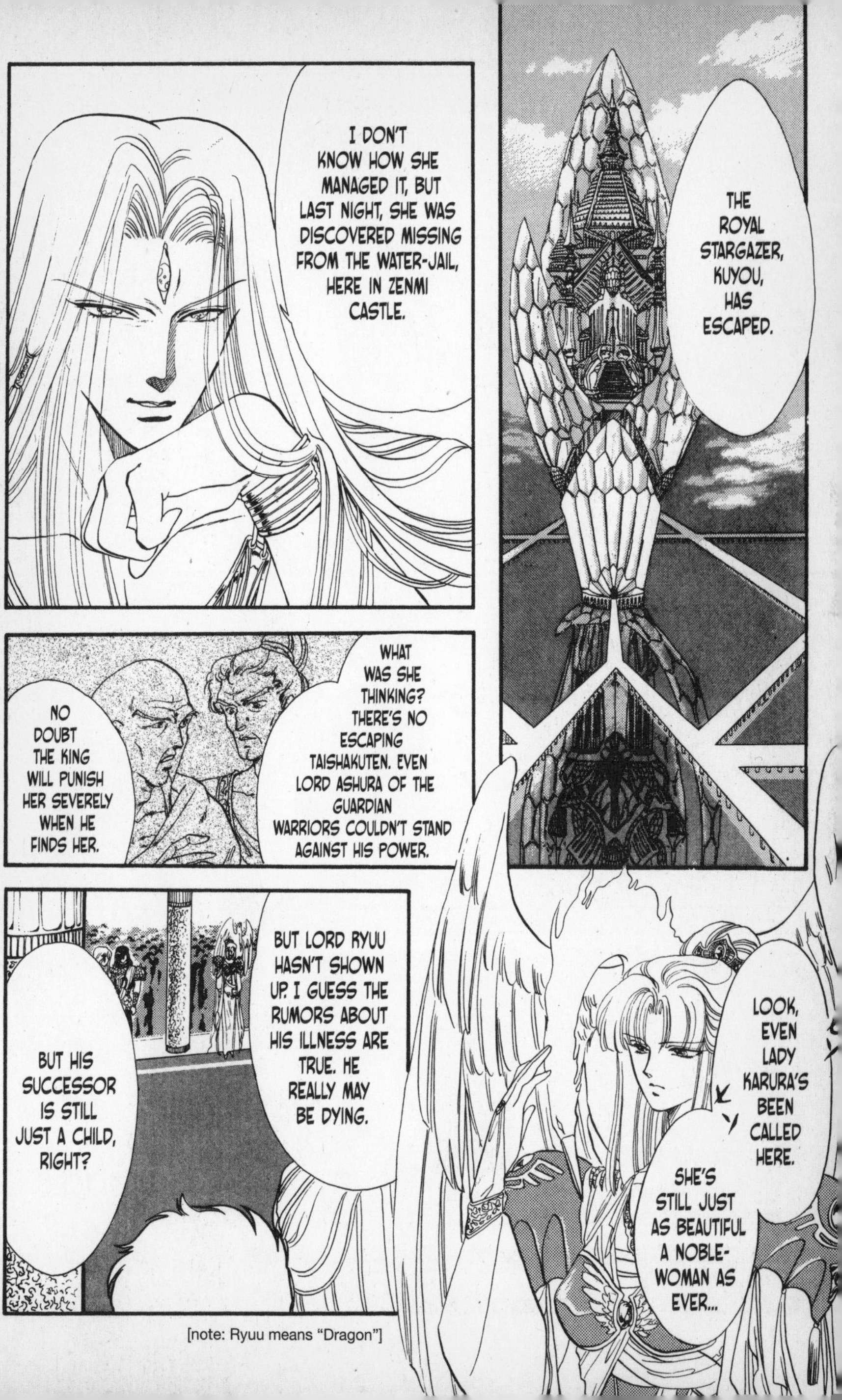
THE ROYAL STARGAZER, KUYOU, HAS ESCAPED.
I DON'T KNOW HOW SHE MANAGED IT, BUT LAST NIGHT, SHE WAS DISCOVERED MISSING FROM THE WATER-JAIL, HERE IN ZENMI CASTLE.
WHAT WAS SHE THINKING? THERE'S NO ESCAPING TAISHAKUTEN. EVEN LORD ASHURA OF THE GUARDIAN WARRIORS COULDN'T STAND AGAINST HIS POWER.
NO DOUBT THE KING WILL PUNISH HER SEVERELY WHEN HE FINDS HER.
LOOK, EVEN LADY KARURA'S BEEN CALLED HERE.
SHE'S STILL JUST AS BEAUTIFUL A NOBLE-WOMAN AS EVER...
BUT LORD RYUU HASN'T SHOWN UP. I GUESS THE RUMORS ABOUT HIS ILLNESS ARE TRUE. HE REALLY MAY BE DYING.
BUT HIS SUCCESSOR IS STILL JUST A CHILD, RIGHT?

[note: Ryuu means "Dragon"]

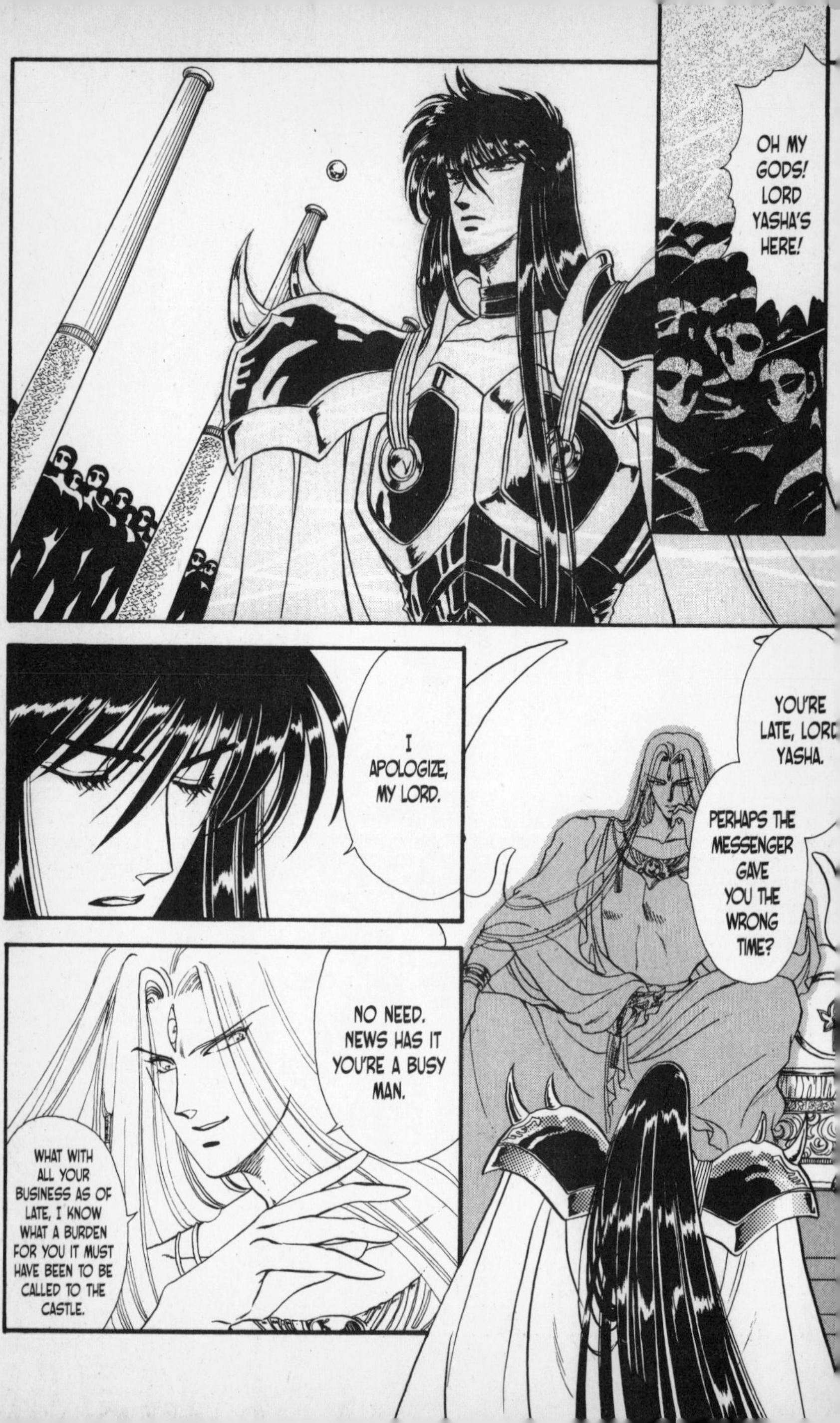
OH MY GODS! LORD YASHA'S HERE!
YOU'RE LATE, LORD YASHA.
PERHAPS THE MESSENGER GAVE YOU THE WRONG TIME?
I APOLOGIZE, MY LORD.
NO NEED. NEWS HAS IT YOU'RE A BUSY MAN.
WHAT WITH ALL YOUR BUSINESS AS OF LATE, I KNOW WHAT A BURDEN FOR YOU IT MUST HAVE BEEN TO BE CALLED TO THE CASTLE.

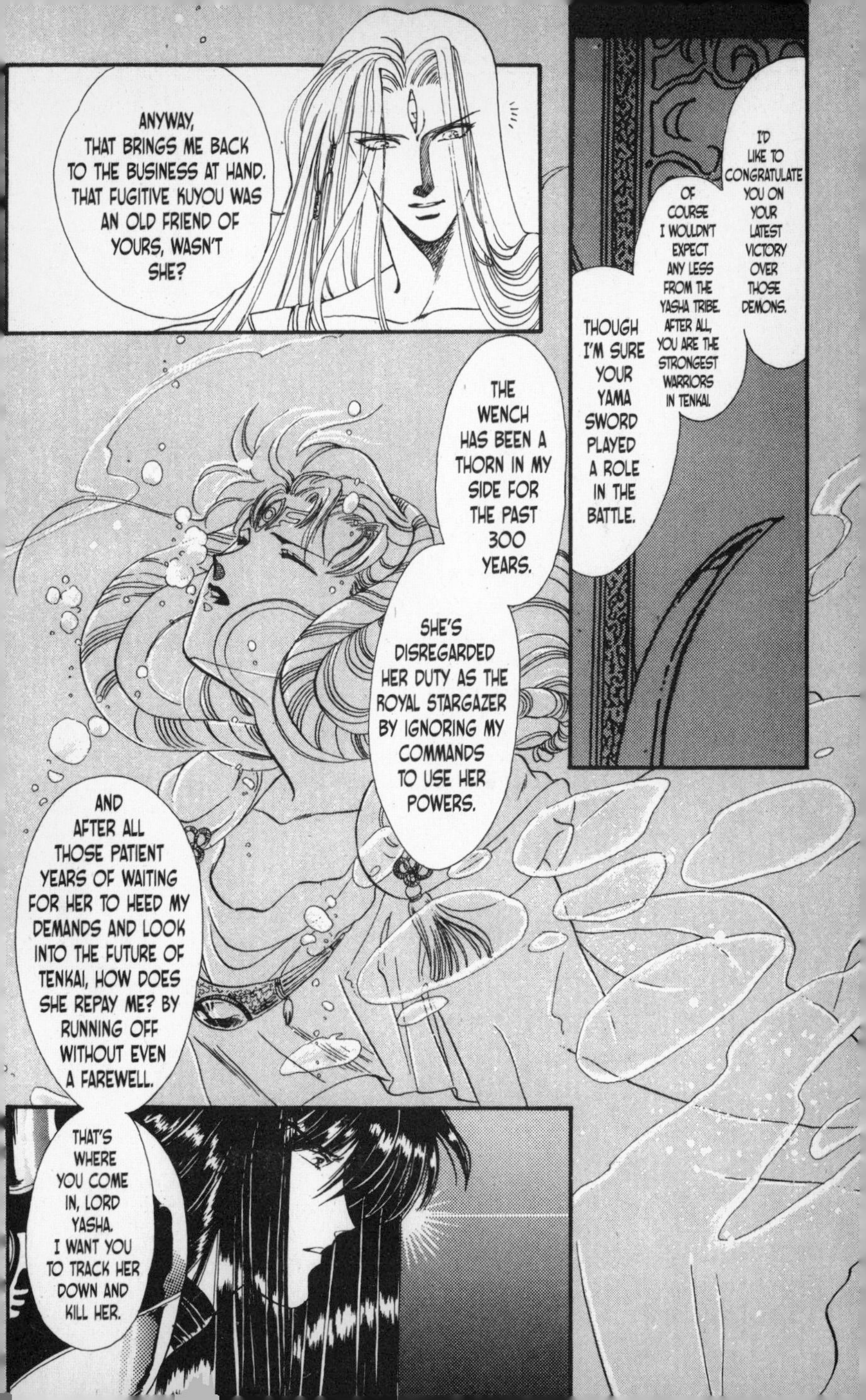
I'D LIKE TO CONGRATULATE YOU ON YOUR LATEST VICTORY OVER THOSE DEMONS.
OF COURSE I WOULDN'T EXPECT ANY LESS FROM THE YASHA TRIBE. AFTER ALL, YOU ARE THE STRONGEST WARRIORS IN TENKAI.
THOUGH I'M SURE YOUR YAMA SWORD PLAYED A ROLE IN THE BATTLE.
ANYWAY, THAT BRINGS ME BACK TO THE BUSINESS AT HAND. THAT FUGITIVE KUYOU WAS AN OLD FRIEND OF YOURS, WASN'T SHE?
THE WENCH HAS BEEN A THORN IN MY SIDE FOR THE PAST 300 YEARS.
SHE'S DISREGARDED HER DUTY AS THE ROYAL STARGAZER BY IGNORING MY COMMANDS TO USE HER POWERS.
AND AFTER ALL THOSE PATIENT YEARS OF WAITING FOR HER TO HEED MY DEMANDS AND LOOK INTO THE FUTURE OF TENKAI, HOW DOES SHE REPAY ME? BY RUNNING OFF WITHOUT EVEN A FAREWELL.
THAT'S WHERE YOU COME IN, LORD YASHA. I WANT YOU TO TRACK HER DOWN AND KILL HER.

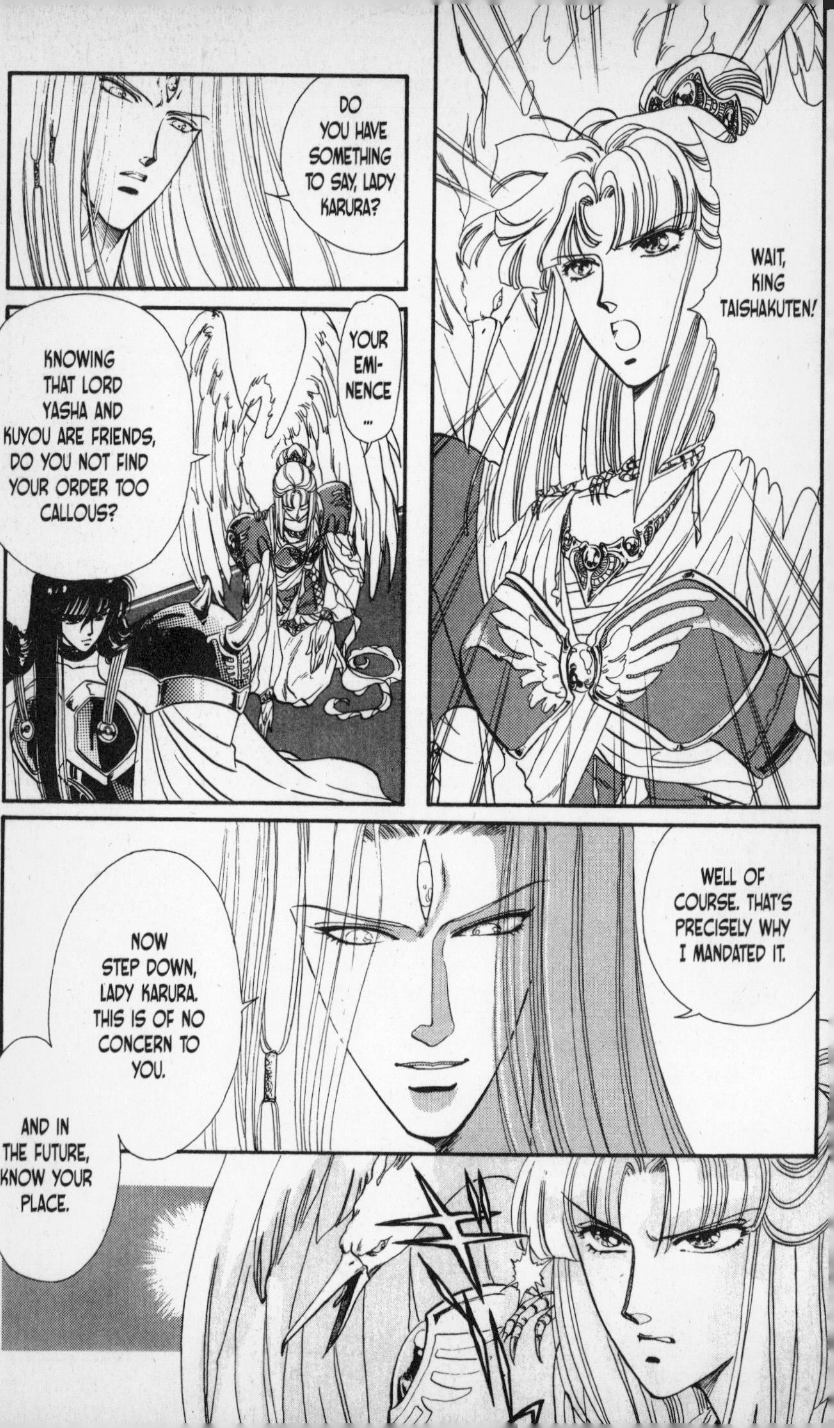
WAIT, KING TAISHAKUTEN!
DO YOU HAVE SOMETHING TO SAY, LADY KARURA?
YOUR EMI-NENCE ...
KNOWING THAT LORD YASHA AND KUYOU ARE FRIENDS, DO YOU NOT FIND YOUR ORDER TOO CALLOUS?
WELL OF COURSE. THAT'S PRECISELY WHY I MANDATED IT.
NOW STEP DOWN, LADY KARURA. THIS IS OF NO CONCERN TO YOU.
AND IN THE FUTURE, KNOW YOUR PLACE.

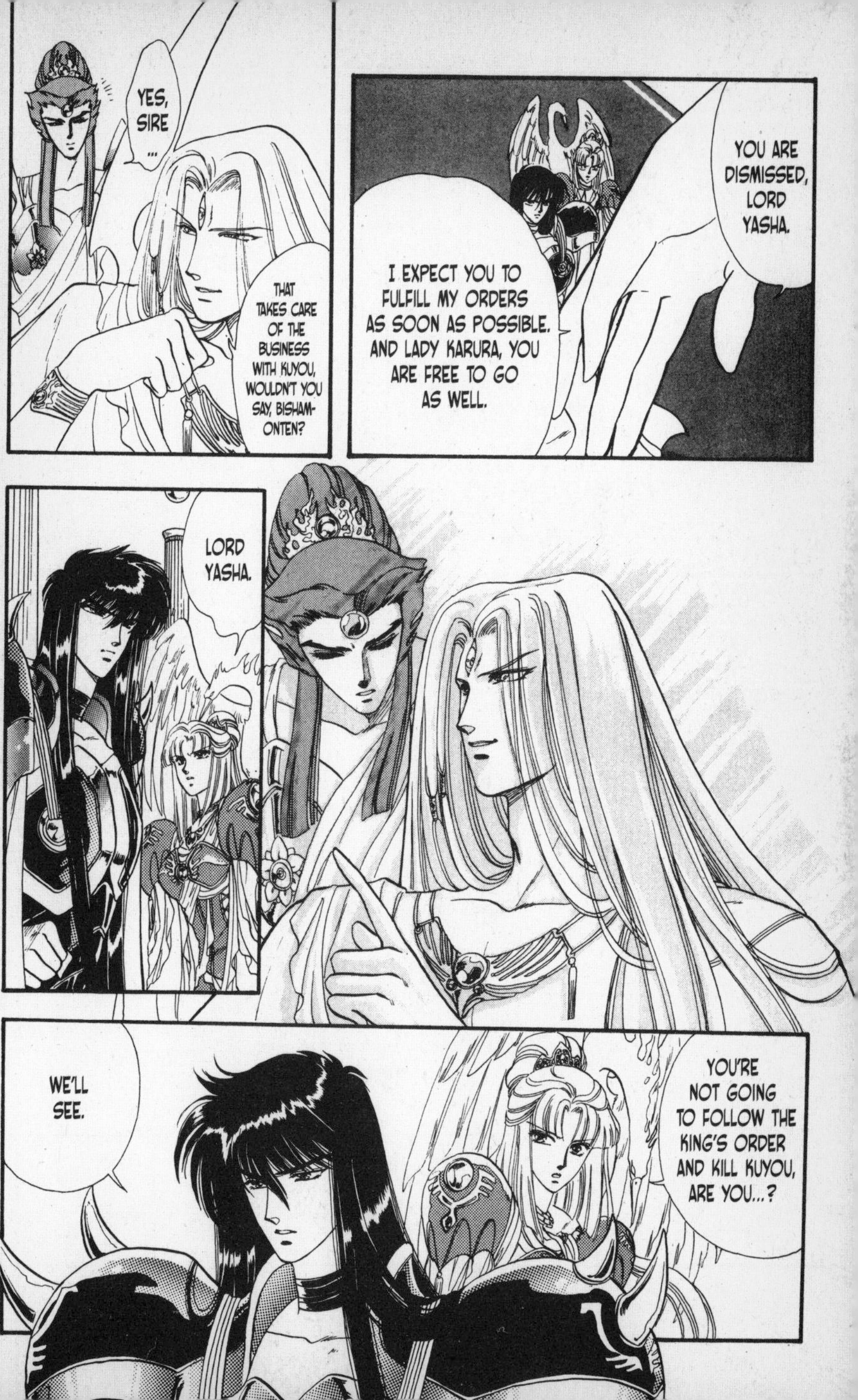
YOU ARE DISMISSED, LORD YASHA.
I EXPECT YOU TO FULFILL MY ORDERS AS SOON AS POSSIBLE. AND LADY KARURA, YOU ARE FREE TO GO AS WELL.
THAT TAKES CARE OF THE BUSINESS WITH KUYOU, WOULDN'T YOU SAY, BISHAM-ONTEN?
YES, SIRE ...
LORD YASHA.
YOU'RE NOT GOING TO FOLLOW THE KING'S ORDER AND KILL KUYOU, ARE YOU...?
WE'LL SEE.

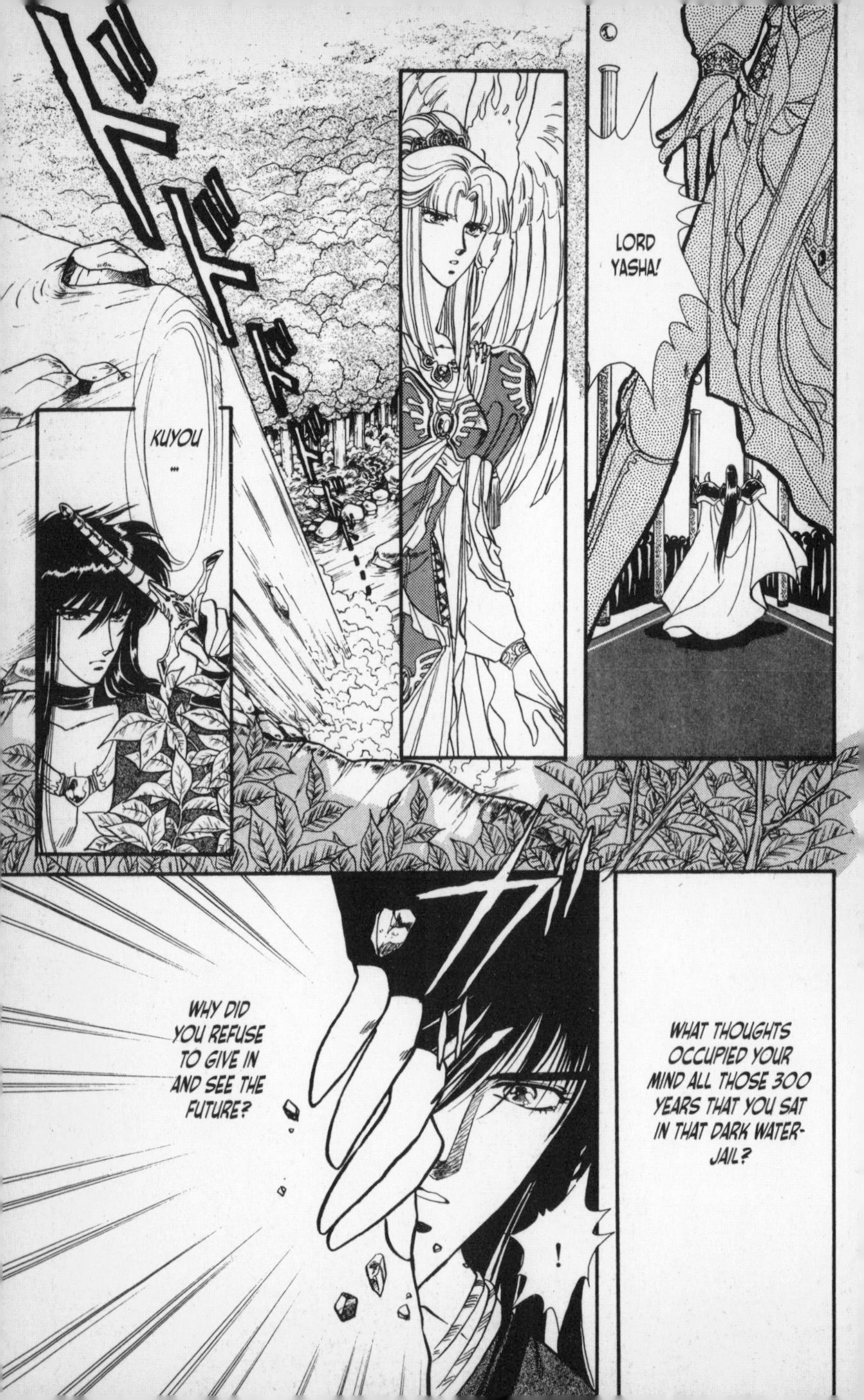
LORD YASHA!
KUYOU ...
WHAT THOUGHTS OCCUPIED YOUR MIND ALL THOSE 300 YEARS THAT YOU SAT IN THAT DARK WATER-JAIL?
WHY DID YOU REFUSE TO GIVE IN AND SEE THE FUTURE?
!

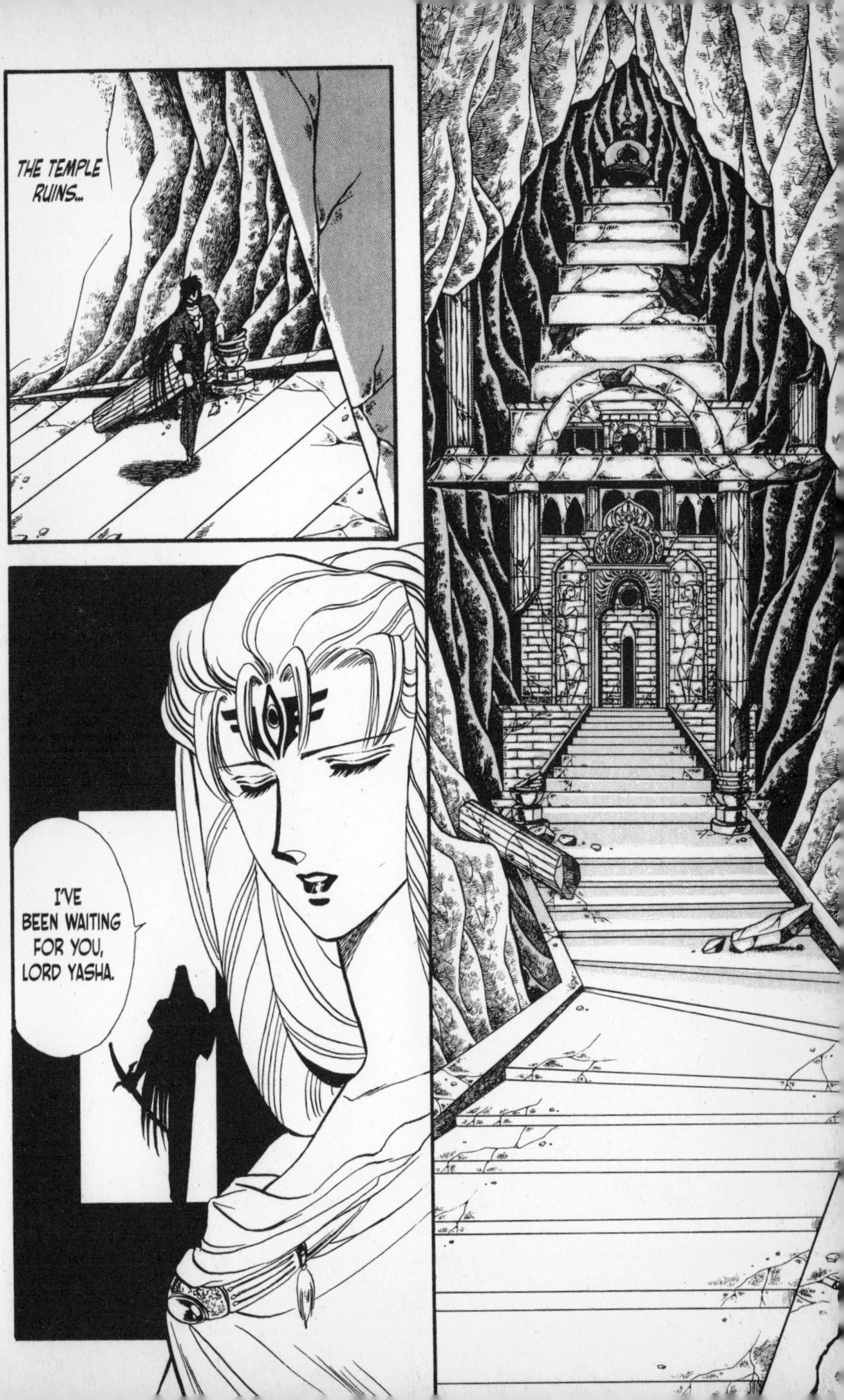
THE TEMPLE RUINS...
I'VE BEEN WAITING FOR YOU, LORD YASHA.

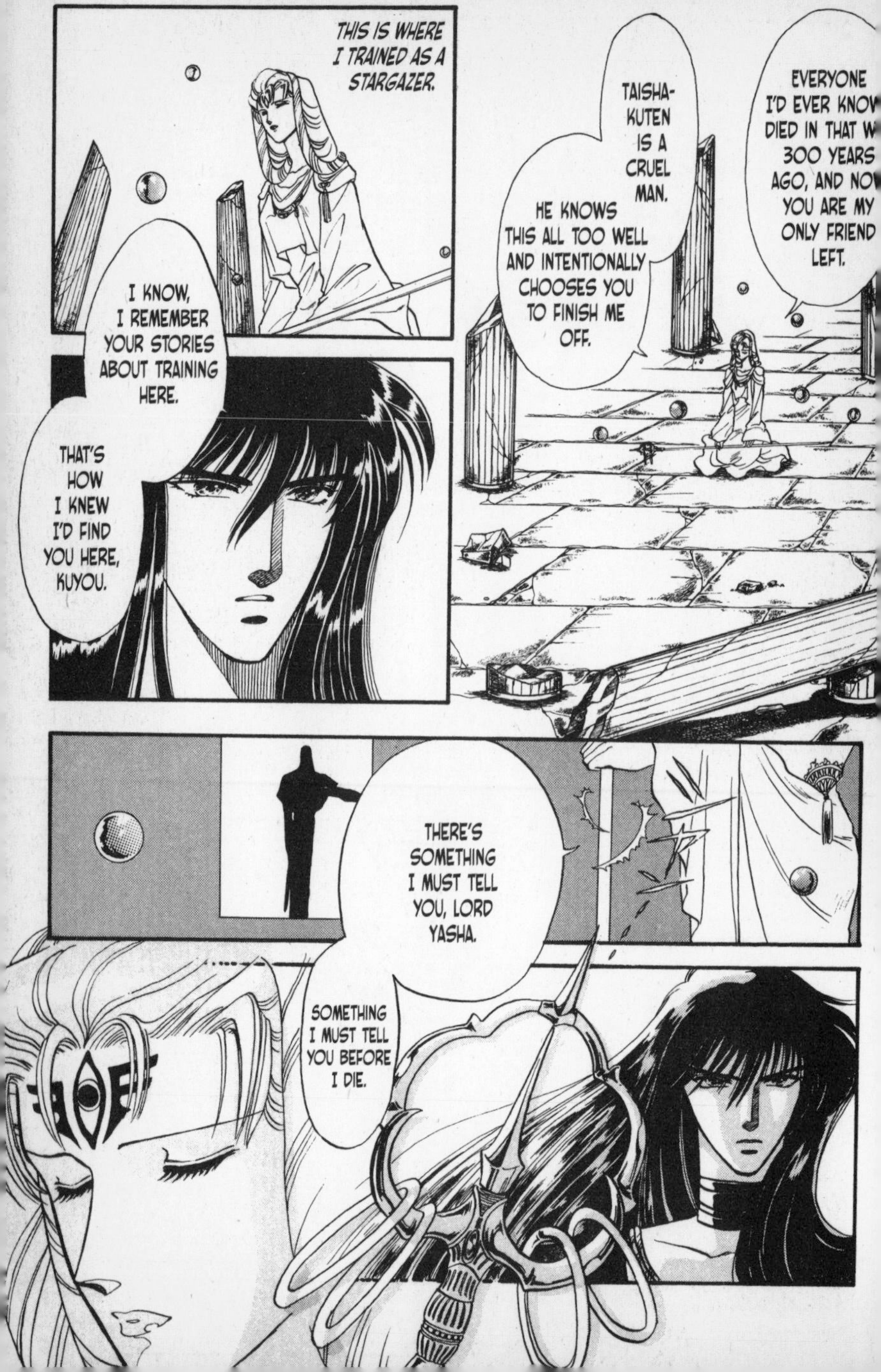
EVERYONE I'D EVER KNOW DIED IN THAT W 300 YEARS AGO, AND NOW YOU ARE MY ONLY FRIEND LEFT.
TAISHA-KUTEN IS A CRUEL MAN.
HE KNOWS THIS ALL TOO WELL AND INTENTIONALLY CHOOSES YOU TO FINISH ME OFF.
THIS IS WHERE I TRAINED AS A STARGAZER.
I KNOW, I REMEMBER YOUR STORIES ABOUT TRAINING HERE.
THAT'S HOW I KNEW I'D FIND YOU HERE, KUYOU.
THERE'S SOMETHING I MUST TELL YOU, LORD YASHA.
SOMETHING I MUST TELL YOU BEFORE I DIE.

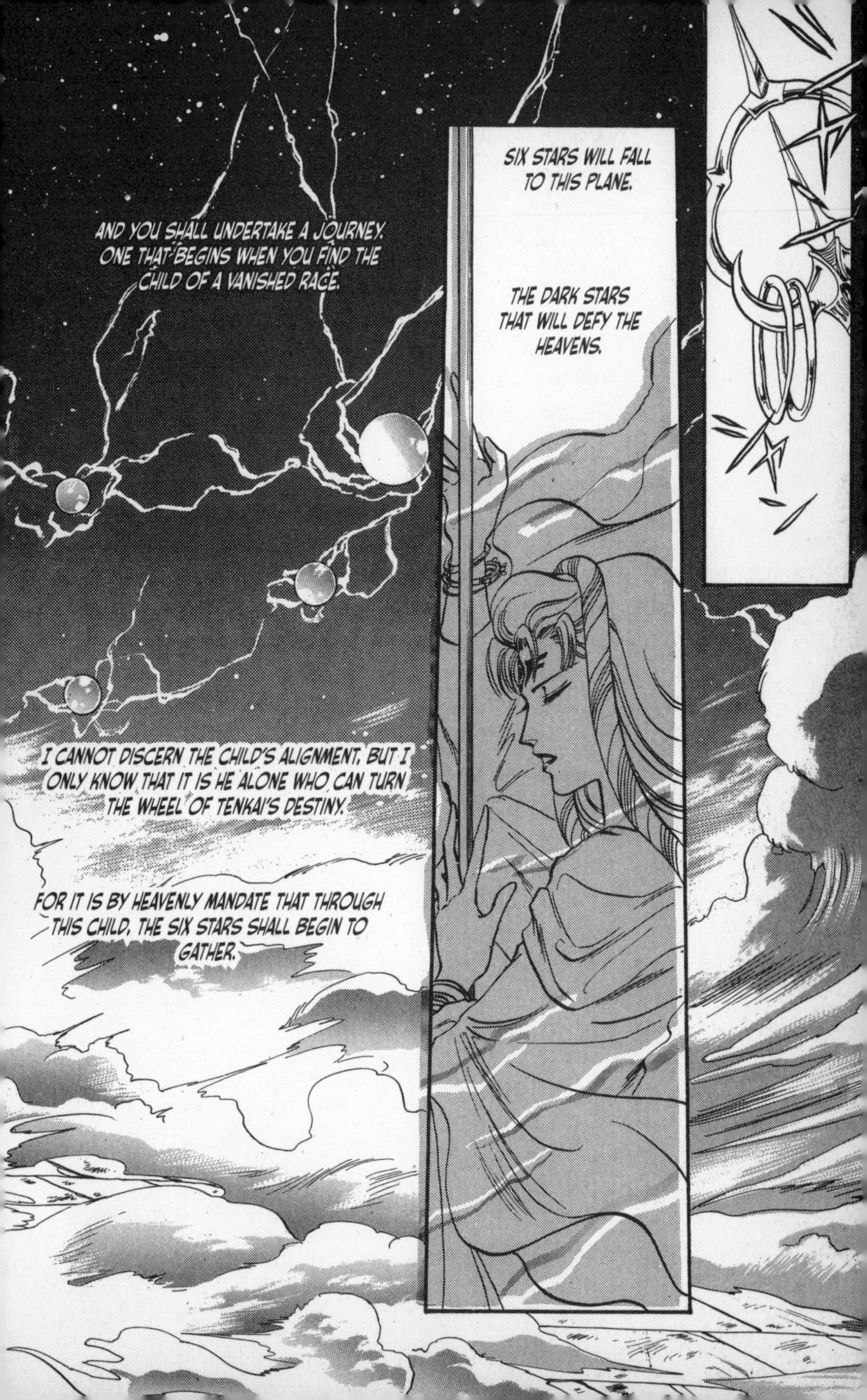
SIX STARS WILL FALL TO THIS PLANE.
THE DARK STARS THAT WILL DEFY THE HEAVENS.
AND YOU SHALL UNDERTAKE A JOURNEY. ONE THAT BEGINS WHEN YOU FIND THE CHILD OF A VANISHED RACE.
I CANNOT DISCERN THE CHILD'S ALIGNMENT, BUT I ONLY KNOW THAT IT IS HE ALONE WHO CAN TURN THE WHEEL OF TENKAI'S DESTINY.
FOR IT IS BY HEAVENLY MANDATE THAT THROUGH THIS CHILD, THE SIX STARS SHALL BEGIN TO GATHER.

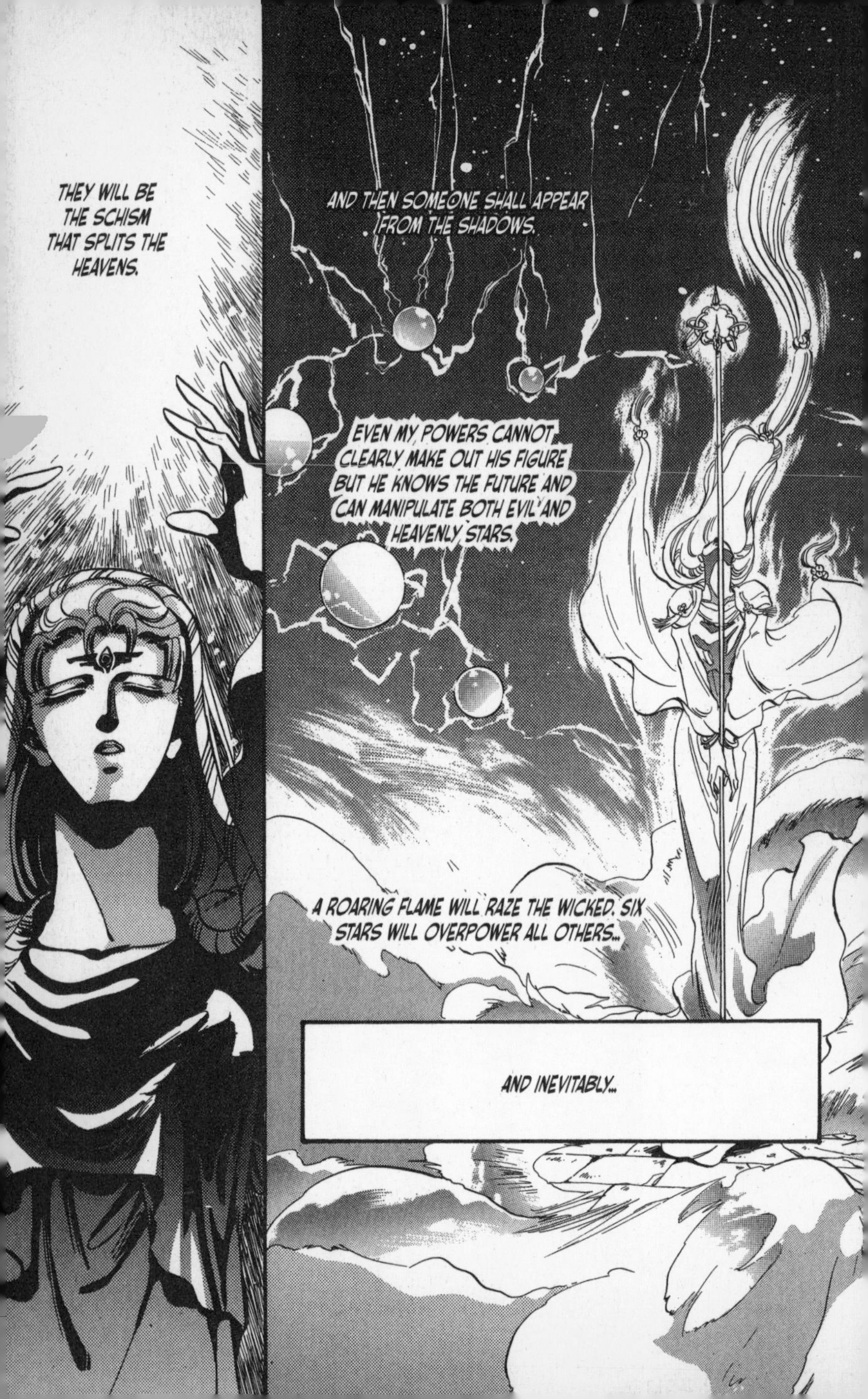
AND THEN SOMEONE SHALL APPEAR FROM THE SHADOWS.
EVEN MY POWERS CANNOT CLEARLY MAKE OUT HIS FIGURE BUT HE KNOWS THE FUTURE AND CAN MANIPULATE BOTH EVIL AND HEAVENLY STARS.
A ROARING FLAME WILL RAZE THE WICKED. SIX STARS WILL OVERPOWER ALL OTHERS...
AND INEVITABLY...
THEY WILL BE THE SCHISM THAT SPLITS THE HEAVENS.

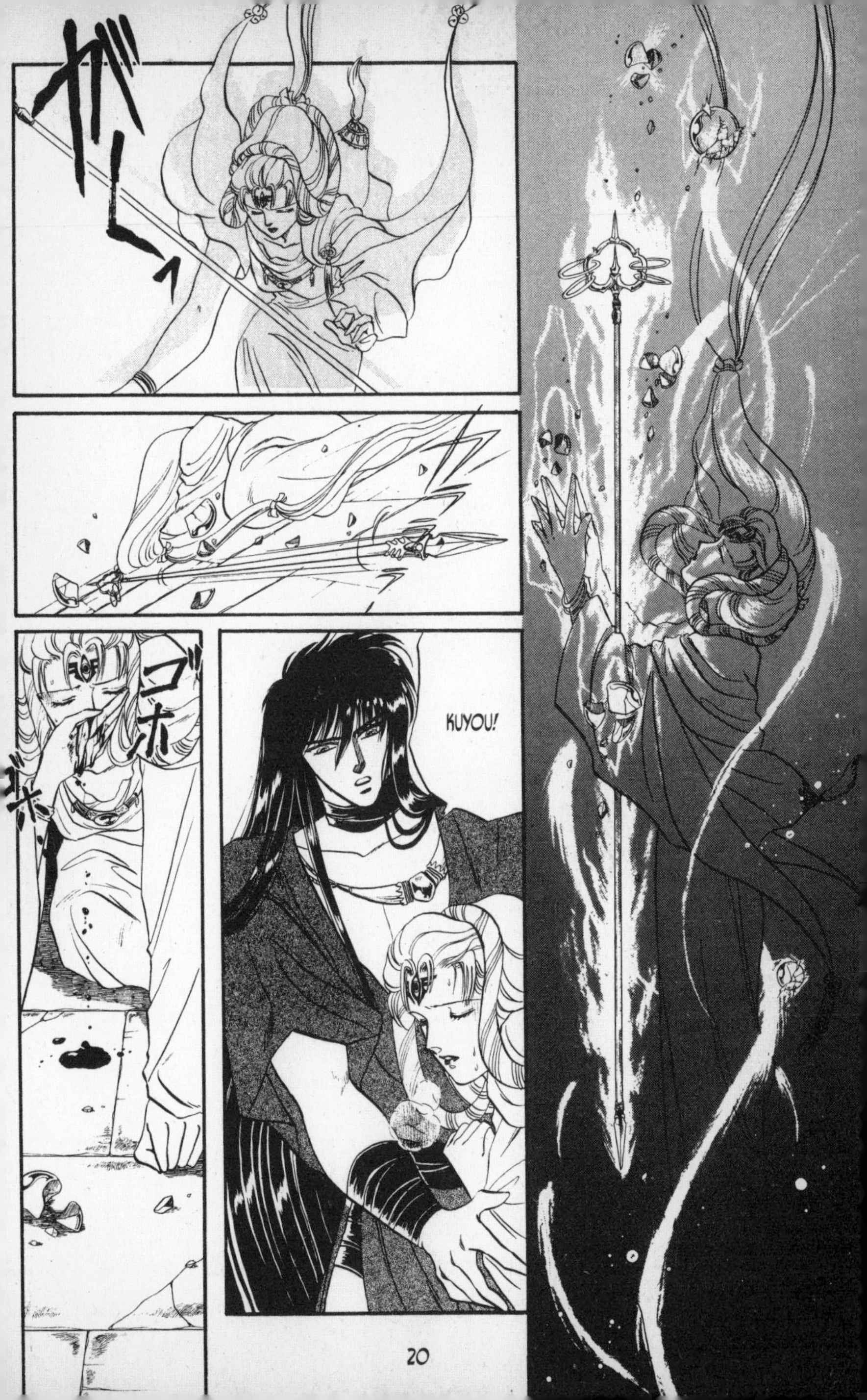
KUYOU!
ゴホ

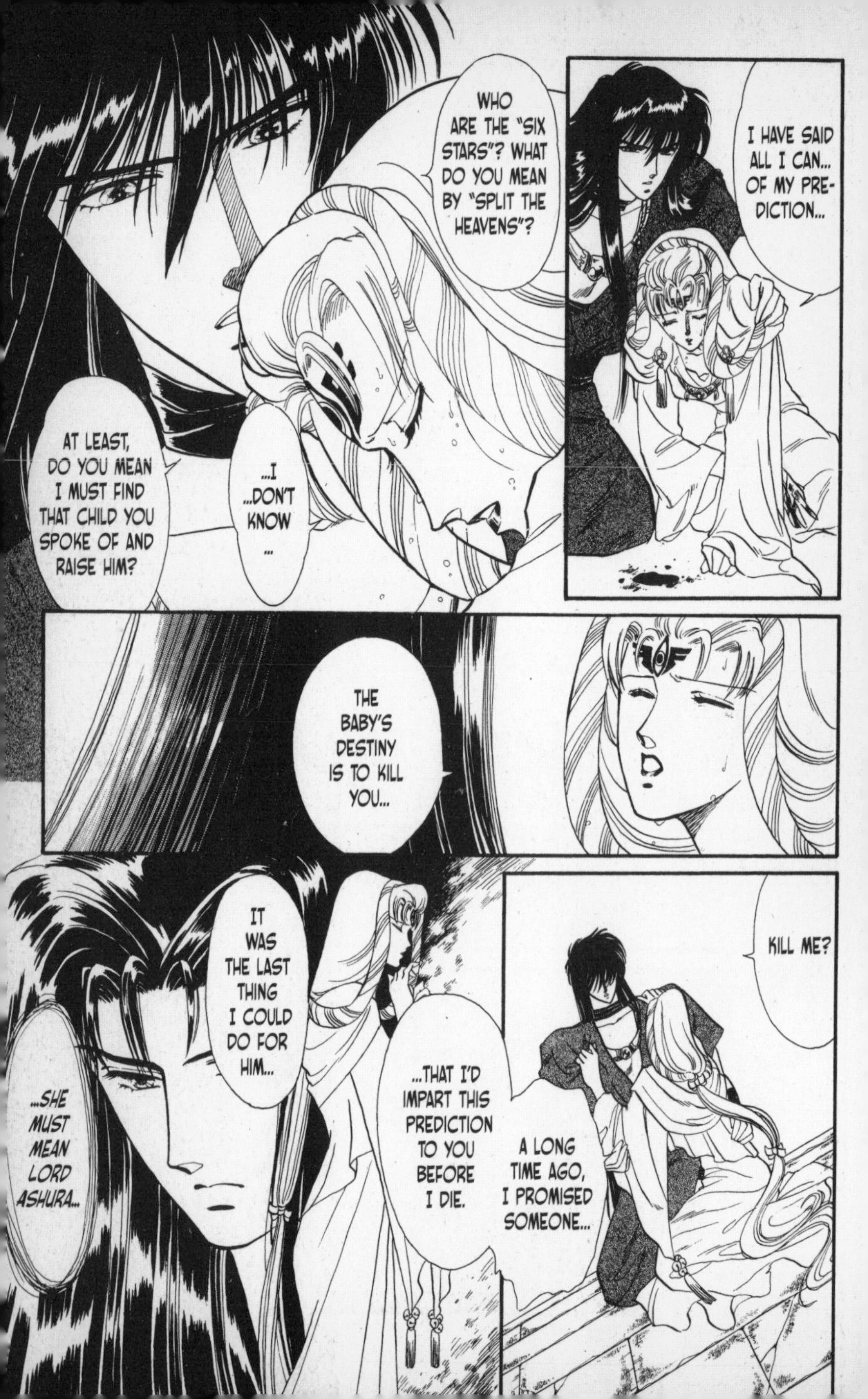
I HAVE SAID ALL I CAN... OF MY PREDICTION...
WHO ARE THE "SIX STARS"? WHAT DO YOU MEAN BY "SPLIT THE HEAVENS"?
...I ...DON'T KNOW ...
AT LEAST, DO YOU MEAN I MUST FIND THAT CHILD YOU SPOKE OF AND RAISE HIM?
THE BABY'S DESTINY IS TO KILL YOU...
KILL ME?
A LONG TIME AGO, I PROMISED SOMEONE...
...THAT I'D IMPART THIS PREDICTION TO YOU BEFORE I DIE.
IT WAS THE LAST THING I COULD DO FOR HIM...
...SHE MUST MEAN LORD ASHURA...

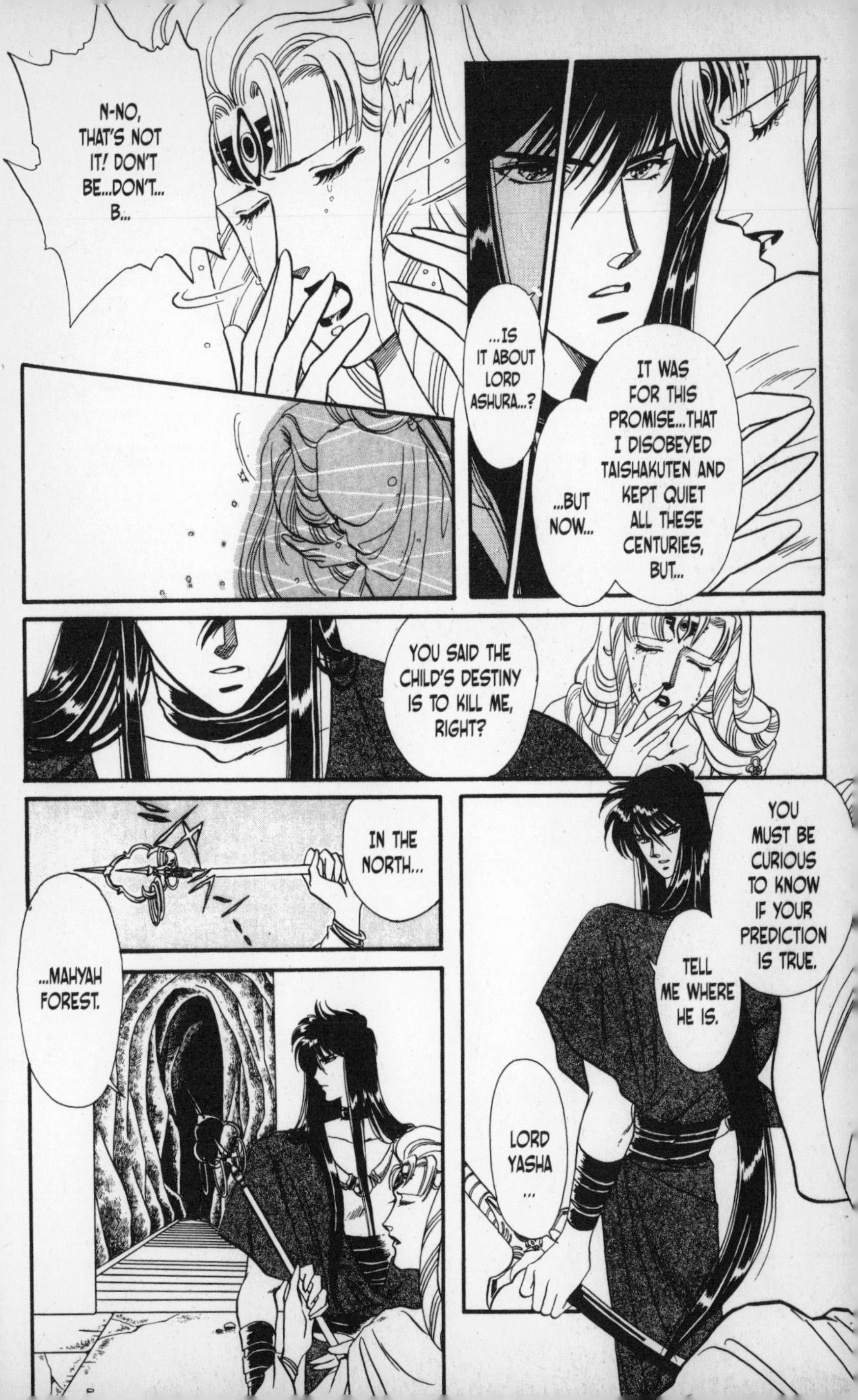
...IS IT ABOUT LORD ASHURA...?
IT WAS FOR THIS PROMISE...THAT I DISOBEYED TAISHAKUTEN AND KEPT QUIET ALL THESE CENTURIES, BUT...
...BUT NOW...
N-NO, THAT'S NOT IT! DON'T BE...DON'T... B...
YOU SAID THE CHILD'S DESTINY IS TO KILL ME, RIGHT?
YOU MUST BE CURIOUS TO KNOW IF YOUR PREDICTION IS TRUE.
TELL ME WHERE HE IS.
LORD YASHA ...
IN THE NORTH...
...MAHYAH FOREST.

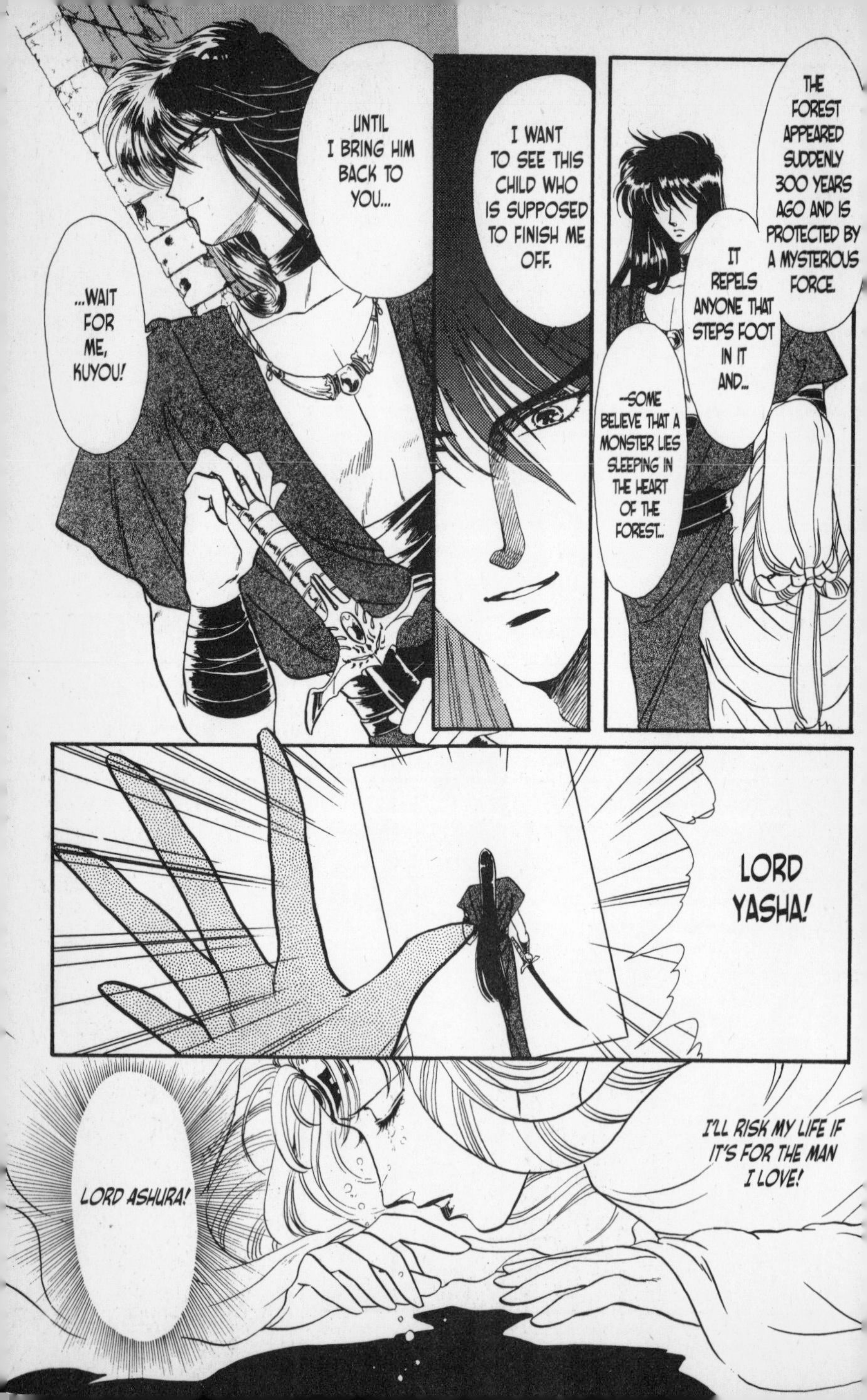
THE FOREST APPEARED SUDDENLY 300 YEARS AGO AND IS PROTECTED BY A MYSTERIOUS FORCE.
IT REPELS ANYONE THAT STEPS FOOT IN IT AND...
--SOME BELIEVE THAT A MONSTER LIES SLEEPING IN THE HEART OF THE FOREST...
I WANT TO SEE THIS CHILD WHO IS SUPPOSED TO FINISH ME OFF.
UNTIL I BRING HIM BACK TO YOU...
...WAIT FOR ME, KUYOU!
LORD YASHA!
I'LL RISK MY LIFE IF IT'S FOR THE MAN I LOVE!
LORD ASHURA!

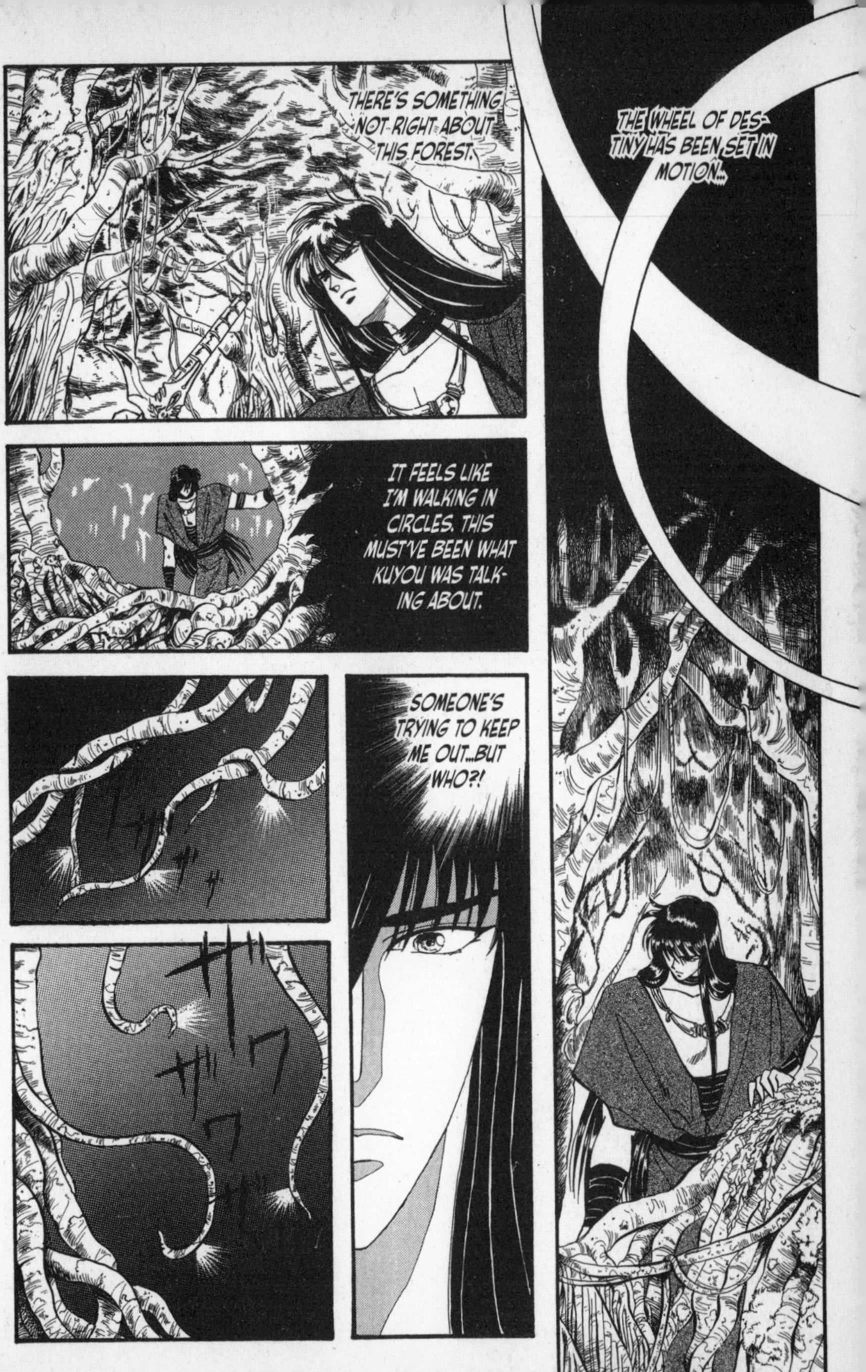
THE WHEEL OF DES-TINY HAS BEEN SET IN MOTION...
THERE'S SOMETHING NOT RIGHT ABOUT THIS FOREST.
IT FEELS LIKE I'M WALKING IN CIRCLES. THIS MUST'VE BEEN WHAT KUYOU WAS TALK-ING ABOUT.
SOMEONE'S TRYING TO KEEP ME OUT...BUT WHO?!

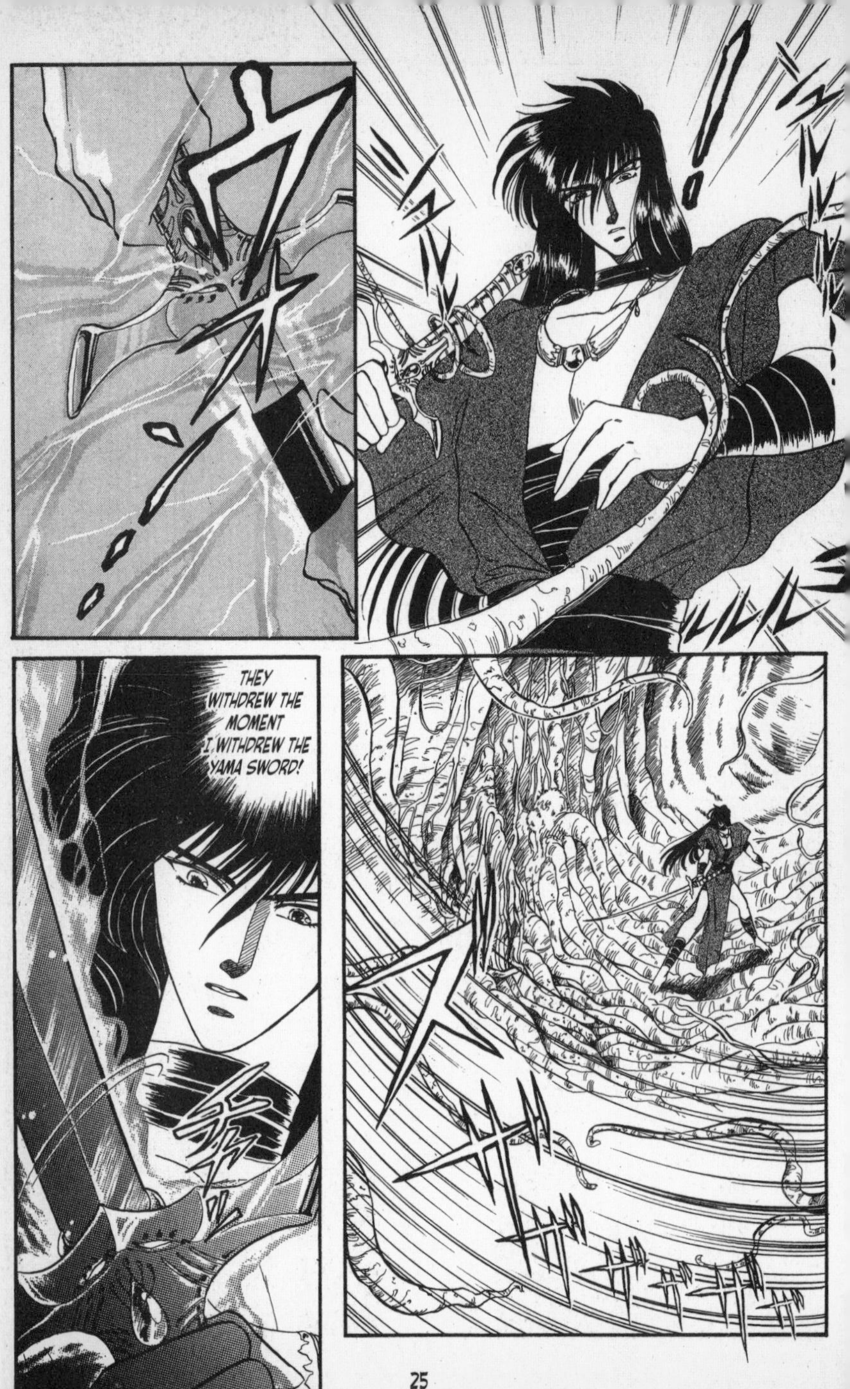
THEY WITHDREW THE MOMENT I WITHDREW THE YAMA SWORD!

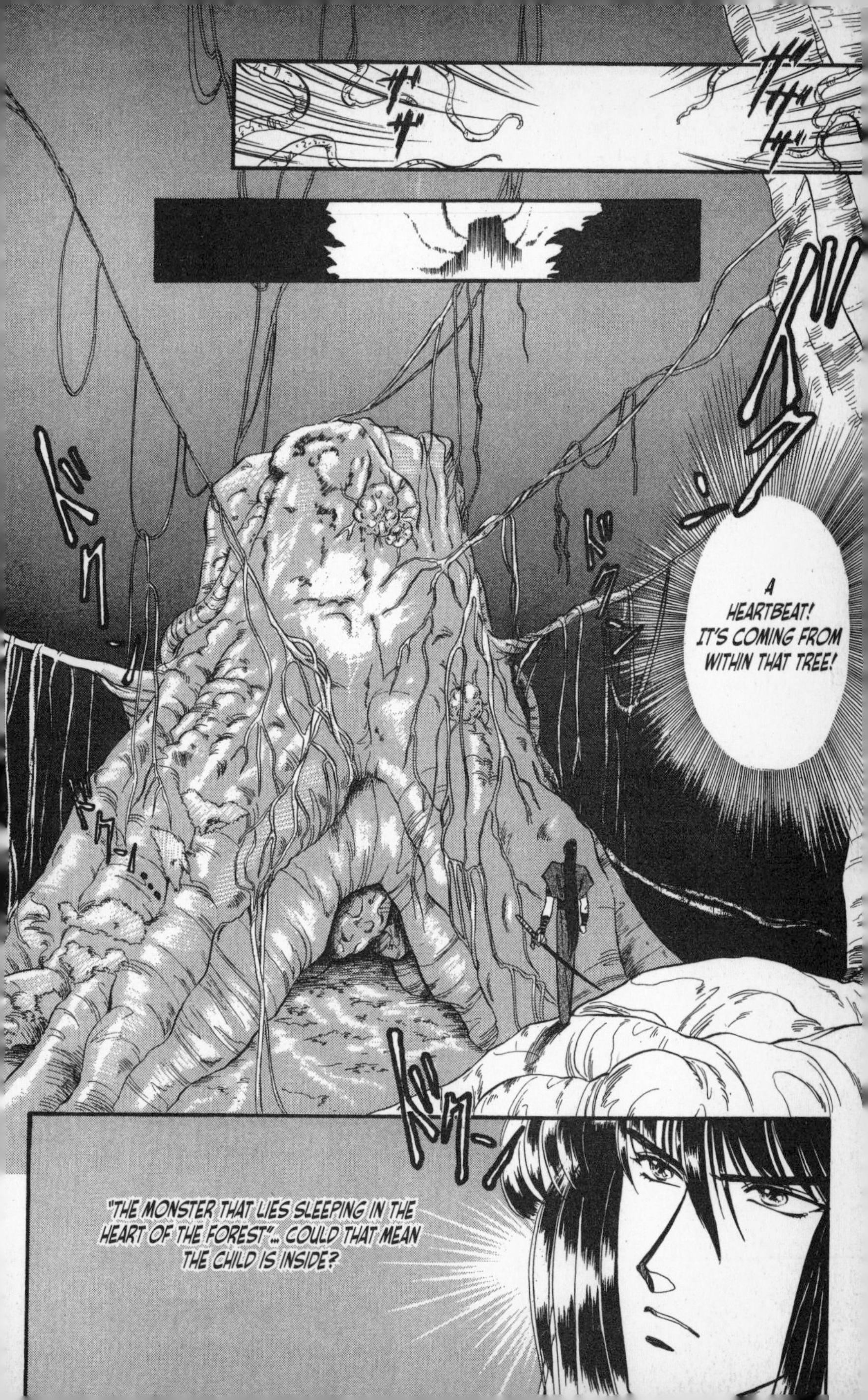
A HEARTBEAT! IT'S COMING FROM WITHIN THAT TREE!
"THE MONSTER THAT LIES SLEEPING IN THE HEART OF THE FOREST"... COULD THAT MEAN THE CHILD IS INSIDE?

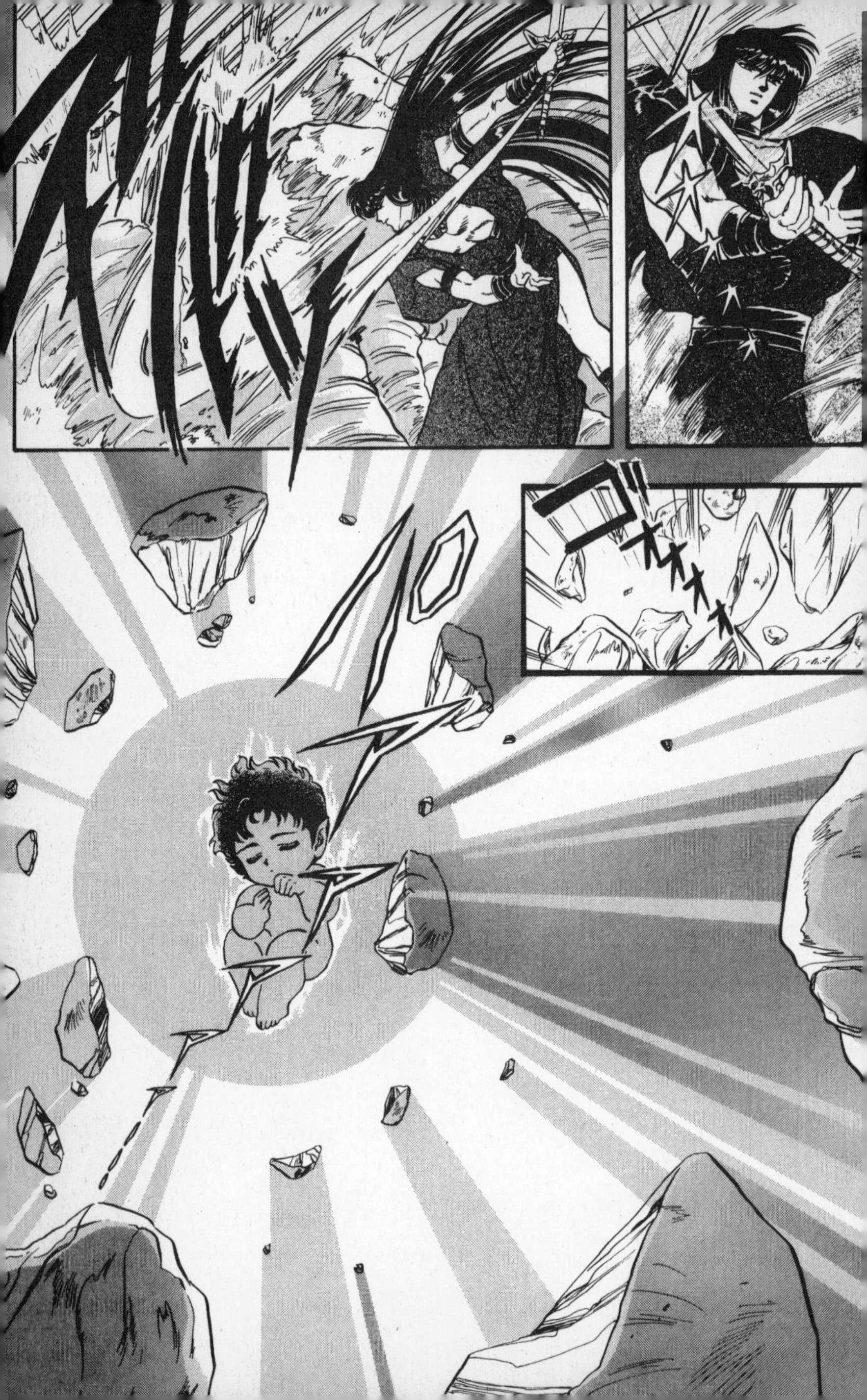
ゴォォォォ

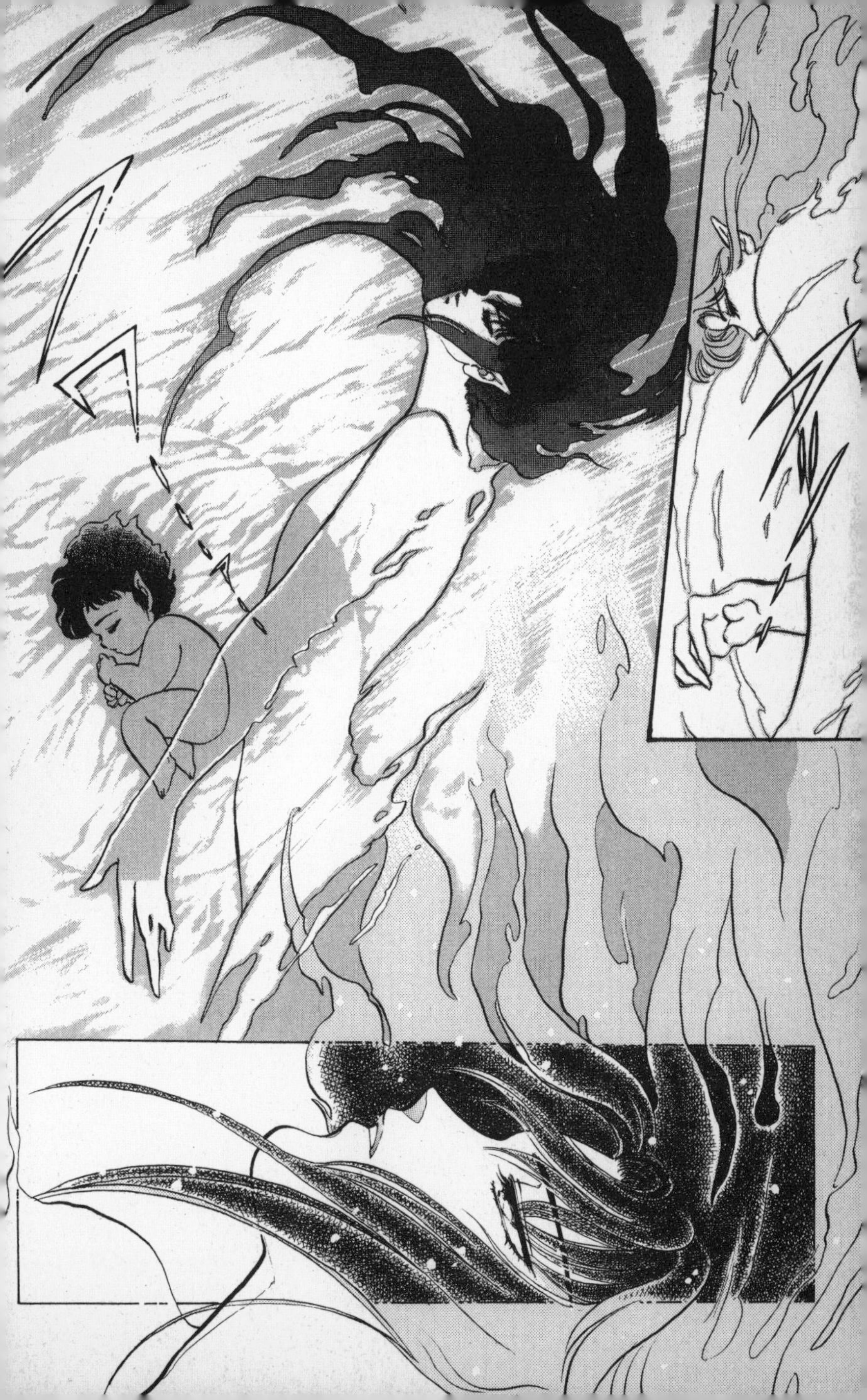

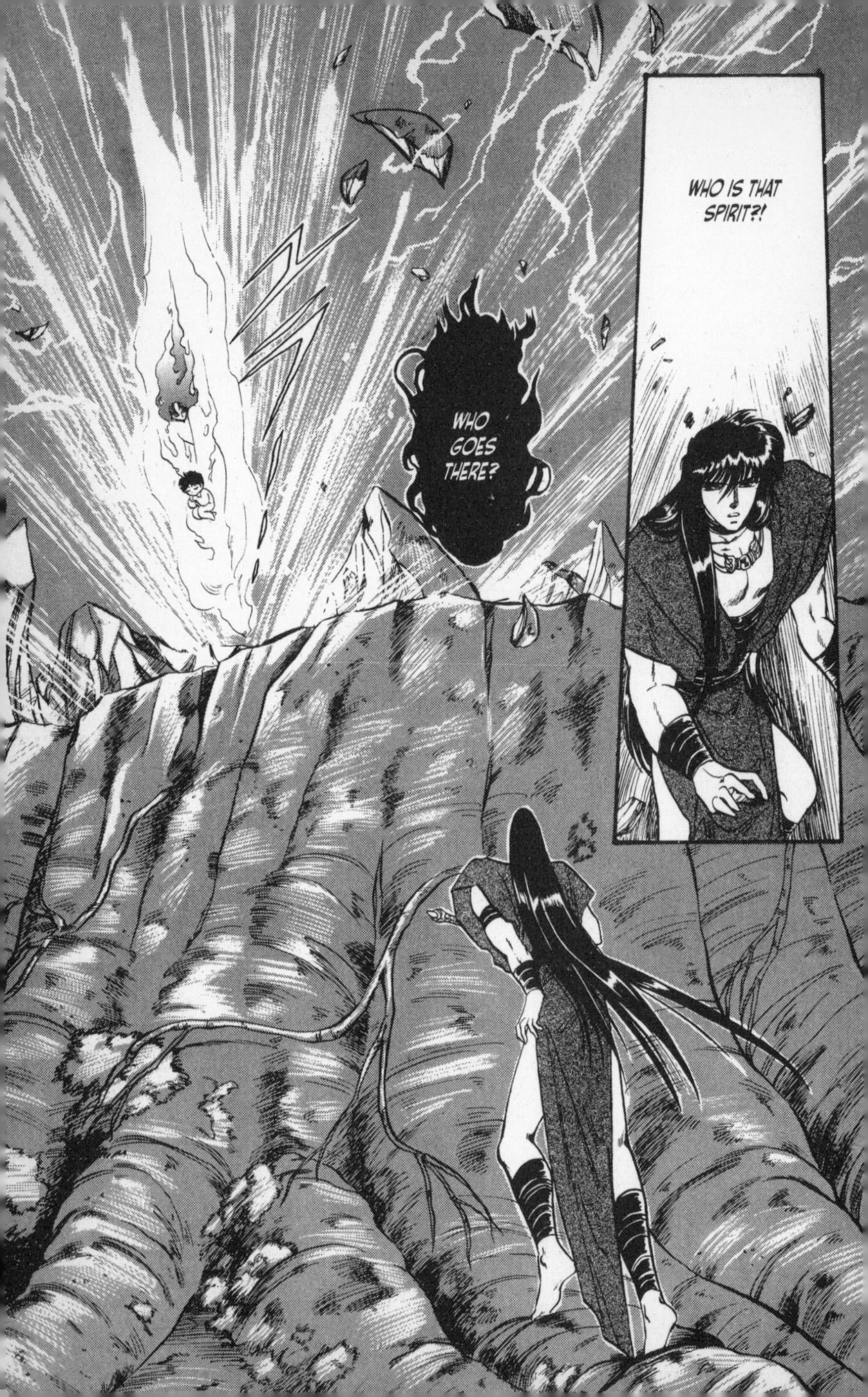
WHO IS THAT SPIRIT?!
WHO GOES THERE?

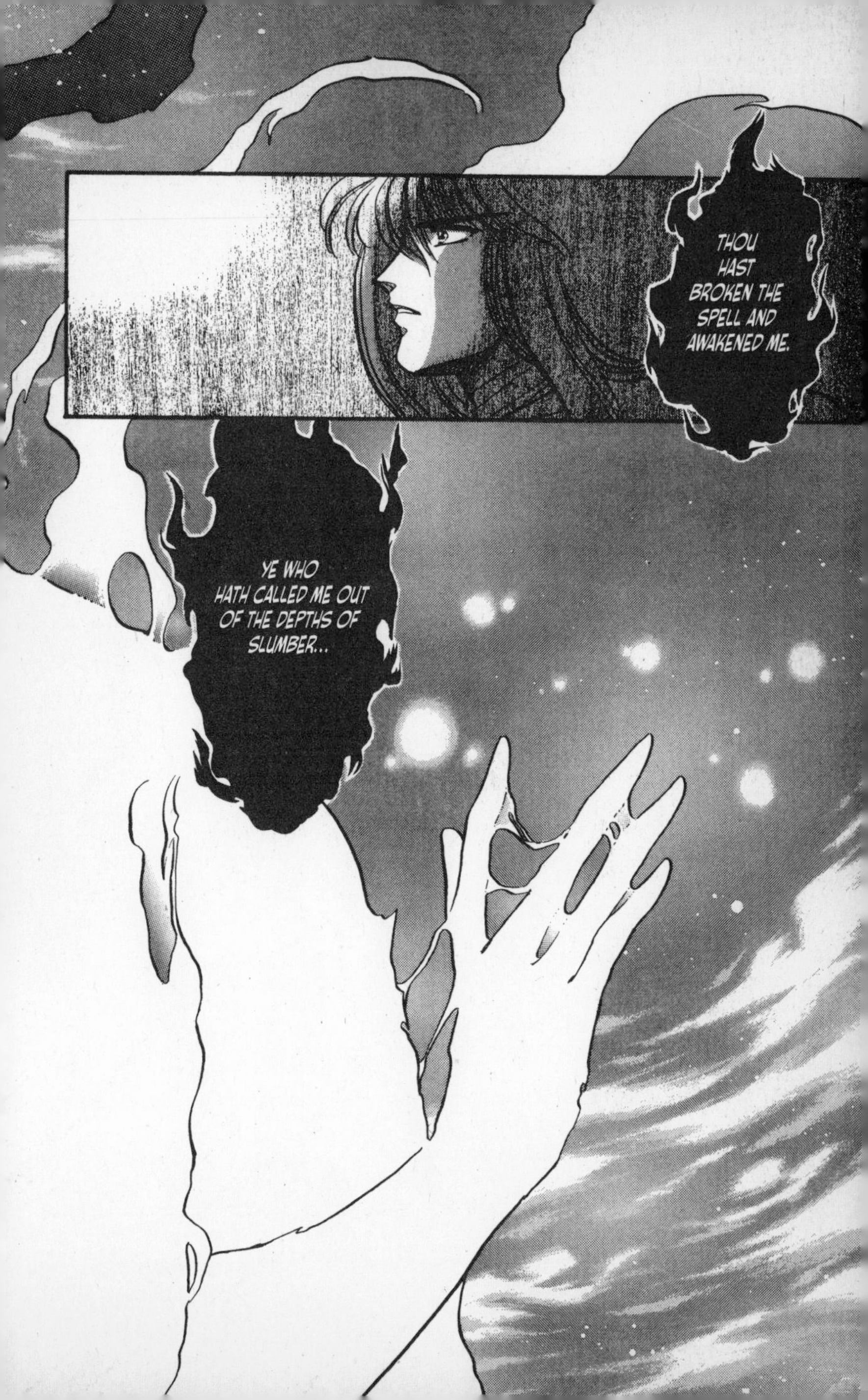
THOU HAST BROKEN THE SPELL AND AWAKENED ME.
YE WHO HATH CALLED ME OUT OF THE DEPTHS OF SLUMBER...

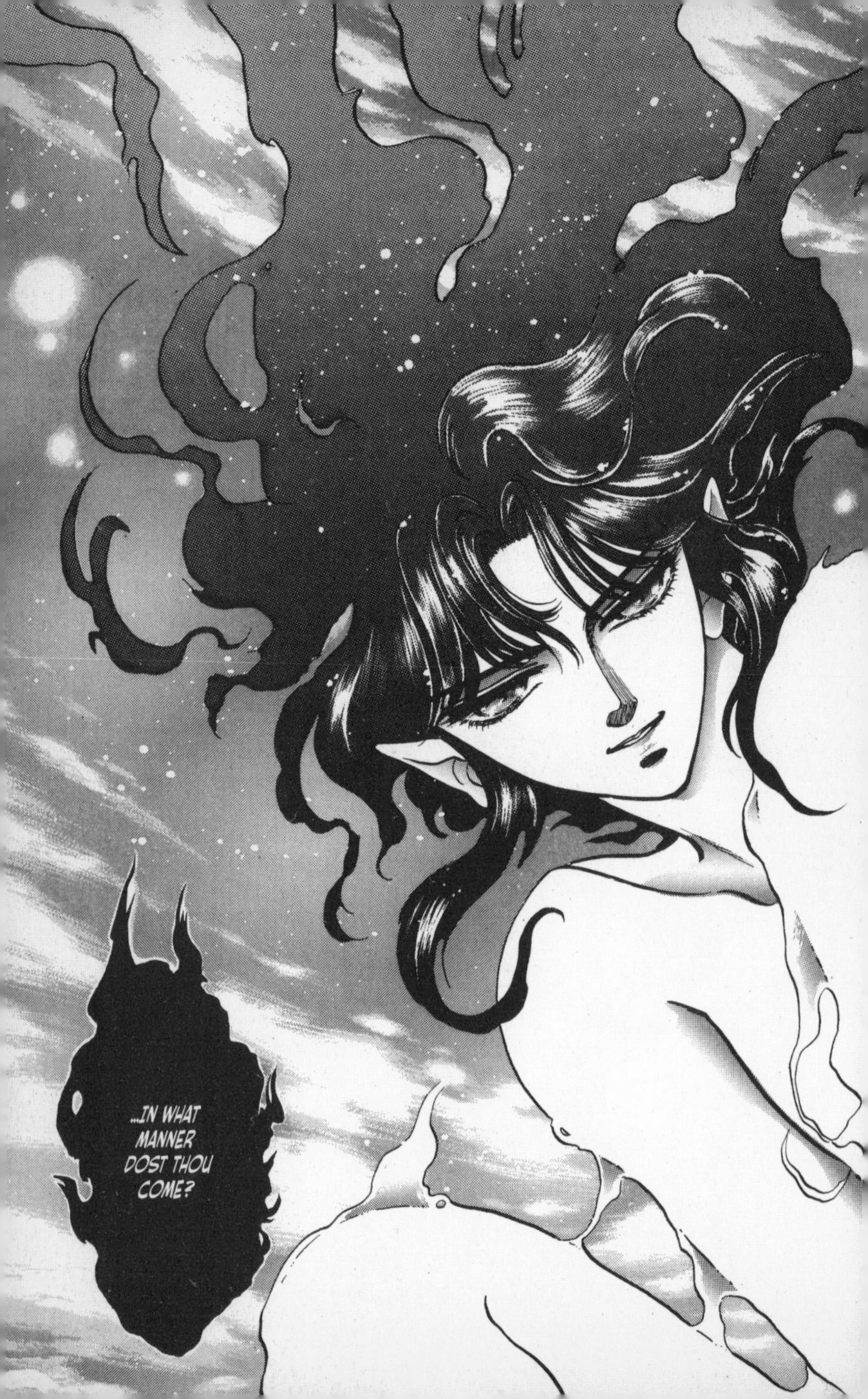
...IN WHAT MANNER DOST THOU COME?

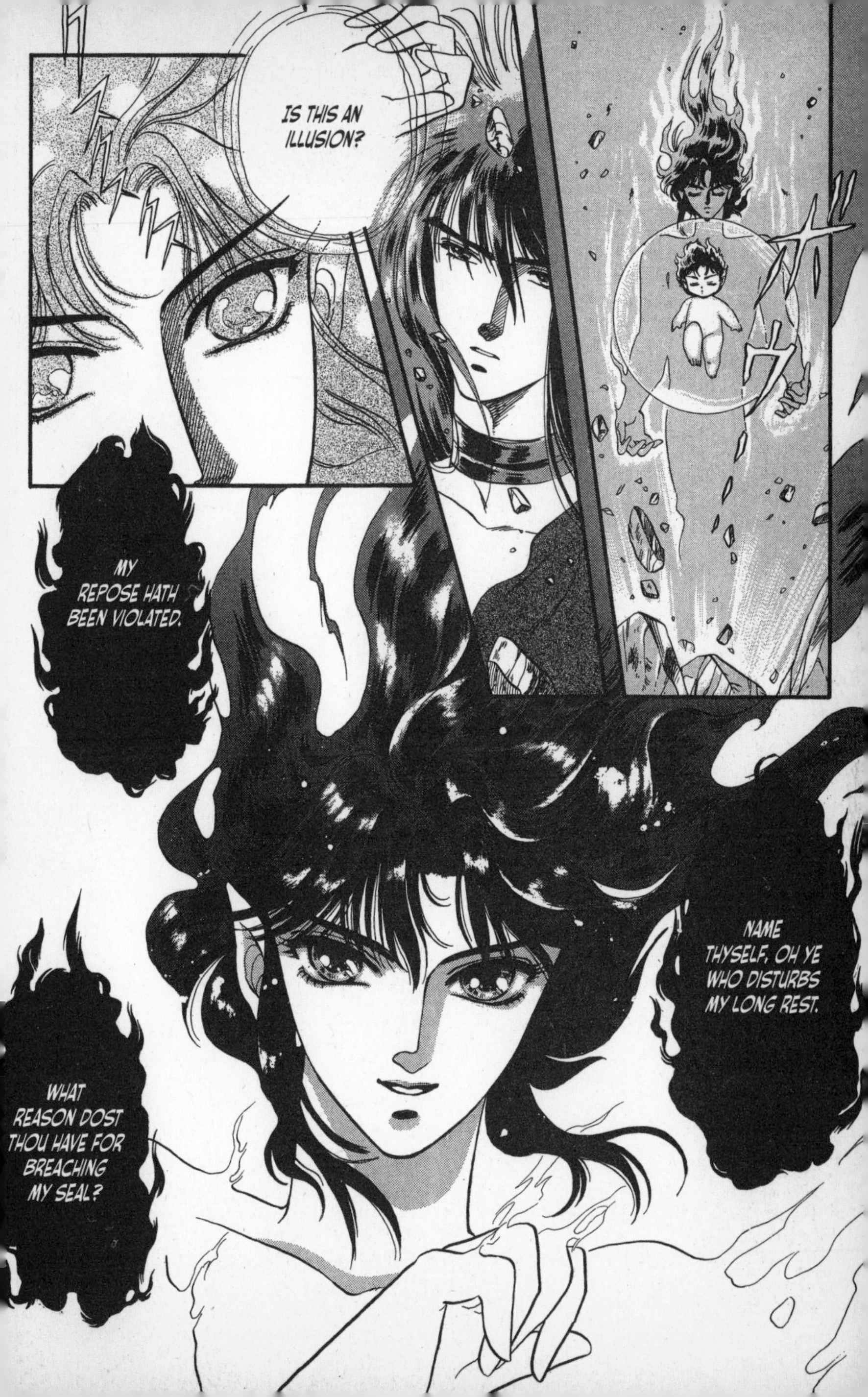
IS THIS AN ILLUSION?
MY REPOSE HATH BEEN VIOLATED.
NAME THYSELF, OH YE WHO DISTURBS MY LONG REST.
WHAT REASON DOST THOU HAVE FOR BREACHING MY SEAL?

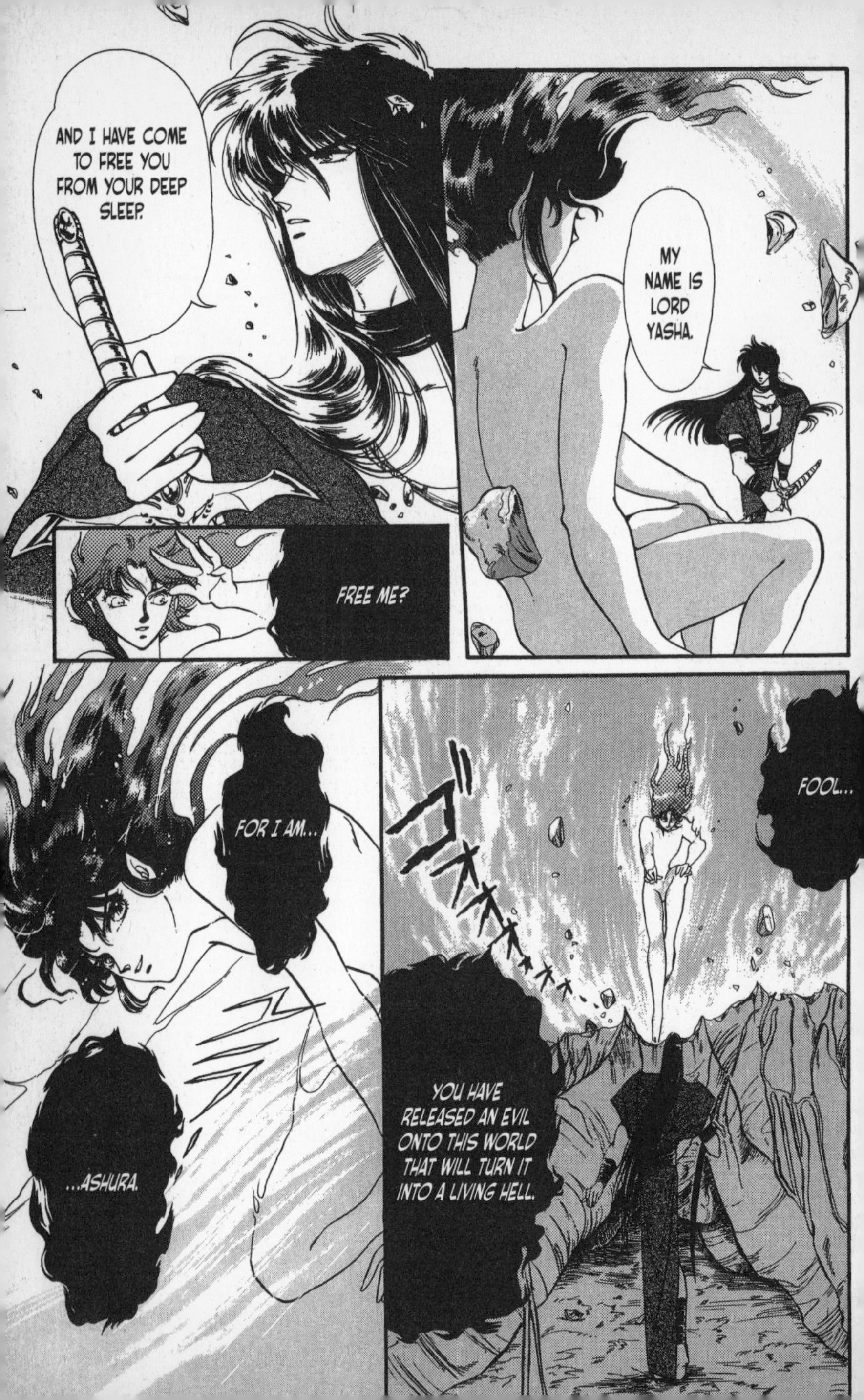
MY NAME IS LORD YASHA.
AND I HAVE COME TO FREE YOU FROM YOUR DEEP SLEEP.
FREE ME?
FOOL...
YOU HAVE RELEASED AN EVIL ONTO THIS WORLD THAT WILL TURN IT INTO A LIVING HELL.
FOR I AM...
...ASHURA.

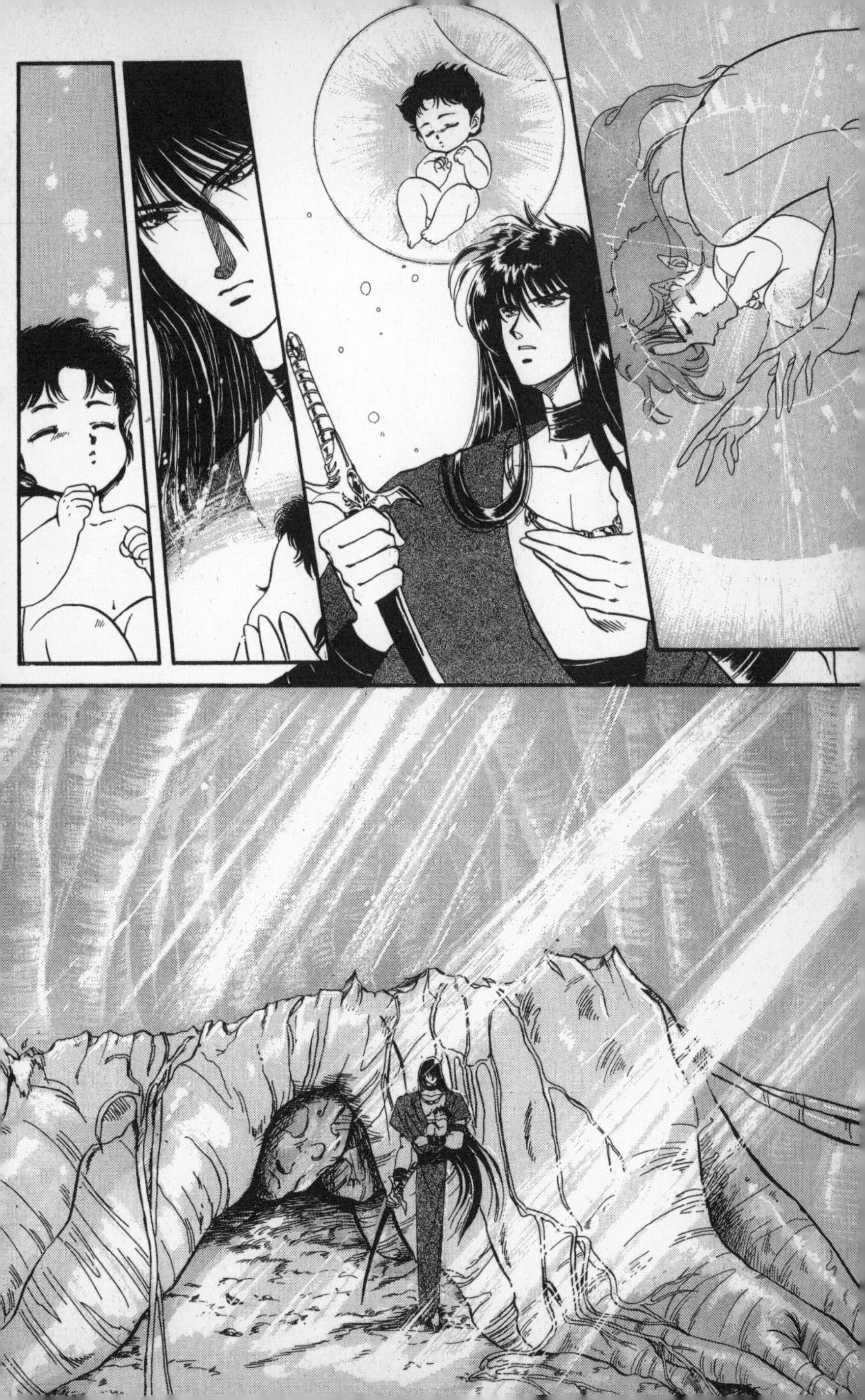

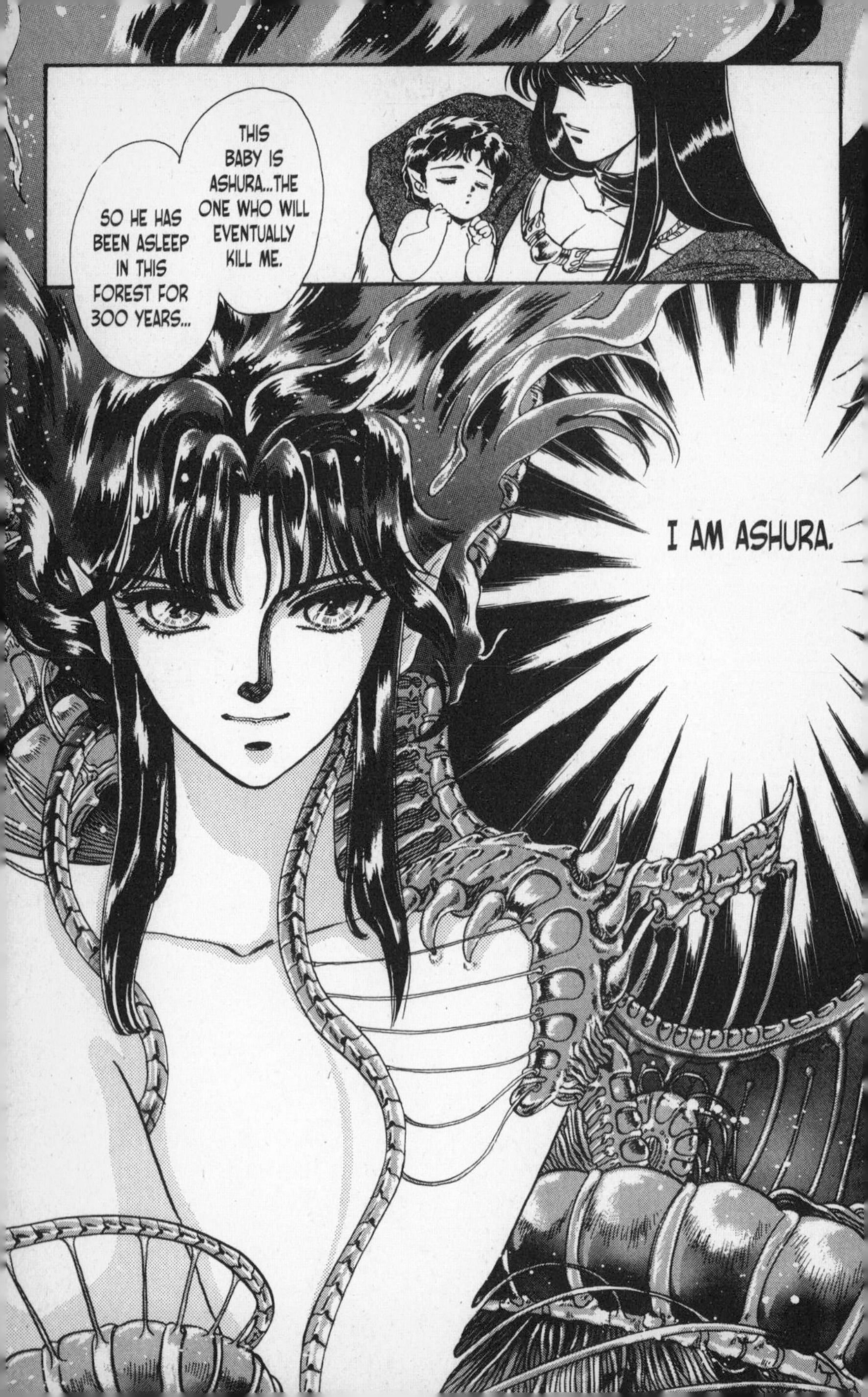
THIS BABY IS ASHURA...THE ONE WHO WILL EVENTUALLY KILL ME.
SO HE HAS BEEN ASLEEP IN THIS FOREST FOR 300 YEARS...
I AM ASHURA.

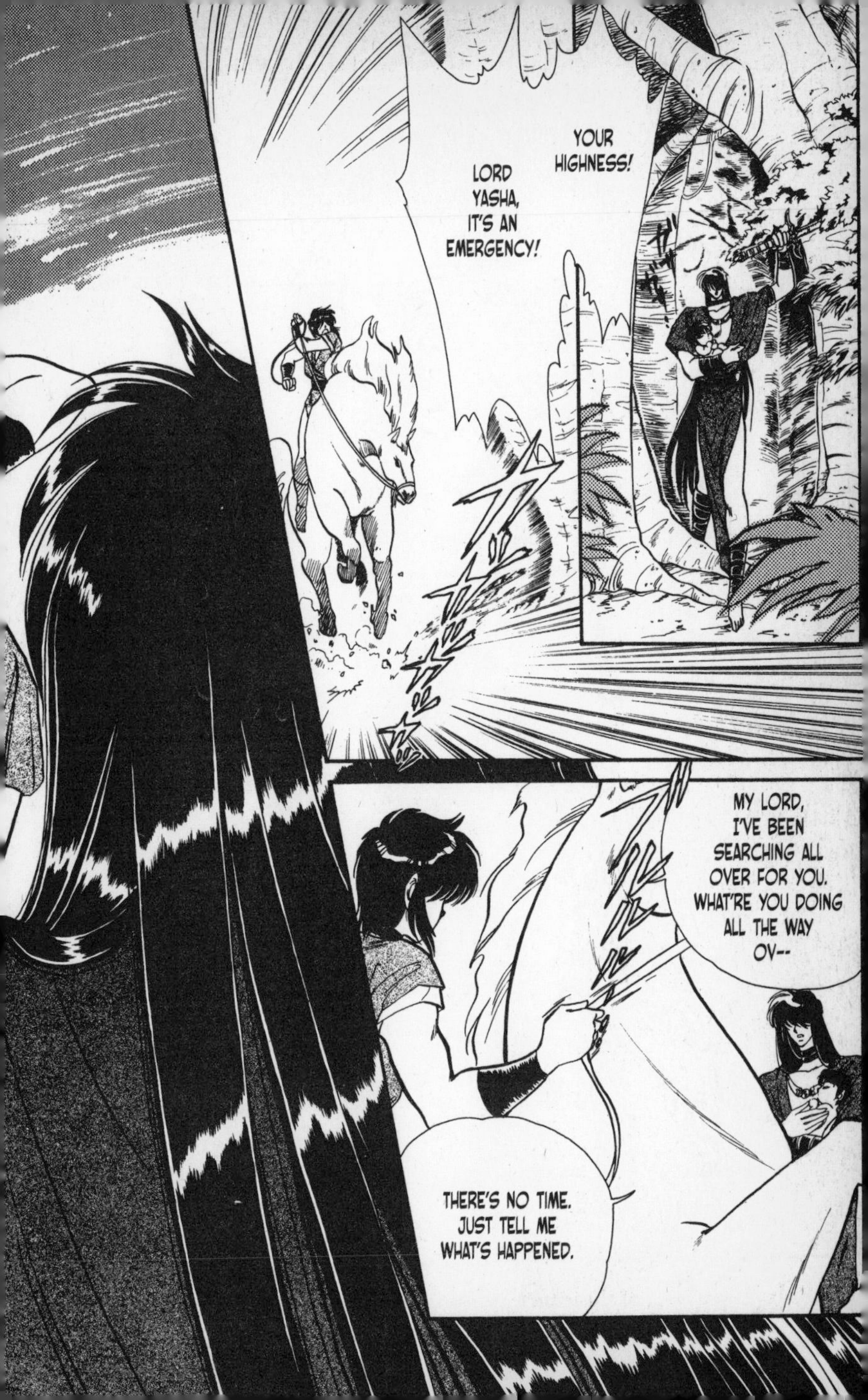
YOUR HIGHNESS!
LORD YASHA, IT'S AN EMERGENCY!
MY LORD, I'VE BEEN SEARCHING ALL OVER FOR YOU. WHAT'RE YOU DOING ALL THE WAY OV--
THERE'S NO TIME. JUST TELL ME WHAT'S HAPPENED.

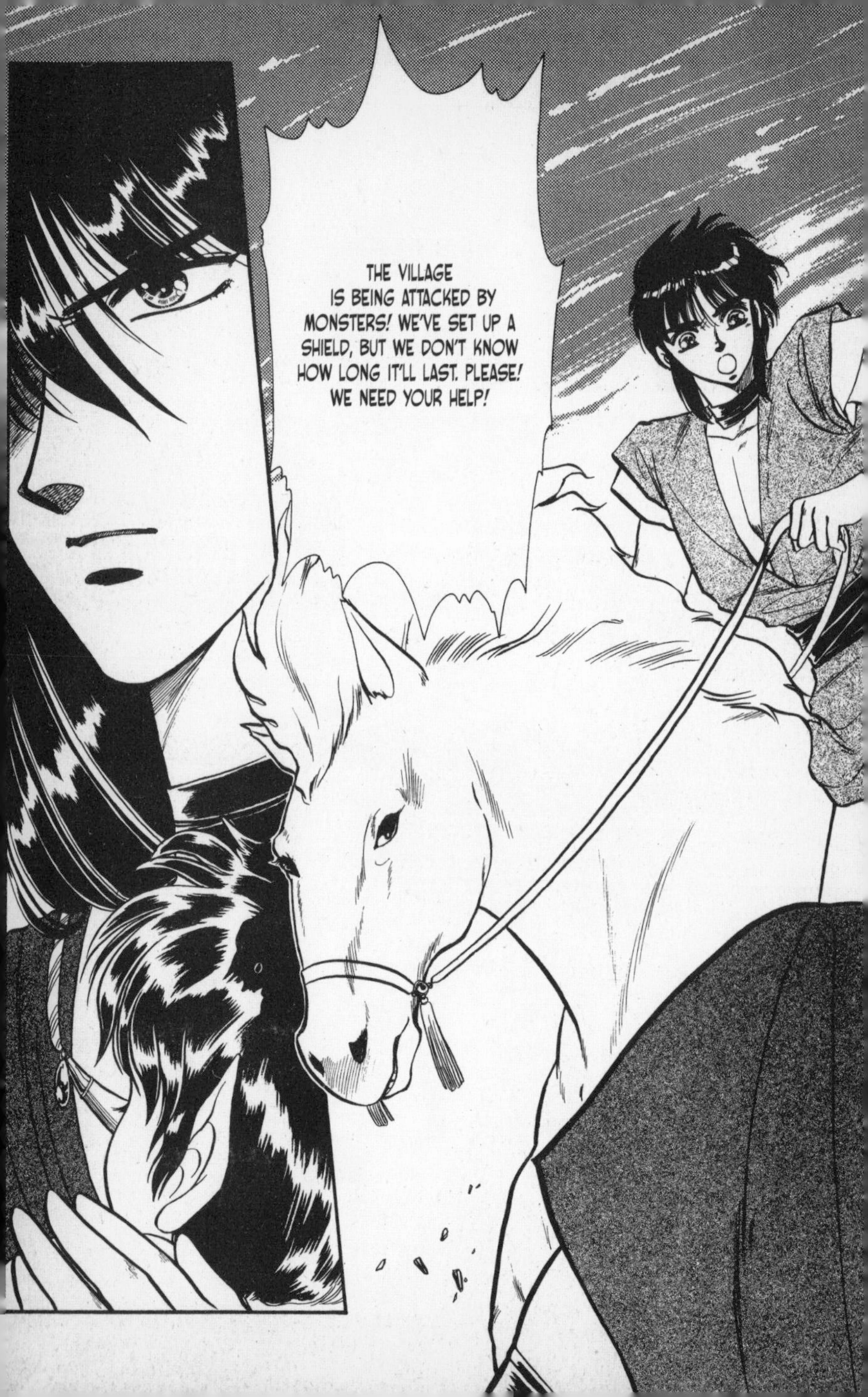
THE VILLAGE IS BEING ATTACKED BY MONSTERS! WE'VE SET UP A SHIELD, BUT WE DON'T KNOW HOW LONG IT'LL LAST. PLEASE! WE NEED YOUR HELP!

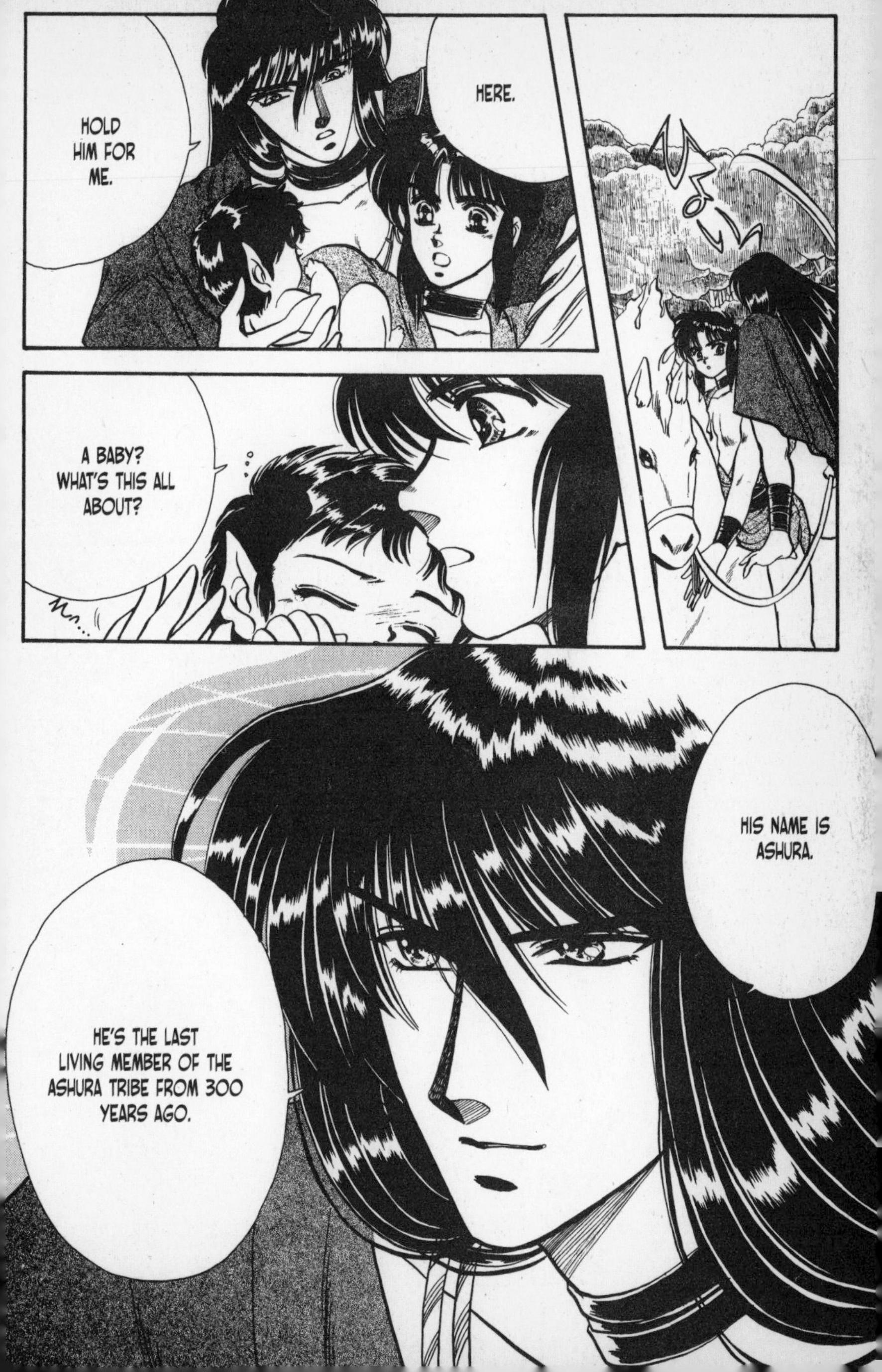
HERE.
HOLD HIM FOR ME.
A BABY? WHAT'S THIS ALL ABOUT?
Mn...
HIS NAME IS ASHURA.
HE'S THE LAST LIVING MEMBER OF THE ASHURA TRIBE FROM 300 YEARS AGO.

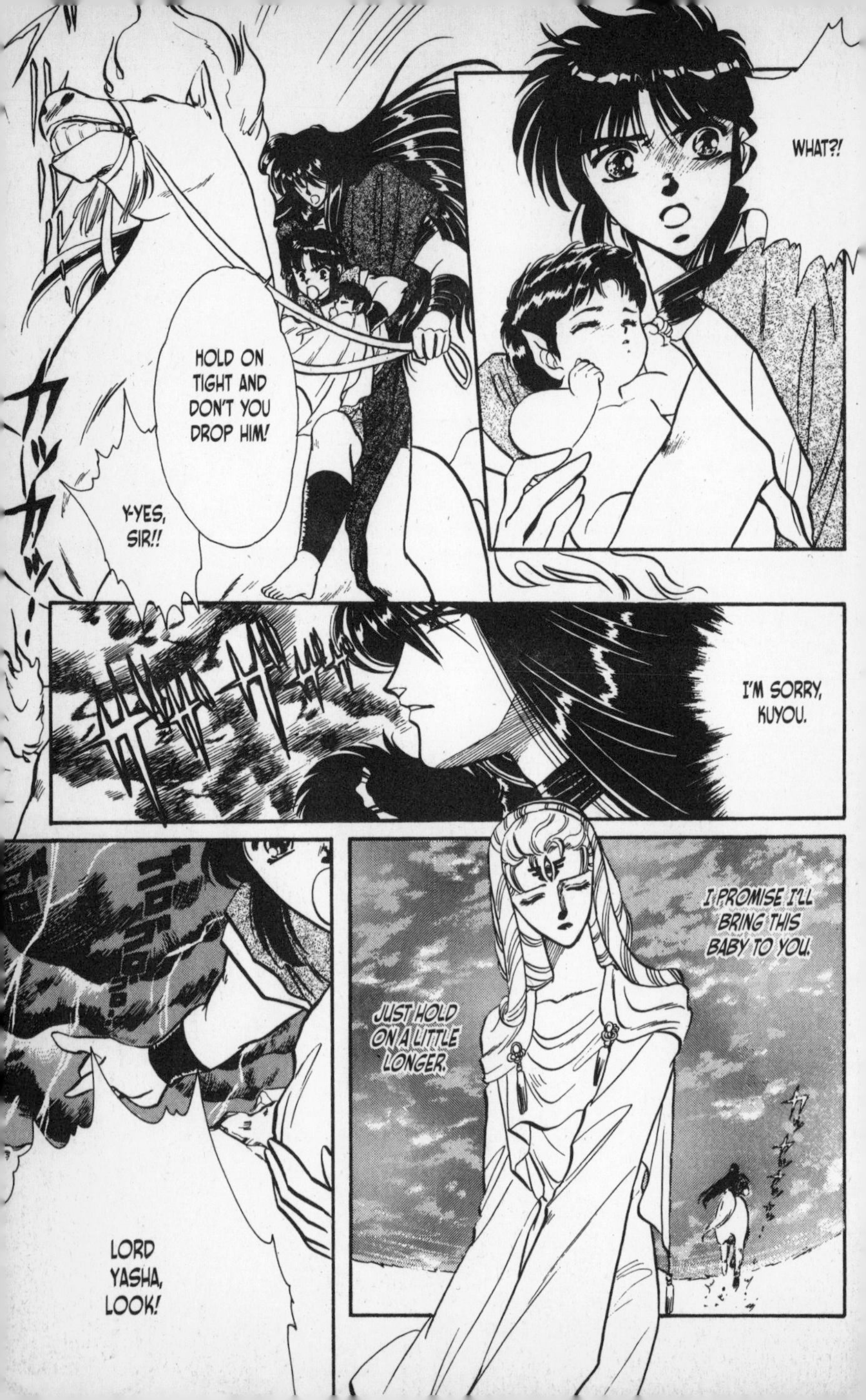
WHAT?!
HOLD ON TIGHT AND DON'T YOU DROP HIM!
Y-YES, SIR!!
I'M SORRY, KUYOU.
I PROMISE I'LL BRING THIS BABY TO YOU.
JUST HOLD ON A LITTLE LONGER.
LORD YASHA, LOOK!

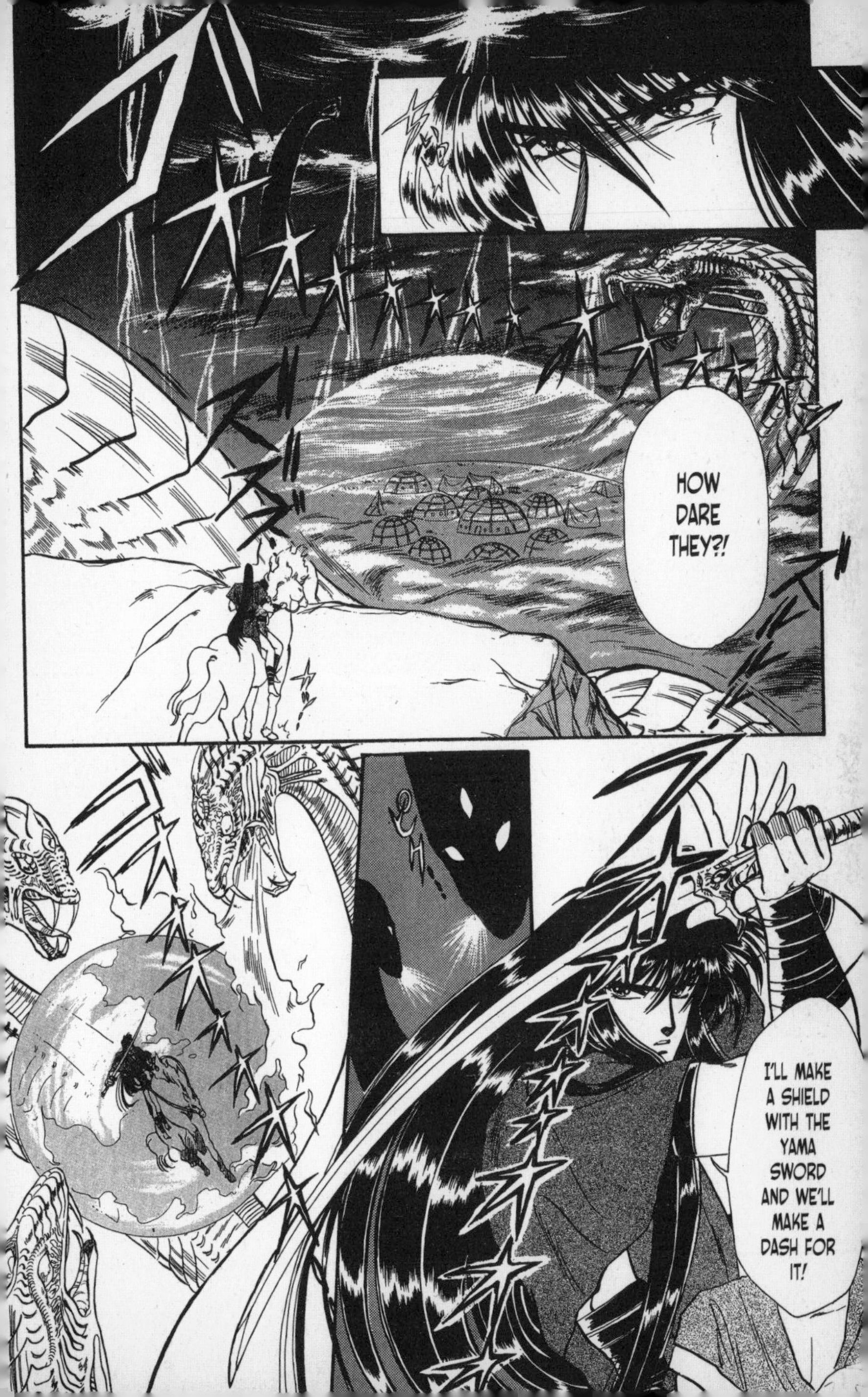
HOW DARE THEY?!
I'LL MAKE A SHIELD WITH THE YAMA SWORD AND WE'LL MAKE A DASH FOR IT!

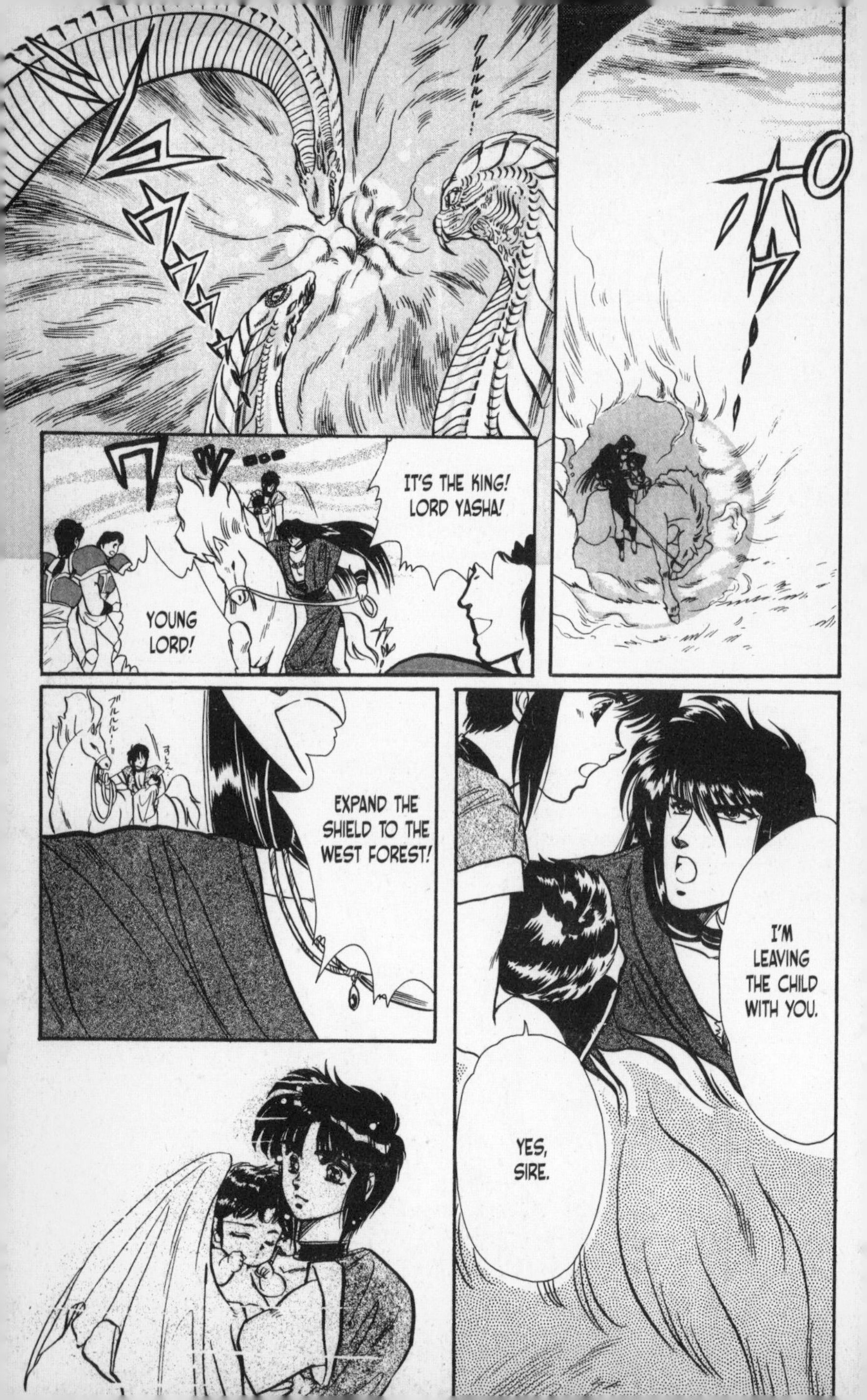
IT'S THE KING! LORD YASHA!
YOUNG LORD!
I'M LEAVING THE CHILD WITH YOU.
YES, SIRE.
EXPAND THE SHIELD TO THE WEST FOREST!

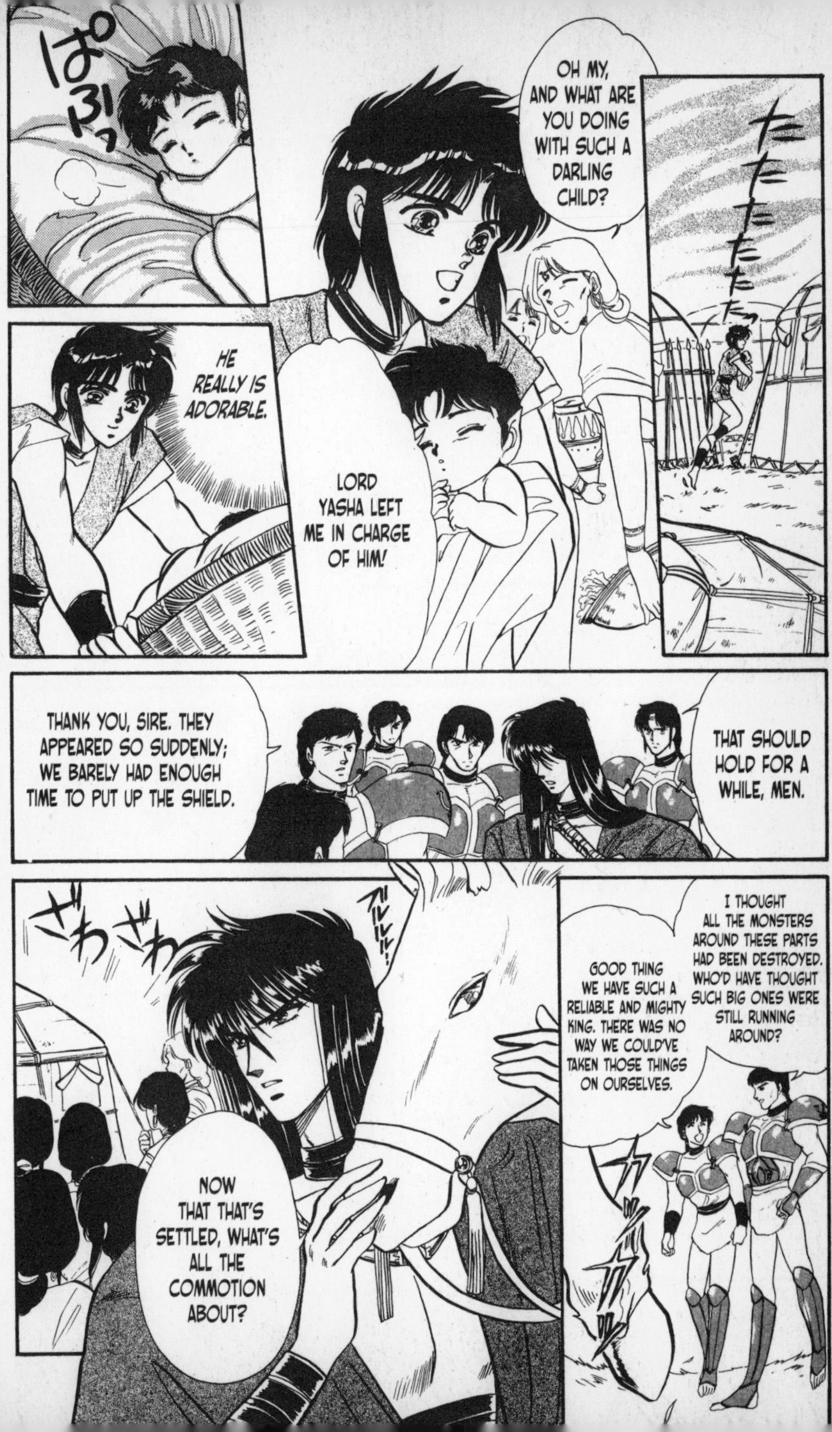
OH MY, AND WHAT ARE YOU DOING WITH SUCH A DARLING CHILD?
LORD YASHA LEFT ME IN CHARGE OF HIM!
HE REALLY IS ADORABLE.
THAT SHOULD HOLD FOR A WHILE, MEN.
THANK YOU, SIRE. THEY APPEARED SO SUDDENLY; WE BARELY HAD ENOUGH TIME TO PUT UP THE SHIELD.
I THOUGHT ALL THE MONSTERS AROUND THESE PARTS HAD BEEN DESTROYED. WHO'D HAVE THOUGHT SUCH BIG ONES WERE STILL RUNNING AROUND?
GOOD THING WE HAVE SUCH A RELIABLE AND MIGHTY KING. THERE WAS NO WAY WE COULD'VE TAKEN THOSE THINGS ON OURSELVES.
ざわざわ
NOW THAT THAT'S SETTLED, WHAT'S ALL THE COMMOTION ABOUT?

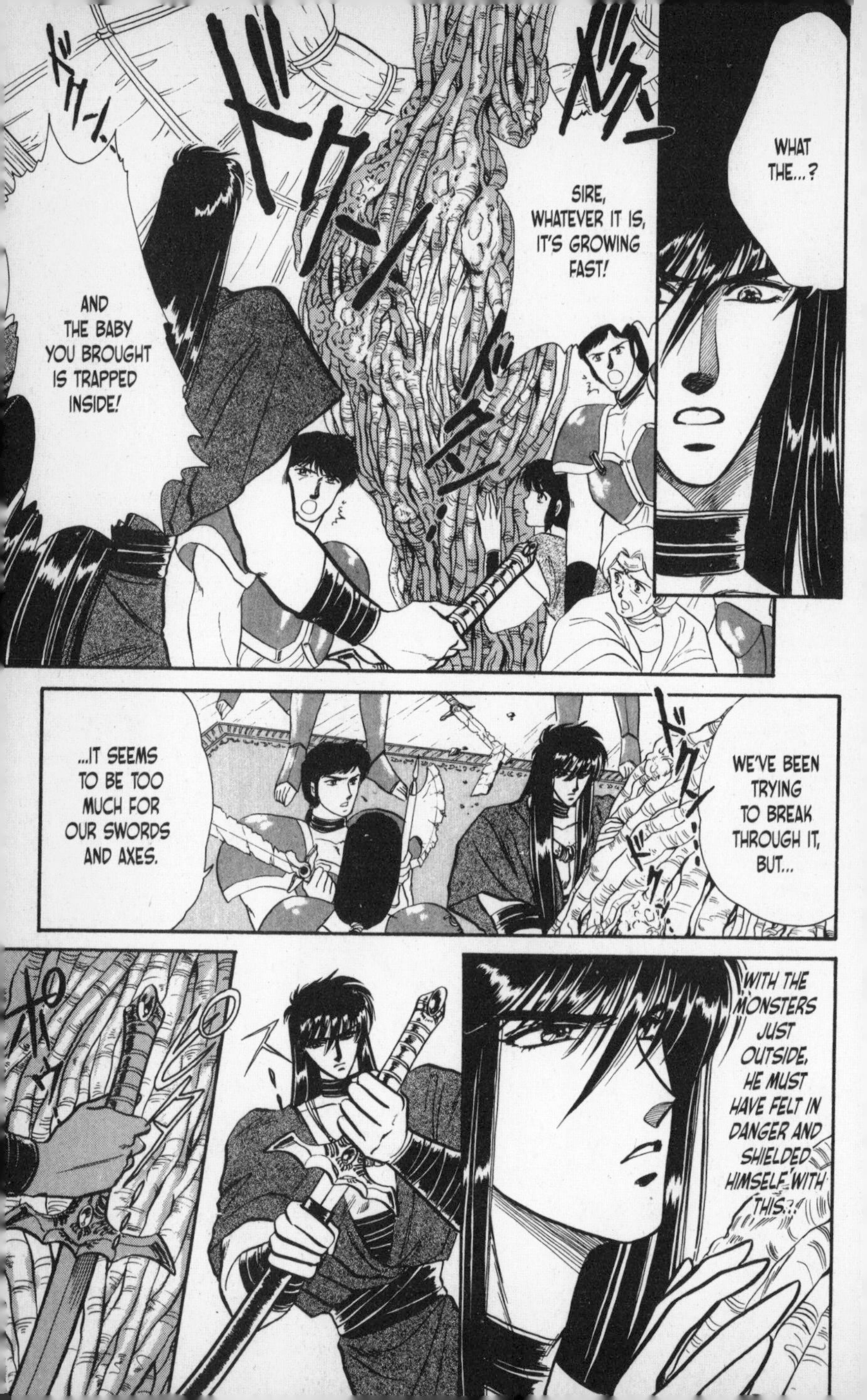
WHAT THE...?
SIRE, WHATEVER IT IS, IT'S GROWING FAST!
AND THE BABY YOU BROUGHT IS TRAPPED INSIDE!
WE'VE BEEN TRYING TO BREAK THROUGH IT, BUT...
...IT SEEMS TO BE TOO MUCH FOR OUR SWORDS AND AXES.
WITH THE MONSTERS JUST OUTSIDE, HE MUST HAVE FELT IN DANGER AND SHIELDED HIMSELF WITH THIS...!

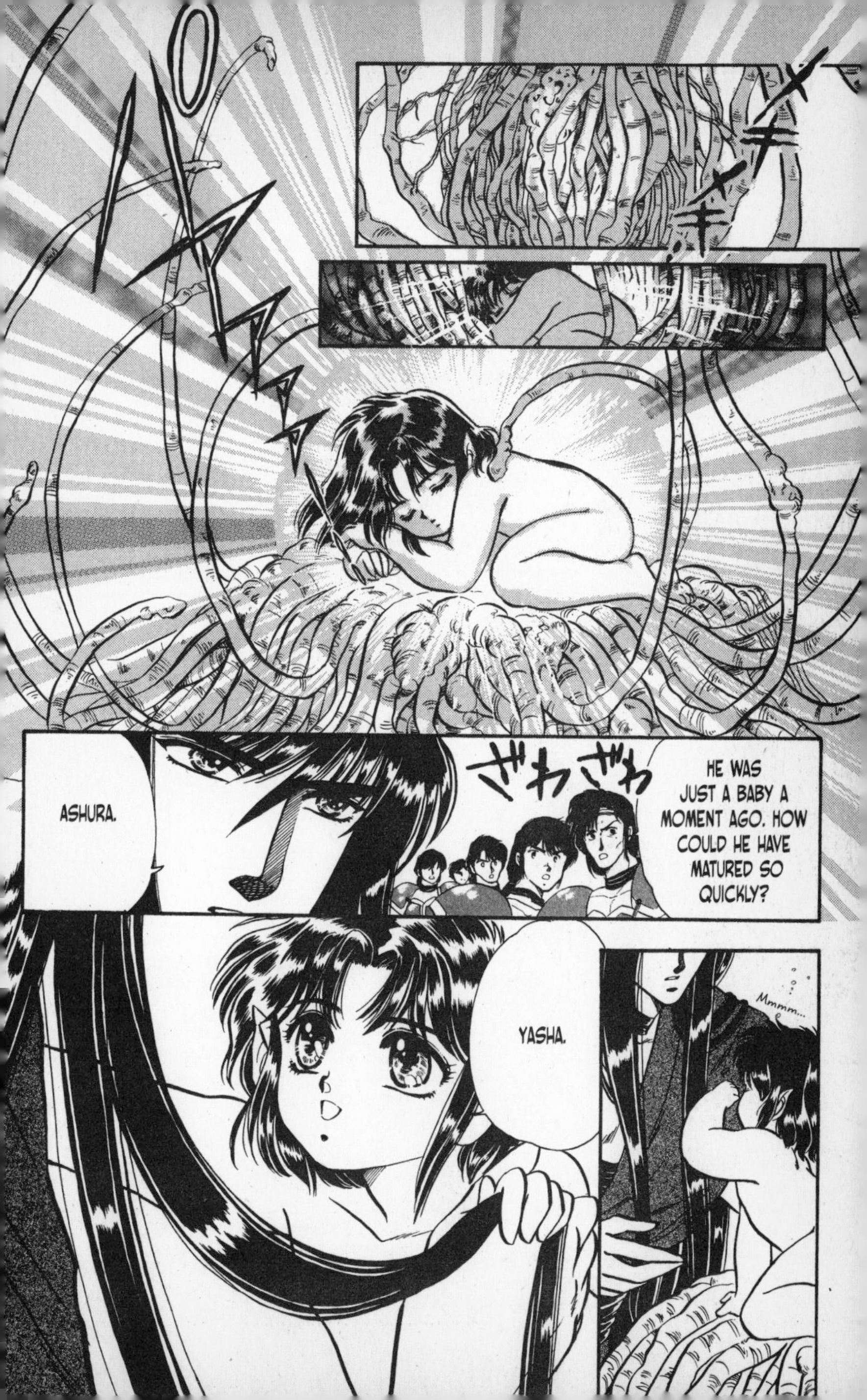
メキメキ
HE WAS JUST A BABY A MOMENT AGO. HOW COULD HE HAVE MATURED SO QUICKLY?
ざわざわ
ASHURA.
Mmmm...
YASHA.

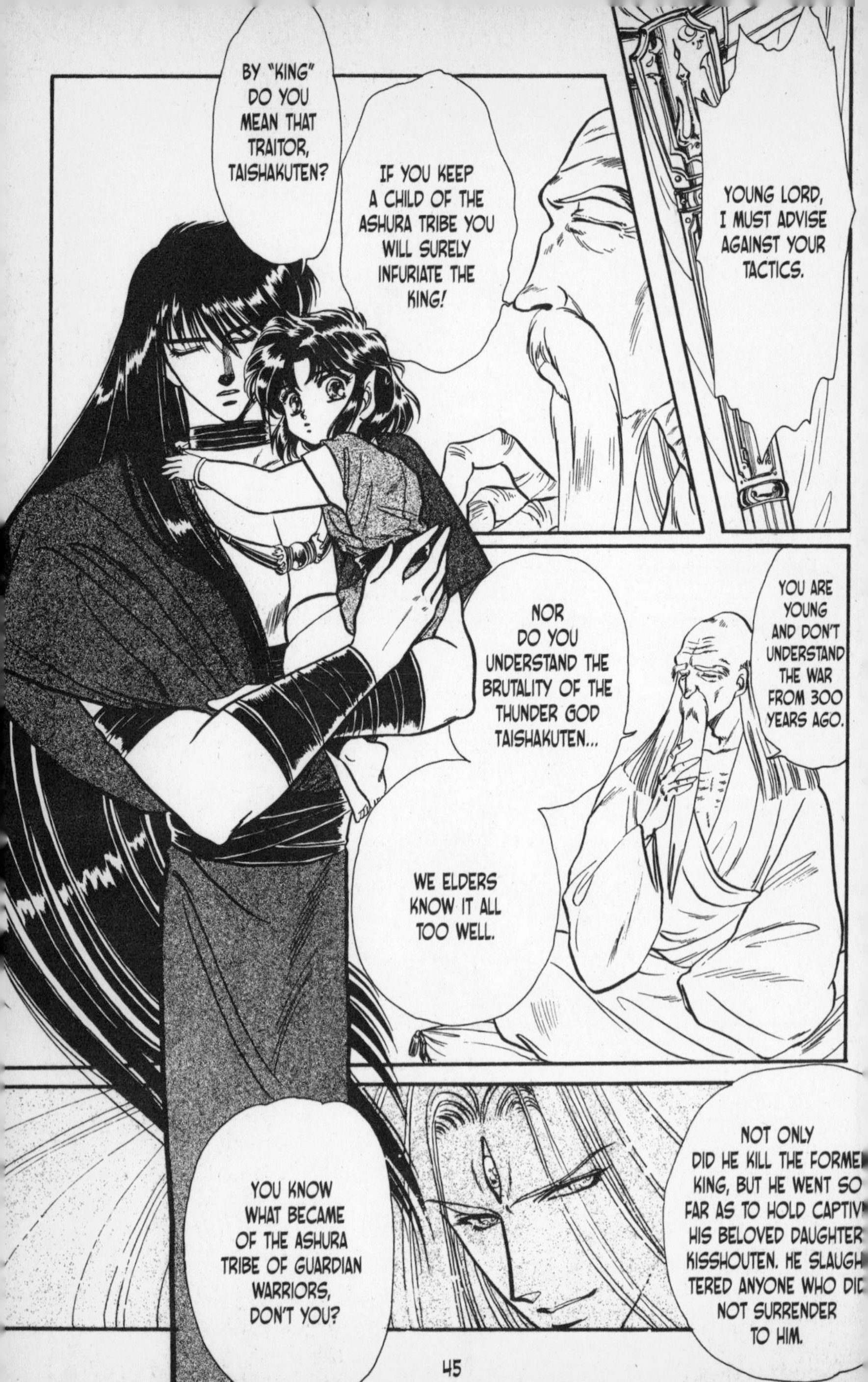
YOUNG LORD, I MUST ADVISE AGAINST YOUR TACTICS.
IF YOU KEEP A CHILD OF THE ASHURA TRIBE YOU WILL SURELY INFURIATE THE KING!
BY "KING" DO YOU MEAN THAT TRAITOR, TAISHAKUTEN?
YOU ARE YOUNG AND DON'T UNDERSTAND THE WAR FROM 300 YEARS AGO.
NOR DO YOU UNDERSTAND THE BRUTALITY OF THE THUNDER GOD TAISHAKUTEN...
WE ELDERS KNOW IT ALL TOO WELL.
NOT ONLY DID HE KILL THE FORME KING, BUT HE WENT SO FAR AS TO HOLD CAPTIV HIS BELOVED DAUGHTER KISSHOUTEN. HE SLAUGH TERED ANYONE WHO DID NOT SURRENDER TO HIM.
YOU KNOW WHAT BECAME OF THE ASHURA TRIBE OF GUARDIAN WARRIORS, DON'T YOU?

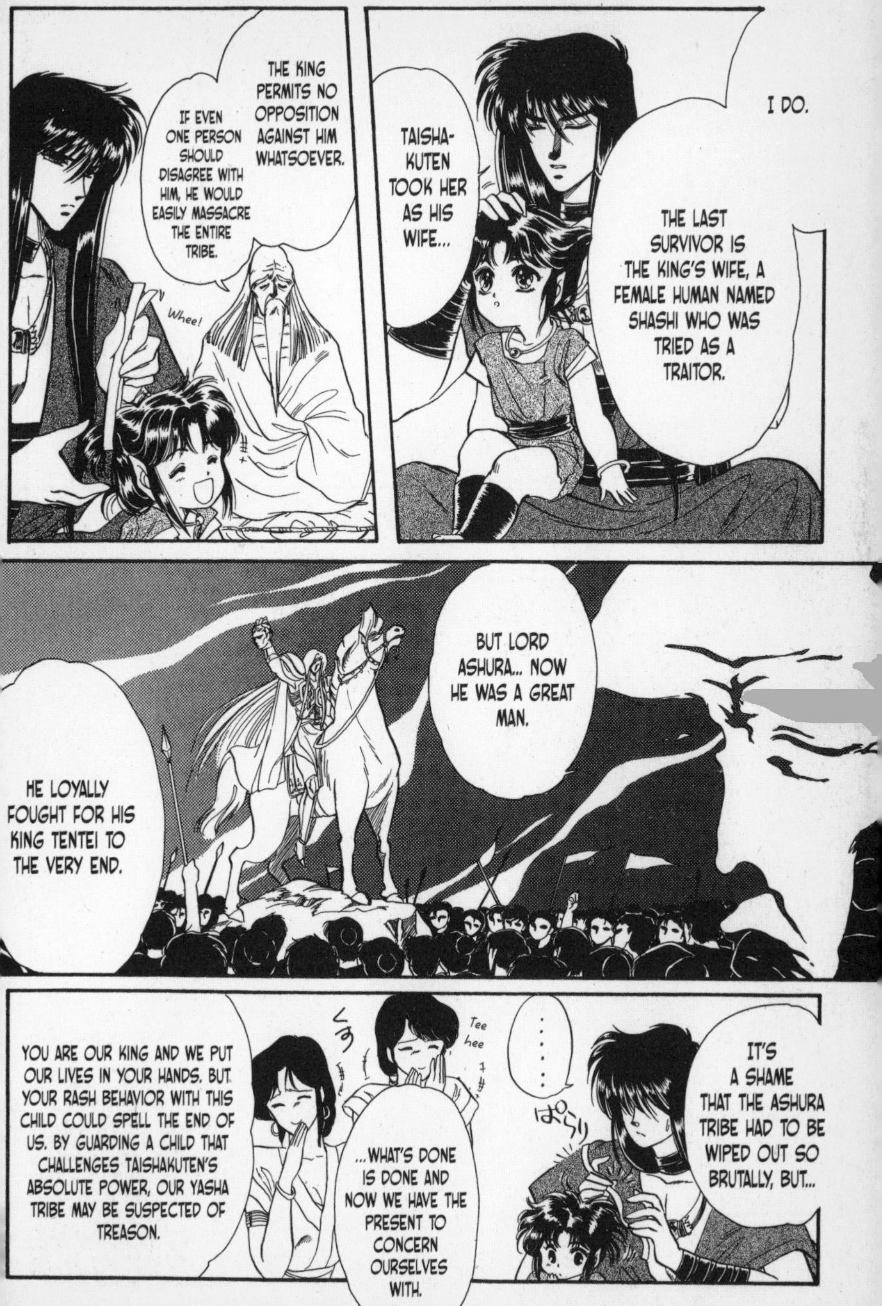
I DO.
THE LAST SURVIVOR IS THE KING'S WIFE, A FEMALE HUMAN NAMED SHASHI WHO WAS TRIED AS A TRAITOR.
TAISHA-KUTEN TOOK HER AS HIS WIFE...
THE KING PERMITS NO OPPOSITION AGAINST HIM WHATSOEVER.
IF EVEN ONE PERSON SHOULD DISAGREE WITH HIM, HE WOULD EASILY MASSACRE THE ENTIRE TRIBE.
Whee!
BUT LORD ASHURA... NOW HE WAS A GREAT MAN.
HE LOYALLY FOUGHT FOR HIS KING TENTEI TO THE VERY END.
IT'S A SHAME THAT THE ASHURA TRIBE HAD TO BE WIPED OUT SO BRUTALLY, BUT...
ぱらり
......
Tee hee
くす
...WHAT'S DONE IS DONE AND NOW WE HAVE THE PRESENT TO CONCERN OURSELVES WITH.
YOU ARE OUR KING AND WE PUT OUR LIVES IN YOUR HANDS. BUT YOUR RASH BEHAVIOR WITH THIS CHILD COULD SPELL THE END OF US. BY GUARDING A CHILD THAT CHALLENGES TAISHAKUTEN'S ABSOLUTE POWER, OUR YASHA TRIBE MAY BE SUSPECTED OF TREASON.

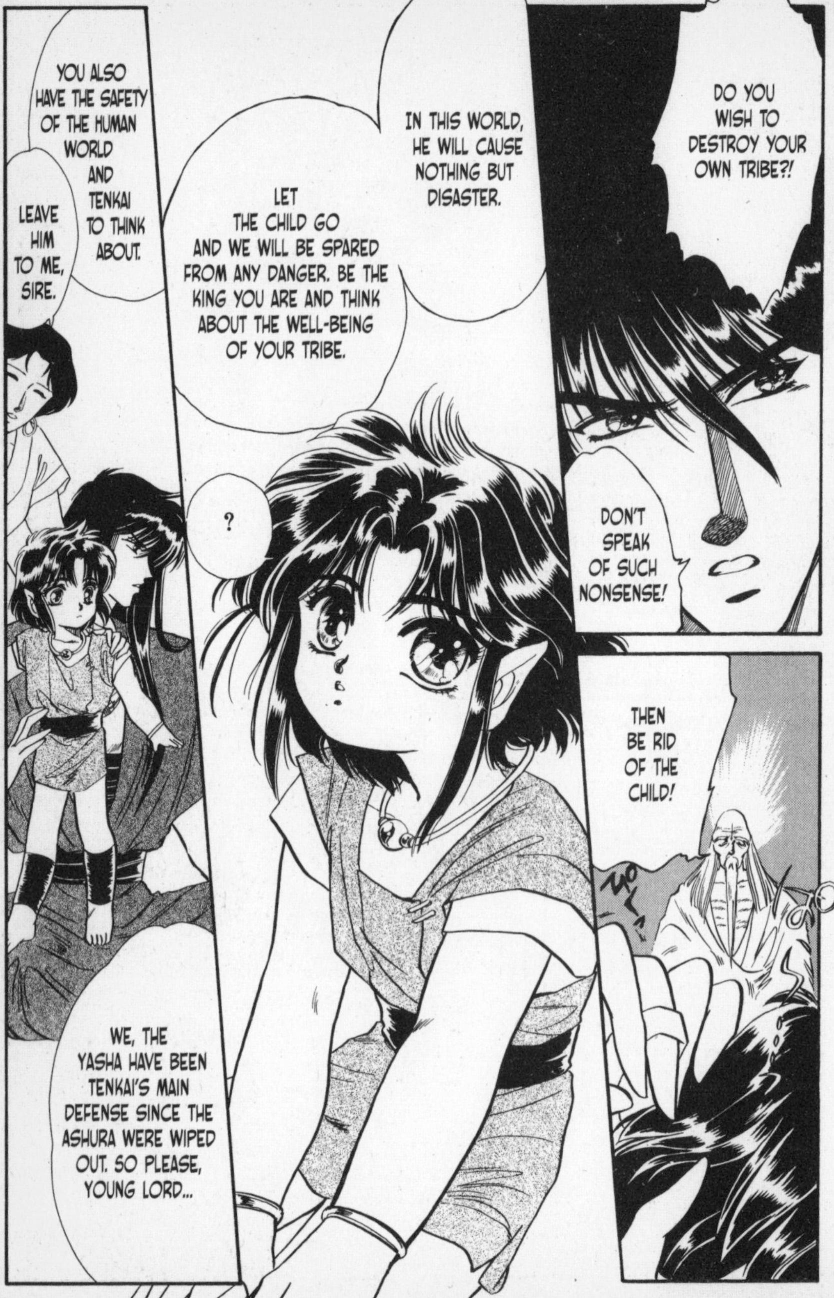
DO YOU WISH TO DESTROY YOUR OWN TRIBE?!
DON'T SPEAK OF SUCH NONSENSE!
THEN BE RID OF THE CHILD!
IN THIS WORLD, HE WILL CAUSE NOTHING BUT DISASTER.
LET THE CHILD GO AND WE WILL BE SPARED FROM ANY DANGER. BE THE KING YOU ARE AND THINK ABOUT THE WELL-BEING OF YOUR TRIBE.
?
YOU ALSO HAVE THE SAFETY OF THE HUMAN WORLD AND TENKAI TO THINK ABOUT.
LEAVE HIM TO ME, SIRE.
WE, THE YASHA HAVE BEEN TENKAI'S MAIN DEFENSE SINCE THE ASHURA WERE WIPED OUT. SO PLEASE, YOUNG LORD...

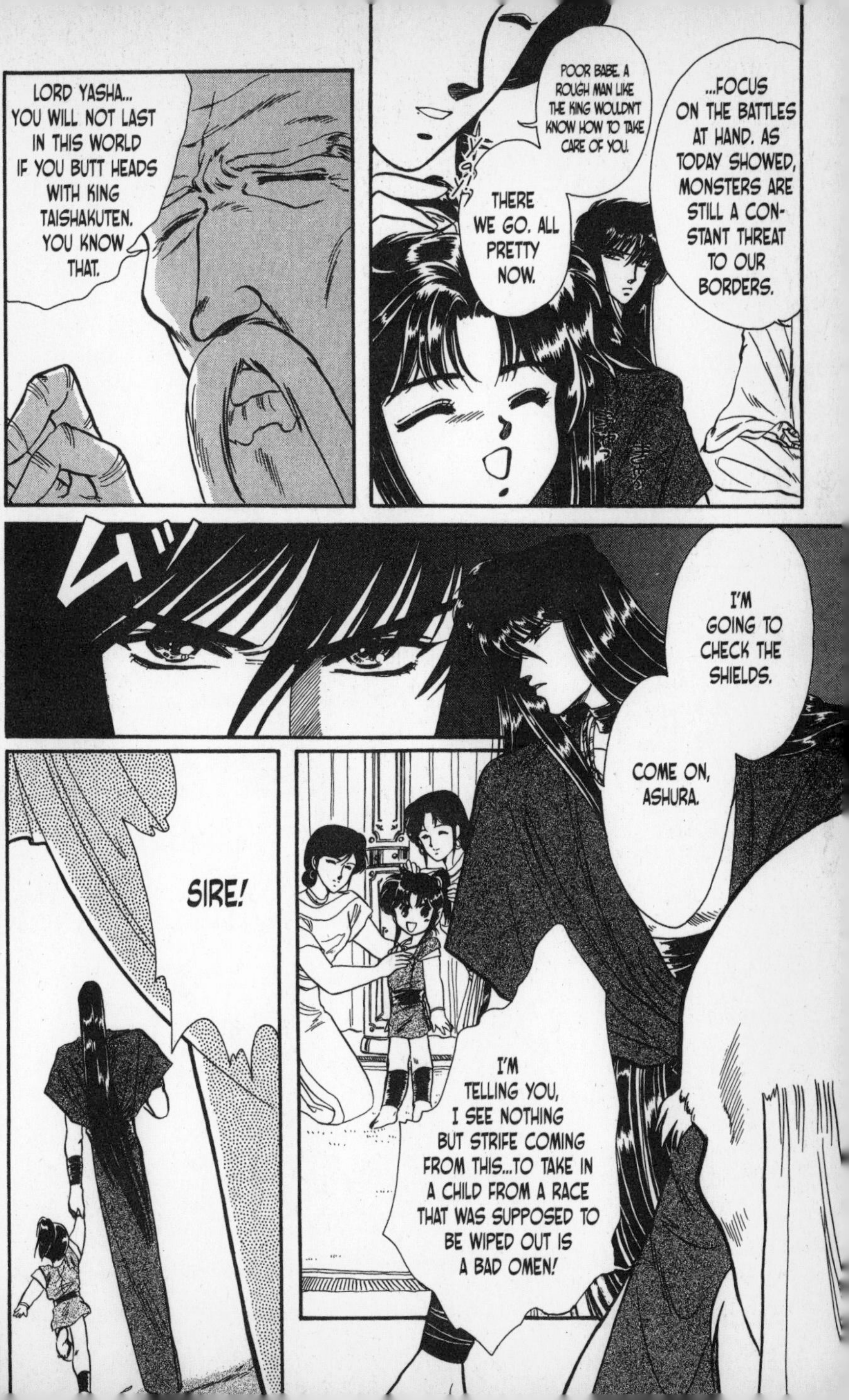
...FOCUS ON THE BATTLES AT HAND. AS TODAY SHOWED, MONSTERS ARE STILL A CONSTANT THREAT TO OUR BORDERS.
POOR BABE. A ROUGH MAN LIKE THE KING WOULDN'T KNOW HOW TO TAKE CARE OF YOU.
THERE WE GO. ALL PRETTY NOW.
LORD YASHA... YOU WILL NOT LAST IN THIS WORLD IF YOU BUTT HEADS WITH KING TAISHAKUTEN. YOU KNOW THAT.
I'M GOING TO CHECK THE SHIELDS.
ムッ
COME ON, ASHURA.
I'M TELLING YOU, I SEE NOTHING BUT STRIFE COMING FROM THIS...TO TAKE IN A CHILD FROM A RACE THAT WAS SUPPOSED TO BE WIPED OUT IS A BAD OMEN!
SIRE!

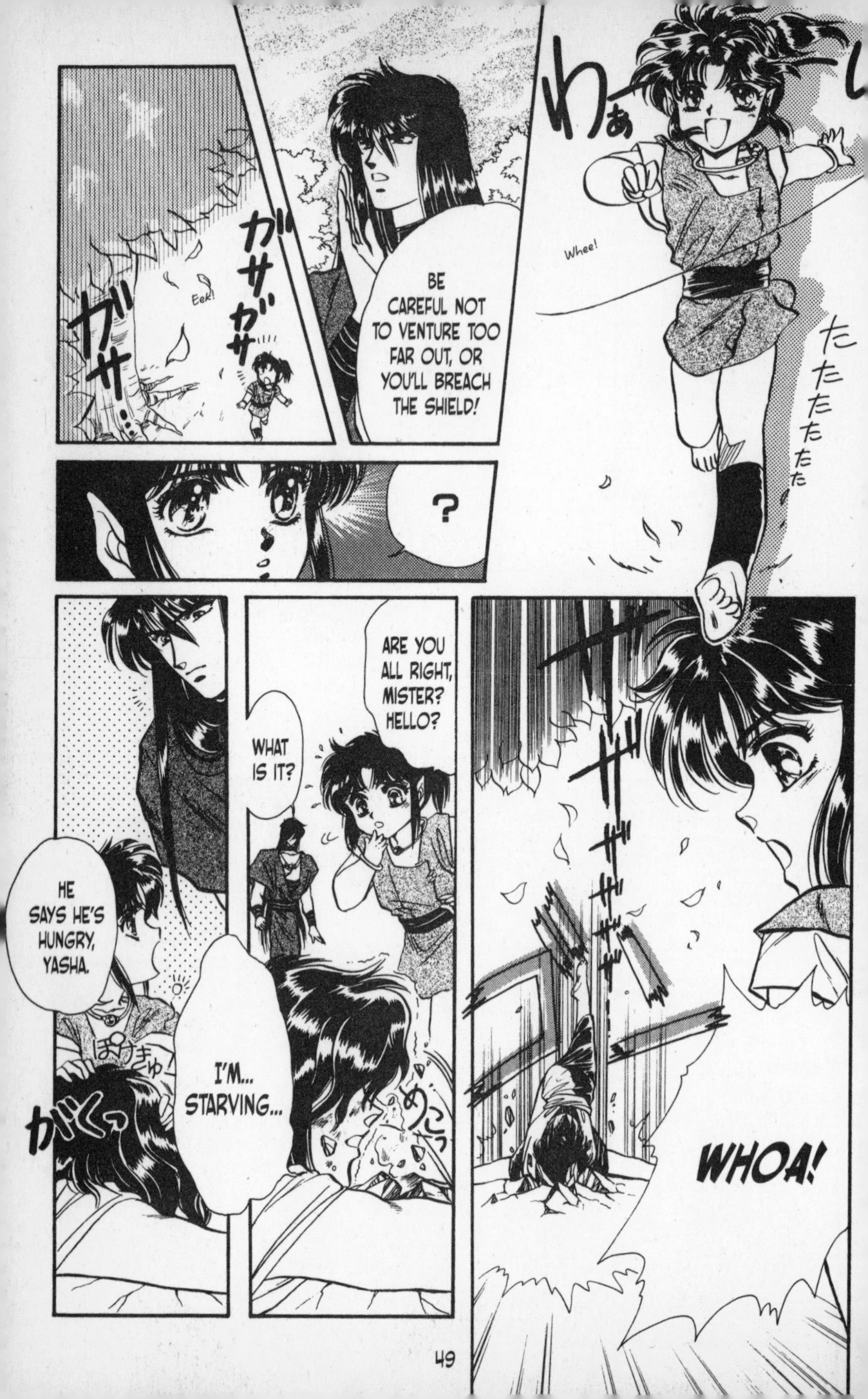
わぁーい
Whee!
たたたたたた
BE CAREFUL NOT TO VENTURE TOO FAR OUT, OR YOU'LL BREACH THE SHIELD!
ガサガサ
ガサ…
Eek!
?
WHOA!
ARE YOU ALL RIGHT, MISTER? HELLO?
WHAT IS IT?
I'M... STARVING...
HE SAYS HE'S HUNGRY, YASHA.
がくっ

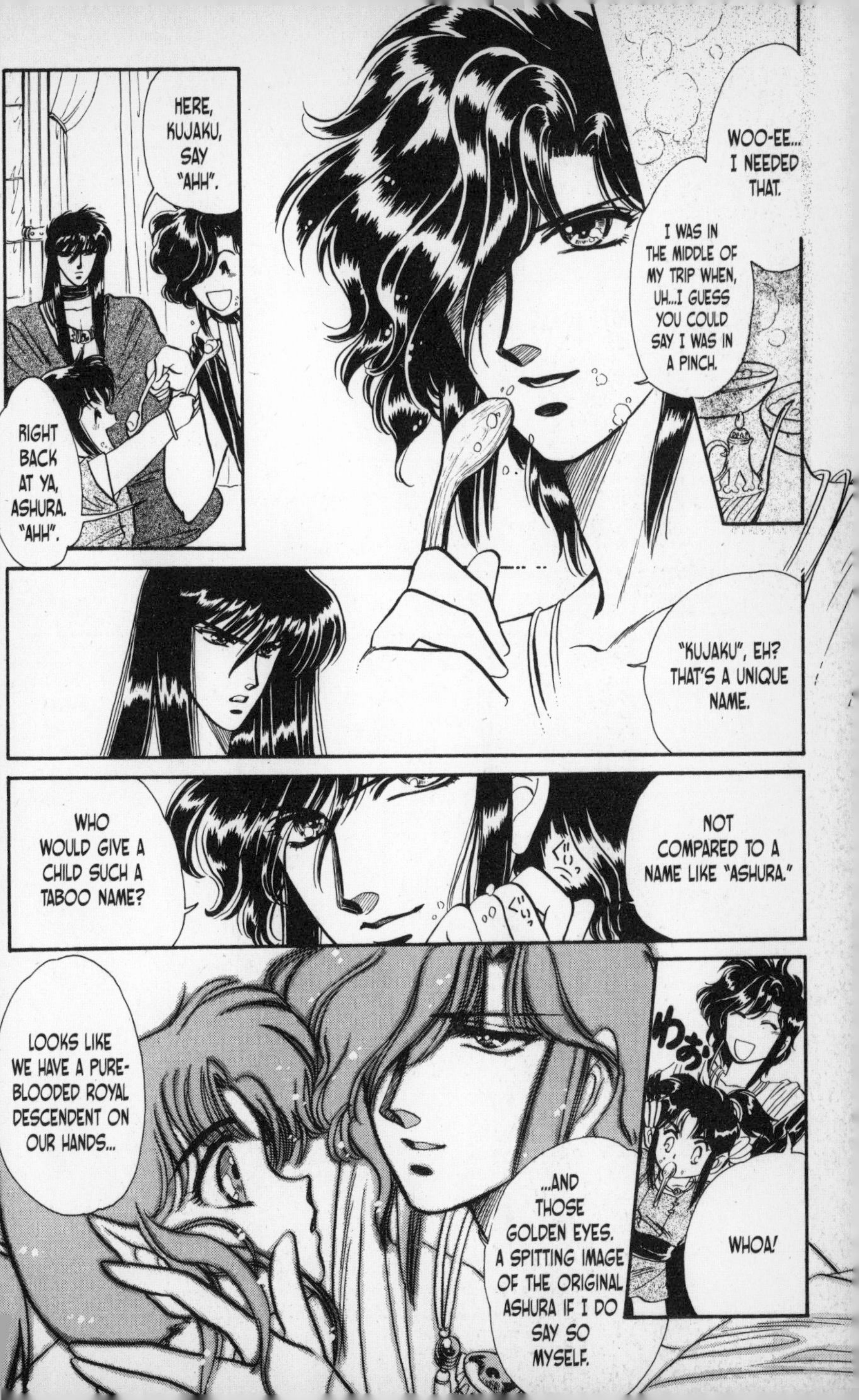
WOO-EE... I NEEDED THAT.
I WAS IN THE MIDDLE OF MY TRIP WHEN, UH...I GUESS YOU COULD SAY I WAS IN A PINCH.
HERE, KUJAKU, SAY "AHH".
RIGHT BACK AT YA, ASHURA. "AHH".
"KUJAKU", EH? THAT'S A UNIQUE NAME.
NOT COMPARED TO A NAME LIKE "ASHURA."
WHO WOULD GIVE A CHILD SUCH A TABOO NAME?
WHOA!
LOOKS LIKE WE HAVE A PURE-BLOODED ROYAL DESCENDENT ON OUR HANDS...
...AND THOSE GOLDEN EYES. A SPITTING IMAGE OF THE ORIGINAL ASHURA IF I DO SAY SO MYSELF.

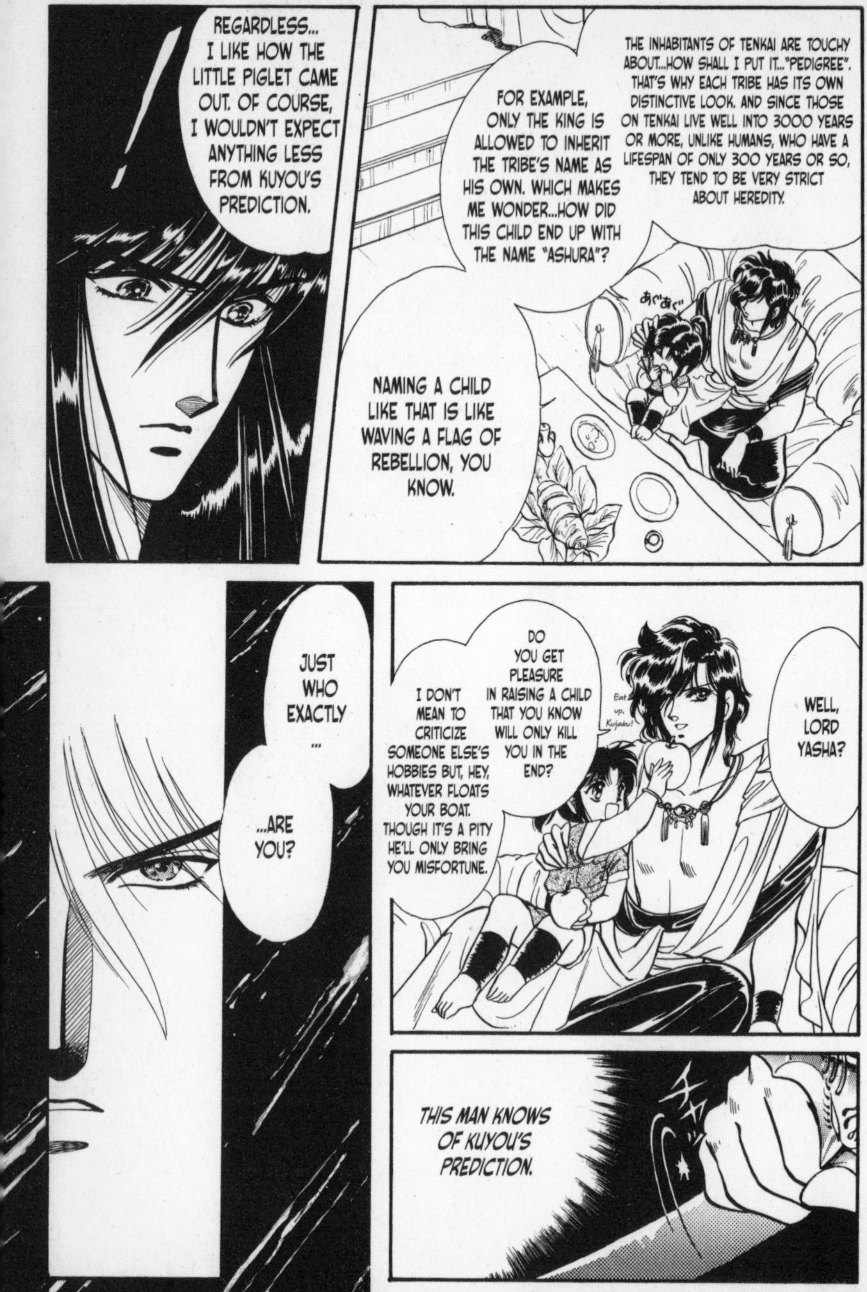
THE INHABITANTS OF TENKAI ARE TOUCHY ABOUT...HOW SHALL I PUT IT..."PEDIGREE". THAT'S WHY EACH TRIBE HAS ITS OWN DISTINCTIVE LOOK. AND SINCE THOSE ON TENKAI LIVE WELL INTO 3000 YEARS OR MORE, UNLIKE HUMANS, WHO HAVE A LIFESPAN OF ONLY 300 YEARS OR SO, THEY TEND TO BE VERY STRICT ABOUT HEREDITY.
FOR EXAMPLE, ONLY THE KING IS ALLOWED TO INHERIT THE TRIBE'S NAME AS HIS OWN. WHICH MAKES ME WONDER...HOW DID THIS CHILD END UP WITH THE NAME "ASHURA"?
あぐあぐ
NAMING A CHILD LIKE THAT IS LIKE WAVING A FLAG OF REBELLION, YOU KNOW.
REGARDLESS... I LIKE HOW THE LITTLE PIGLET CAME OUT. OF COURSE, I WOULDN'T EXPECT ANYTHING LESS FROM KUYOU'S PREDICTION.
WELL, LORD YASHA?
Eat up, Kujaku!
DO YOU GET PLEASURE IN RAISING A CHILD THAT YOU KNOW WILL ONLY KILL YOU IN THE END?
I DON'T MEAN TO CRITICIZE SOMEONE ELSE'S HOBBIES BUT, HEY, WHATEVER FLOATS YOUR BOAT. THOUGH IT'S A PITY HE'LL ONLY BRING YOU MISFORTUNE.
THIS MAN KNOWS OF KUYOU'S PREDICTION.
JUST WHO EXACTLY ...
...ARE YOU?

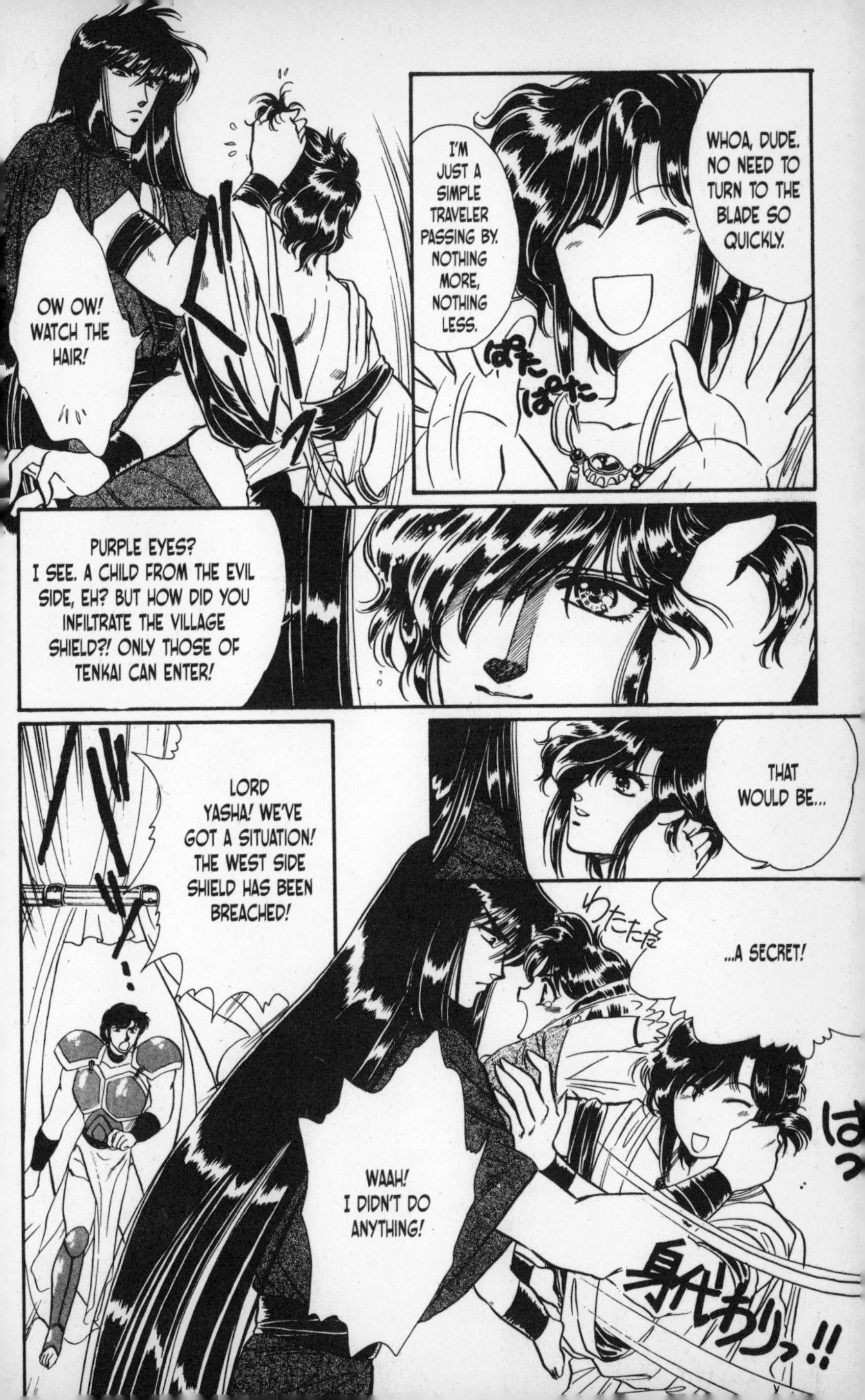
WHOA, DUDE. NO NEED TO TURN TO THE BLADE SO QUICKLY.
I'M JUST A SIMPLE TRAVELER PASSING BY. NOTHING MORE, NOTHING LESS.
ぱたぱた
OW OW! WATCH THE HAIR!
PURPLE EYES? I SEE. A CHILD FROM THE EVIL SIDE, EH? BUT HOW DID YOU INFILTRATE THE VILLAGE SHIELD?! ONLY THOSE OF TENKAI CAN ENTER!
THAT WOULD BE...
わたたた
...A SECRET!
はっ
身代わりっ!!
WAAH! I DIDN'T DO ANYTHING!
LORD YASHA! WE'VE GOT A SITUATION! THE WEST SIDE SHIELD HAS BEEN BREACHED!

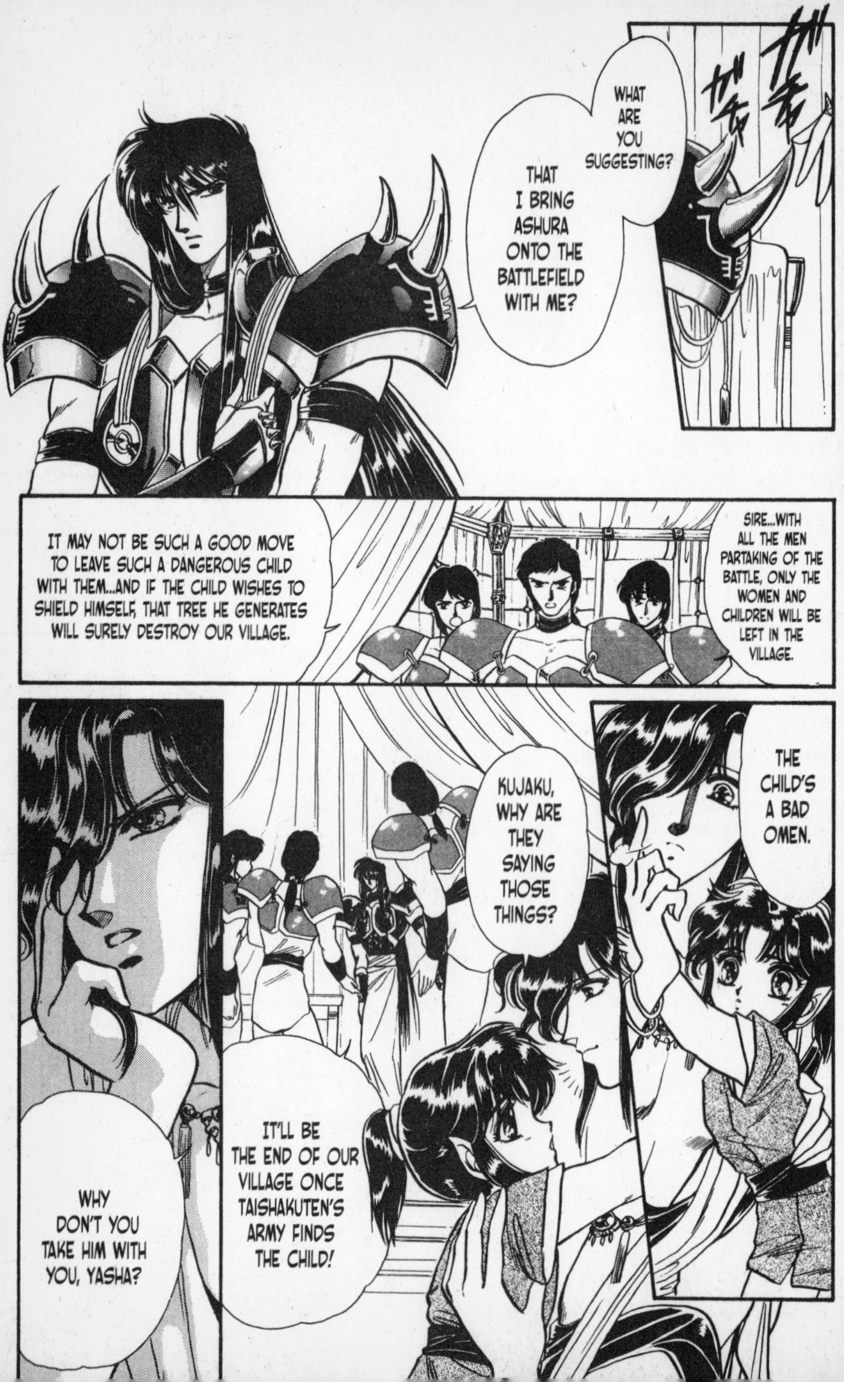
WHAT ARE YOU SUGGESTING?
THAT I BRING ASHURA ONTO THE BATTLEFIELD WITH ME?
SIRE...WITH ALL THE MEN PARTAKING OF THE BATTLE, ONLY THE WOMEN AND CHILDREN WILL BE LEFT IN THE VILLAGE.
IT MAY NOT BE SUCH A GOOD MOVE TO LEAVE SUCH A DANGEROUS CHILD WITH THEM...AND IF THE CHILD WISHES TO SHIELD HIMSELF, THAT TREE HE GENERATES WILL SURELY DESTROY OUR VILLAGE.
THE CHILD'S A BAD OMEN.
KUJAKU, WHY ARE THEY SAYING THOSE THINGS?
IT'LL BE THE END OF OUR VILLAGE ONCE TAISHAKUTEN'S ARMY FINDS THE CHILD!
WHY DON'T YOU TAKE HIM WITH YOU, YASHA?

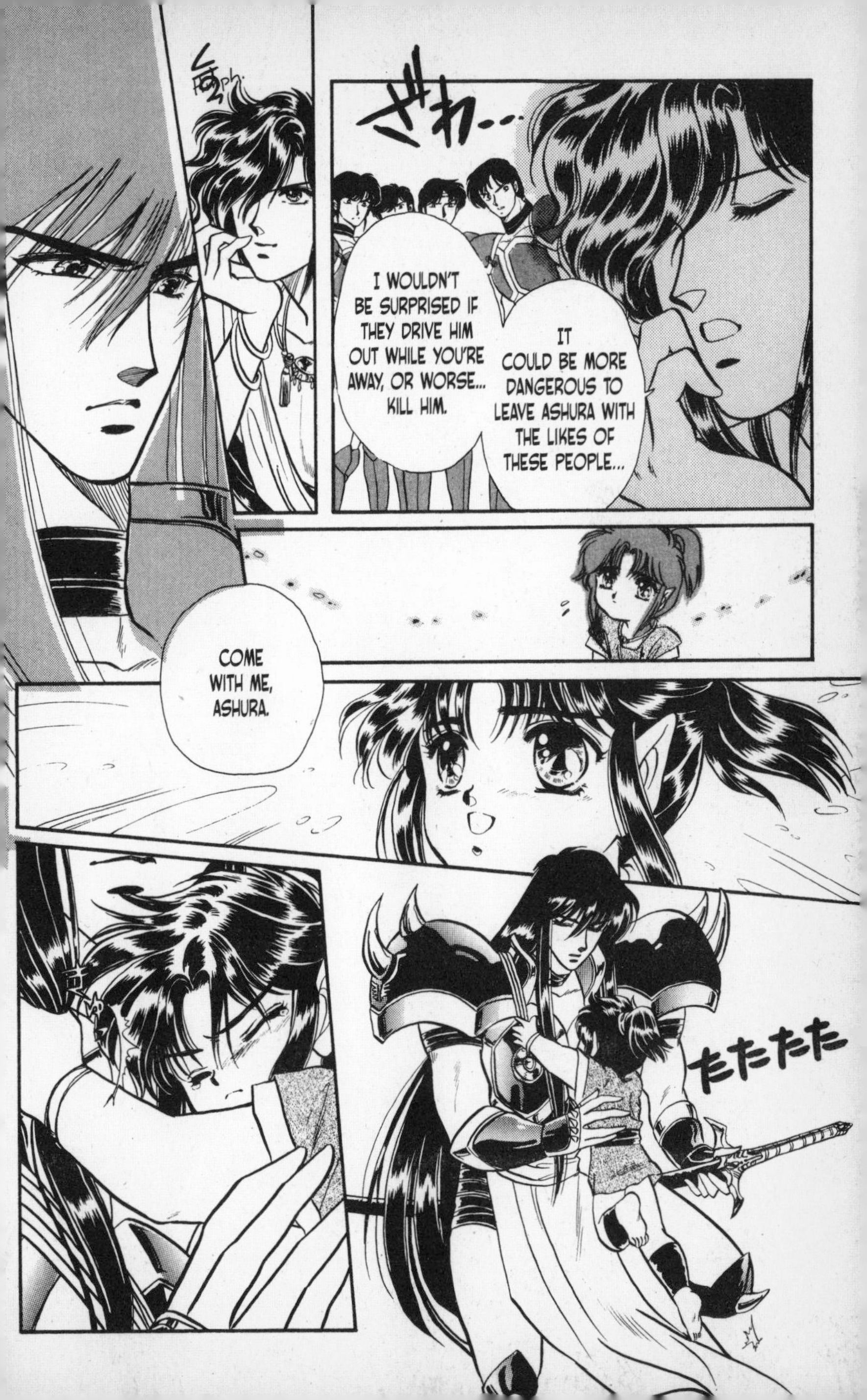
ざわ…
IT COULD BE MORE DANGEROUS TO LEAVE ASHURA WITH THE LIKES OF THESE PEOPLE...
I WOULDN'T BE SURPRISED IF THEY DRIVE HIM OUT WHILE YOU'RE AWAY, OR WORSE... KILL HIM.
Hmph.
COME WITH ME, ASHURA.
たたたた

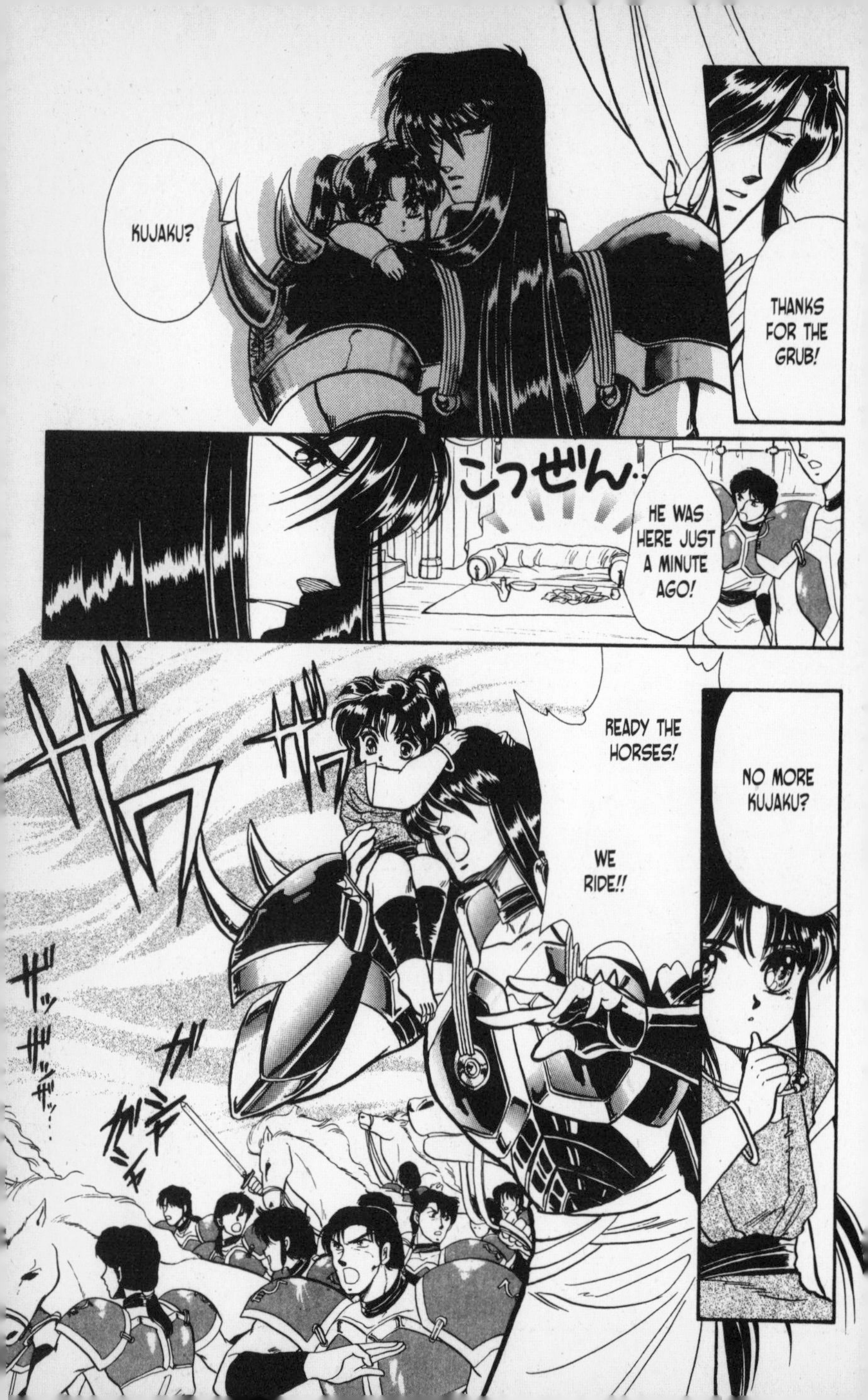
THANKS FOR THE GRUB!
KUJAKU?
HE WAS HERE JUST A MINUTE AGO!
こつぜん…
NO MORE KUJAKU?
READY THE HORSES!
WE RIDE!!
ザワ
ザワ
ガチャ
ガチャ
ザッザッザッ…

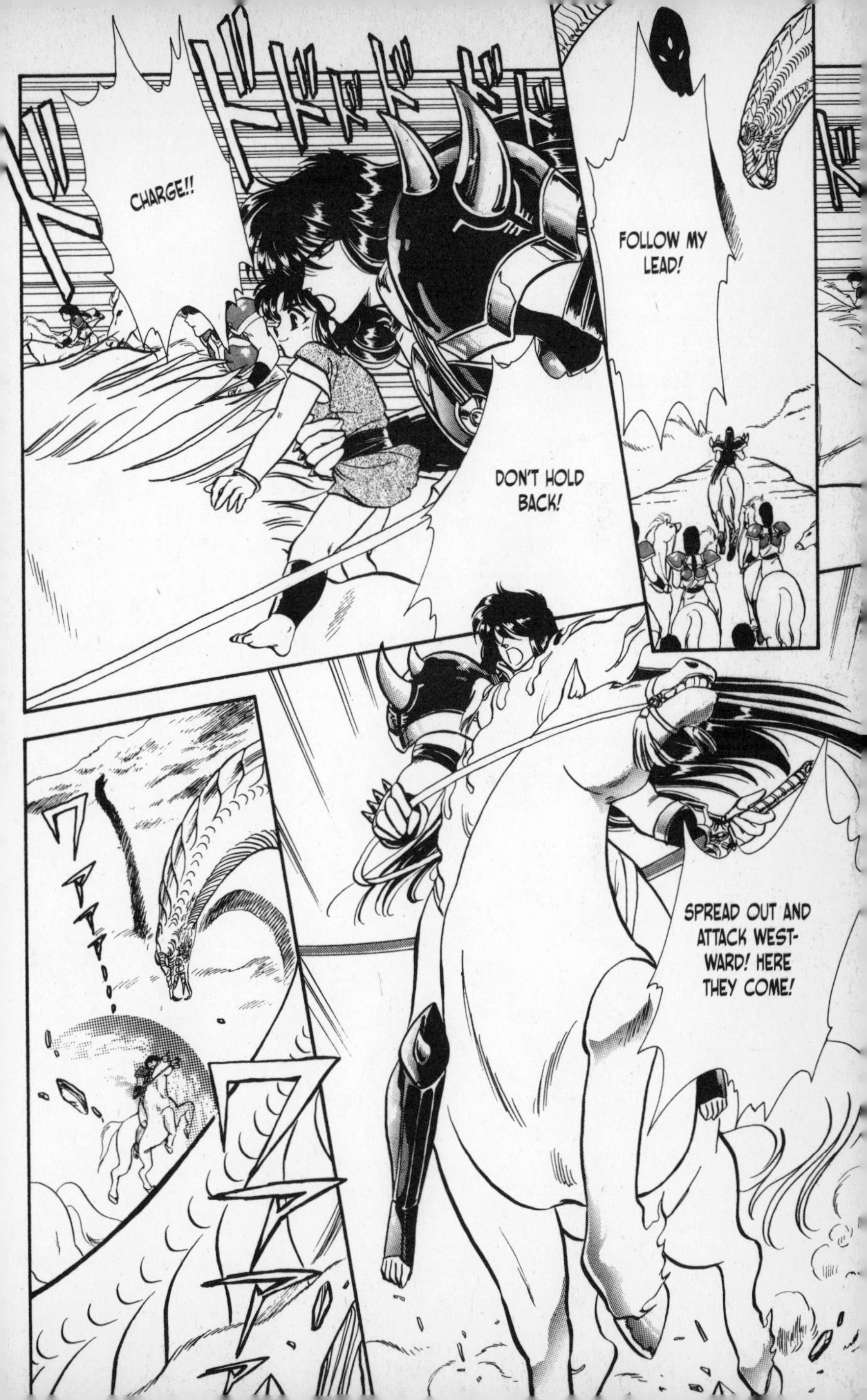
FOLLOW MY LEAD!
CHARGE!!
DON'T HOLD BACK!
SPREAD OUT AND ATTACK WEST-WARD! HERE THEY COME!

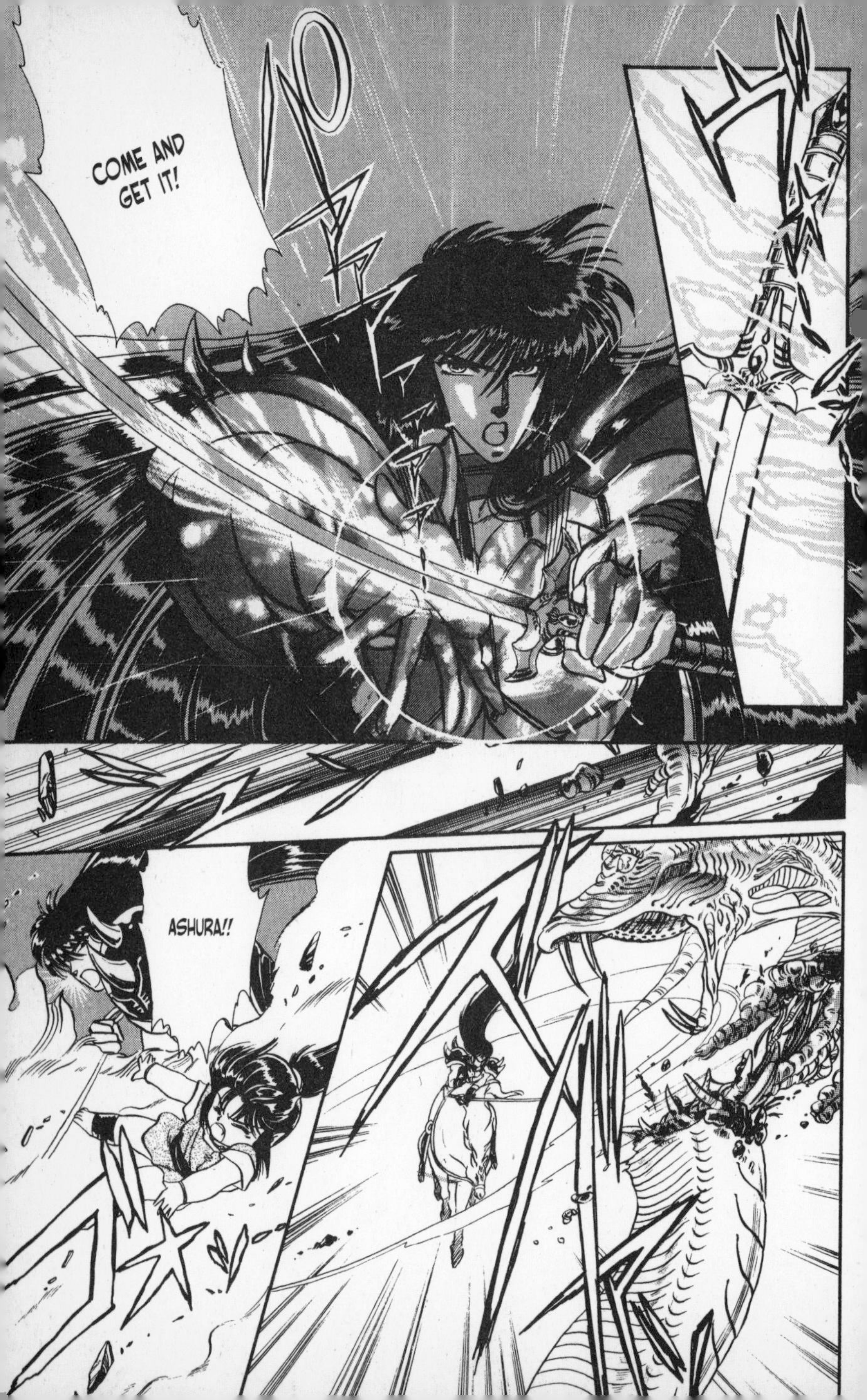
COME AND GET IT!
ASHURA!!

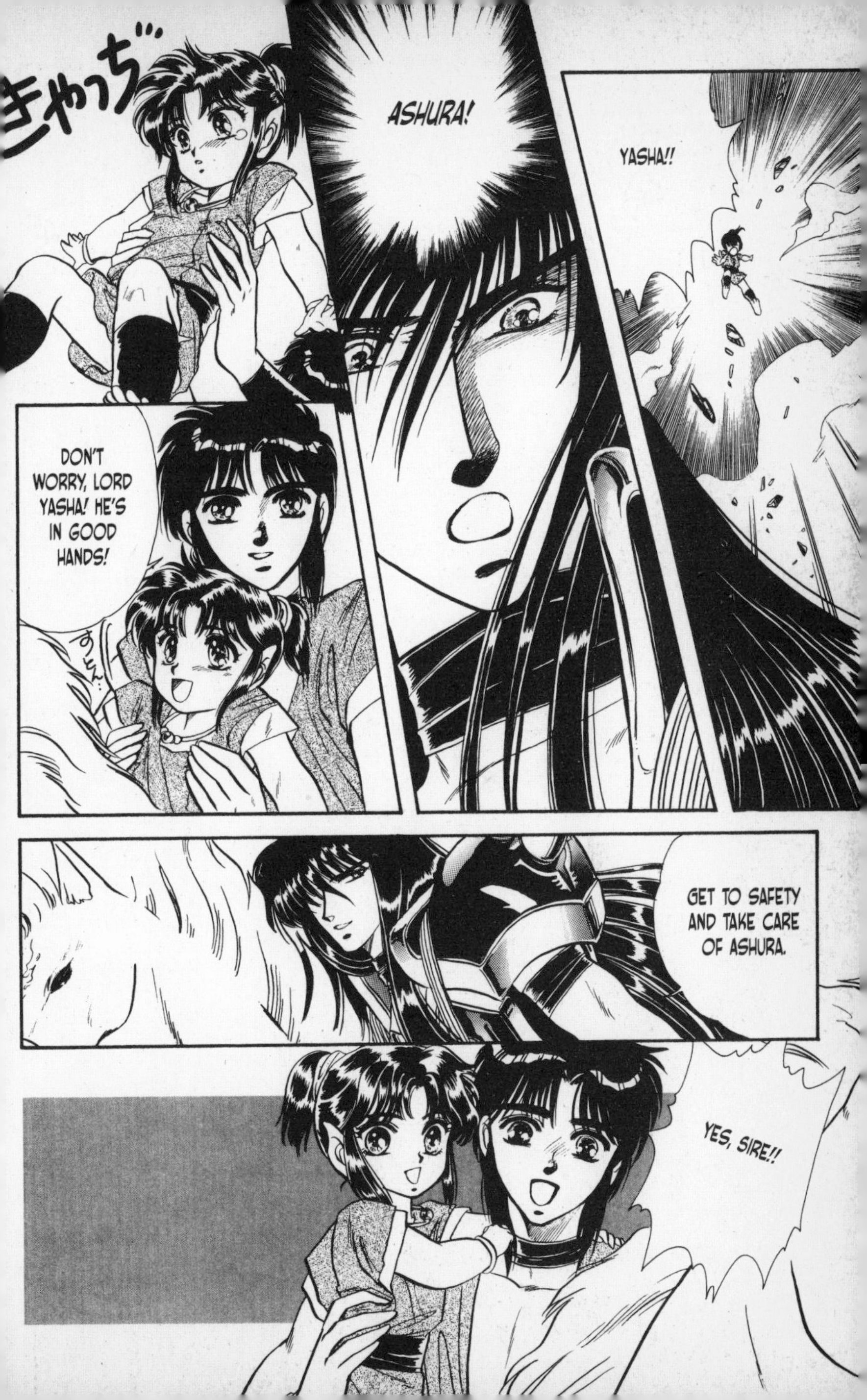
YASHA!!
ASHURA!
きゃっぢ
DON'T WORRY, LORD YASHA! HE'S IN GOOD HANDS!
すとん…
GET TO SAFETY AND TAKE CARE OF ASHURA.
YES, SIRE!!

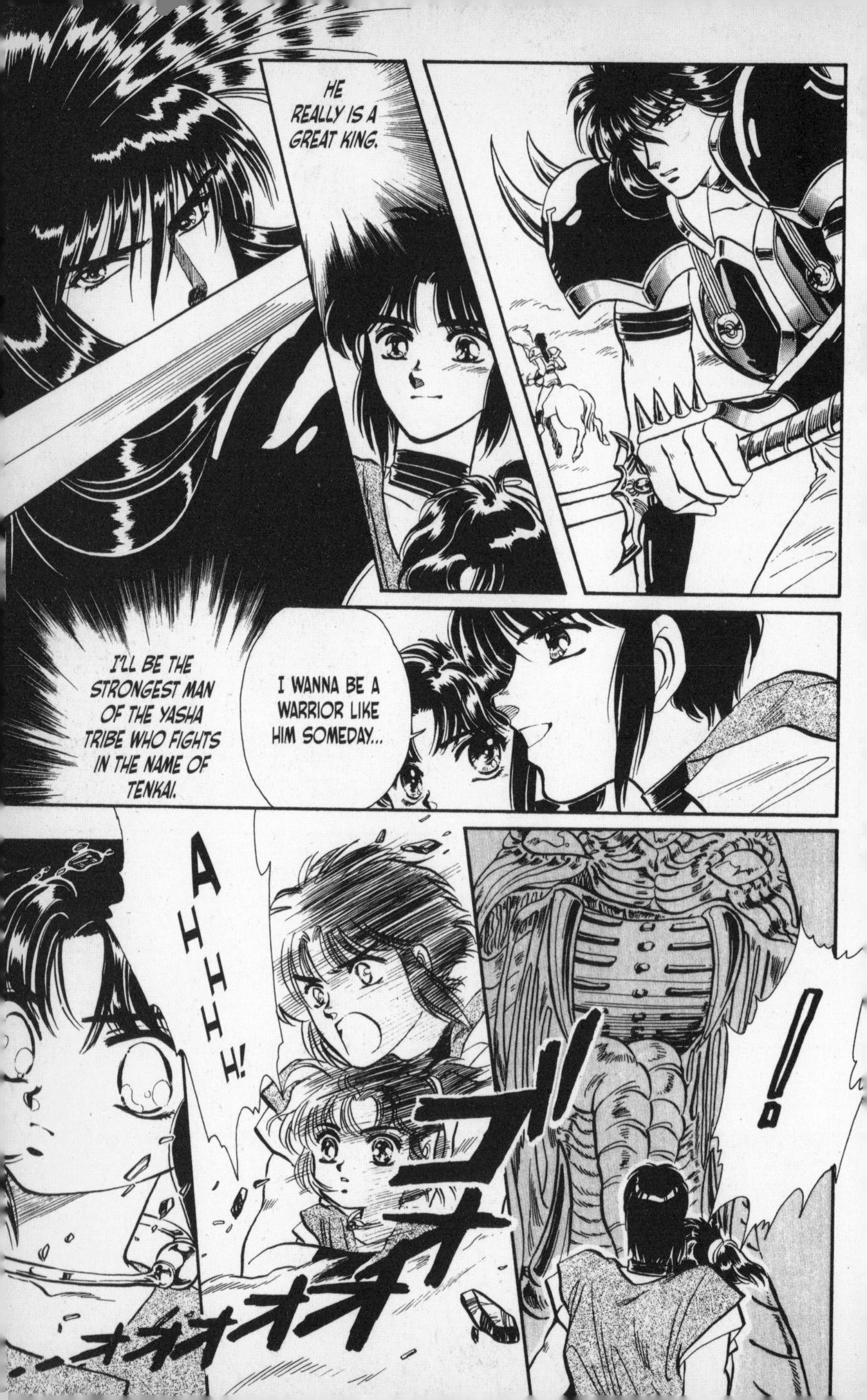
HE REALLY IS A GREAT KING.
I WANNA BE A WARRIOR LIKE HIM SOMEDAY...
I'LL BE THE STRONGEST MAN OF THE YASHA TRIBE WHO FIGHTS IN THE NAME OF TENKAI.
!
AHHHHH!

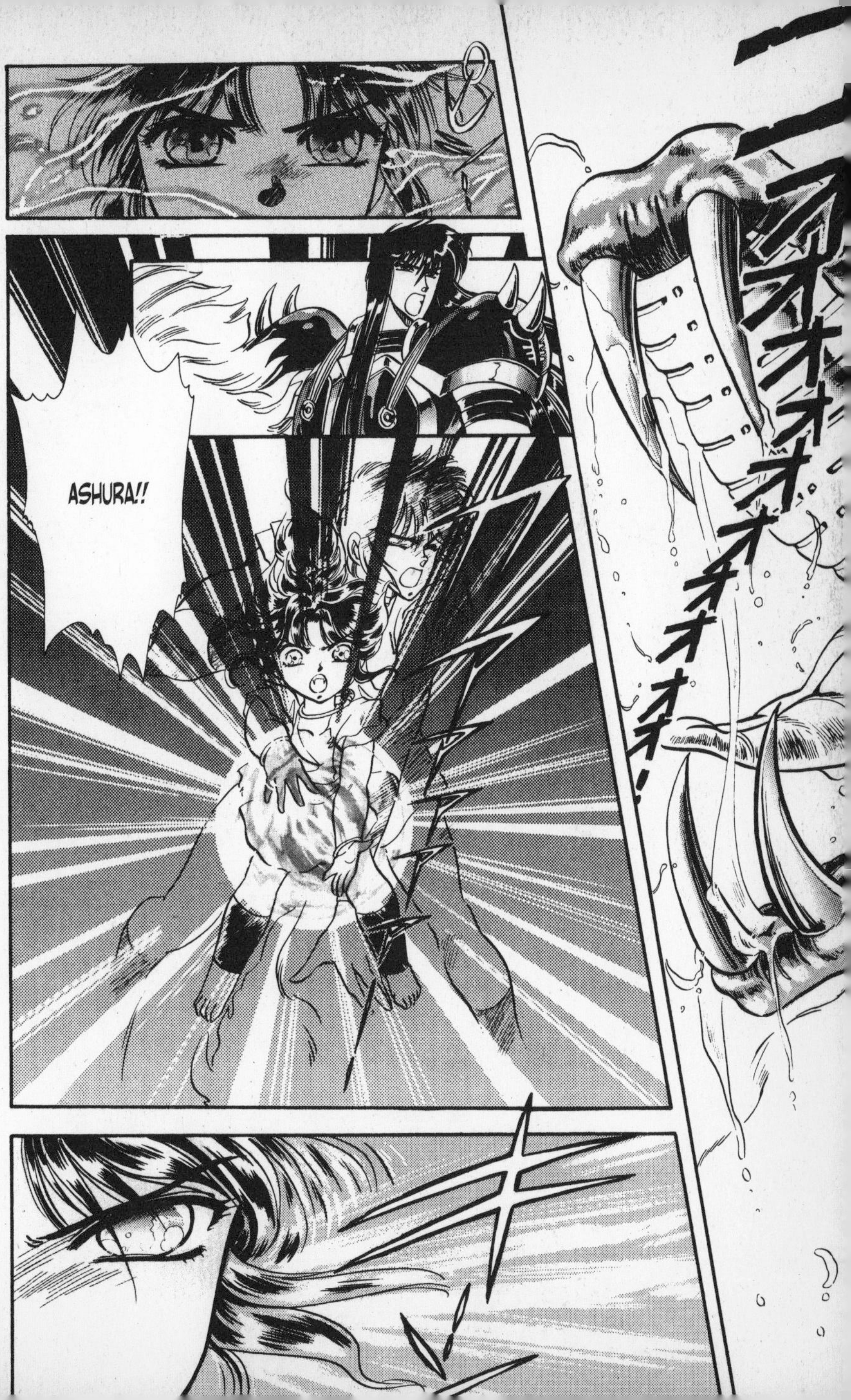
ASHURA!!

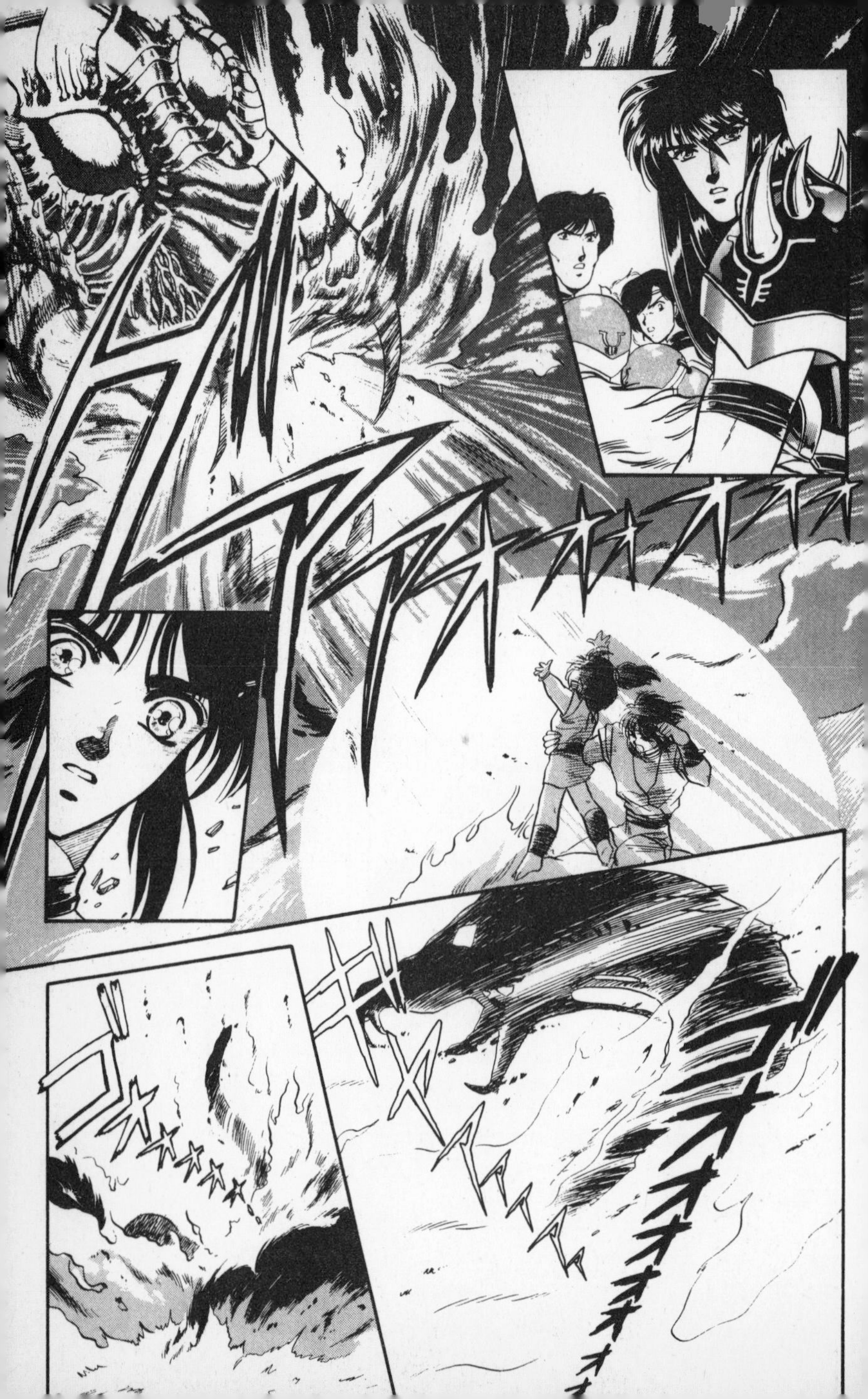

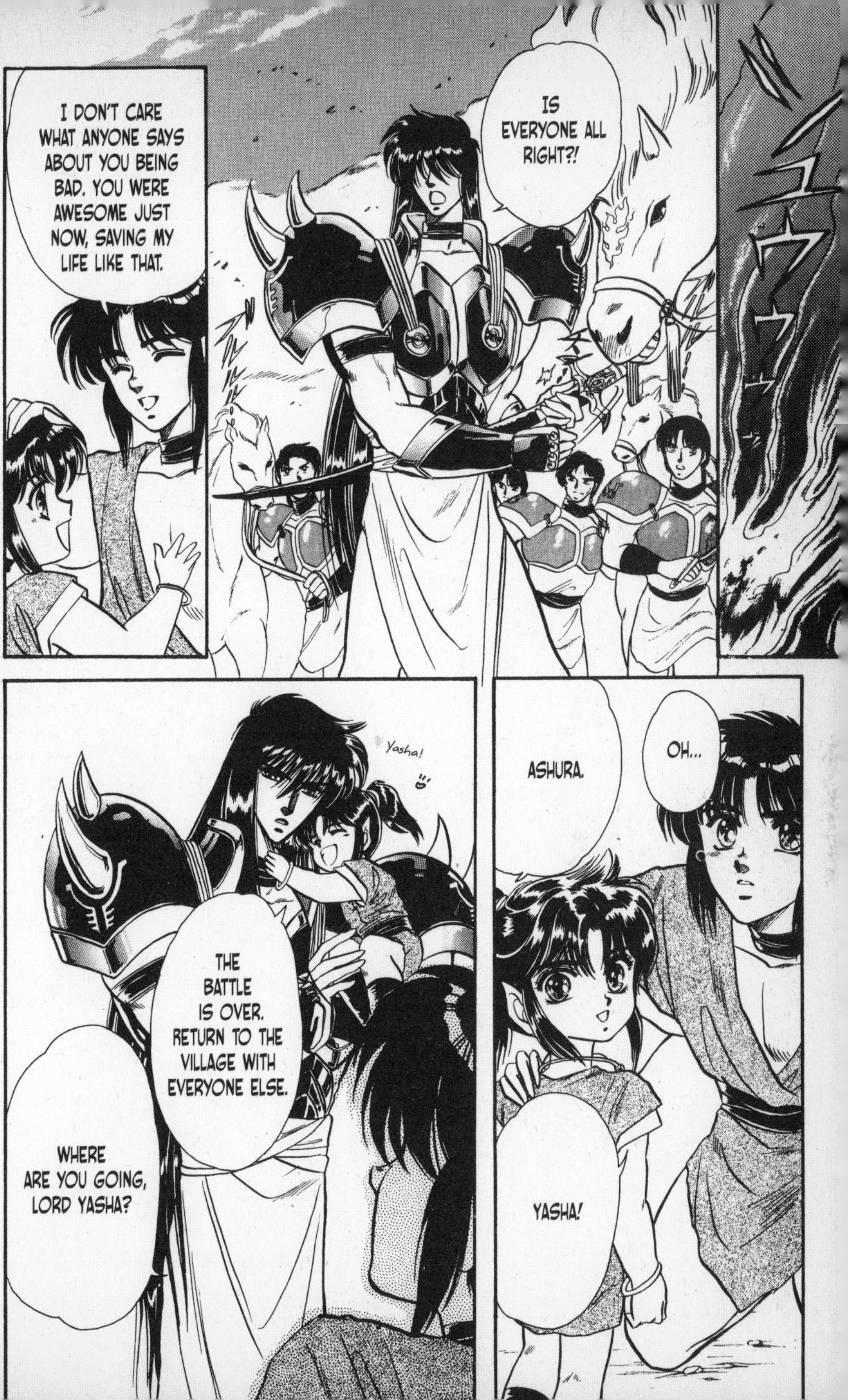
IS EVERYONE ALL RIGHT?!
I DON'T CARE WHAT ANYONE SAYS ABOUT YOU BEING BAD. YOU WERE AWESOME JUST NOW, SAVING MY LIFE LIKE THAT.
OH...
ASHURA.
YASHA!
Yasha!
THE BATTLE IS OVER. RETURN TO THE VILLAGE WITH EVERYONE ELSE.
WHERE ARE YOU GOING, LORD YASHA?

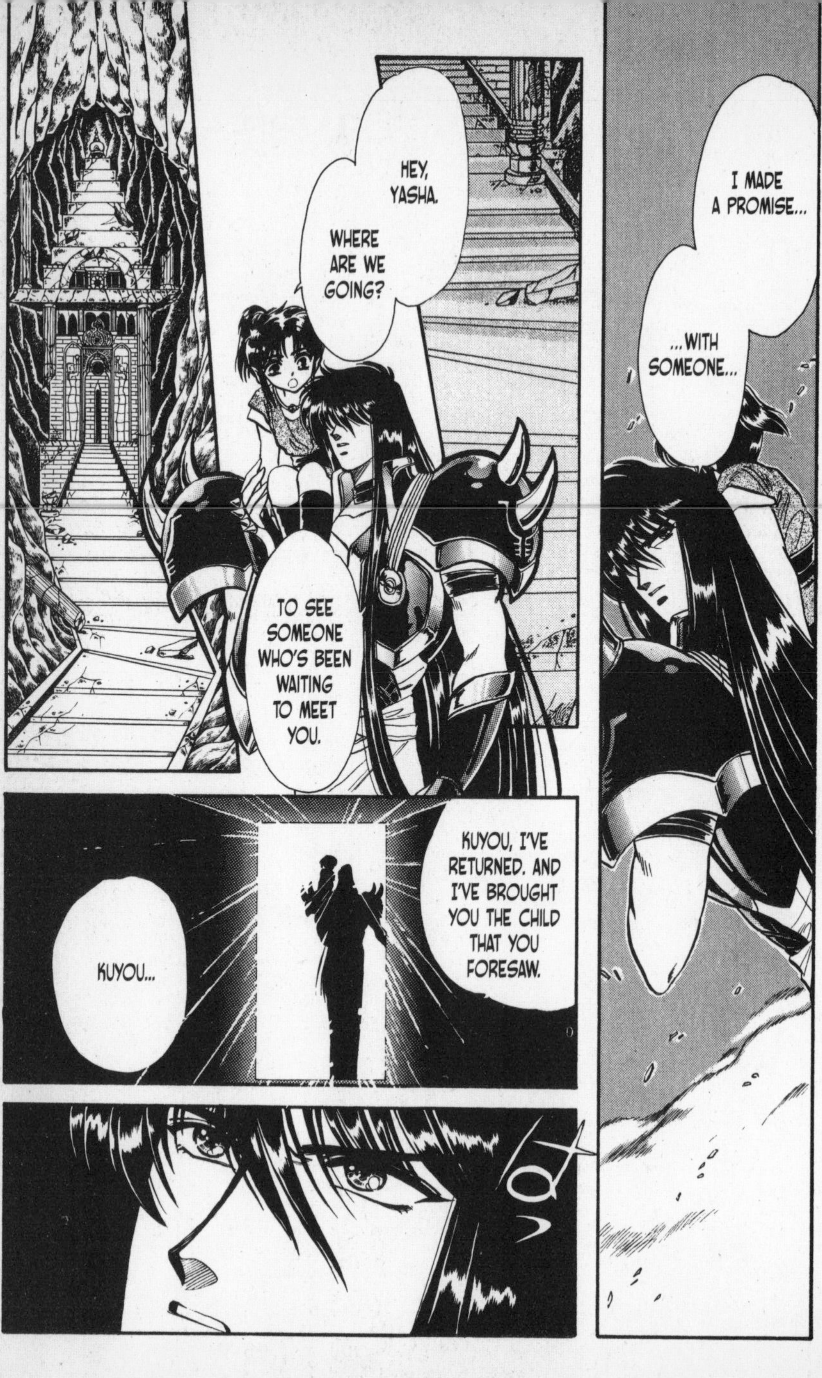
I MADE A PROMISE...
...WITH SOMEONE...
HEY, YASHA.
WHERE ARE WE GOING?
TO SEE SOMEONE WHO'S BEEN WAITING TO MEET YOU.
KUYOU, I'VE RETURNED. AND I'VE BROUGHT YOU THE CHILD THAT YOU FORESAW.
KUYOU...

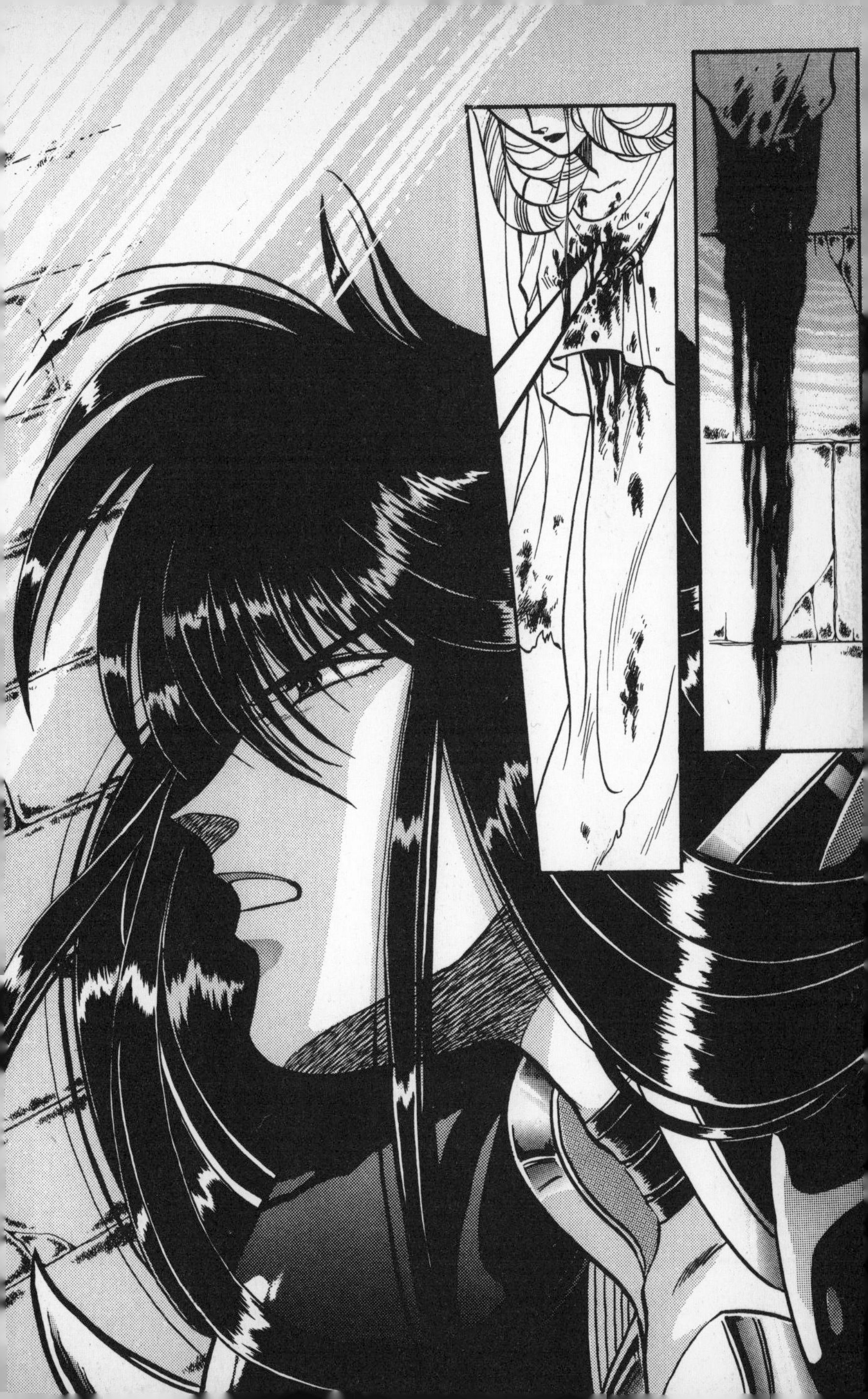

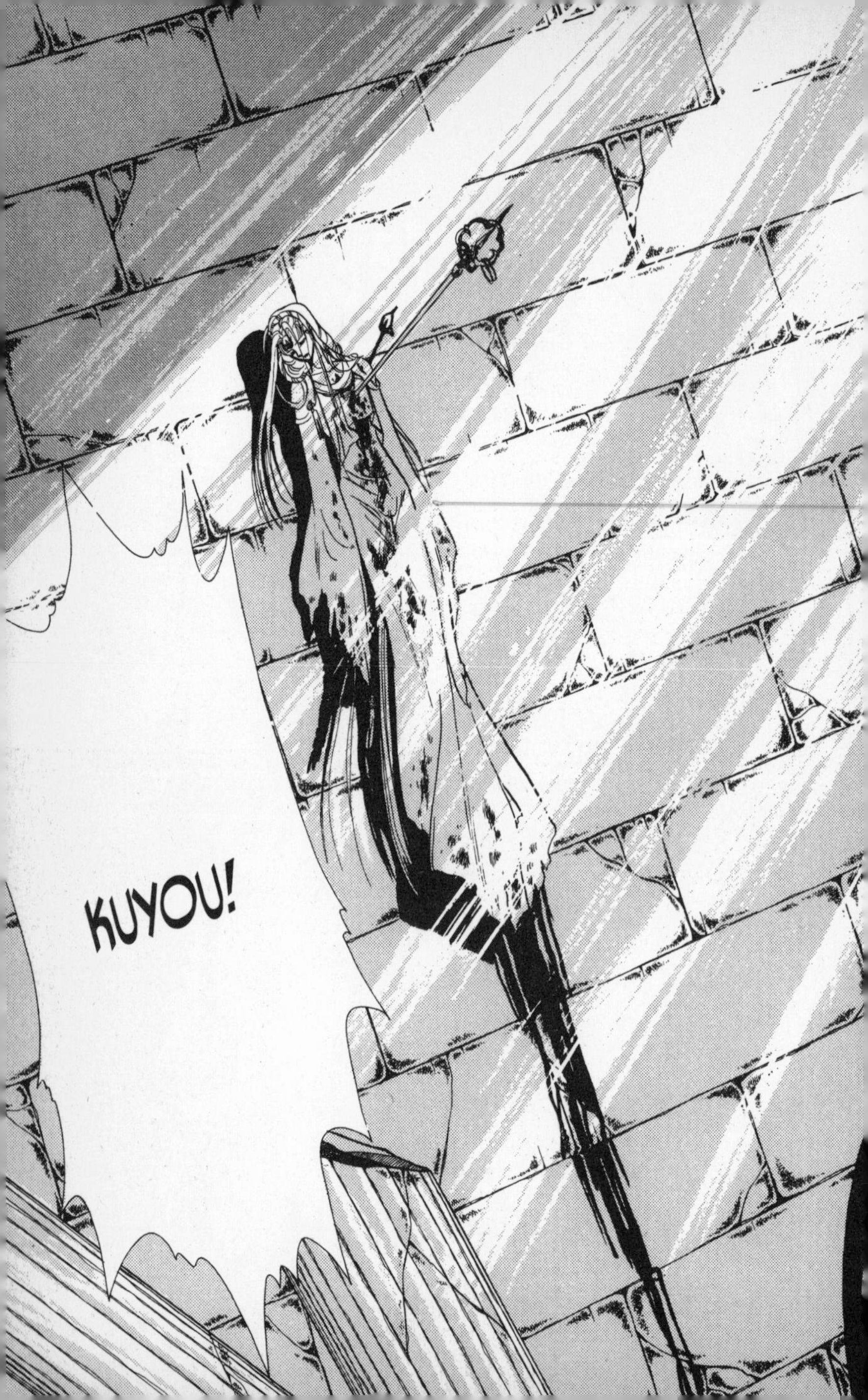
KUYOU!

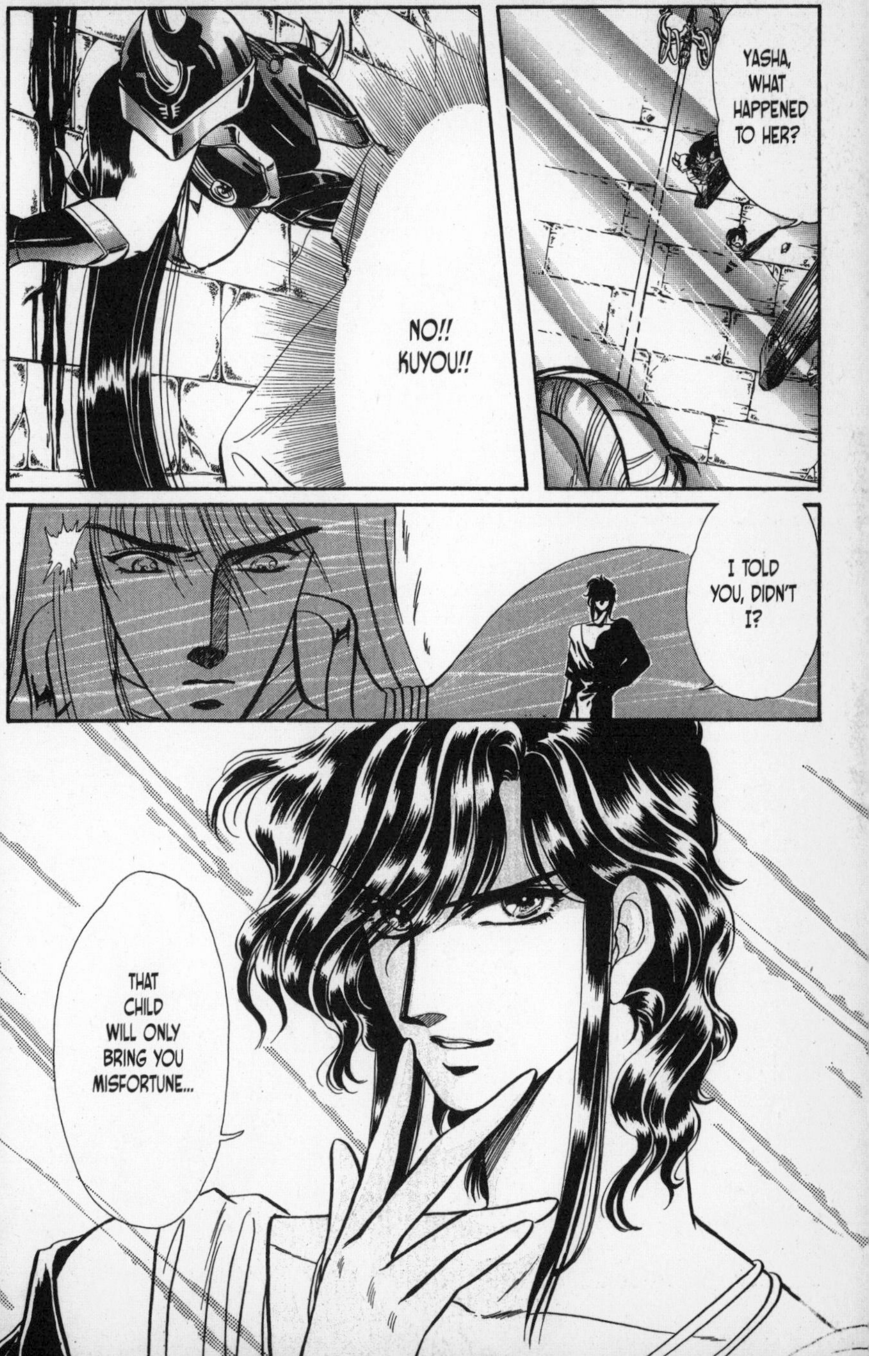
YASHA, WHAT HAPPENED TO HER?
NO!! KUYOU!!
I TOLD YOU, DIDN'T I?
THAT CHILD WILL ONLY BRING YOU MISFORTUNE...

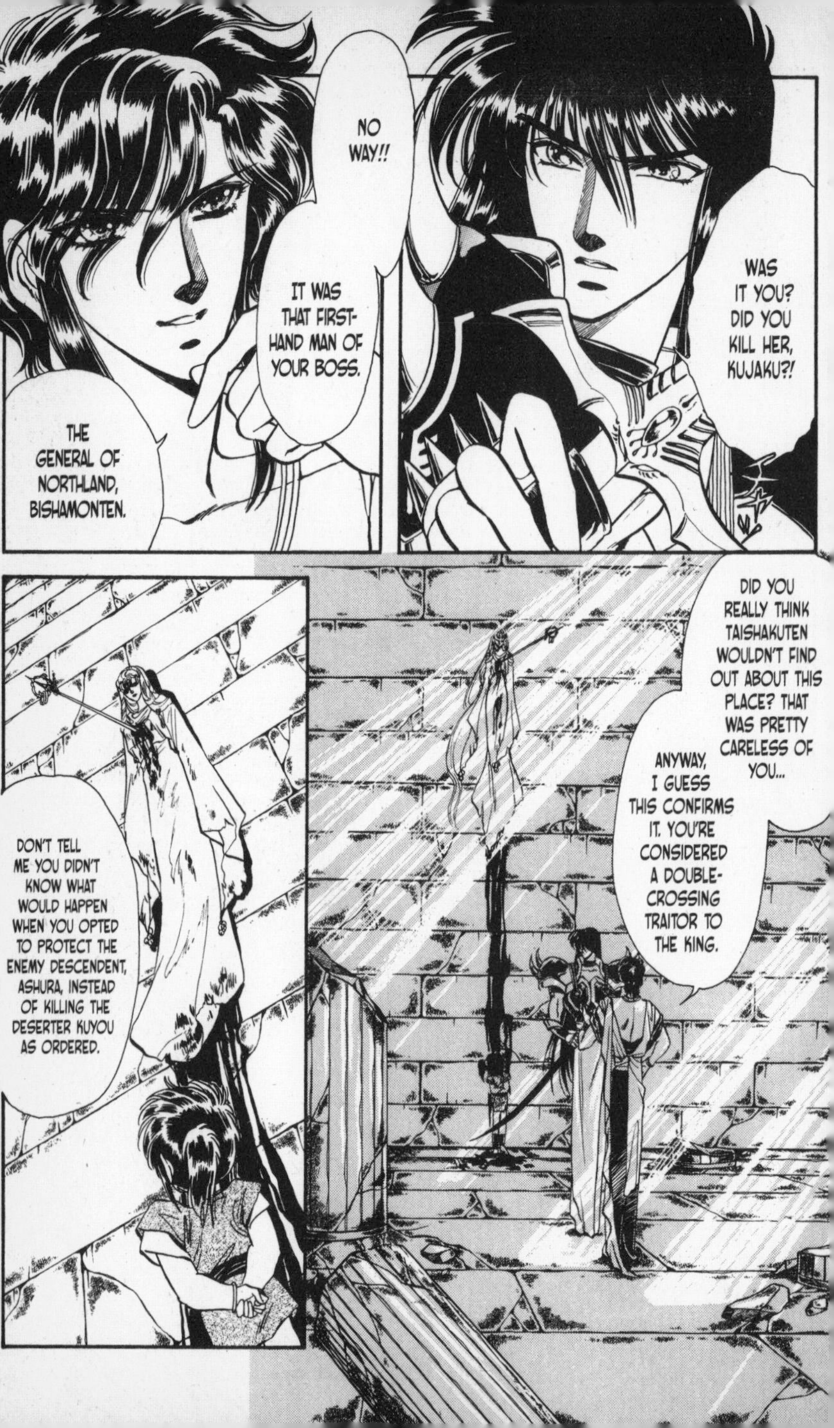
WAS IT YOU? DID YOU KILL HER, KUJAKU?!
NO WAY!!
IT WAS THAT FIRST-HAND MAN OF YOUR BOSS.
THE GENERAL OF NORTHLAND, BISHAMONTEN.
DID YOU REALLY THINK TAISHAKUTEN WOULDN'T FIND OUT ABOUT THIS PLACE? THAT WAS PRETTY CARELESS OF YOU...
ANYWAY, I GUESS THIS CONFIRMS IT. YOU'RE CONSIDERED A DOUBLE-CROSSING TRAITOR TO THE KING.
DON'T TELL ME YOU DIDN'T KNOW WHAT WOULD HAPPEN WHEN YOU OPTED TO PROTECT THE ENEMY DESCENDENT, ASHURA, INSTEAD OF KILLING THE DESERTER KUYOU AS ORDERED.

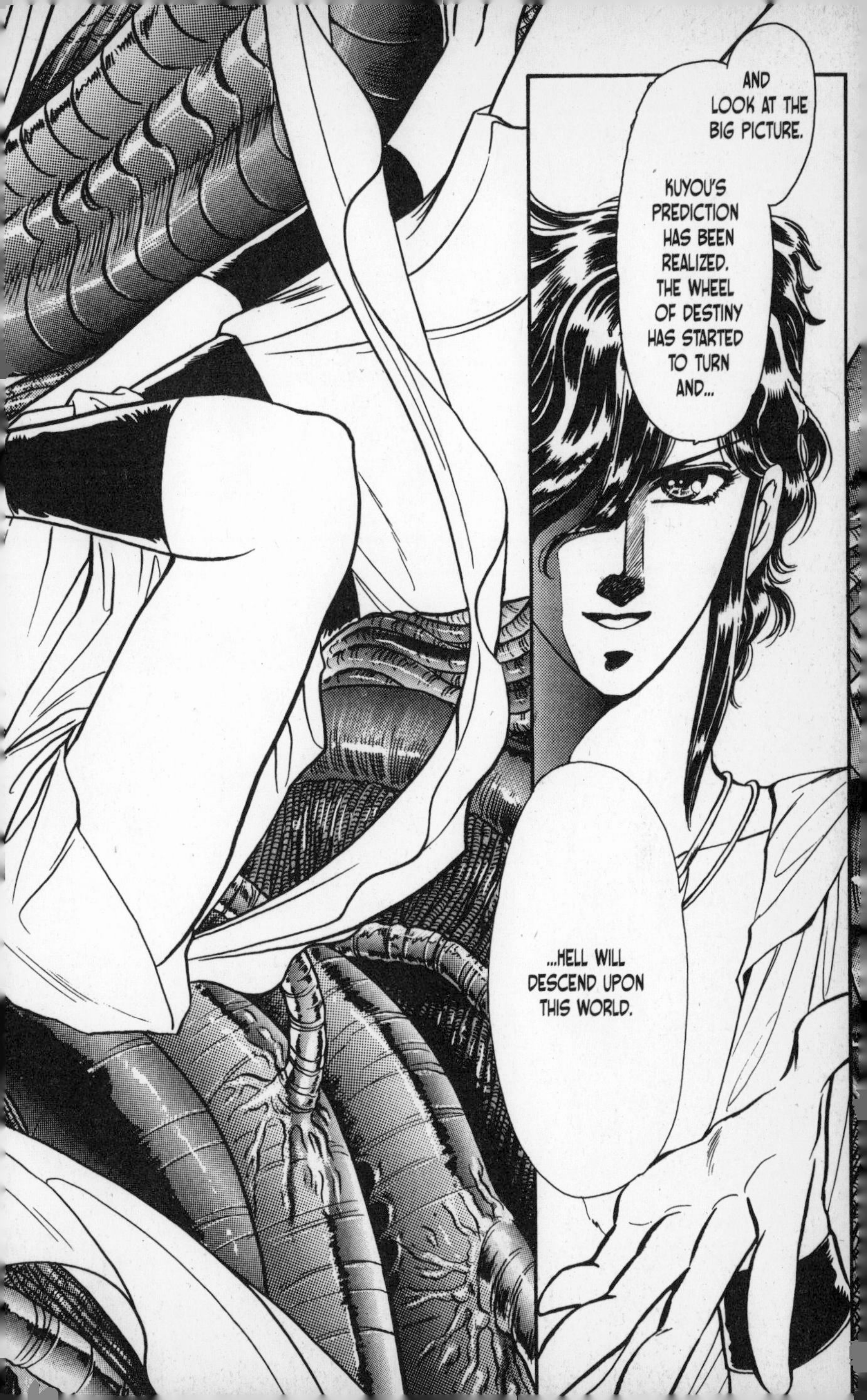
AND LOOK AT THE BIG PICTURE.
KUYOU'S PREDICTION HAS BEEN REALIZED. THE WHEEL OF DESTINY HAS STARTED TO TURN AND...
...HELL WILL DESCEND UPON THIS WORLD.

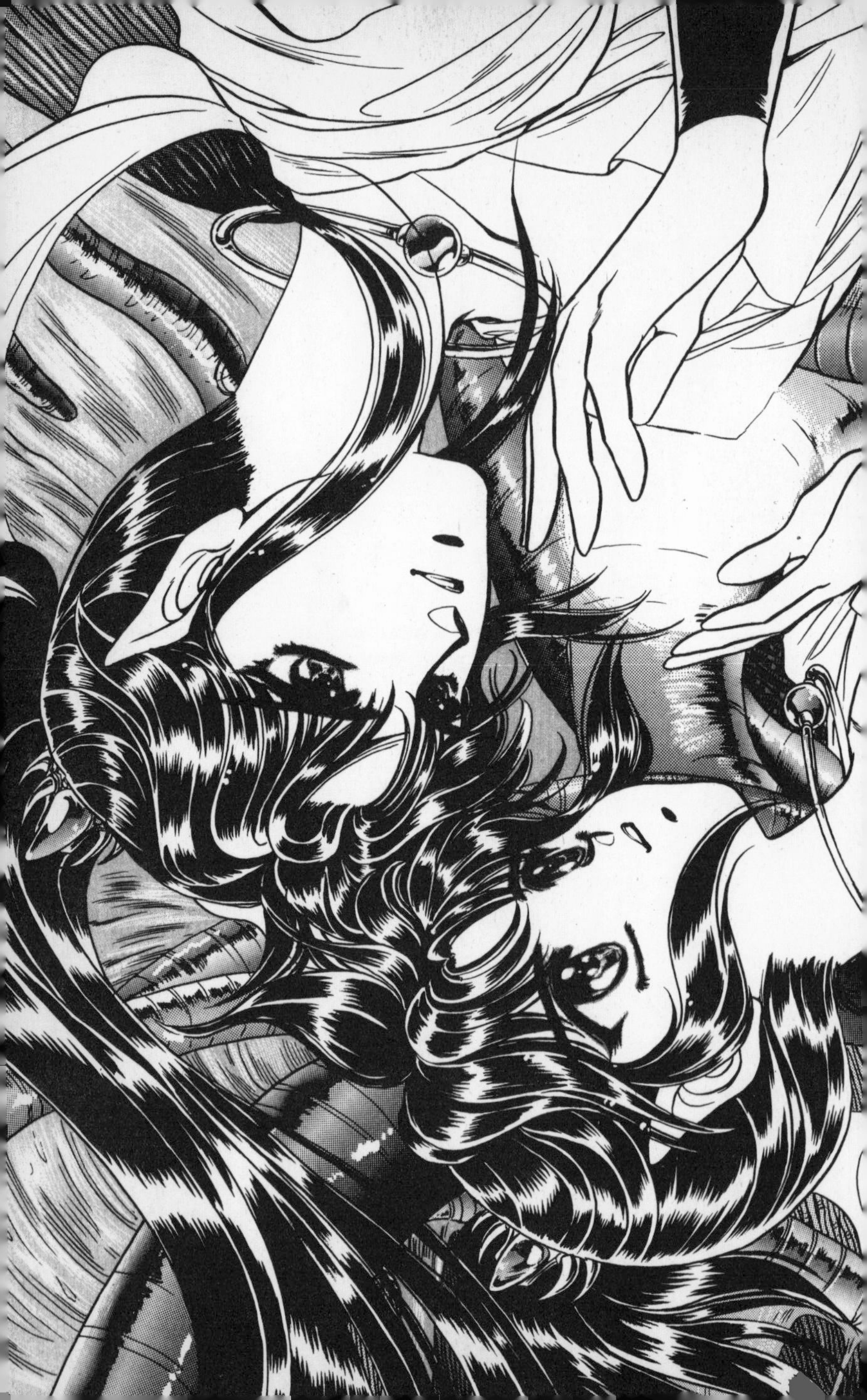

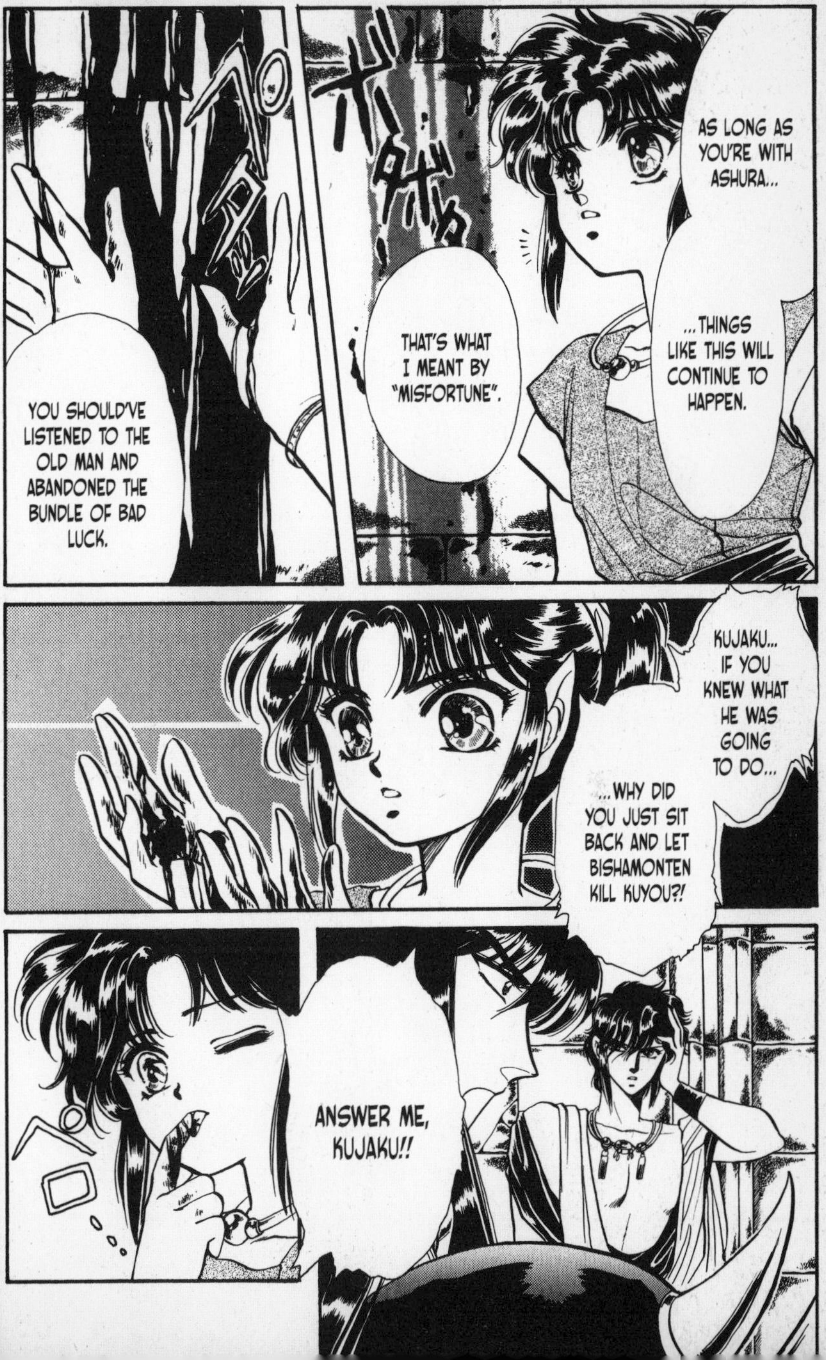
AS LONG AS YOU'RE WITH ASHURA...
...THINGS LIKE THIS WILL CONTINUE TO HAPPEN.
THAT'S WHAT I MEANT BY "MISFORTUNE".
YOU SHOULD'VE LISTENED TO THE OLD MAN AND ABANDONED THE BUNDLE OF BAD LUCK.
KUJAKU... IF YOU KNEW WHAT HE WAS GOING TO DO...
...WHY DID YOU JUST SIT BACK AND LET BISHAMONTEN KILL KUYOU?!
ANSWER ME, KUJAKU!!

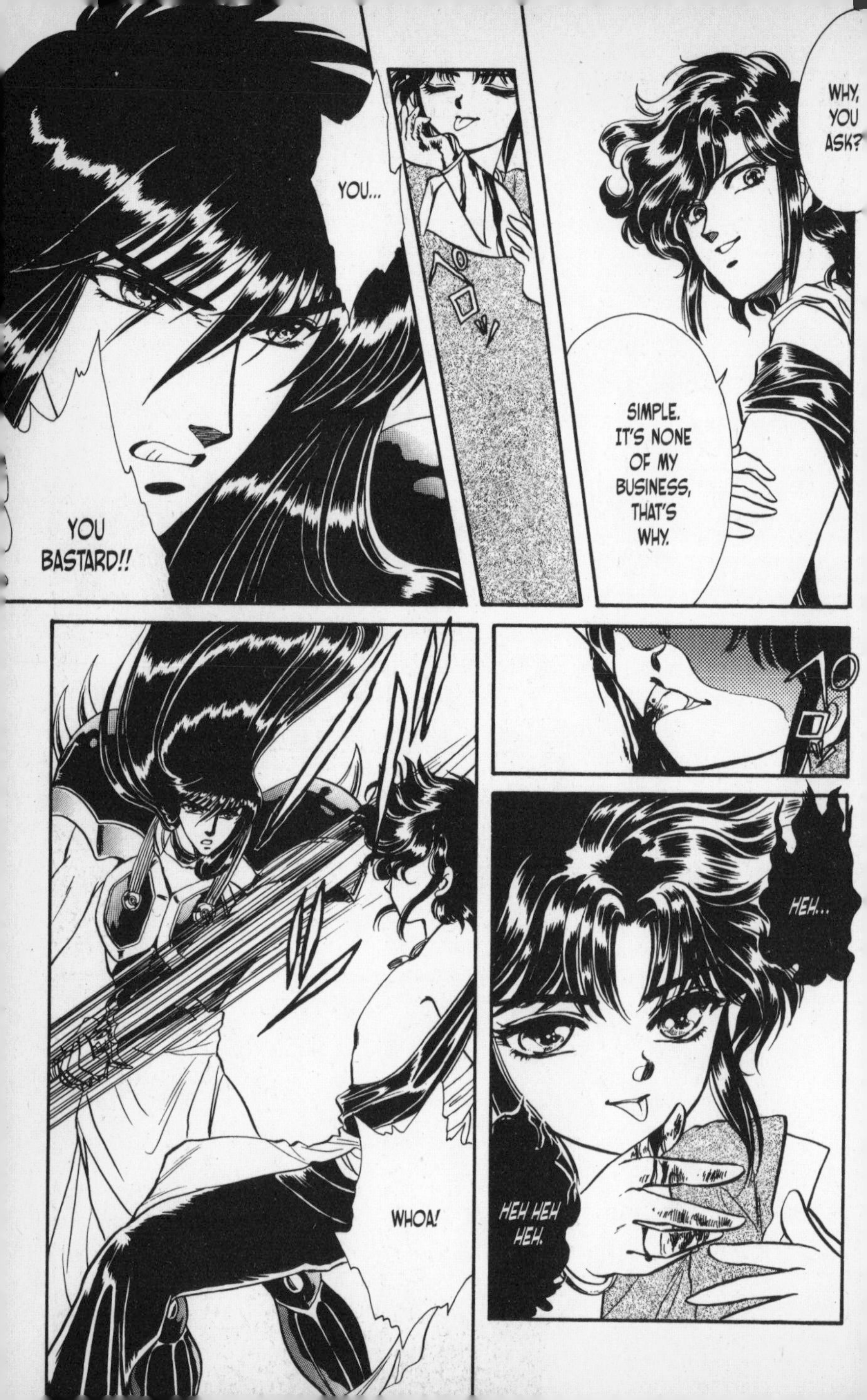
WHY, YOU ASK?
SIMPLE. IT'S NONE OF MY BUSINESS, THAT'S WHY.
YOU...
YOU BASTARD!!
HEH...
HEH HEH HEH.
WHOA!

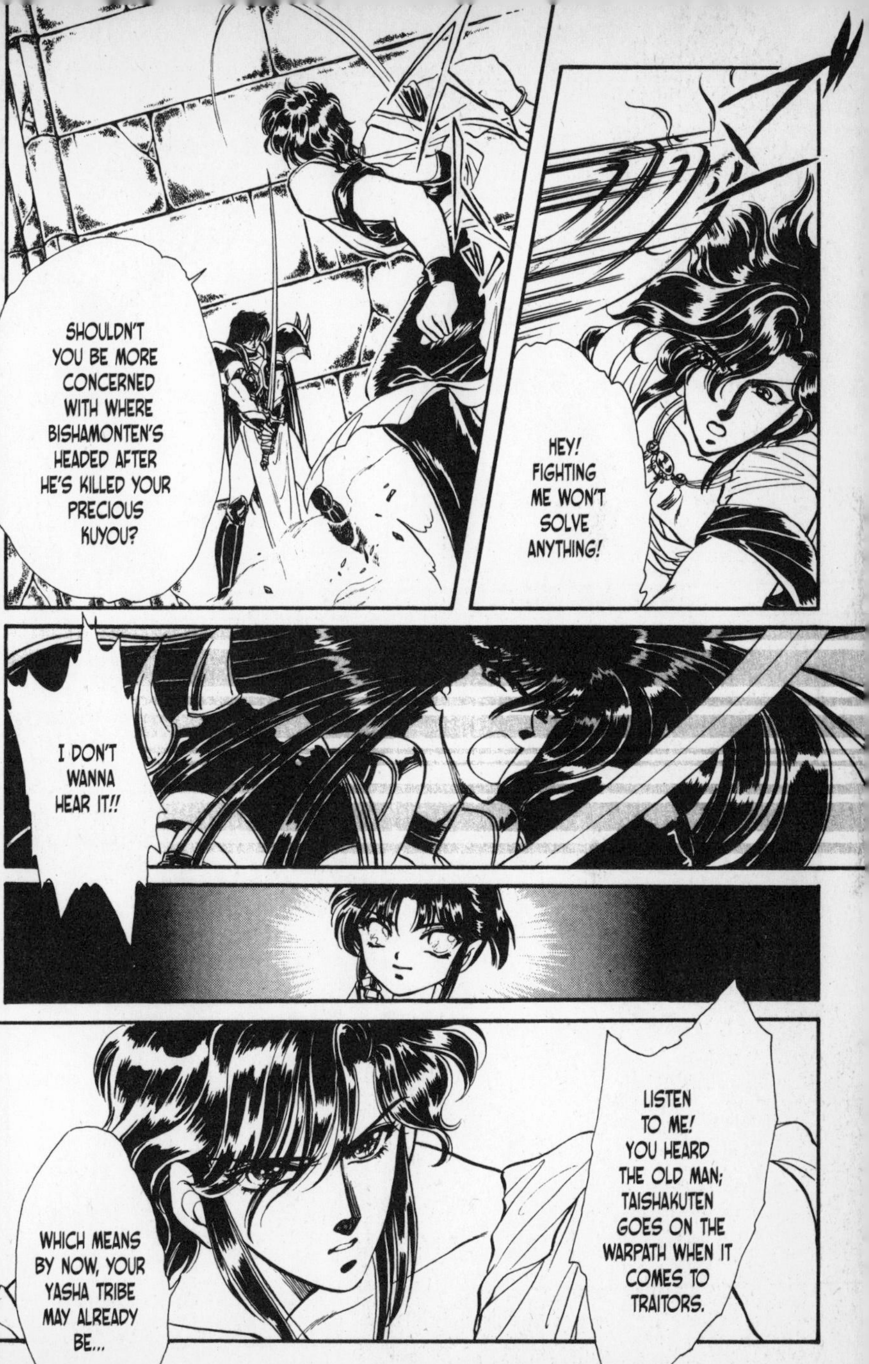
HEY! FIGHTING ME WON'T SOLVE ANYTHING!
SHOULDN'T YOU BE MORE CONCERNED WITH WHERE BISHAMONTEN'S HEADED AFTER HE'S KILLED YOUR PRECIOUS KUYOU?
I DON'T WANNA HEAR IT!!
LISTEN TO ME! YOU HEARD THE OLD MAN; TAISHAKUTEN GOES ON THE WARPATH WHEN IT COMES TO TRAITORS.
WHICH MEANS BY NOW, YOUR YASHA TRIBE MAY ALREADY BE...

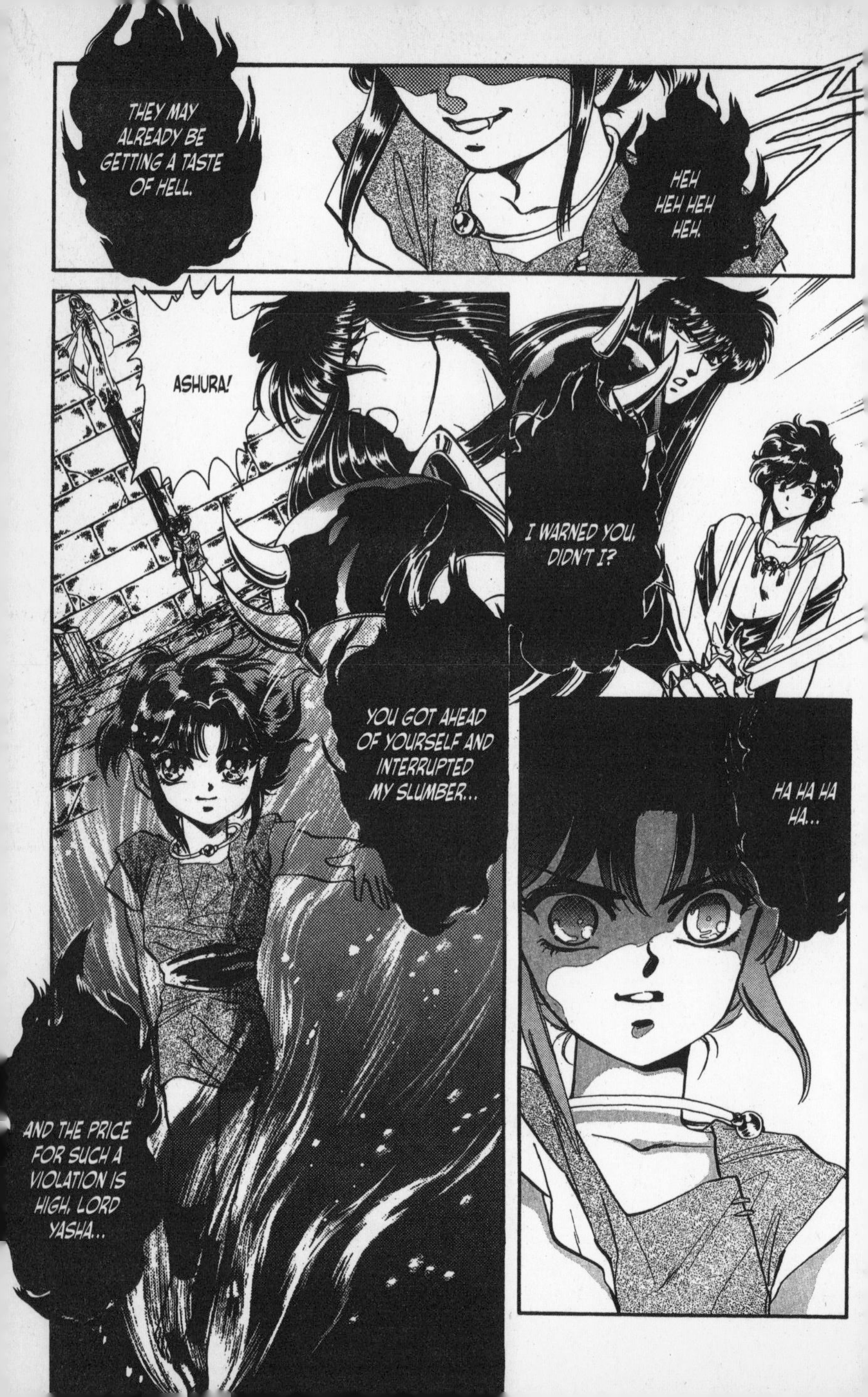
HEH HEH HEH HEH.
THEY MAY ALREADY BE GETTING A TASTE OF HELL.
I WARNED YOU, DIDN'T I?
HA HA HA HA...
ASHURA!
YOU GOT AHEAD OF YOURSELF AND INTERRUPTED MY SLUMBER...
AND THE PRICE FOR SUCH A VIOLATION IS HIGH, LORD YASHA...

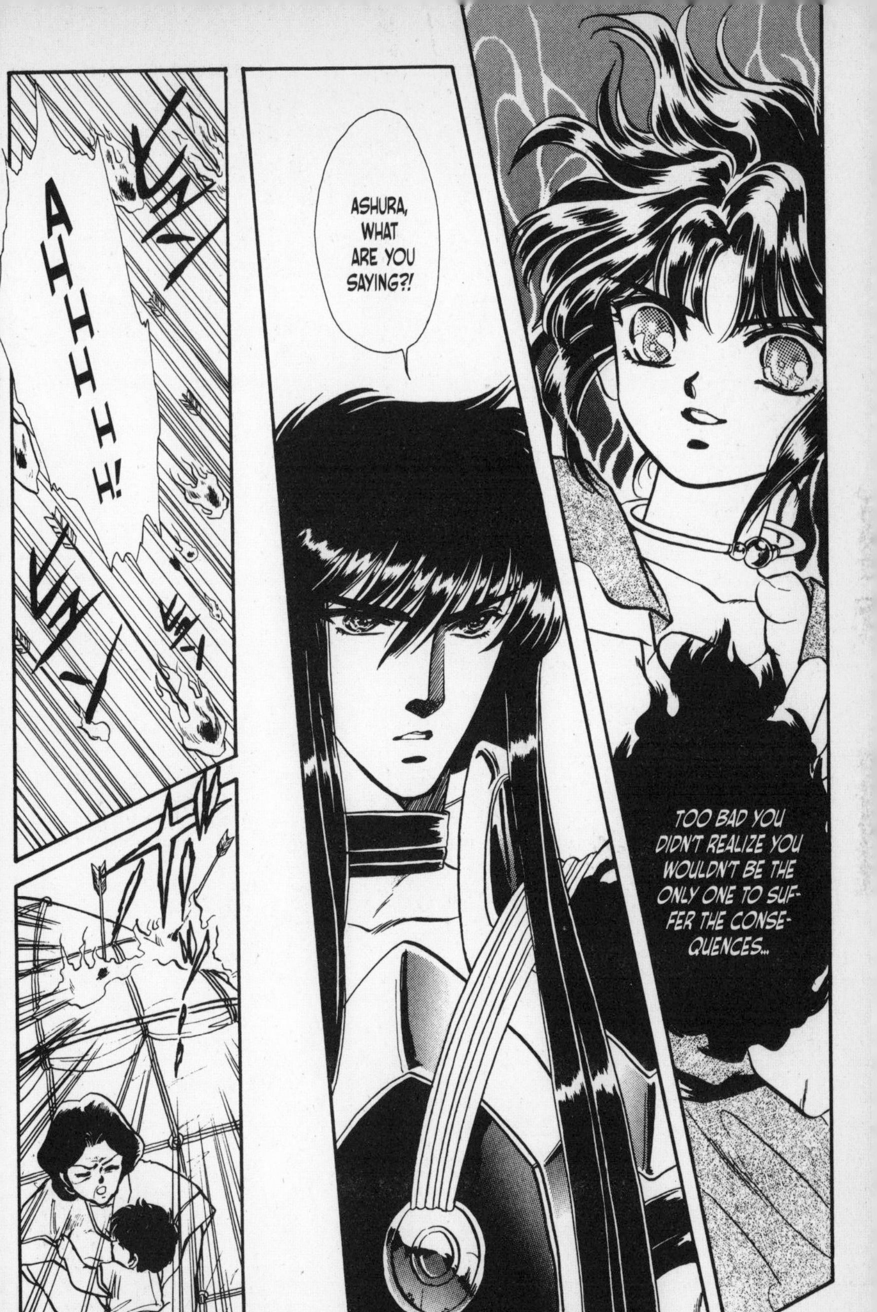
TOO BAD YOU DIDN'T REALIZE YOU WOULDN'T BE THE ONLY ONE TO SUFFER THE CONSEQUENCES...
ASHURA, WHAT ARE YOU SAYING?!
AHHHHHH!

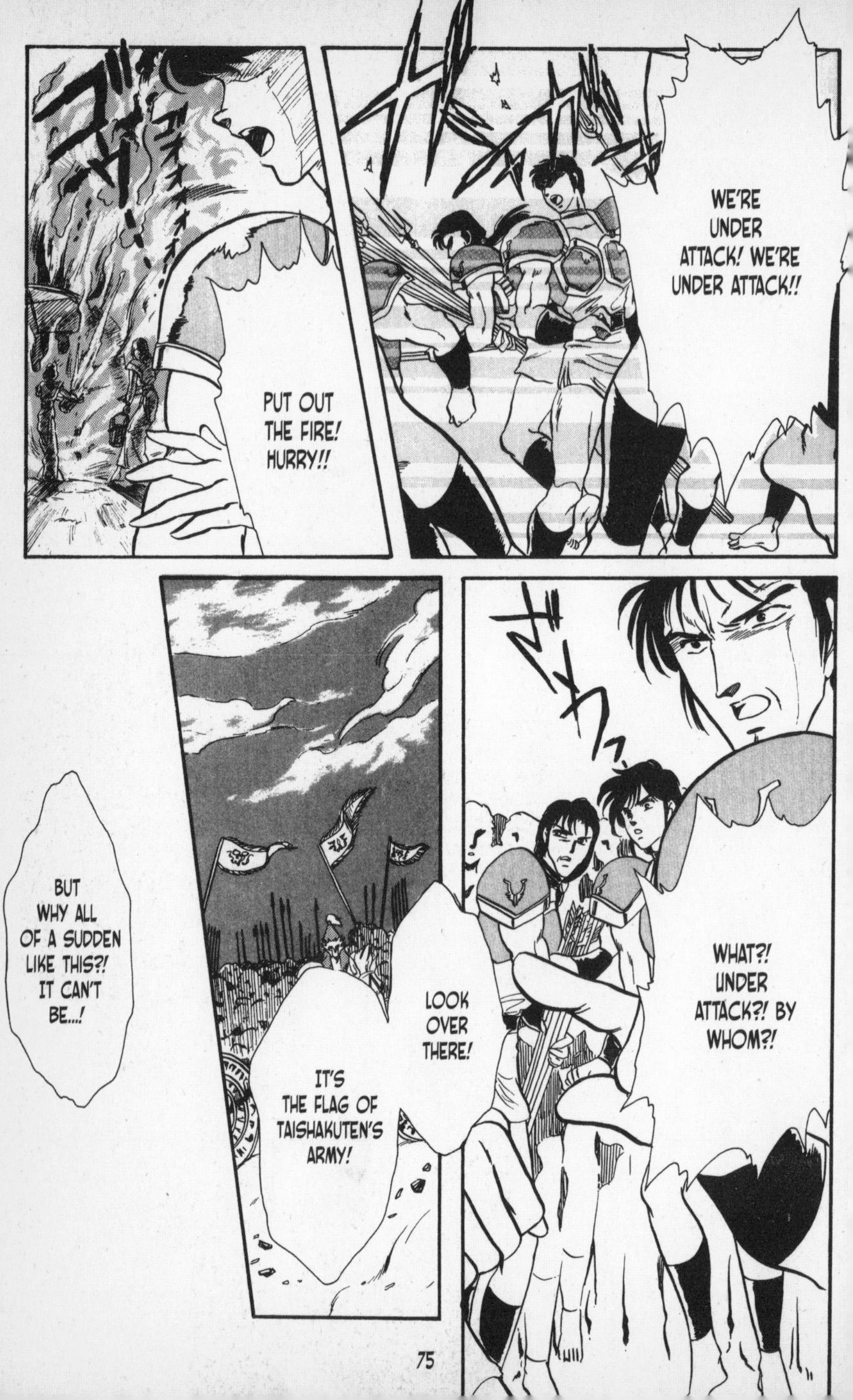
WE'RE UNDER ATTACK! WE'RE UNDER ATTACK!!
PUT OUT THE FIRE! HURRY!!
WHAT?! UNDER ATTACK?! BY WHOM?!
LOOK OVER THERE!
IT'S THE FLAG OF TAISHAKUTEN'S ARMY!
BUT WHY ALL OF A SUDDEN LIKE THIS?! IT CAN'T BE...!

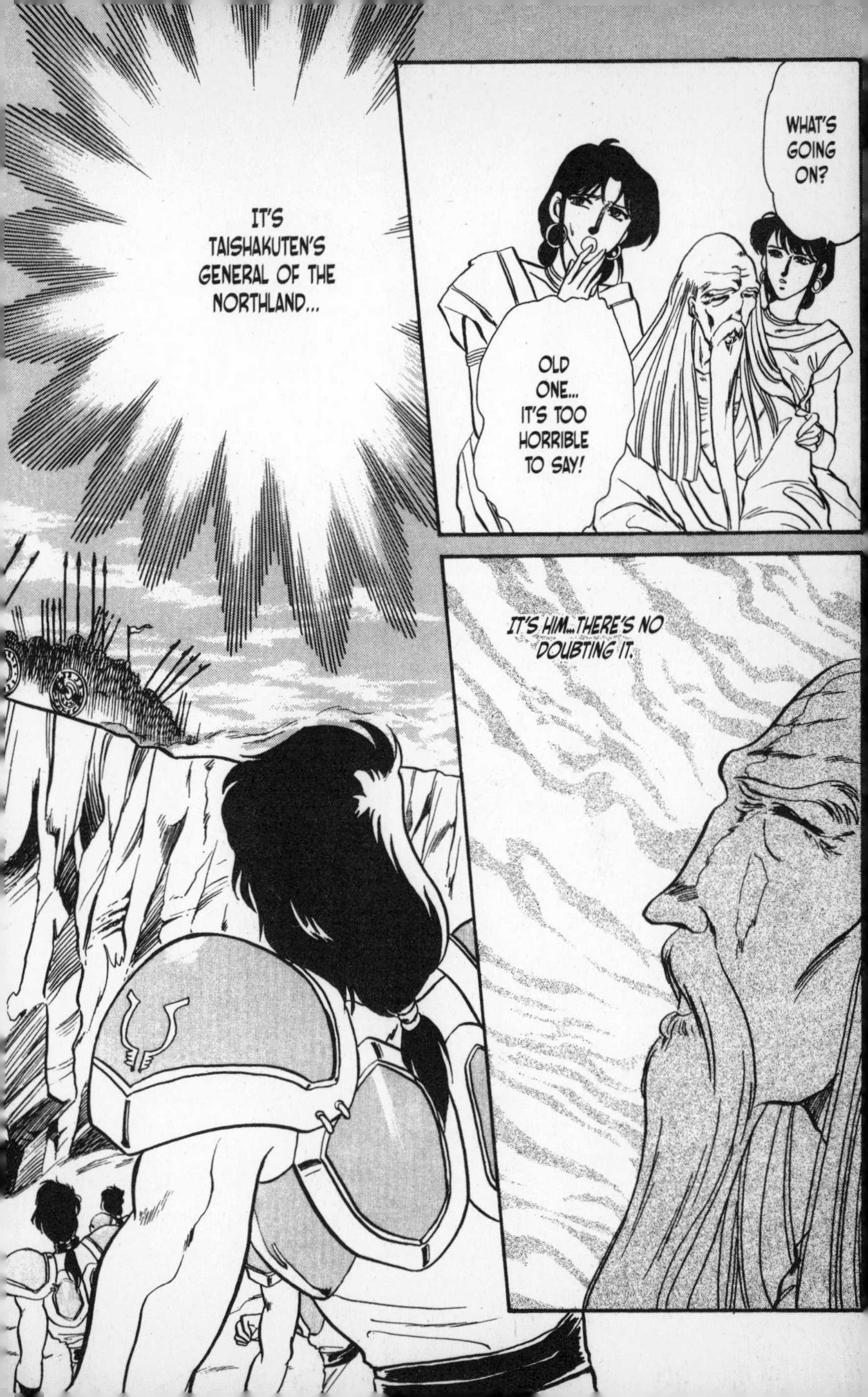
WHAT'S GOING ON?
OLD ONE... IT'S TOO HORRIBLE TO SAY!
IT'S HIM...THERE'S NO DOUBTING IT.
IT'S TAISHAKUTEN'S GENERAL OF THE NORTHLAND...

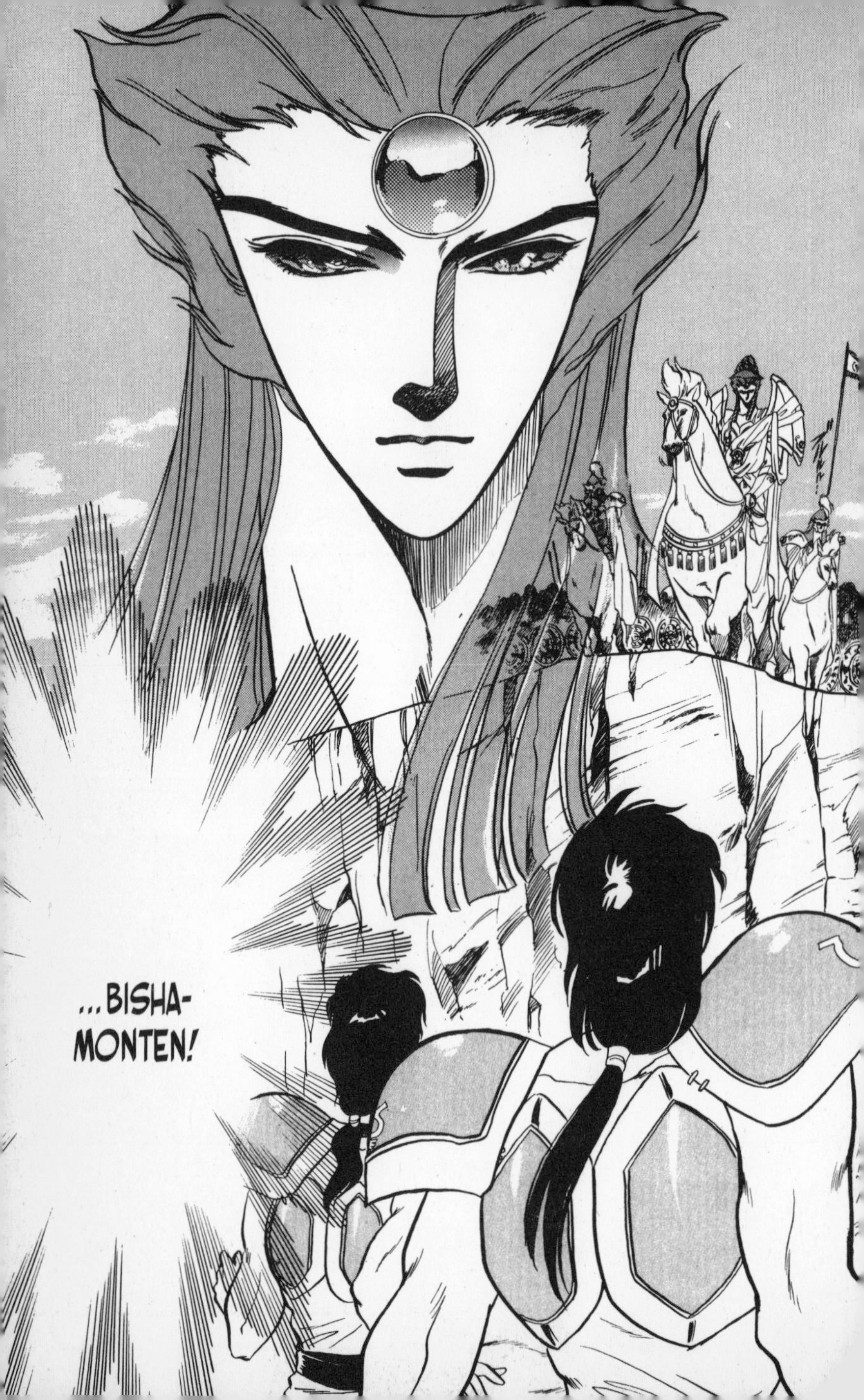
...BISHA-
MONTEN!

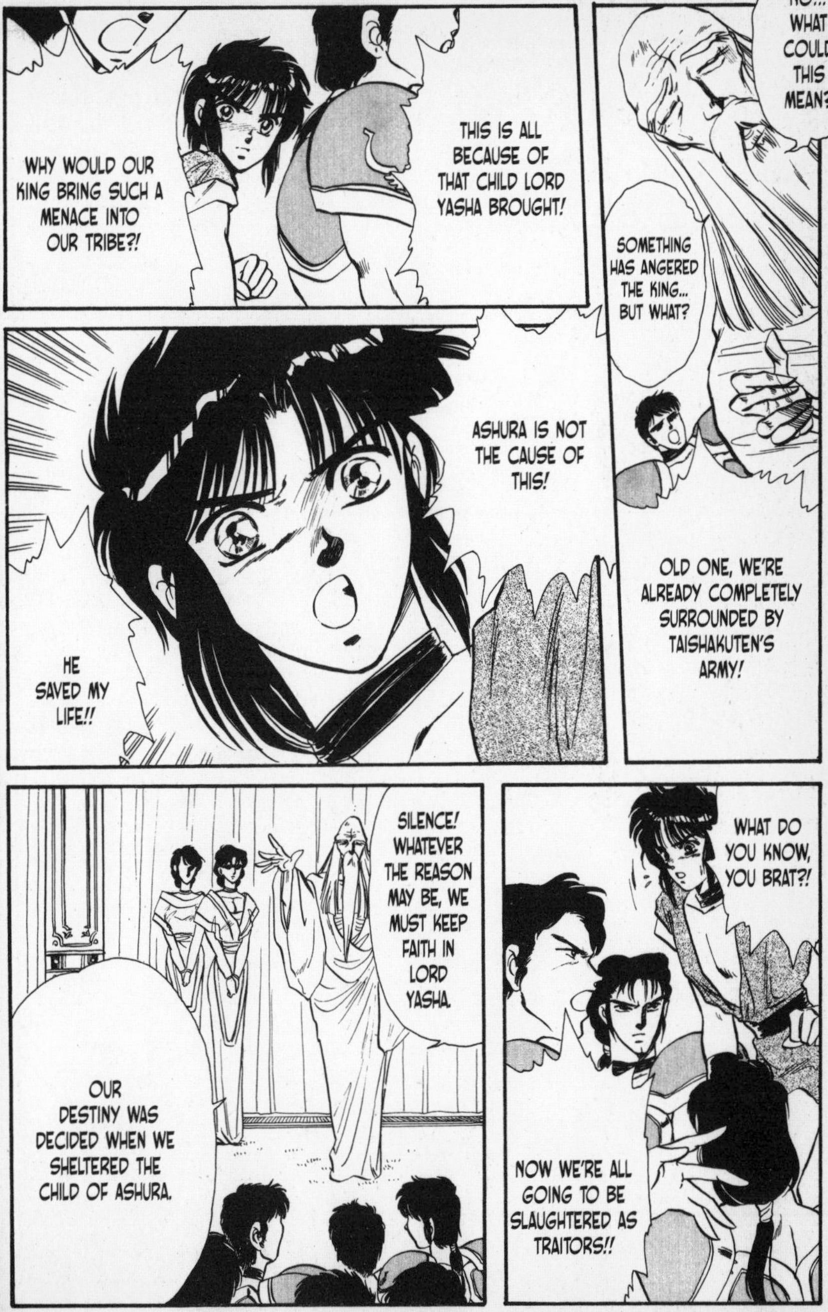
NO... WHAT COULD THIS MEAN?
SOMETHING HAS ANGERED THE KING... BUT WHAT?
OLD ONE, WE'RE ALREADY COMPLETELY SURROUNDED BY TAISHAKUTEN'S ARMY!
THIS IS ALL BECAUSE OF THAT CHILD LORD YASHA BROUGHT!
WHY WOULD OUR KING BRING SUCH A MENACE INTO OUR TRIBE?!
ASHURA IS NOT THE CAUSE OF THIS!
HE SAVED MY LIFE!!
WHAT DO YOU KNOW, YOU BRAT?!
NOW WE'RE ALL GOING TO BE SLAUGHTERED AS TRAITORS!!
SILENCE! WHATEVER THE REASON MAY BE, WE MUST KEEP FAITH IN LORD YASHA.
OUR DESTINY WAS DECIDED WHEN WE SHELTERED THE CHILD OF ASHURA.

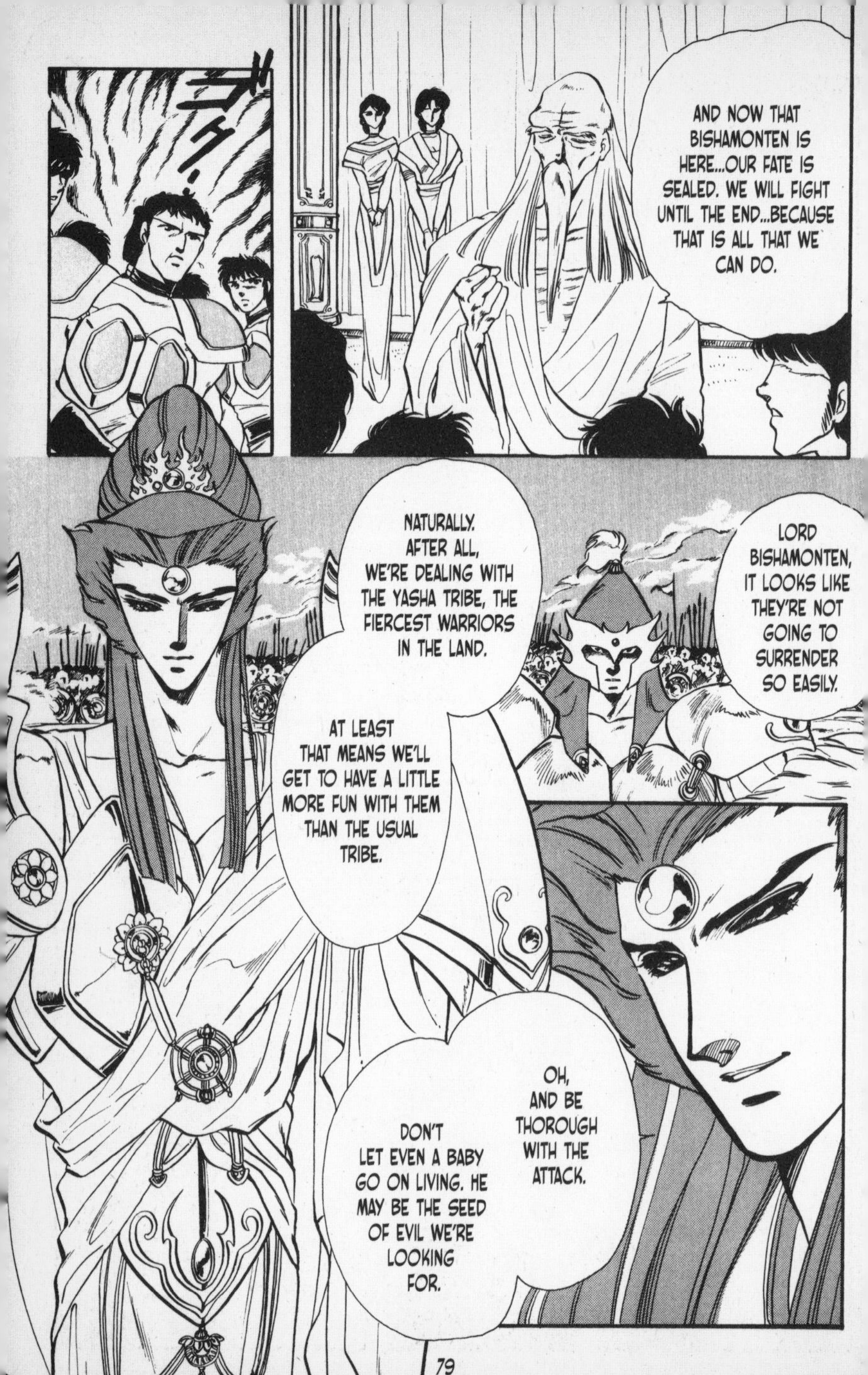
AND NOW THAT BISHAMONTEN IS HERE...OUR FATE IS SEALED. WE WILL FIGHT UNTIL THE END...BECAUSE THAT IS ALL THAT WE CAN DO.
ゴク…
LORD BISHAMONTEN, IT LOOKS LIKE THEY'RE NOT GOING TO SURRENDER SO EASILY.
NATURALLY. AFTER ALL, WE'RE DEALING WITH THE YASHA TRIBE, THE FIERCEST WARRIORS IN THE LAND.
AT LEAST THAT MEANS WE'LL GET TO HAVE A LITTLE MORE FUN WITH THEM THAN THE USUAL TRIBE.
OH, AND BE THOROUGH WITH THE ATTACK.
DON'T LET EVEN A BABY GO ON LIVING. HE MAY BE THE SEED OF EVIL WE'RE LOOKING FOR.

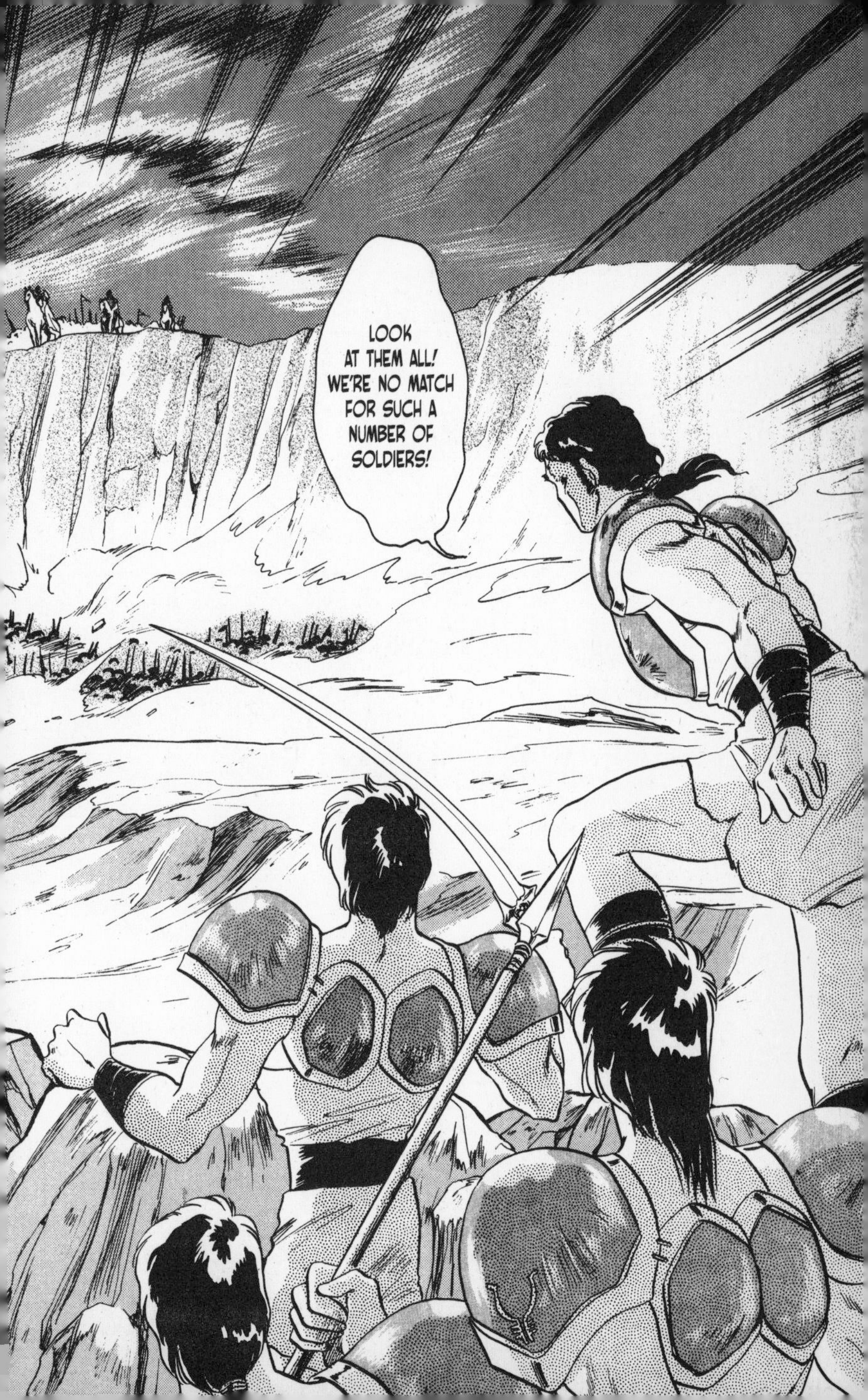
LOOK AT THEM ALL! WE'RE NO MATCH FOR SUCH A NUMBER OF SOLDIERS!

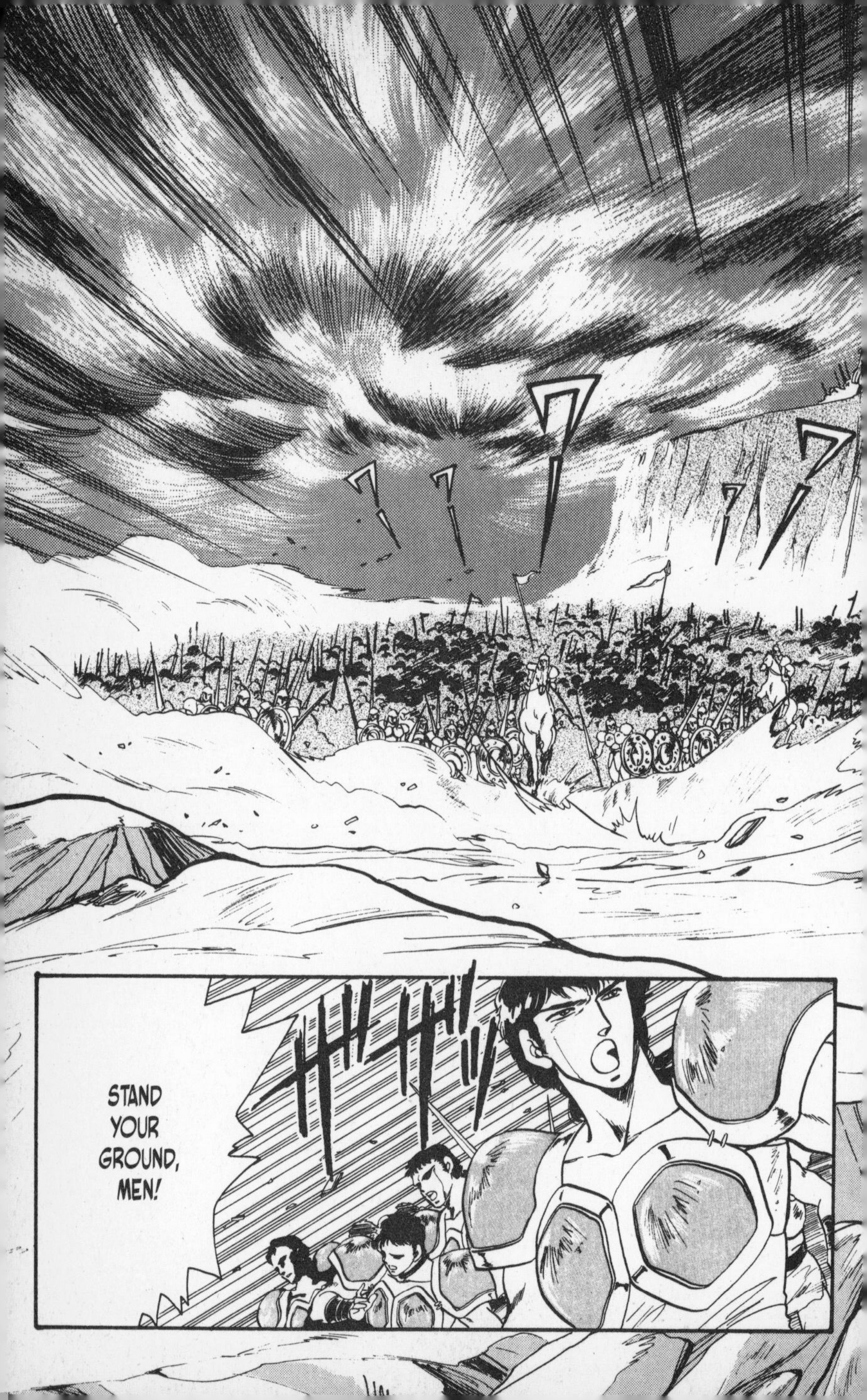
STAND YOUR GROUND, MEN!

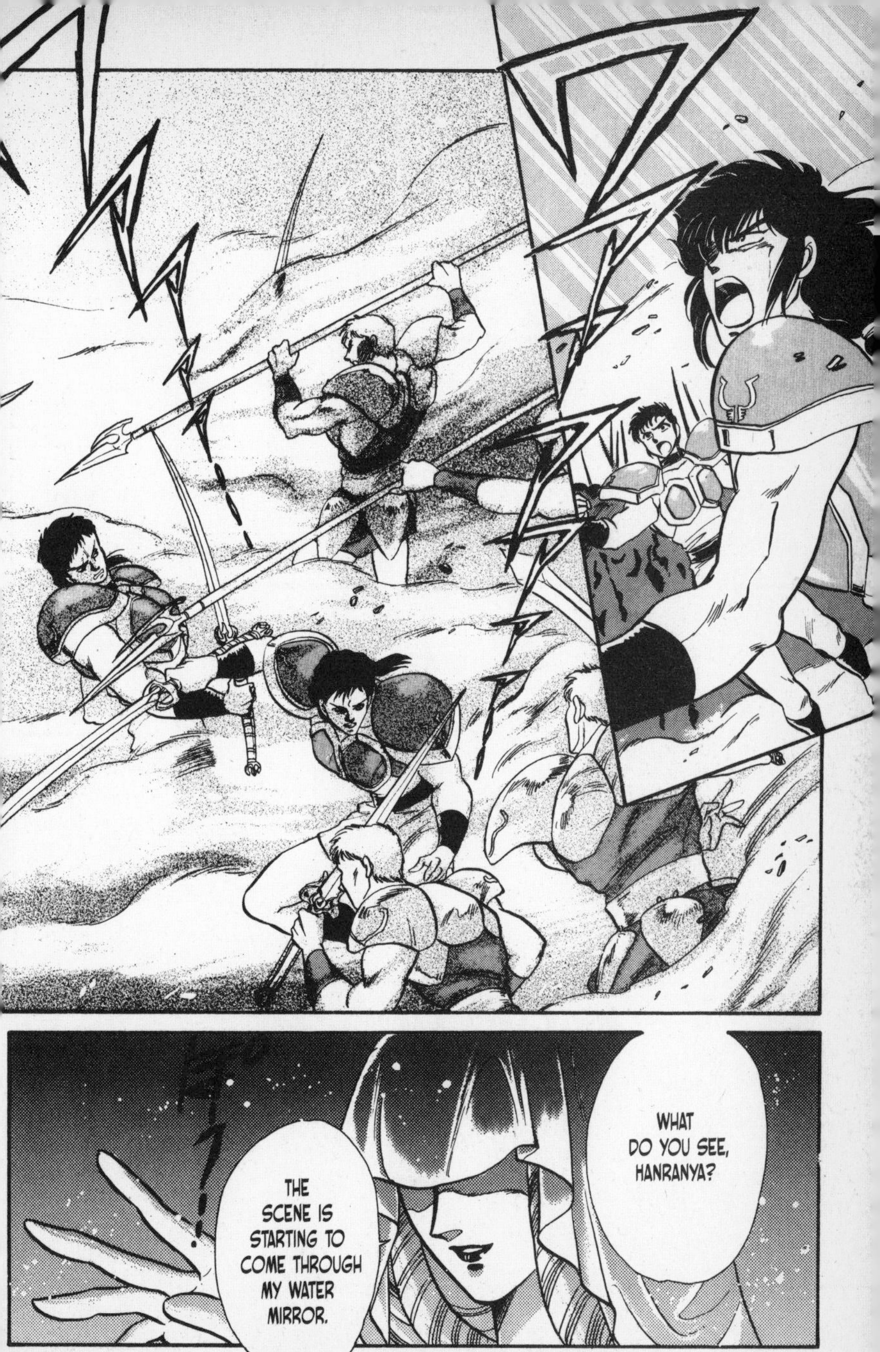
WHAT DO YOU SEE, HANRANYA?
THE SCENE IS STARTING TO COME THROUGH MY WATER MIRROR.

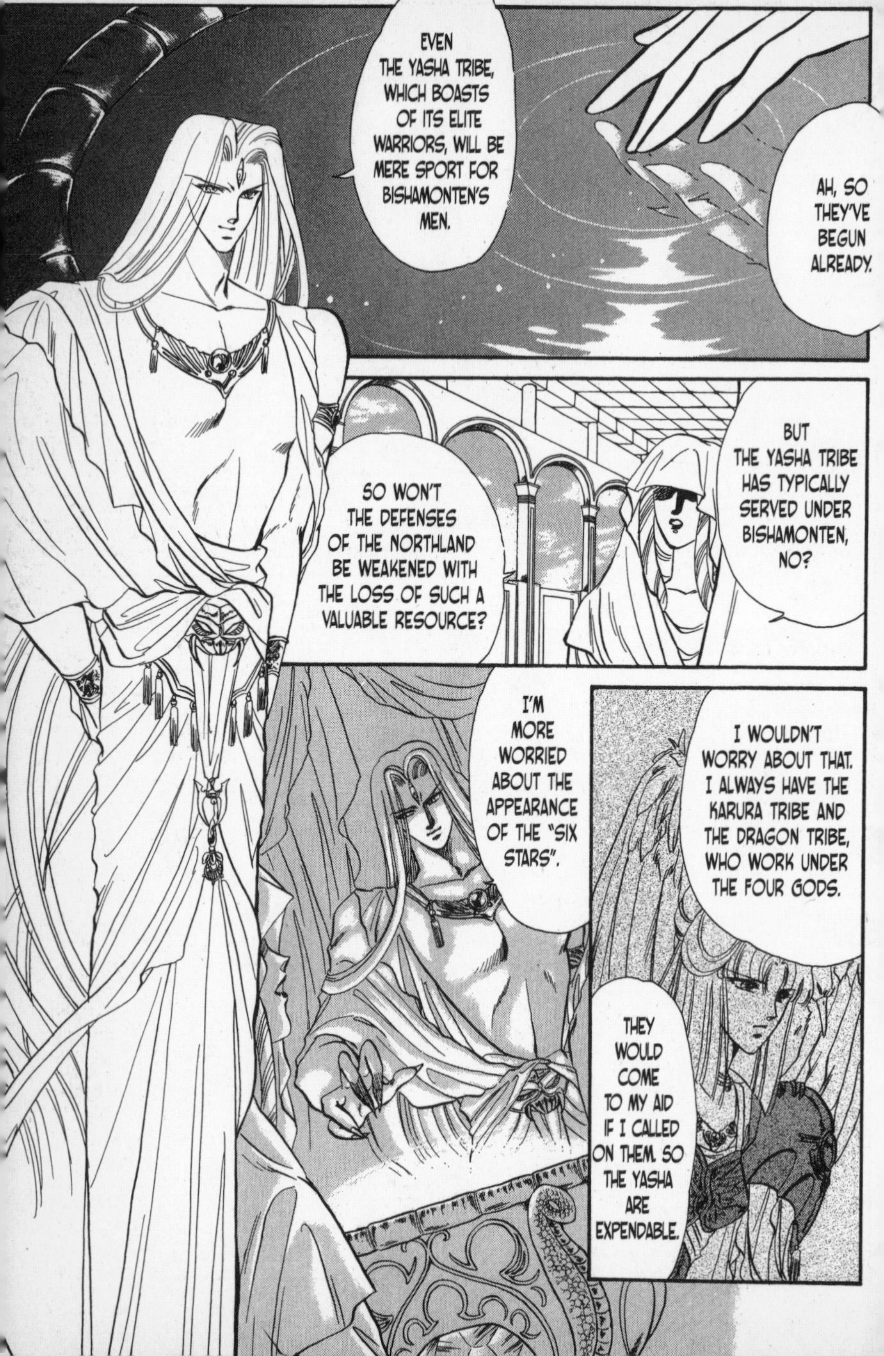
AH, SO THEY'VE BEGUN ALREADY.
EVEN THE YASHA TRIBE, WHICH BOASTS OF ITS ELITE WARRIORS, WILL BE MERE SPORT FOR BISHAMONTEN'S MEN.
BUT THE YASHA TRIBE HAS TYPICALLY SERVED UNDER BISHAMONTEN, NO?
SO WON'T THE DEFENSES OF THE NORTHLAND BE WEAKENED WITH THE LOSS OF SUCH A VALUABLE RESOURCE?
I WOULDN'T WORRY ABOUT THAT. I ALWAYS HAVE THE KARURA TRIBE AND THE DRAGON TRIBE, WHO WORK UNDER THE FOUR GODS.
THEY WOULD COME TO MY AID IF I CALLED ON THEM. SO THE YASHA ARE EXPENDABLE.
I'M MORE WORRIED ABOUT THE APPEARANCE OF THE "SIX STARS".

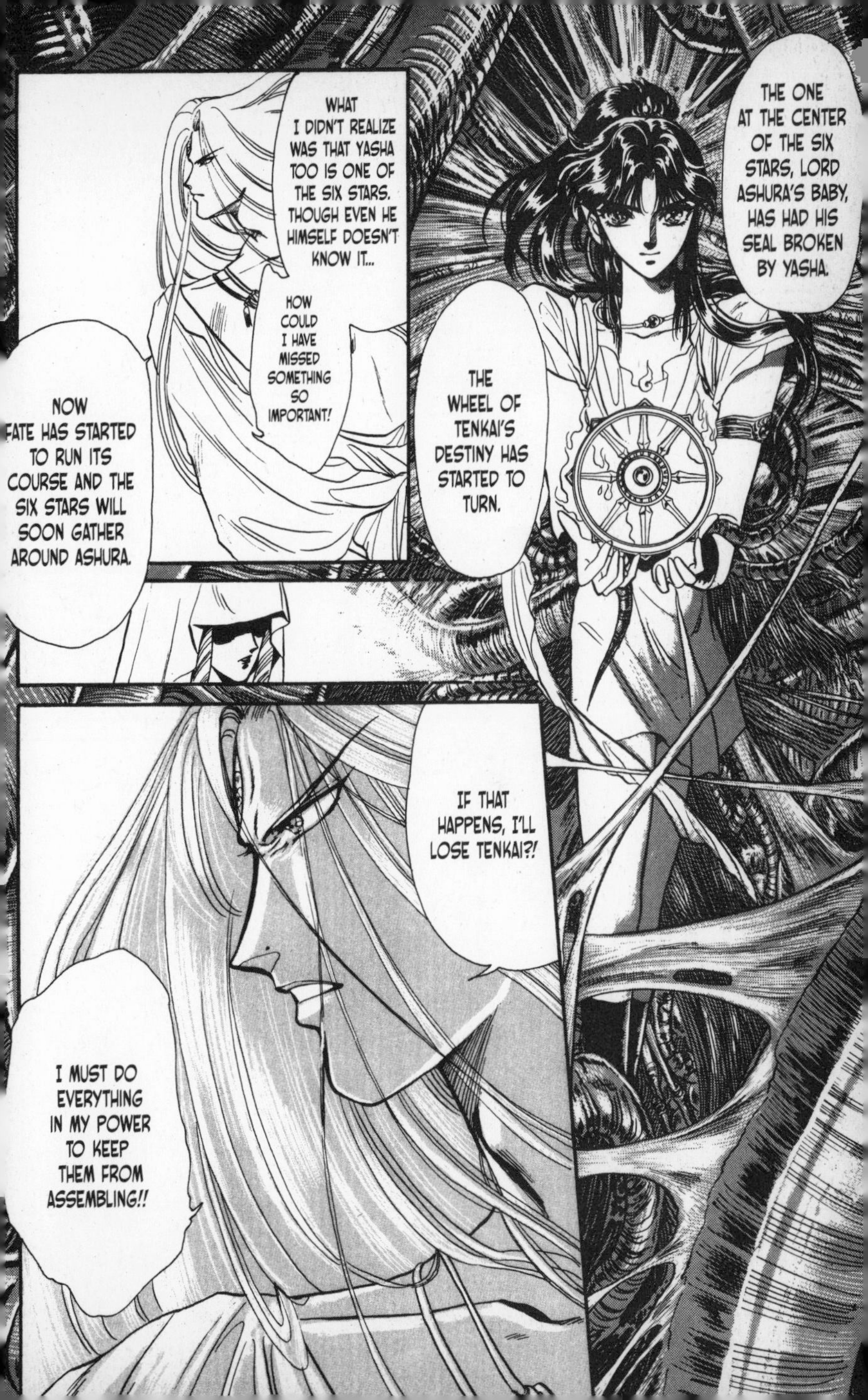
THE ONE AT THE CENTER OF THE SIX STARS, LORD ASHURA'S BABY, HAS HAD HIS SEAL BROKEN BY YASHA.
THE WHEEL OF TENKAI'S DESTINY HAS STARTED TO TURN.
WHAT I DIDN'T REALIZE WAS THAT YASHA TOO IS ONE OF THE SIX STARS. THOUGH EVEN HE HIMSELF DOESN'T KNOW IT...
HOW COULD I HAVE MISSED SOMETHING SO IMPORTANT!
NOW FATE HAS STARTED TO RUN ITS COURSE AND THE SIX STARS WILL SOON GATHER AROUND ASHURA.
IF THAT HAPPENS, I'LL LOSE TENKAI?!
I MUST DO EVERYTHING IN MY POWER TO KEEP THEM FROM ASSEMBLING!!

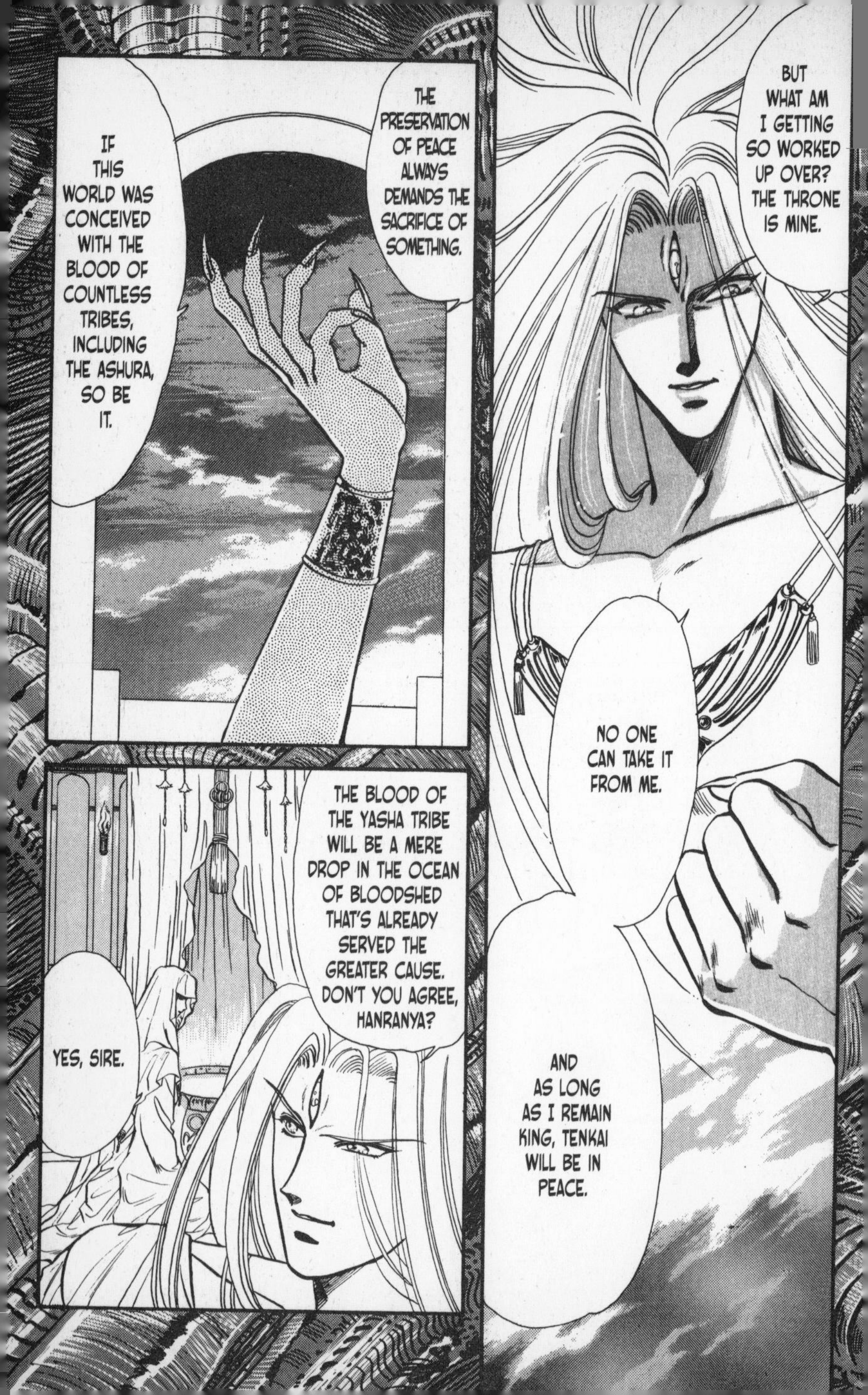
BUT WHAT AM I GETTING SO WORKED UP OVER? THE THRONE IS MINE.
NO ONE CAN TAKE IT FROM ME.
AND AS LONG AS I REMAIN KING, TENKAI WILL BE IN PEACE.
THE PRESERVATION OF PEACE ALWAYS DEMANDS THE SACRIFICE OF SOMETHING.
IF THIS WORLD WAS CONCEIVED WITH THE BLOOD OF COUNTLESS TRIBES, INCLUDING THE ASHURA, SO BE IT.
THE BLOOD OF THE YASHA TRIBE WILL BE A MERE DROP IN THE OCEAN OF BLOODSHED THAT'S ALREADY SERVED THE GREATER CAUSE. DON'T YOU AGREE, HANRANYA?
YES, SIRE.

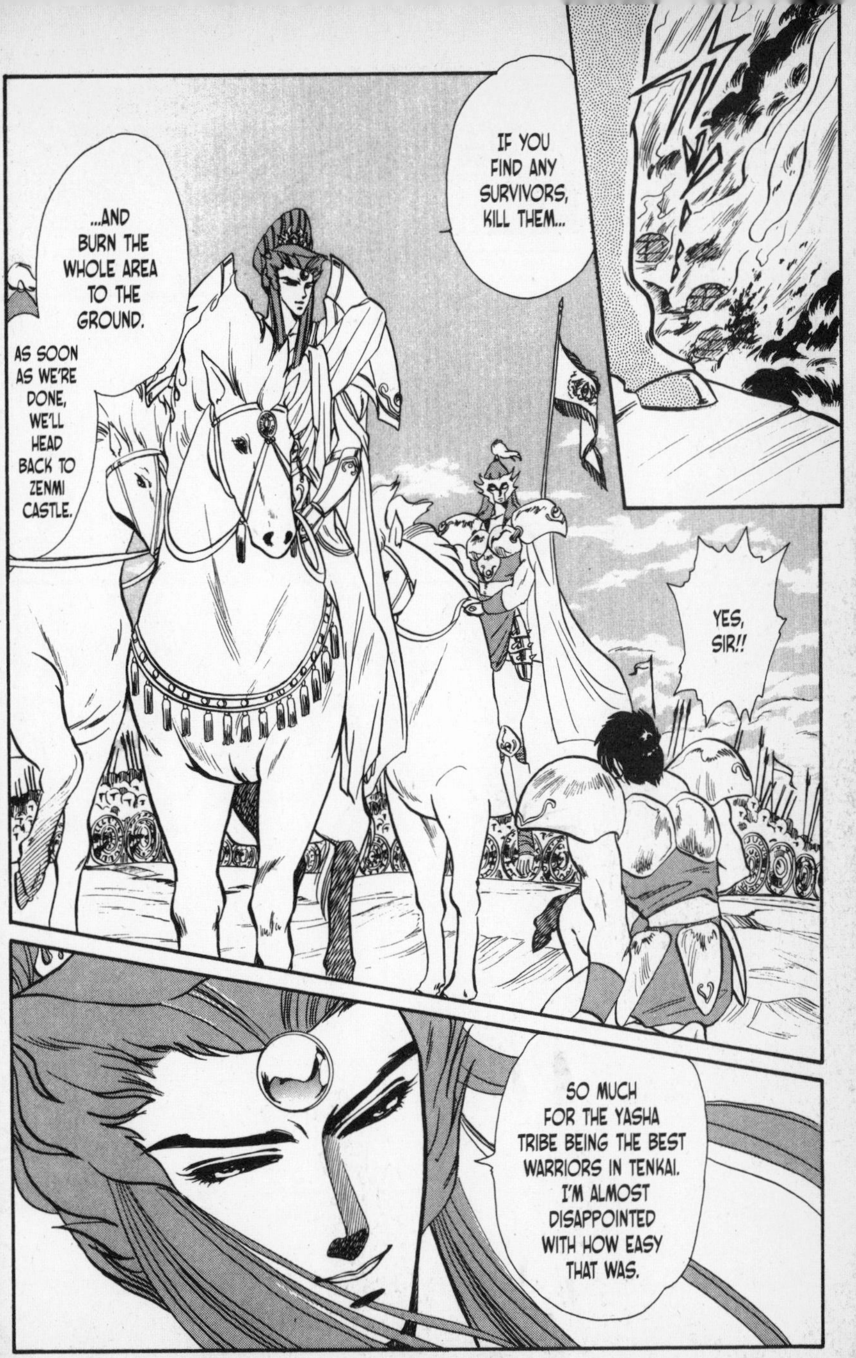
IF YOU FIND ANY SURVIVORS, KILL THEM...
...AND BURN THE WHOLE AREA TO THE GROUND.
AS SOON AS WE'RE DONE, WE'LL HEAD BACK TO ZENMI CASTLE.
YES, SIR!!
SO MUCH FOR THE YASHA TRIBE BEING THE BEST WARRIORS IN TENKAI. I'M ALMOST DISAPPOINTED WITH HOW EASY THAT WAS.

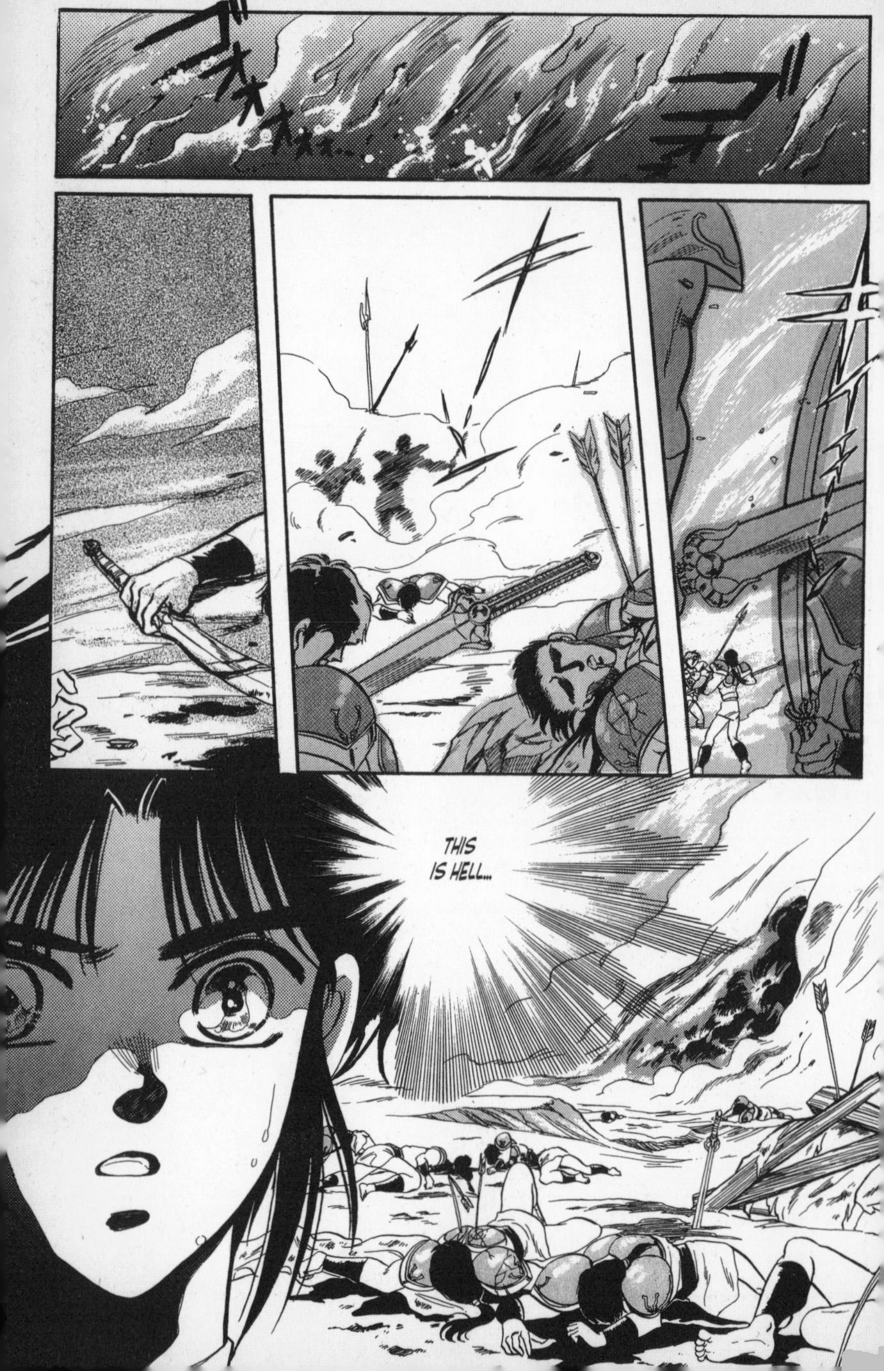
THIS IS HELL...

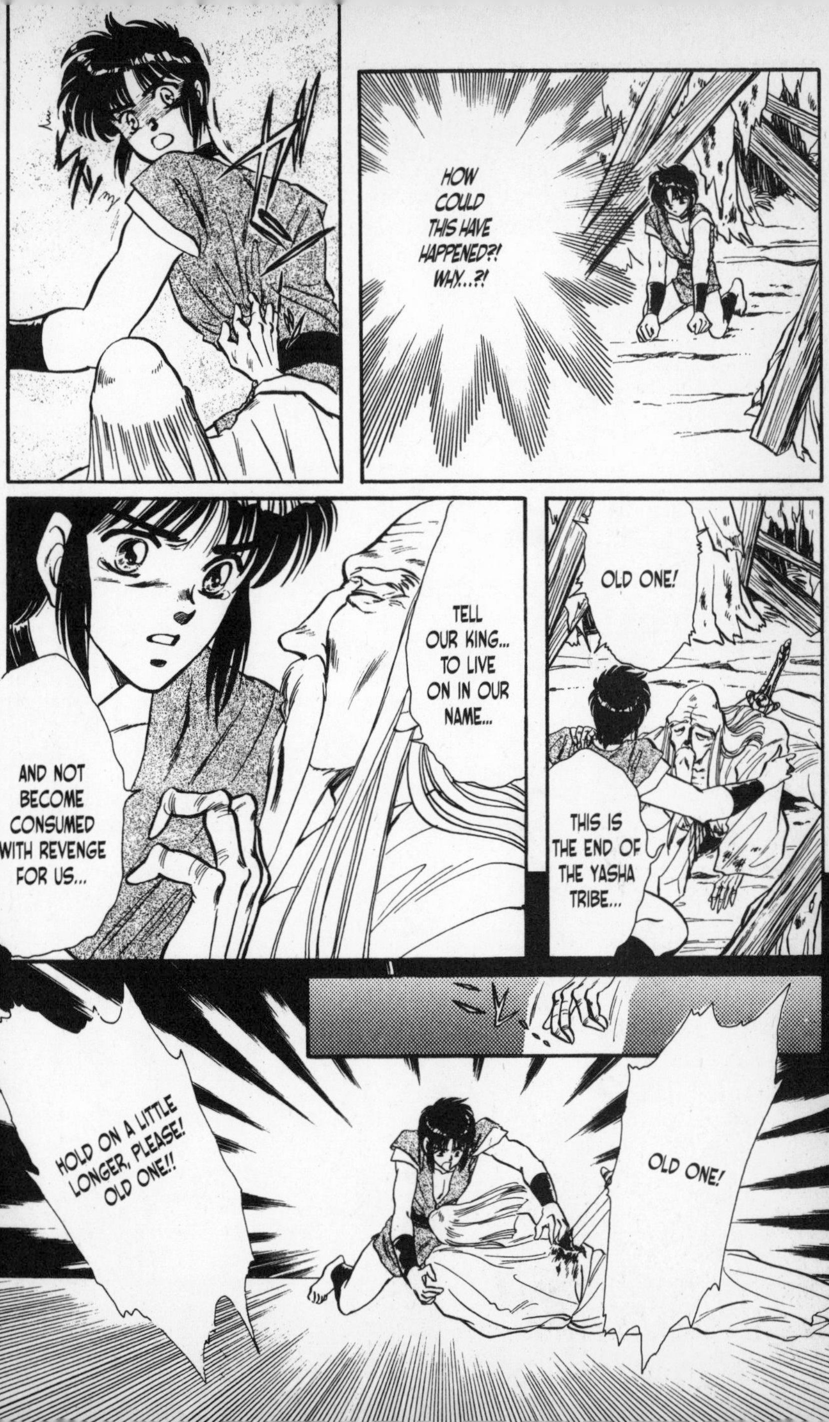
HOW COULD THIS HAVE HAPPENED?! WHY...?!
OLD ONE!
THIS IS THE END OF THE YASHA TRIBE...
TELL OUR KING... TO LIVE ON IN OUR NAME...
AND NOT BECOME CONSUMED WITH REVENGE FOR US...
OLD ONE!
HOLD ON A LITTLE LONGER, PLEASE! OLD ONE!!

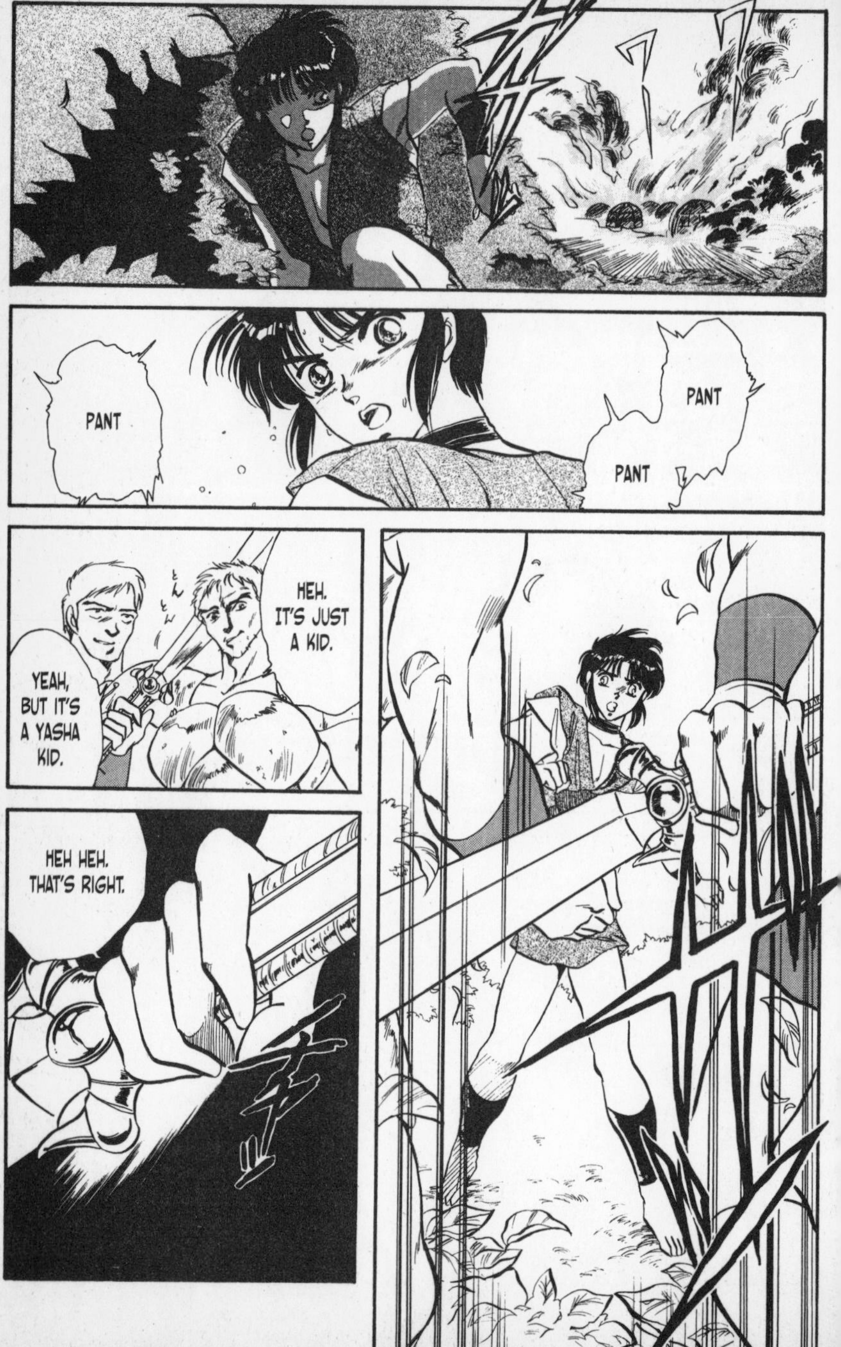
PANT
PANT
PANT
HEH. IT'S JUST A KID.
YEAH, BUT IT'S A YASHA KID.
HEH HEH. THAT'S RIGHT.

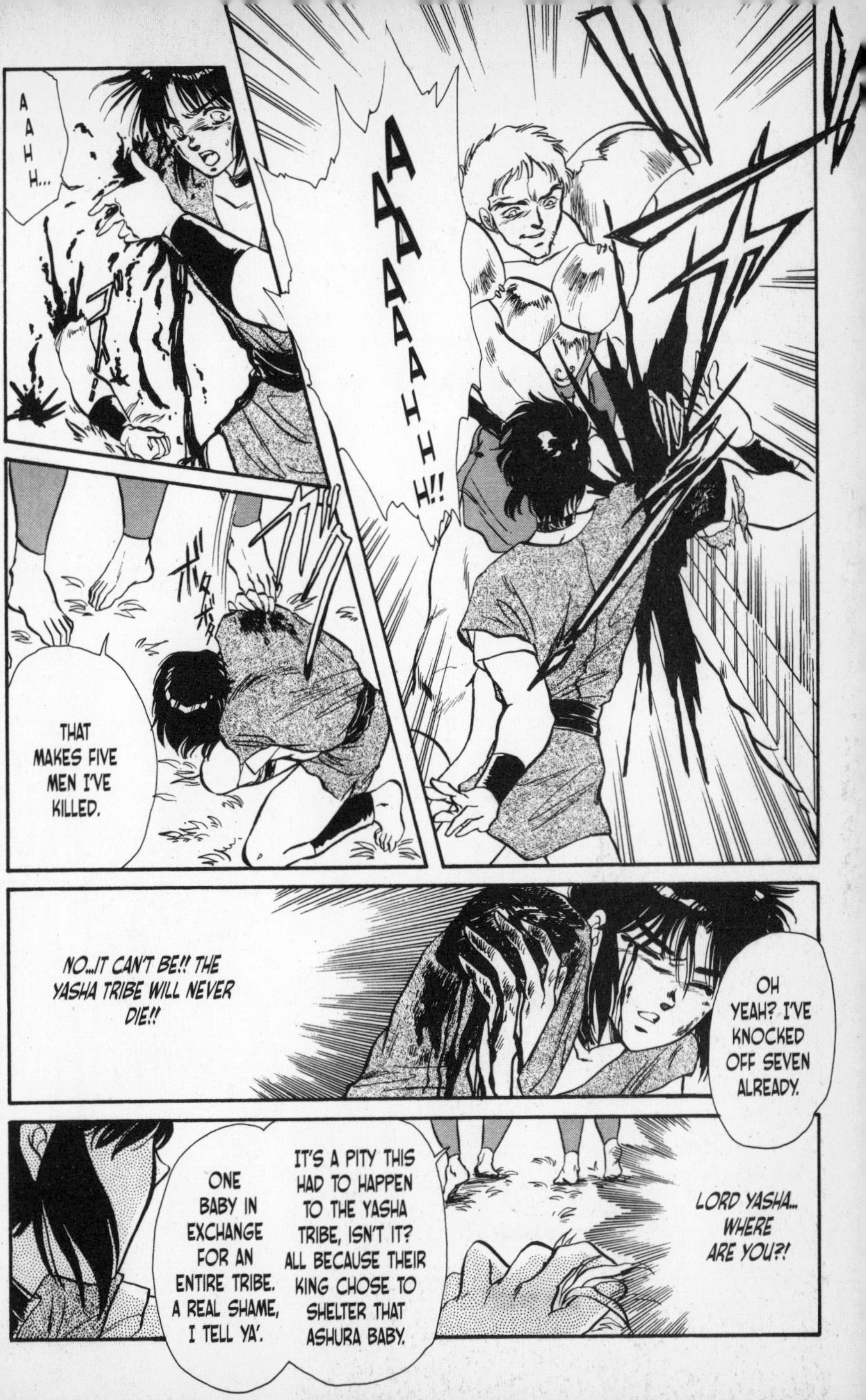
AAAAAAAHHH!!
AAHH...
THAT MAKES FIVE MEN I'VE KILLED.
OH YEAH? I'VE KNOCKED OFF SEVEN ALREADY.
NO...IT CAN'T BE!! THE YASHA TRIBE WILL NEVER DIE!!
LORD YASHA... WHERE ARE YOU?!
IT'S A PITY THIS HAD TO HAPPEN TO THE YASHA TRIBE, ISN'T IT? ALL BECAUSE THEIR KING CHOSE TO SHELTER THAT ASHURA BABY.
ONE BABY IN EXCHANGE FOR AN ENTIRE TRIBE. A REAL SHAME, I TELL YA'.

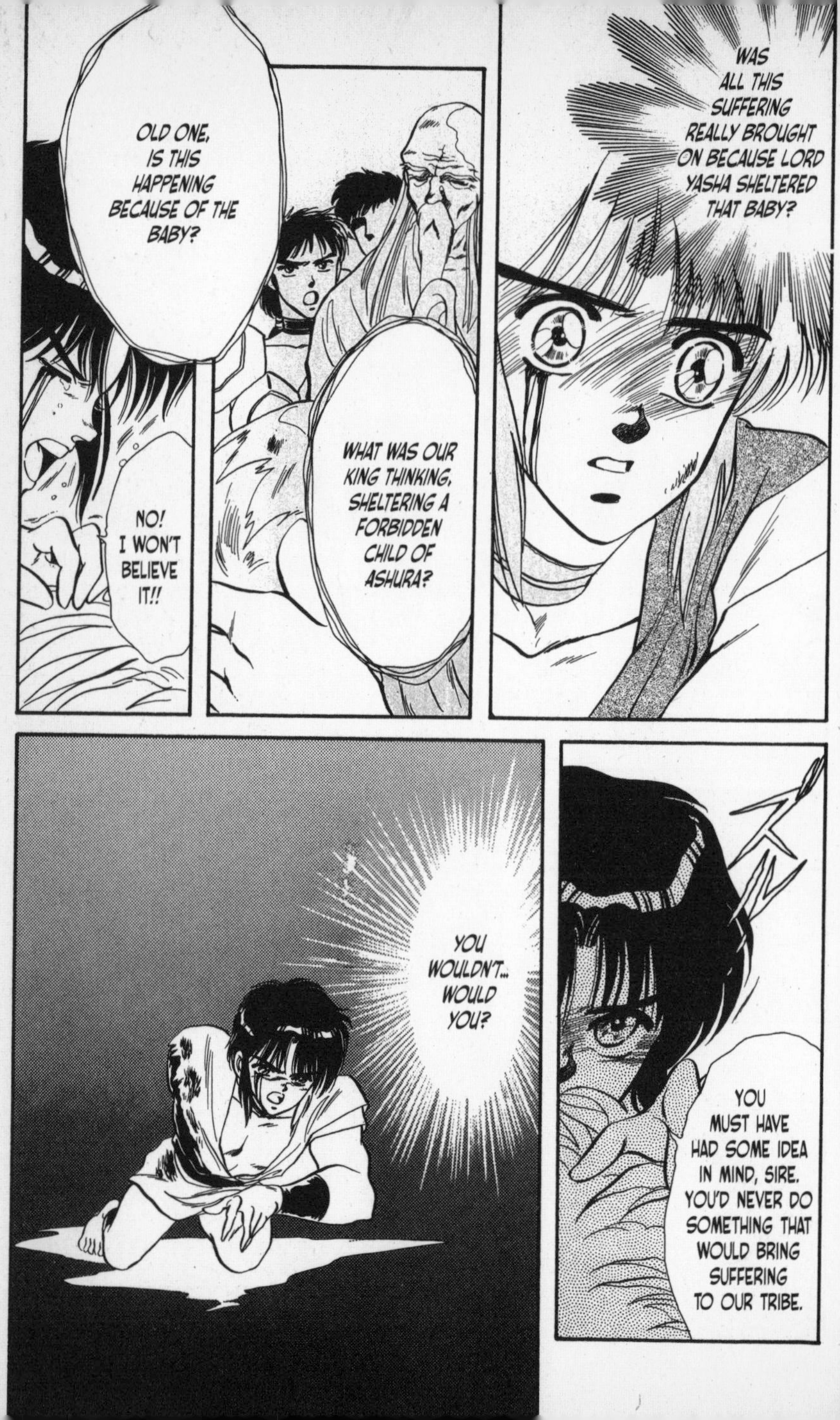
WAS ALL THIS SUFFERING REALLY BROUGHT ON BECAUSE LORD YASHA SHELTERED THAT BABY?
OLD ONE, IS THIS HAPPENING BECAUSE OF THE BABY?
WHAT WAS OUR KING THINKING, SHELTERING A FORBIDDEN CHILD OF ASHURA?
NO! I WON'T BELIEVE IT!!
YOU MUST HAVE HAD SOME IDEA IN MIND, SIRE. YOU'D NEVER DO SOMETHING THAT WOULD BRING SUFFERING TO OUR TRIBE.
YOU WOULDN'T... WOULD YOU?

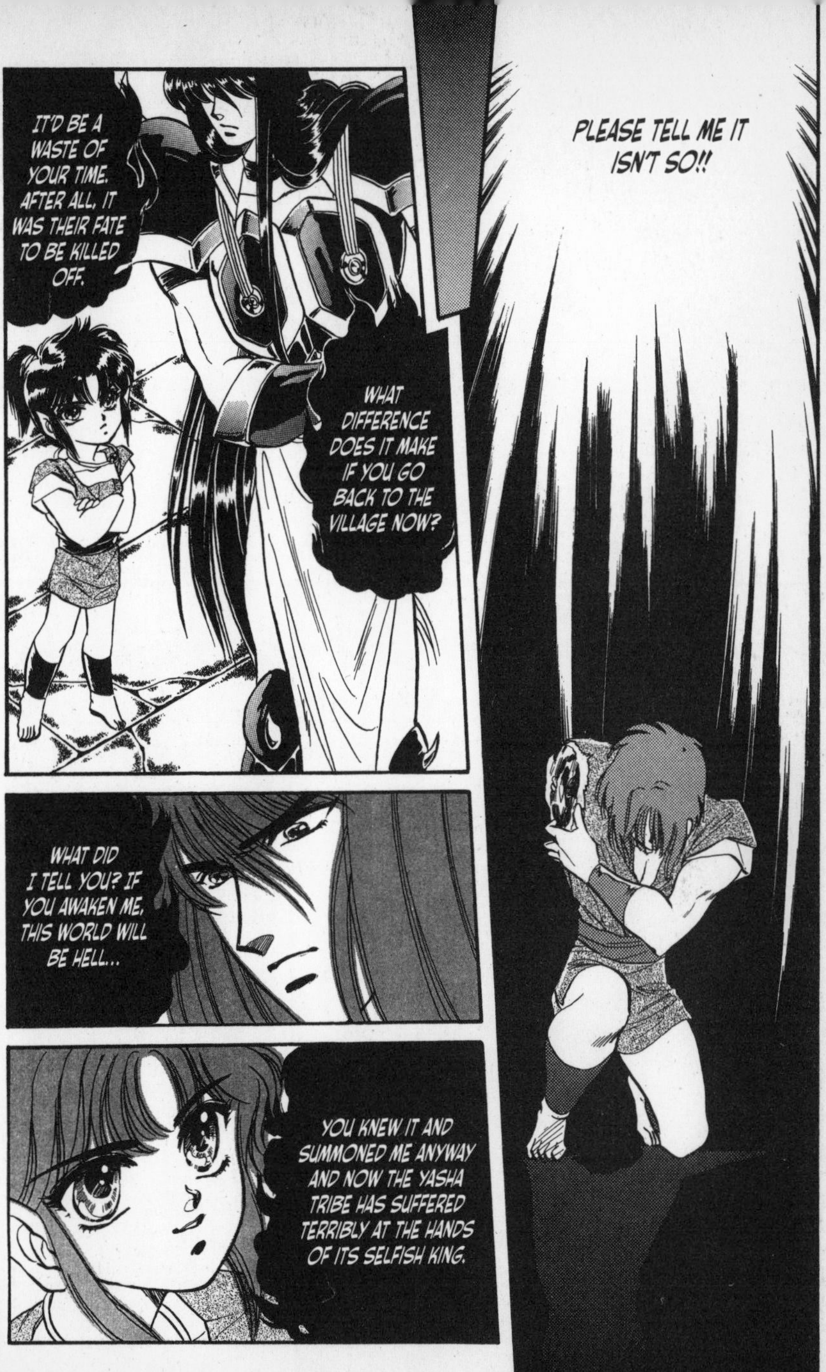
PLEASE TELL ME IT ISN'T SO!!
IT'D BE A WASTE OF YOUR TIME. AFTER ALL, IT WAS THEIR FATE TO BE KILLED OFF.
WHAT DIFFERENCE DOES IT MAKE IF YOU GO BACK TO THE VILLAGE NOW?
WHAT DID I TELL YOU? IF YOU AWAKEN ME, THIS WORLD WILL BE HELL...
YOU KNEW IT AND SUMMONED ME ANYWAY AND NOW THE YASHA TRIBE HAS SUFFERED TERRIBLY AT THE HANDS OF ITS SELFISH KING.

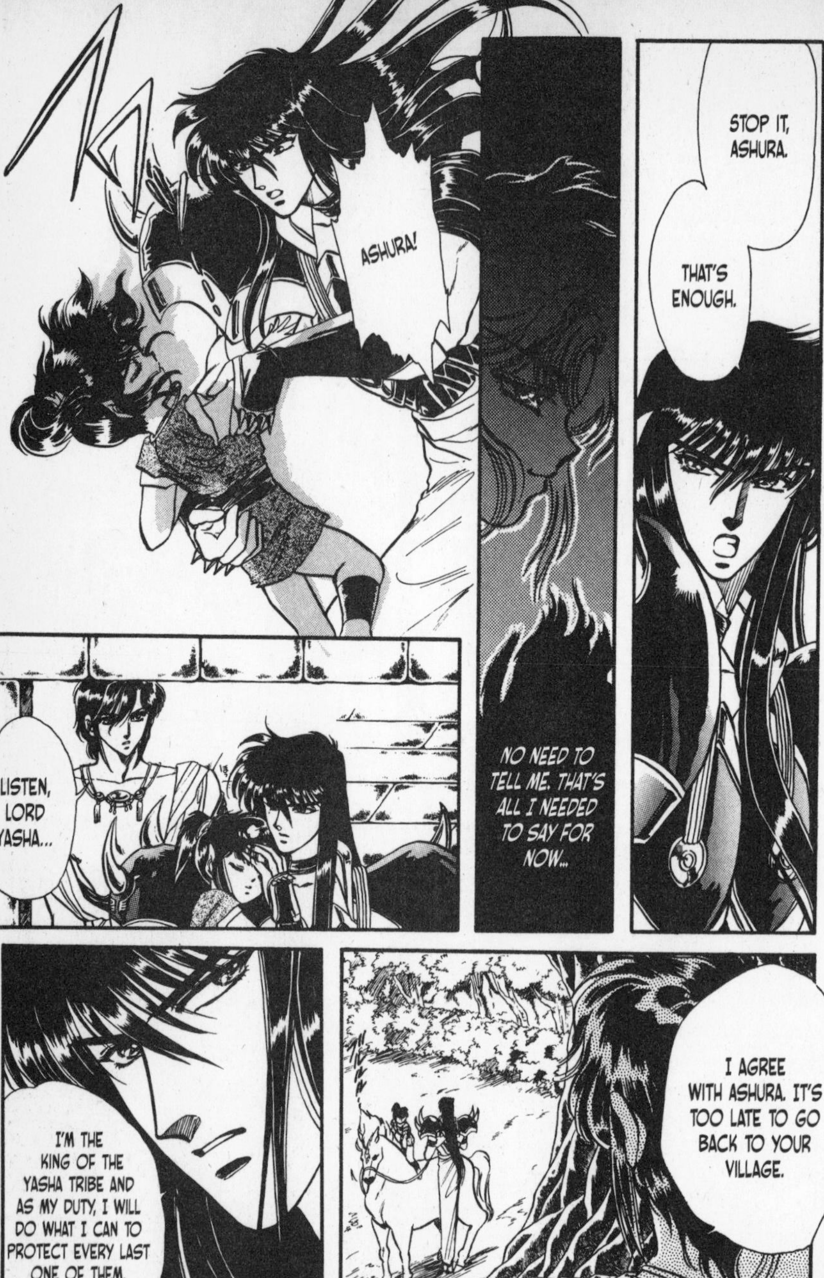
STOP IT, ASHURA.
THAT'S ENOUGH.
NO NEED TO TELL ME. THAT'S ALL I NEEDED TO SAY FOR NOW...
ASHURA!
LISTEN, LORD YASHA...
I AGREE WITH ASHURA. IT'S TOO LATE TO GO BACK TO YOUR VILLAGE.
I'M THE KING OF THE YASHA TRIBE AND AS MY DUTY, I WILL DO WHAT I CAN TO PROTECT EVERY LAST ONE OF THEM.

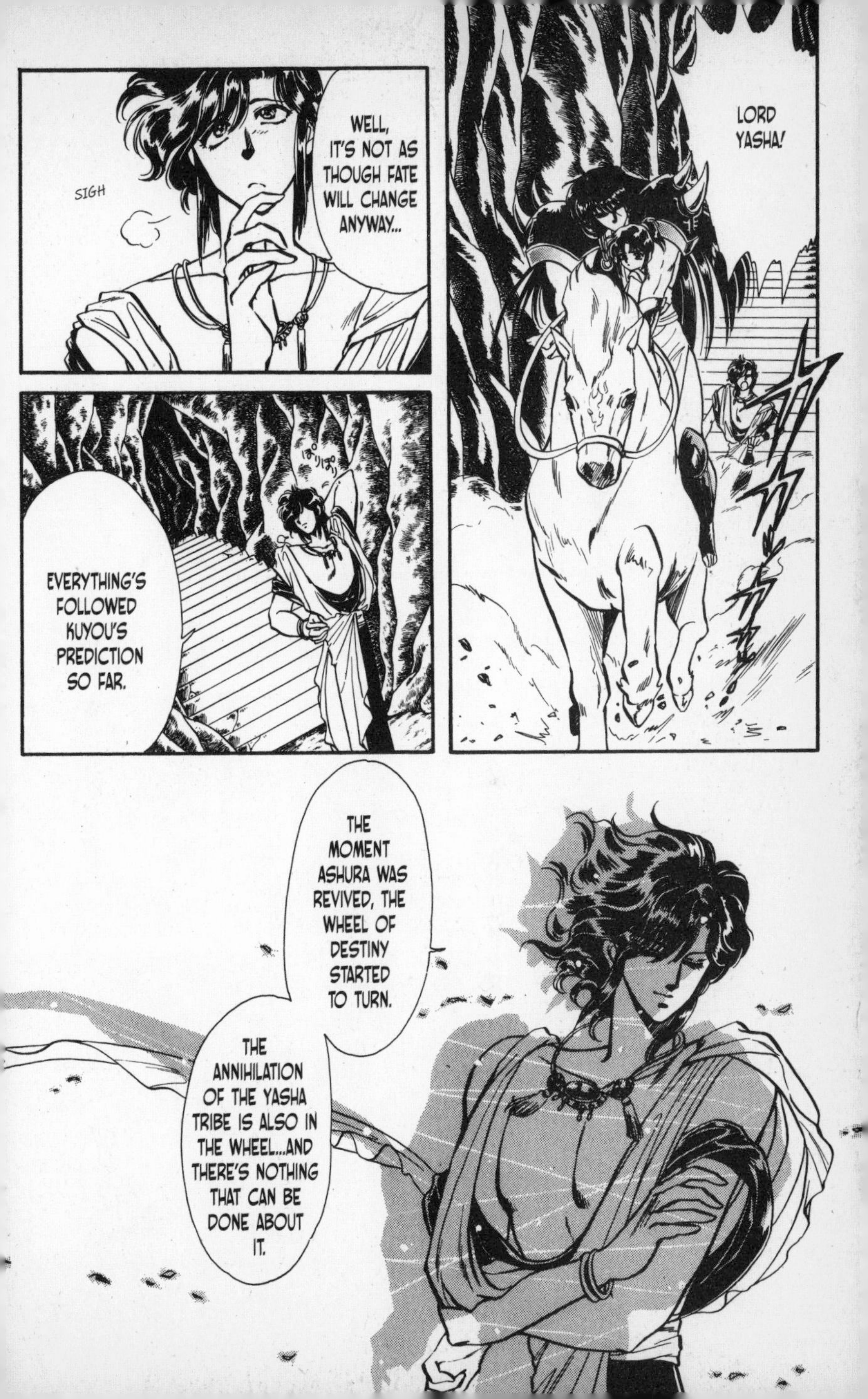
LORD YASHA!
WELL, IT'S NOT AS THOUGH FATE WILL CHANGE ANYWAY...
SIGH
ぽりぽり
EVERYTHING'S FOLLOWED KUYOU'S PREDICTION SO FAR.
THE MOMENT ASHURA WAS REVIVED, THE WHEEL OF DESTINY STARTED TO TURN.
THE ANNIHILATION OF THE YASHA TRIBE IS ALSO IN THE WHEEL...AND THERE'S NOTHING THAT CAN BE DONE ABOUT IT.

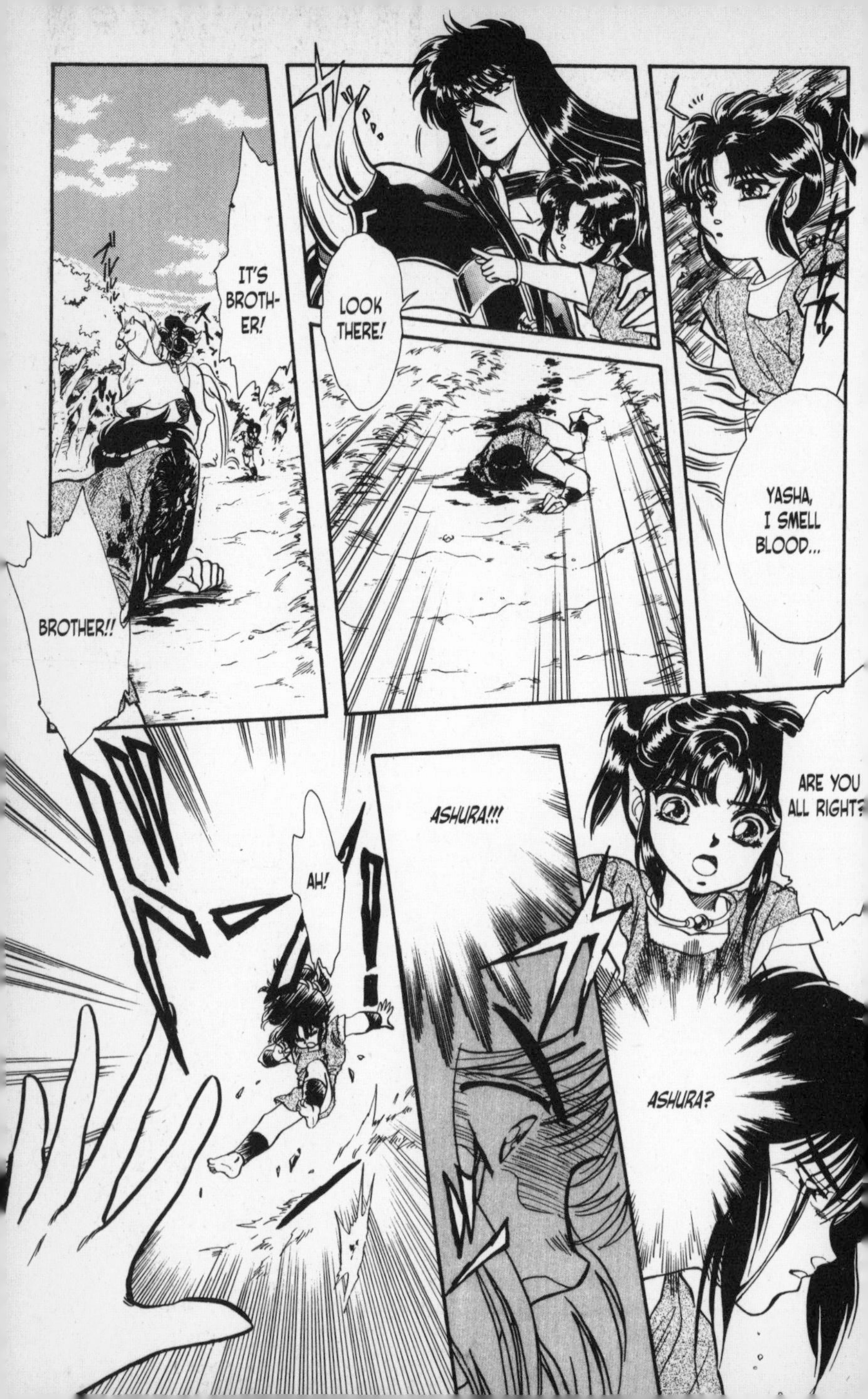
YASHA, I SMELL BLOOD...
LOOK THERE!
IT'S BROTHER!
BROTHER!!
ARE YOU ALL RIGHT?
ASHURA?
ASHURA!!!
AH!

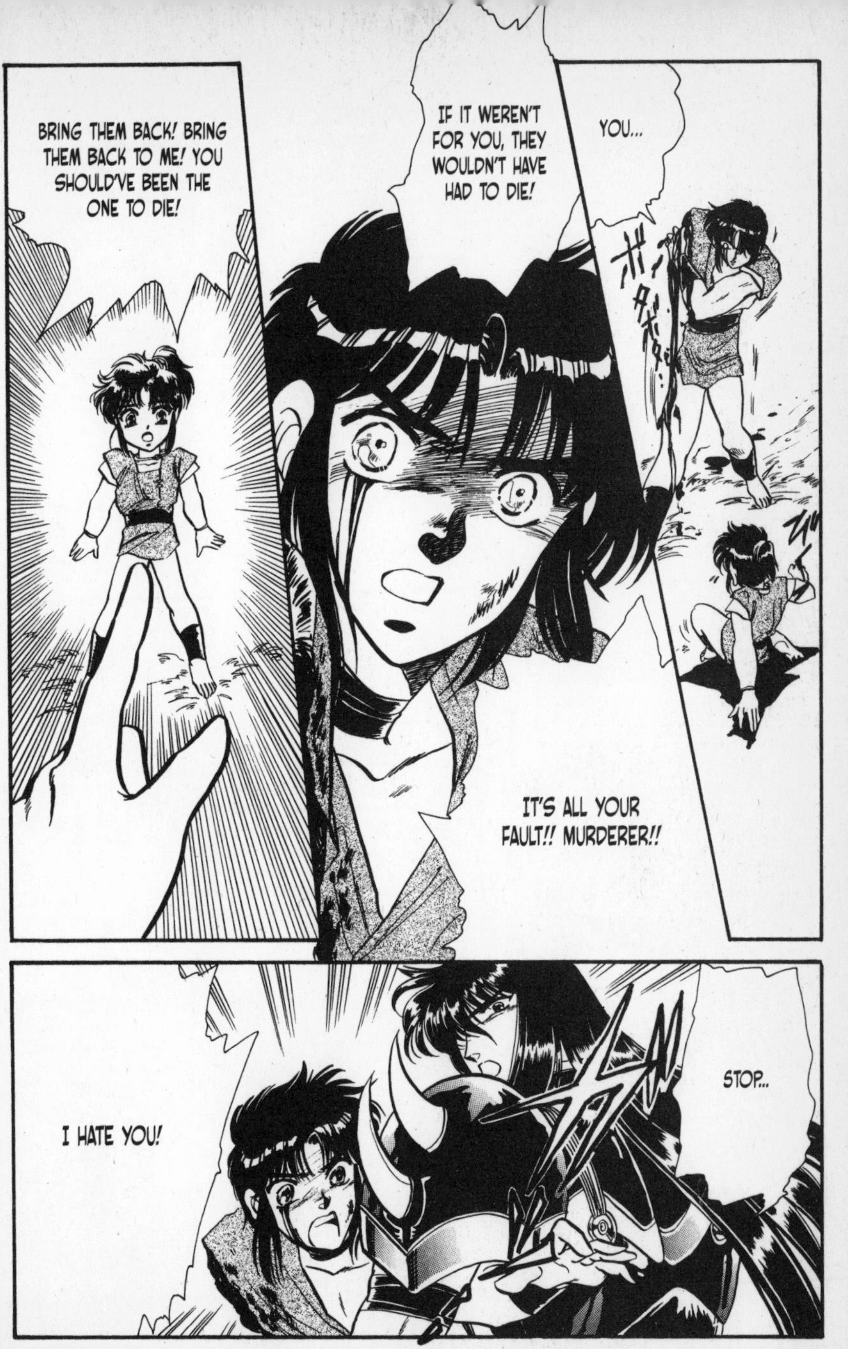
YOU...
IF IT WEREN'T FOR YOU, THEY WOULDN'T HAVE HAD TO DIE!
IT'S ALL YOUR FAULT!! MURDERER!!
BRING THEM BACK! BRING THEM BACK TO ME! YOU SHOULD'VE BEEN THE ONE TO DIE!
STOP...
I HATE YOU!

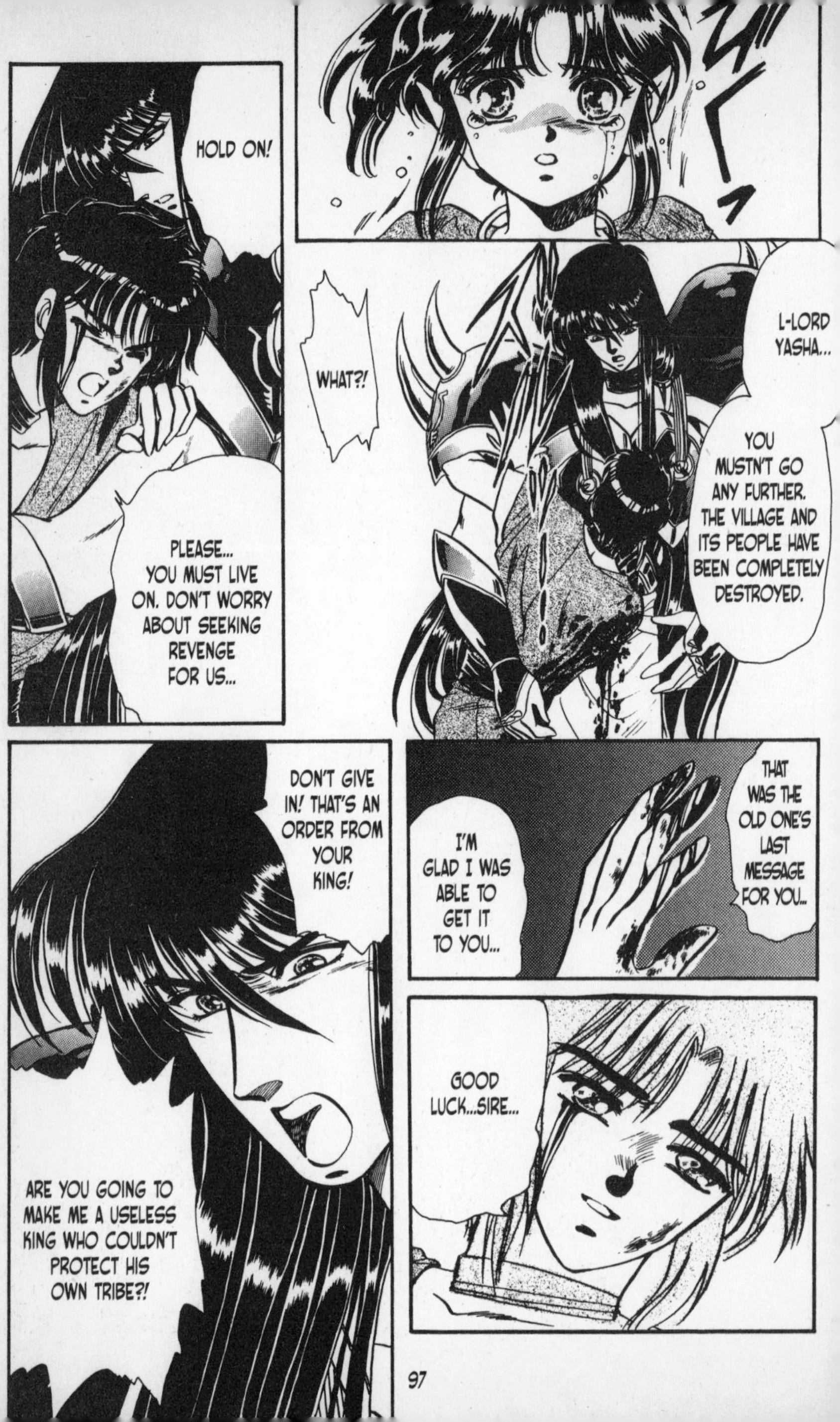
L-LORD YASHA...
YOU MUSTN'T GO ANY FURTHER. THE VILLAGE AND ITS PEOPLE HAVE BEEN COMPLETELY DESTROYED.
WHAT?!
HOLD ON!
PLEASE... YOU MUST LIVE ON. DON'T WORRY ABOUT SEEKING REVENGE FOR US...
THAT WAS THE OLD ONE'S LAST MESSAGE FOR YOU...
I'M GLAD I WAS ABLE TO GET IT TO YOU...
GOOD LUCK...SIRE...
DON'T GIVE IN! THAT'S AN ORDER FROM YOUR KING!
ARE YOU GOING TO MAKE ME A USELESS KING WHO COULDN'T PROTECT HIS OWN TRIBE?!

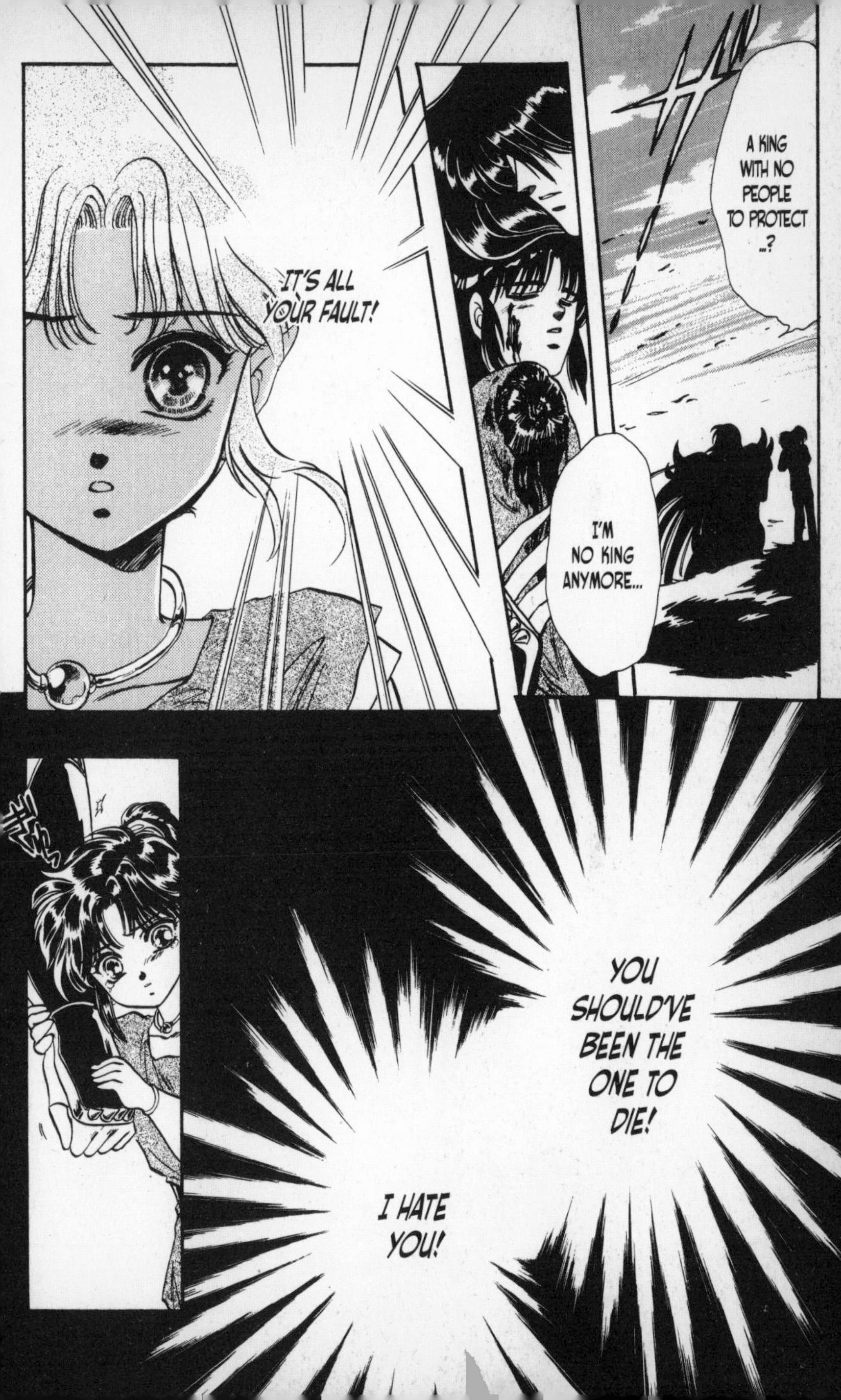
A KING WITH NO PEOPLE TO PROTECT ...?
I'M NO KING ANYMORE...
IT'S ALL YOUR FAULT!
YOU SHOULD'VE BEEN THE ONE TO DIE!
I HATE YOU!

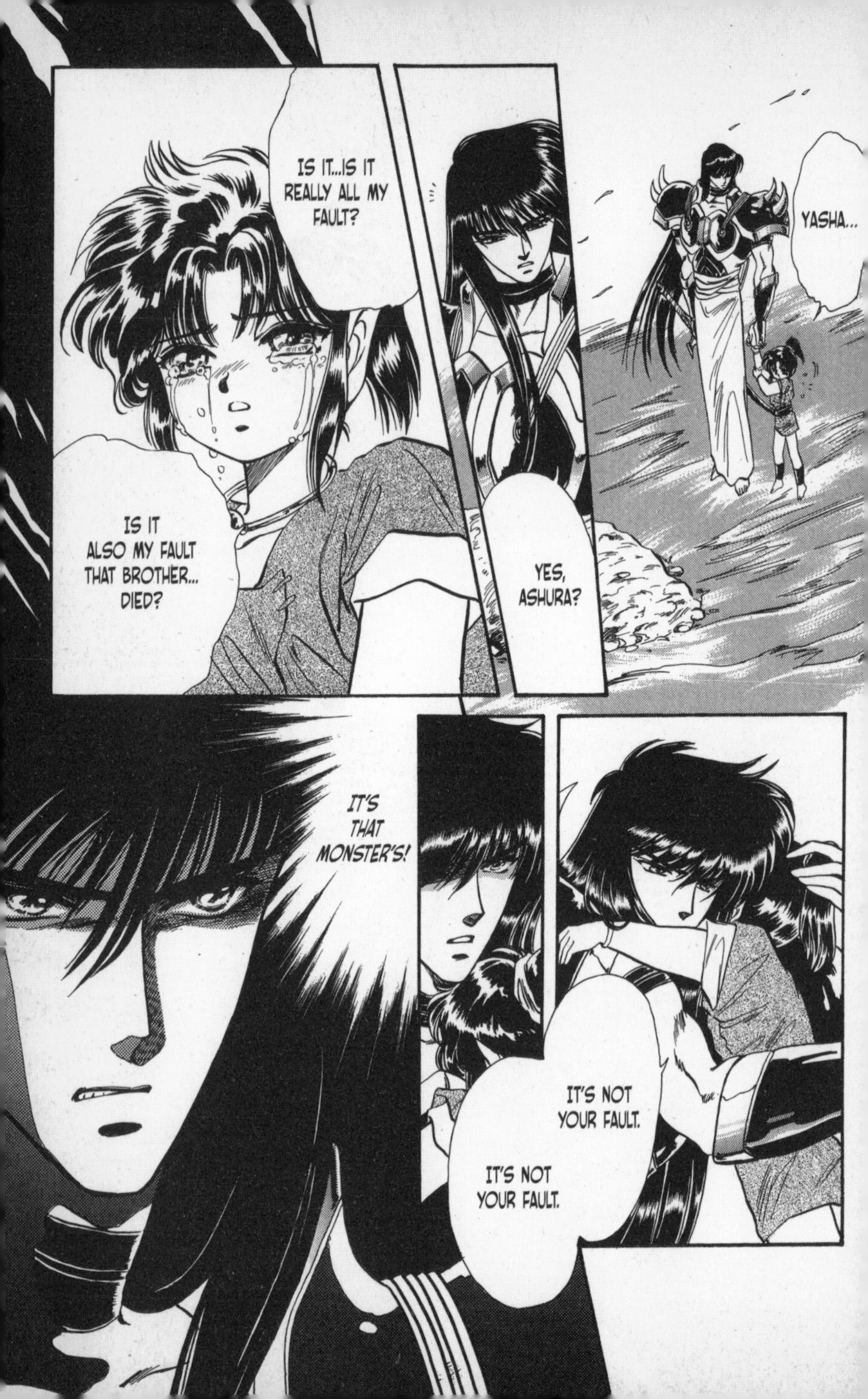
YASHA...
YES, ASHURA?
IS IT...IS IT REALLY ALL MY FAULT?
IS IT ALSO MY FAULT THAT BROTHER... DIED?
IT'S NOT YOUR FAULT.
IT'S NOT YOUR FAULT.
IT'S THAT MONSTER'S!

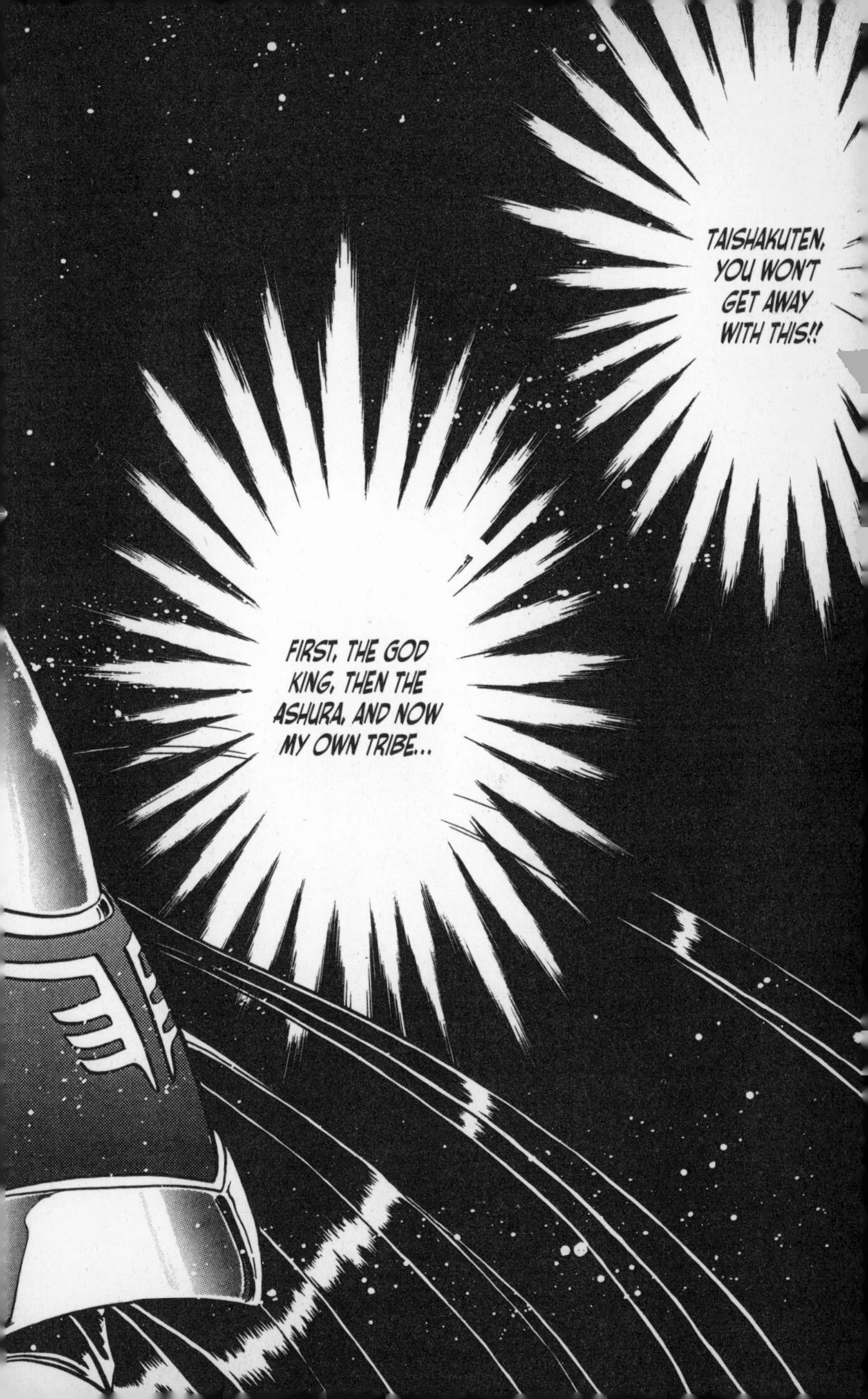
TAISHAKUTEN, YOU WON'T GET AWAY WITH THIS!!
FIRST, THE GOD KING, THEN THE ASHURA, AND NOW MY OWN TRIBE...

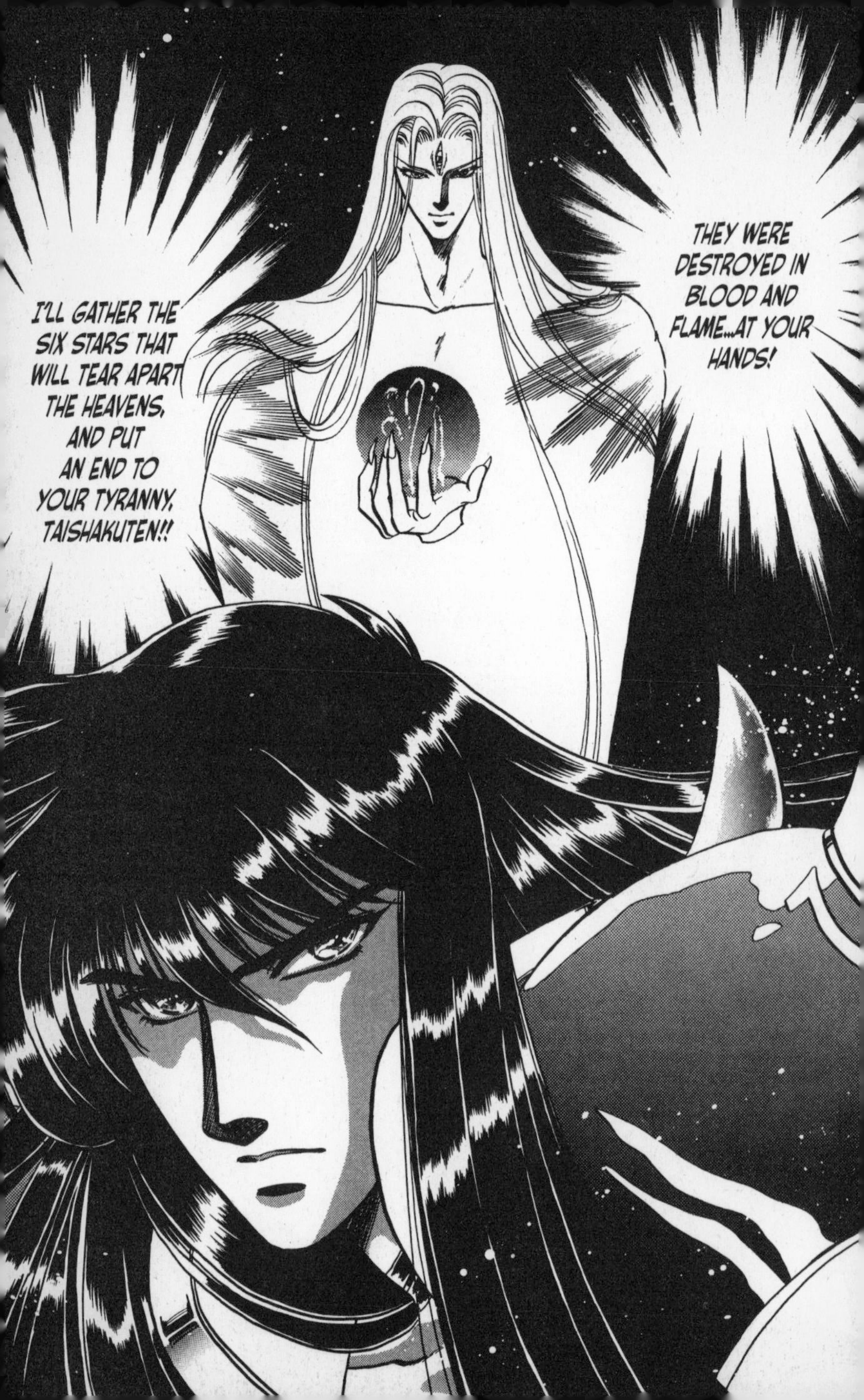
THEY WERE DESTROYED IN BLOOD AND FLAME...AT YOUR HANDS!
I'LL GATHER THE SIX STARS THAT WILL TEAR APART THE HEAVENS, AND PUT AN END TO YOUR TYRANNY, TAISHAKUTEN!!

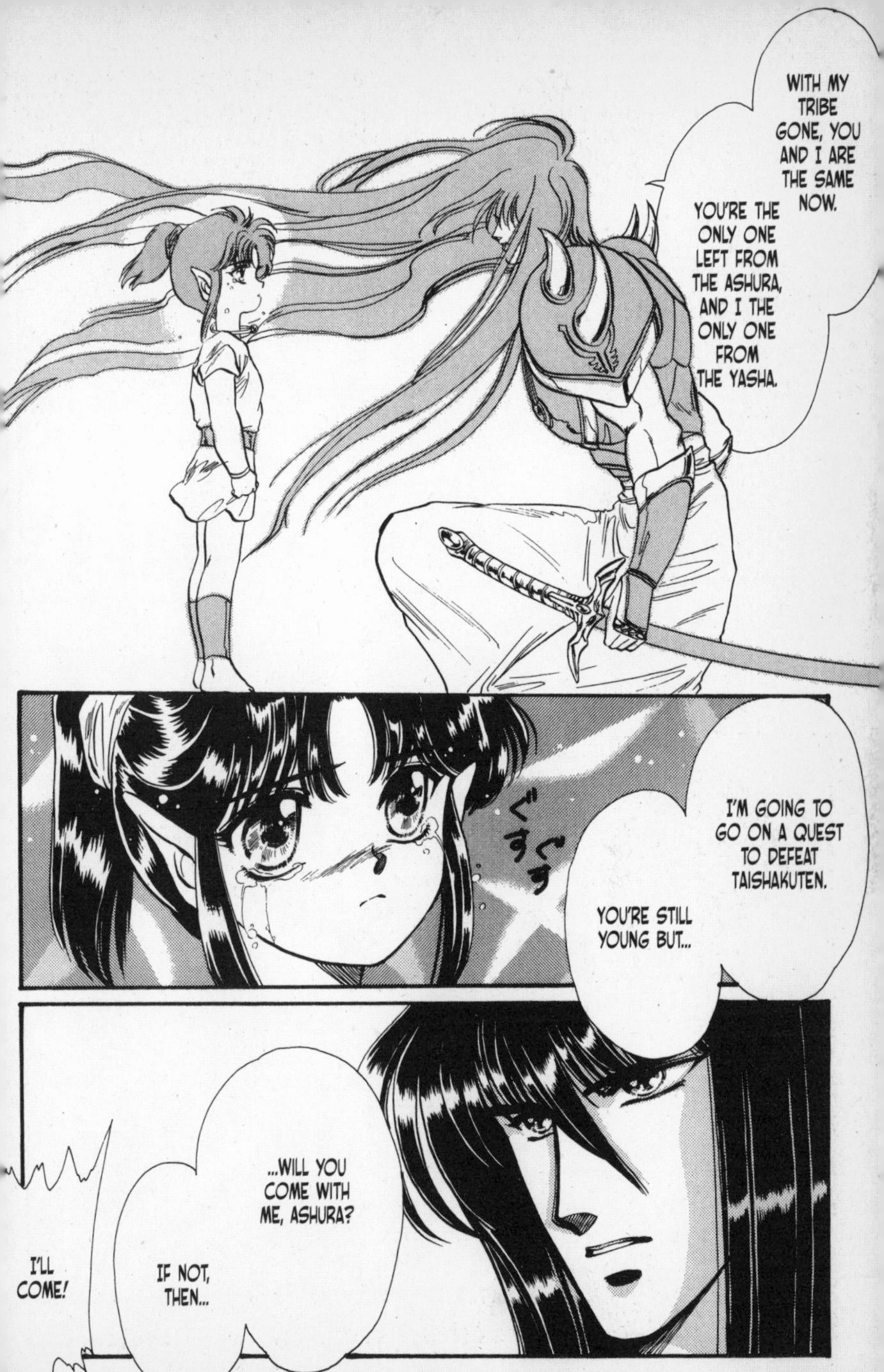
WITH MY TRIBE GONE, YOU AND I ARE THE SAME NOW.
YOU'RE THE ONLY ONE LEFT FROM THE ASHURA, AND I THE ONLY ONE FROM THE YASHA.
ぐすぐす
I'M GOING TO GO ON A QUEST TO DEFEAT TAISHAKUTEN.
YOU'RE STILL YOUNG BUT...
...WILL YOU COME WITH ME, ASHURA?
IF NOT, THEN...
I'LL COME!

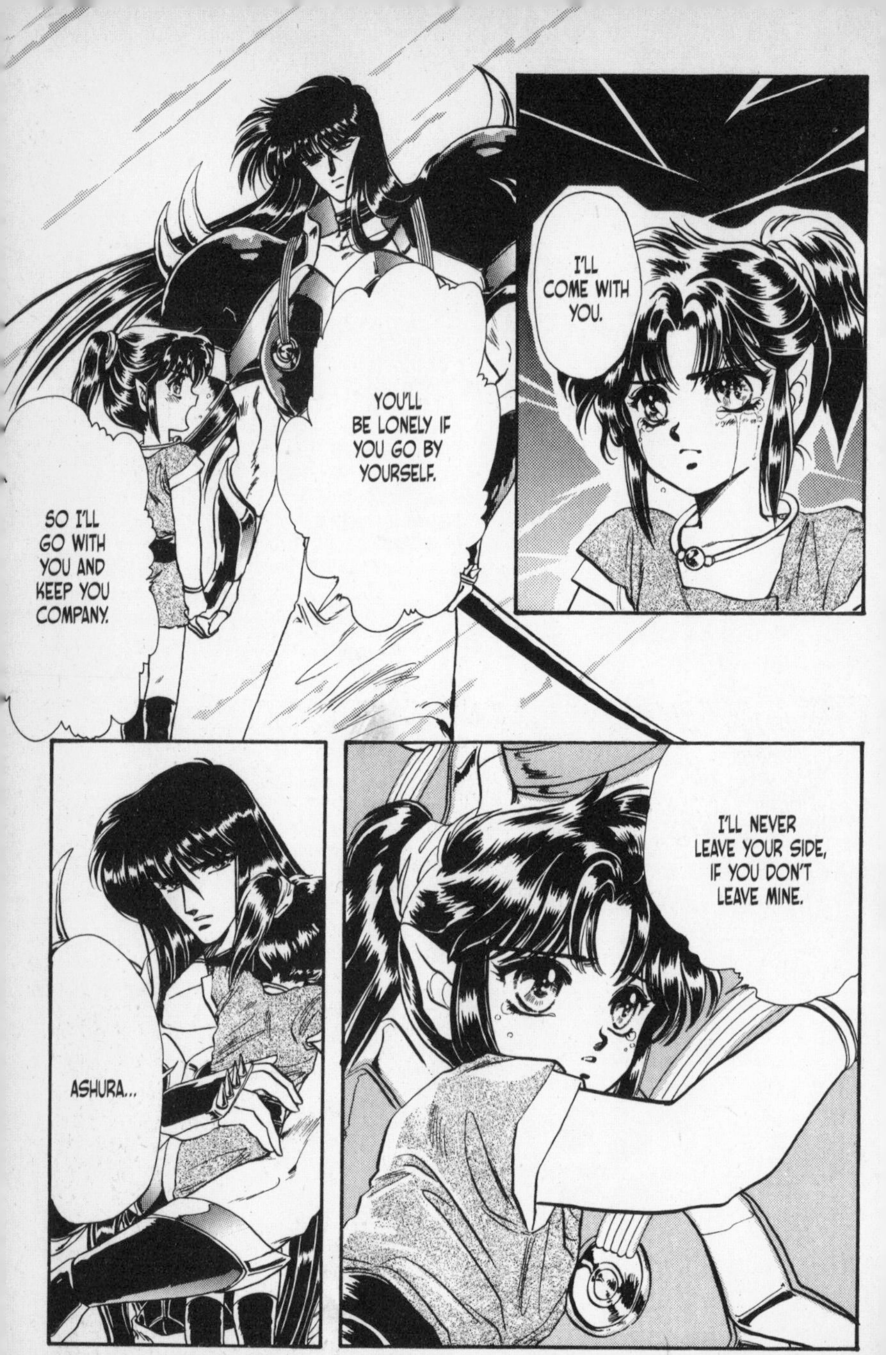
I'LL COME WITH YOU.
YOU'LL BE LONELY IF YOU GO BY YOURSELF.
SO I'LL GO WITH YOU AND KEEP YOU COMPANY.
I'LL NEVER LEAVE YOUR SIDE, IF YOU DON'T LEAVE MINE.
ASHURA...

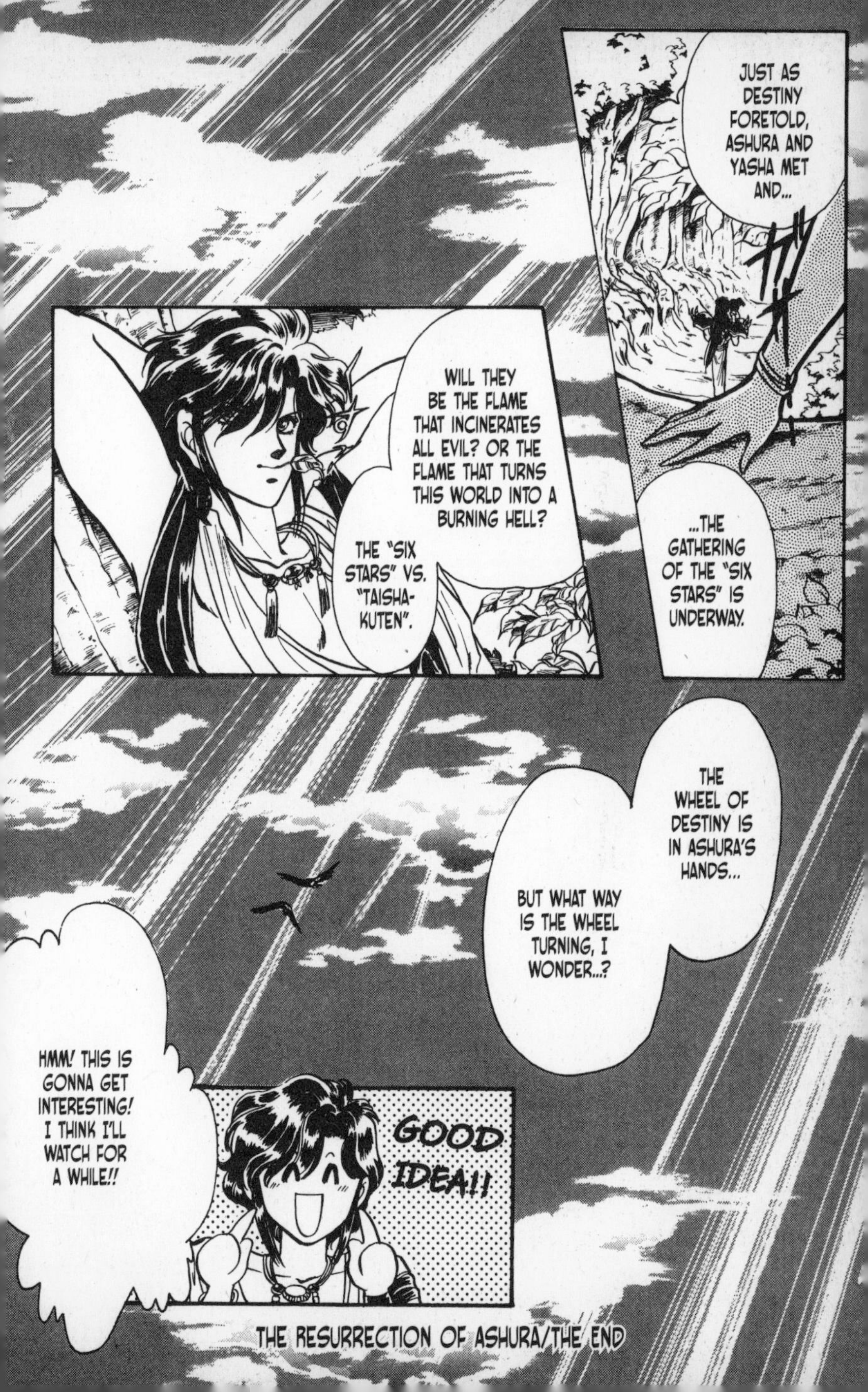
JUST AS DESTINY FORETOLD, ASHURA AND YASHA MET AND...
...THE GATHERING OF THE "SIX STARS" IS UNDERWAY.
WILL THEY BE THE FLAME THAT INCINERATES ALL EVIL? OR THE FLAME THAT TURNS THIS WORLD INTO A BURNING HELL?
THE "SIX STARS" VS. "TAISHA-KUTEN".
THE WHEEL OF DESTINY IS IN ASHURA'S HANDS...
BUT WHAT WAY IS THE WHEEL TURNING, I WONDER...?
HMM! THIS IS GONNA GET INTERESTING! I THINK I'LL WATCH FOR A WHILE!!
GOOD IDEA!!
THE RESURRECTION OF ASHURA/THE END

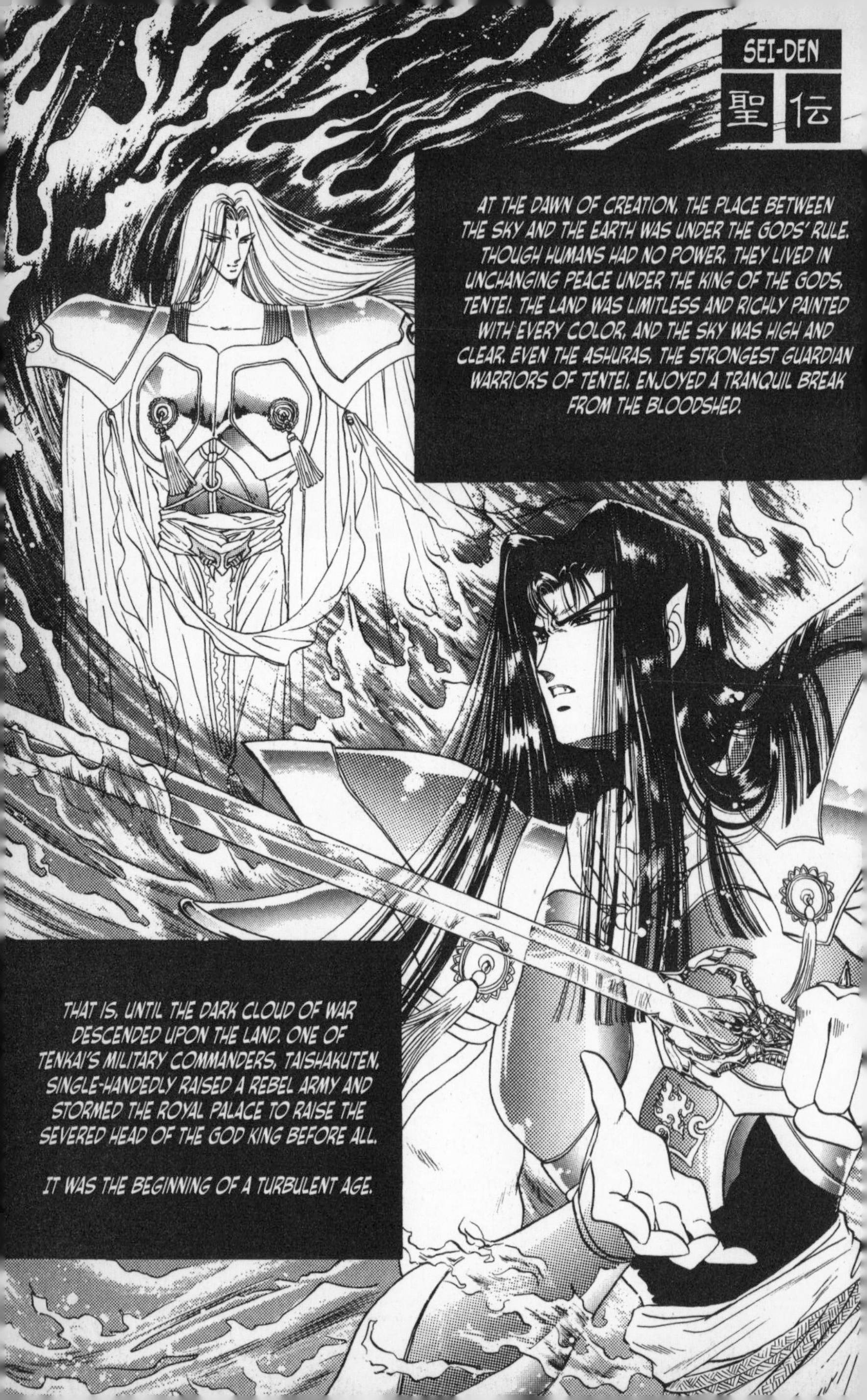
SEI-DEN
聖伝
AT THE DAWN OF CREATION, THE PLACE BETWEEN THE SKY AND THE EARTH WAS UNDER THE GODS' RULE. THOUGH HUMANS HAD NO POWER, THEY LIVED IN UNCHANGING PEACE UNDER THE KING OF THE GODS, TENTEI. THE LAND WAS LIMITLESS AND RICHLY PAINTED WITH EVERY COLOR, AND THE SKY WAS HIGH AND CLEAR. EVEN THE ASHURAS, THE STRONGEST GUARDIAN WARRIORS OF TENTEI, ENJOYED A TRANQUIL BREAK FROM THE BLOODSHED.
THAT IS, UNTIL THE DARK CLOUD OF WAR DESCENDED UPON THE LAND. ONE OF TENKAI'S MILITARY COMMANDERS, TAISHAKUTEN, SINGLE-HANDEDLY RAISED A REBEL ARMY AND STORMED THE ROYAL PALACE TO RAISE THE SEVERED HEAD OF THE GOD KING BEFORE ALL.
IT WAS THE BEGINNING OF A TURBULENT AGE.

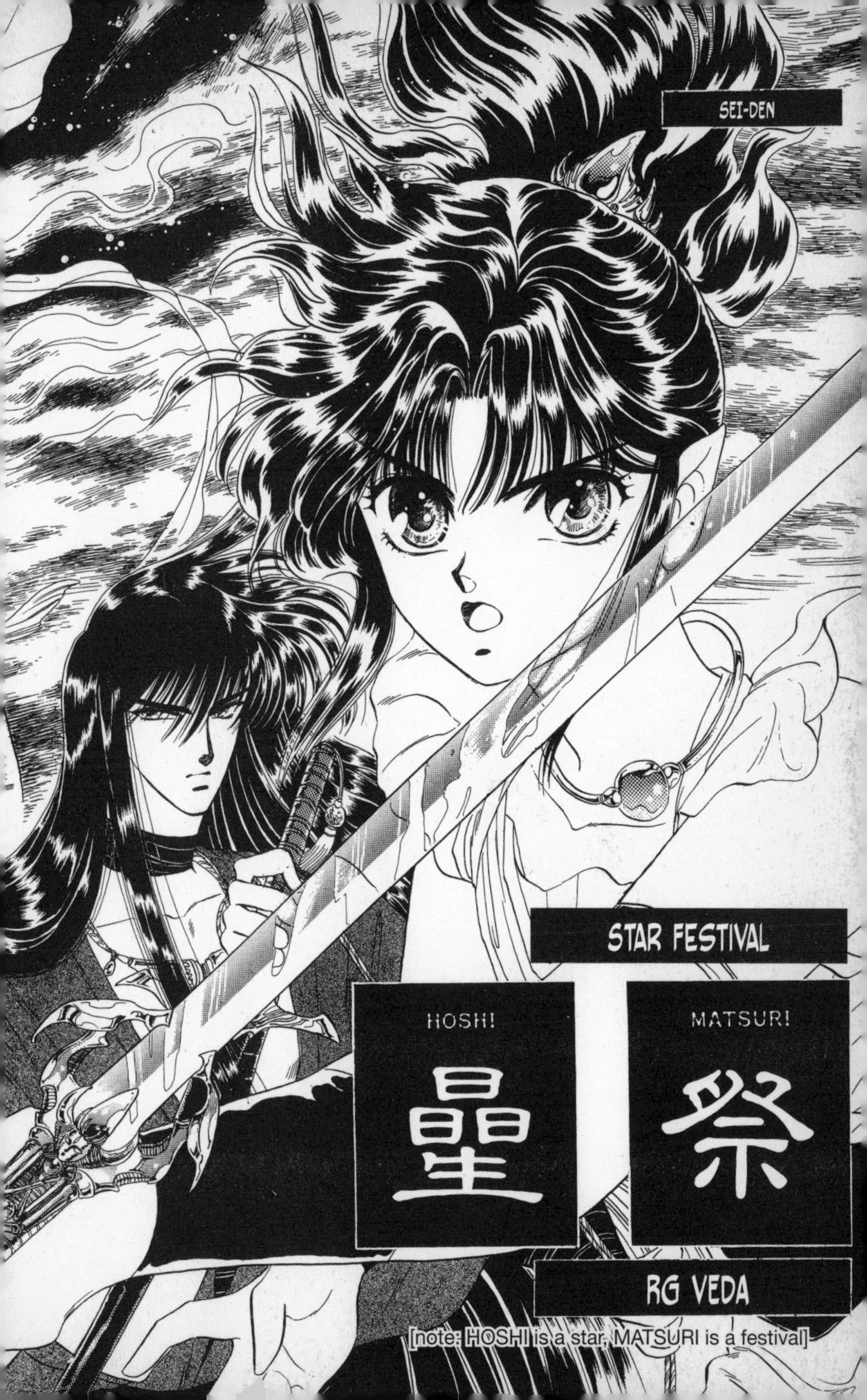
SEI-DEN
STAR FESTIVAL
HOSHI
MATSURI
星
祭
RG VEDA
[note: HOSHI is a star, MATSURI is a festival]

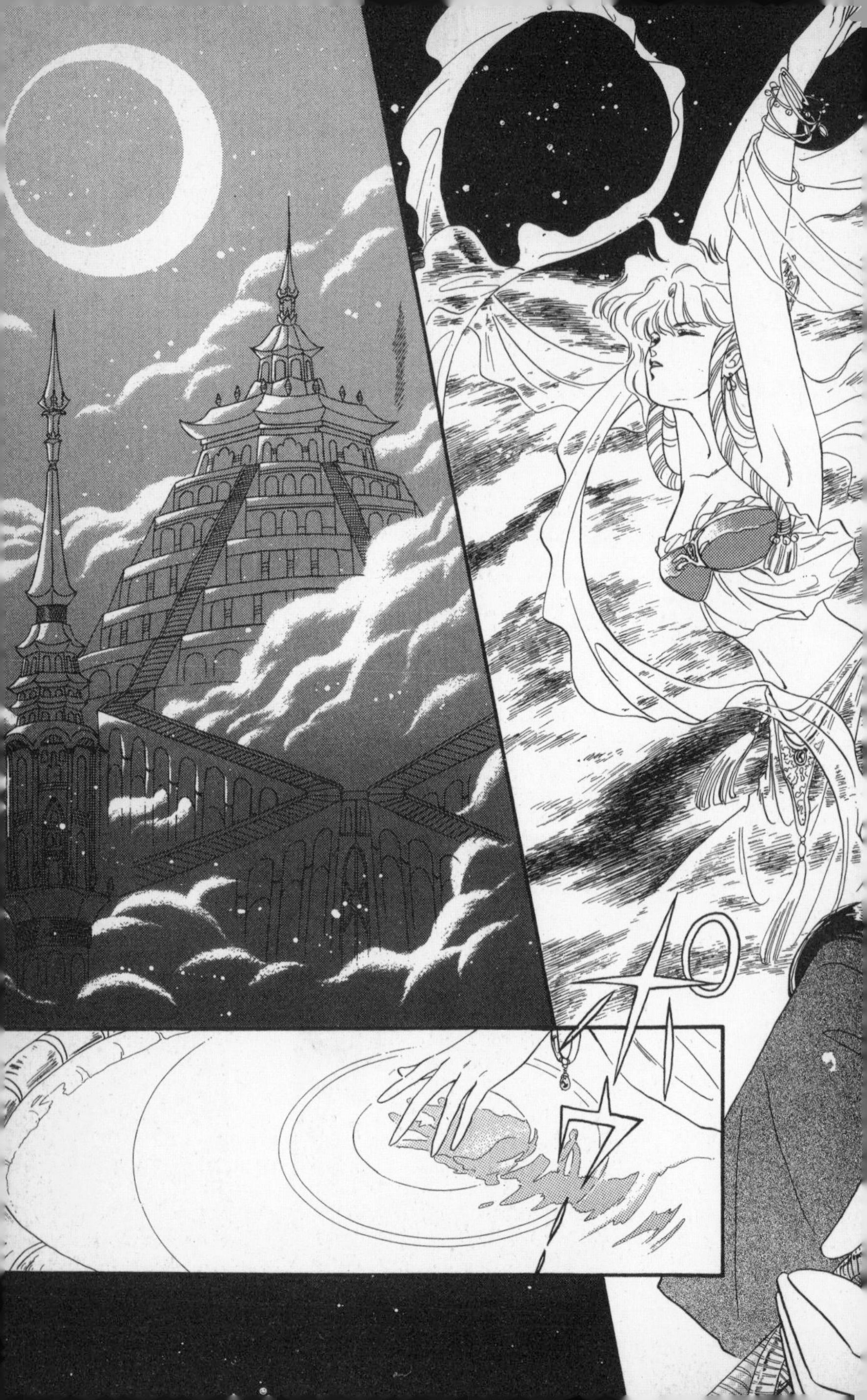

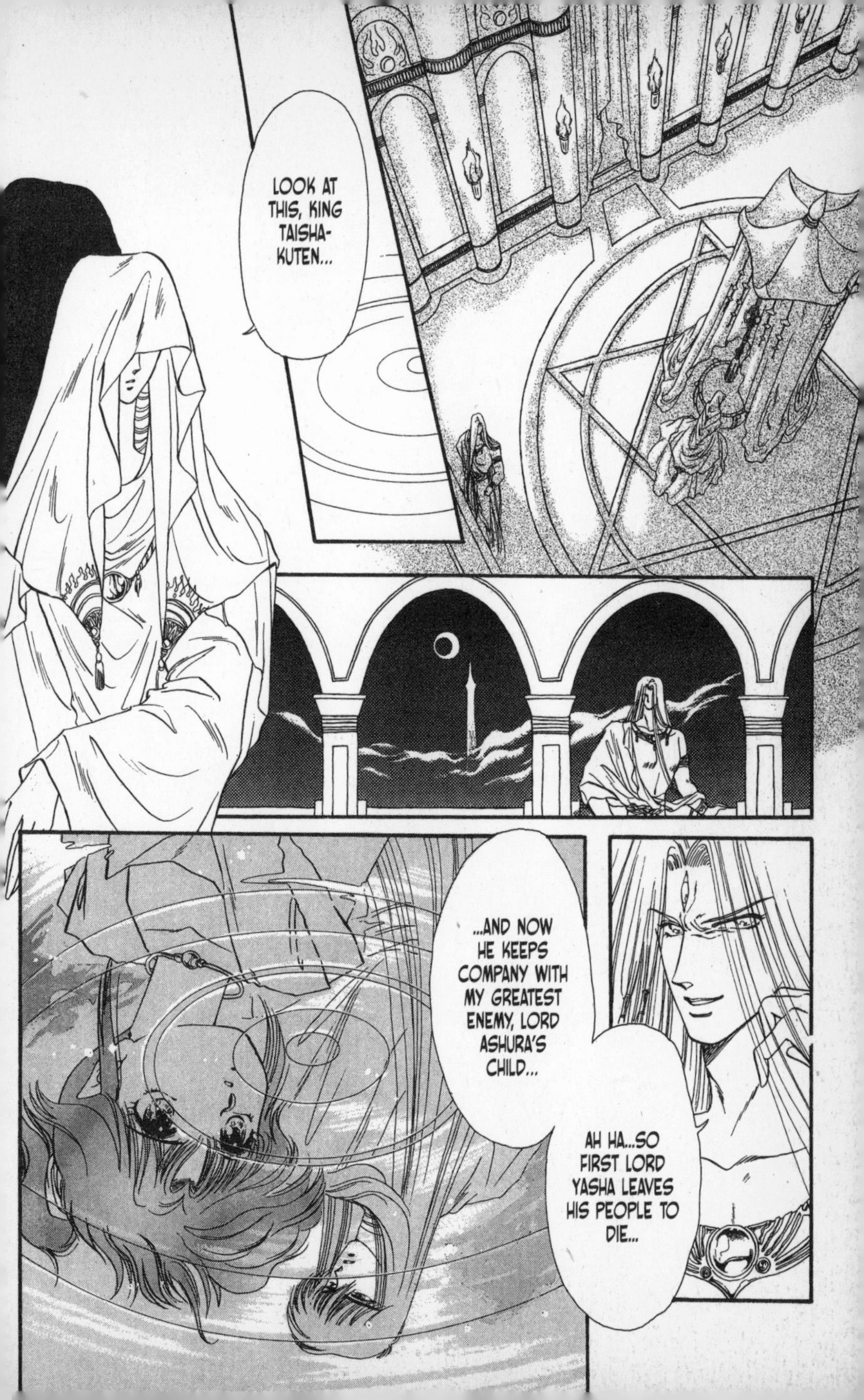
LOOK AT THIS, KING TAISHAKUTEN...
AH HA...SO FIRST LORD YASHA LEAVES HIS PEOPLE TO DIE...
...AND NOW HE KEEPS COMPANY WITH MY GREATEST ENEMY, LORD ASHURA'S CHILD...

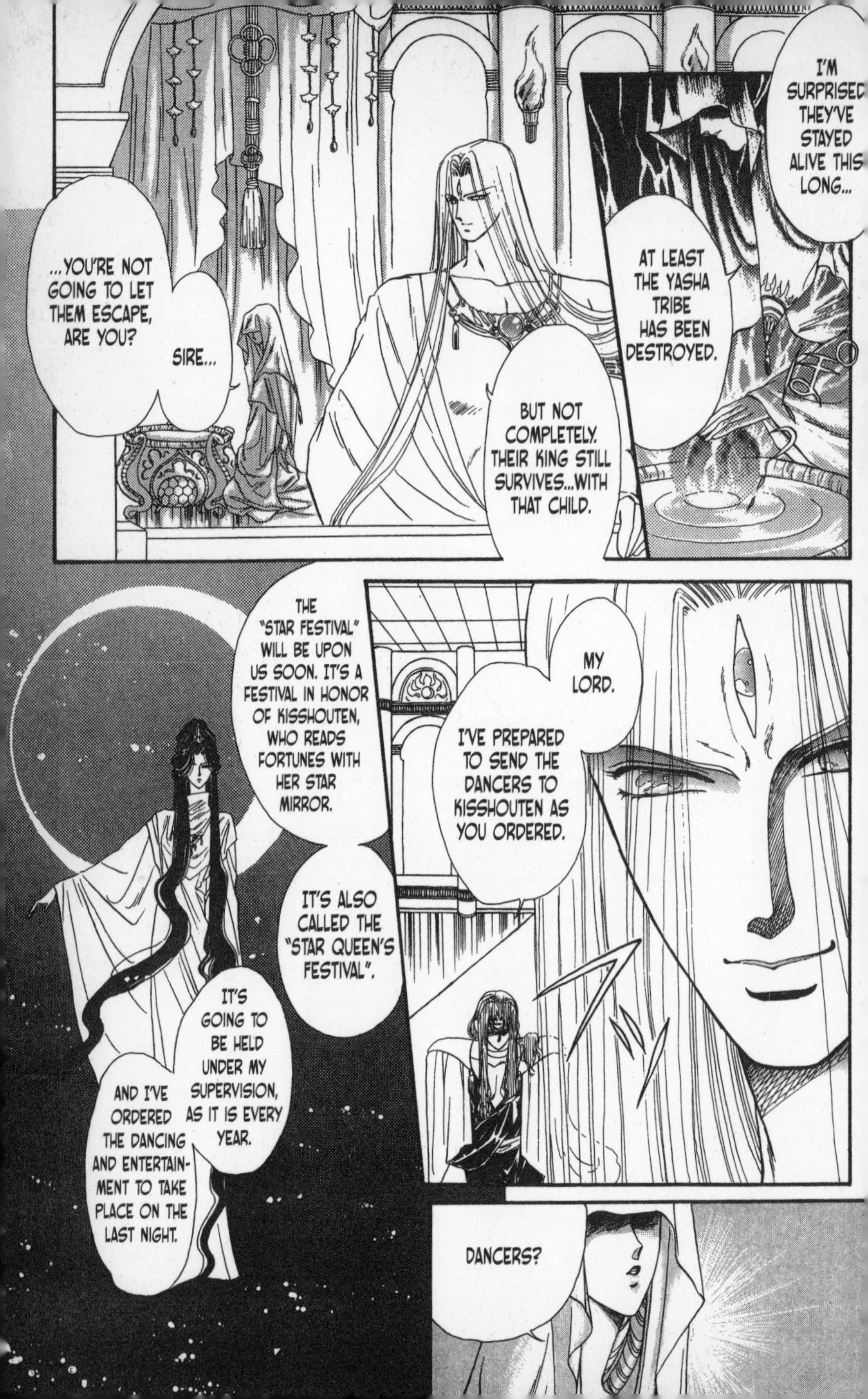
I'M SURPRISED THEY'VE STAYED ALIVE THIS LONG...
AT LEAST THE YASHA TRIBE HAS BEEN DESTROYED.
BUT NOT COMPLETELY. THEIR KING STILL SURVIVES...WITH THAT CHILD.
...YOU'RE NOT GOING TO LET THEM ESCAPE, ARE YOU?
SIRE...
MY LORD.
I'VE PREPARED TO SEND THE DANCERS TO KISSHOUTEN AS YOU ORDERED.
DANCERS?
THE "STAR FESTIVAL" WILL BE UPON US SOON. IT'S A FESTIVAL IN HONOR OF KISSHOUTEN, WHO READS FORTUNES WITH HER STAR MIRROR.
IT'S ALSO CALLED THE "STAR QUEEN'S FESTIVAL".
IT'S GOING TO BE HELD UNDER MY SUPERVISION, AS IT IS EVERY YEAR.
AND I'VE ORDERED THE DANCING AND ENTERTAINMENT TO TAKE PLACE ON THE LAST NIGHT.

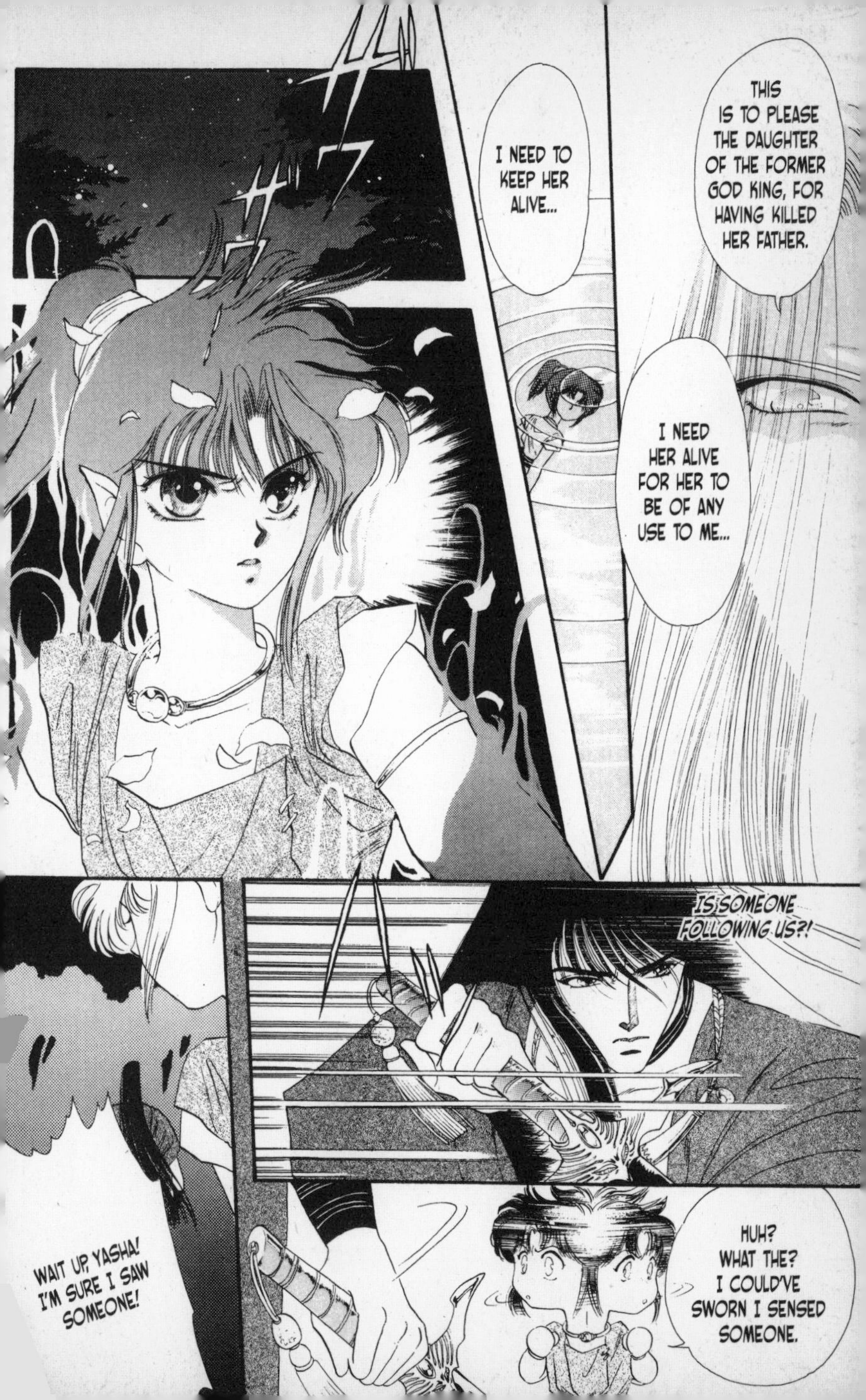
THIS IS TO PLEASE THE DAUGHTER OF THE FORMER GOD KING, FOR HAVING KILLED HER FATHER.
I NEED HER ALIVE FOR HER TO BE OF ANY USE TO ME...
I NEED TO KEEP HER ALIVE...
IS SOMEONE FOLLOWING US?!
HUH? WHAT THE? I COULD'VE SWORN I SENSED SOMEONE.
WAIT UP, YASHA! I'M SURE I SAW SOMEONE!

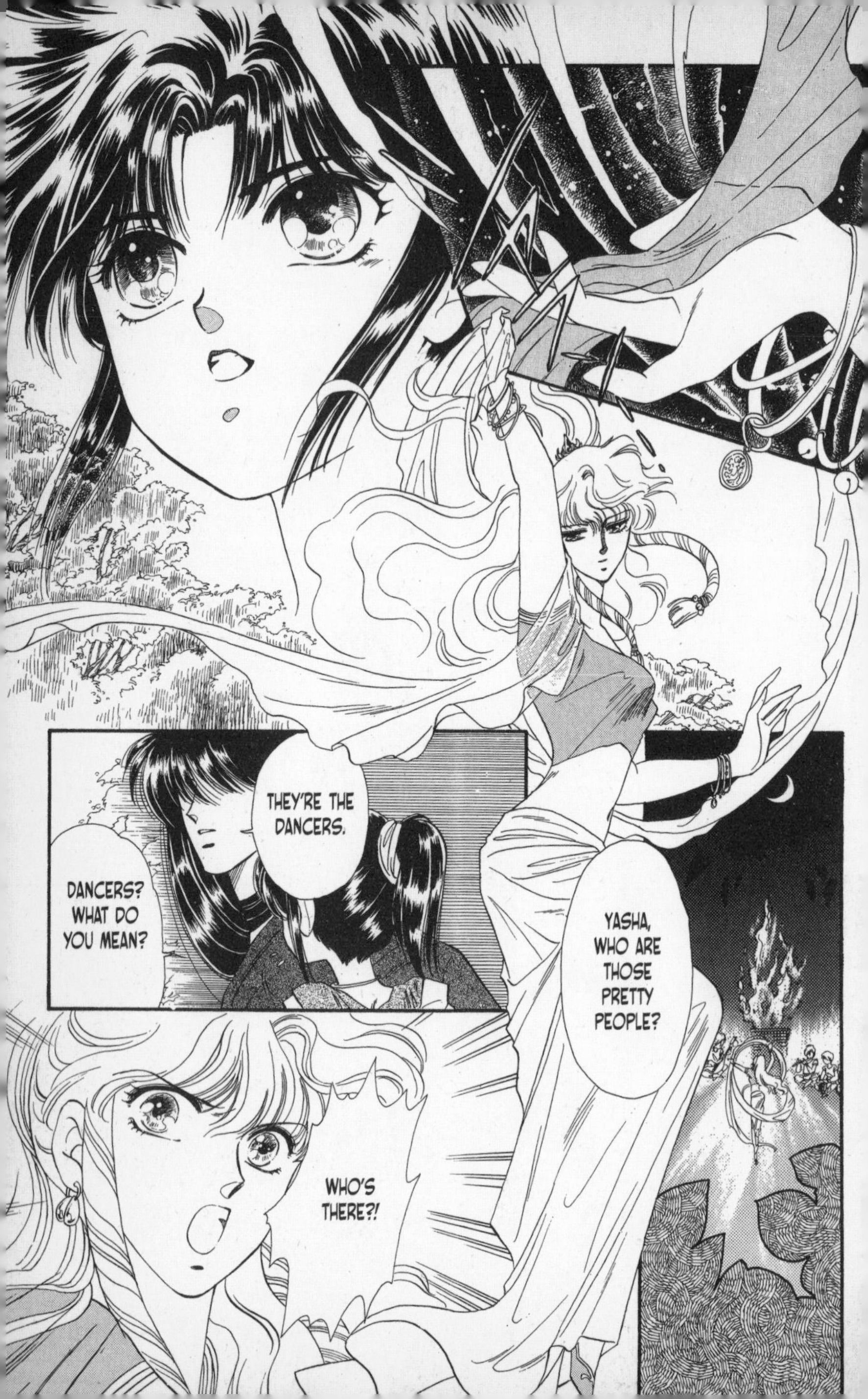
YASHA, WHO ARE THOSE PRETTY PEOPLE?
THEY'RE THE DANCERS.
DANCERS? WHAT DO YOU MEAN?
WHO'S THERE?!

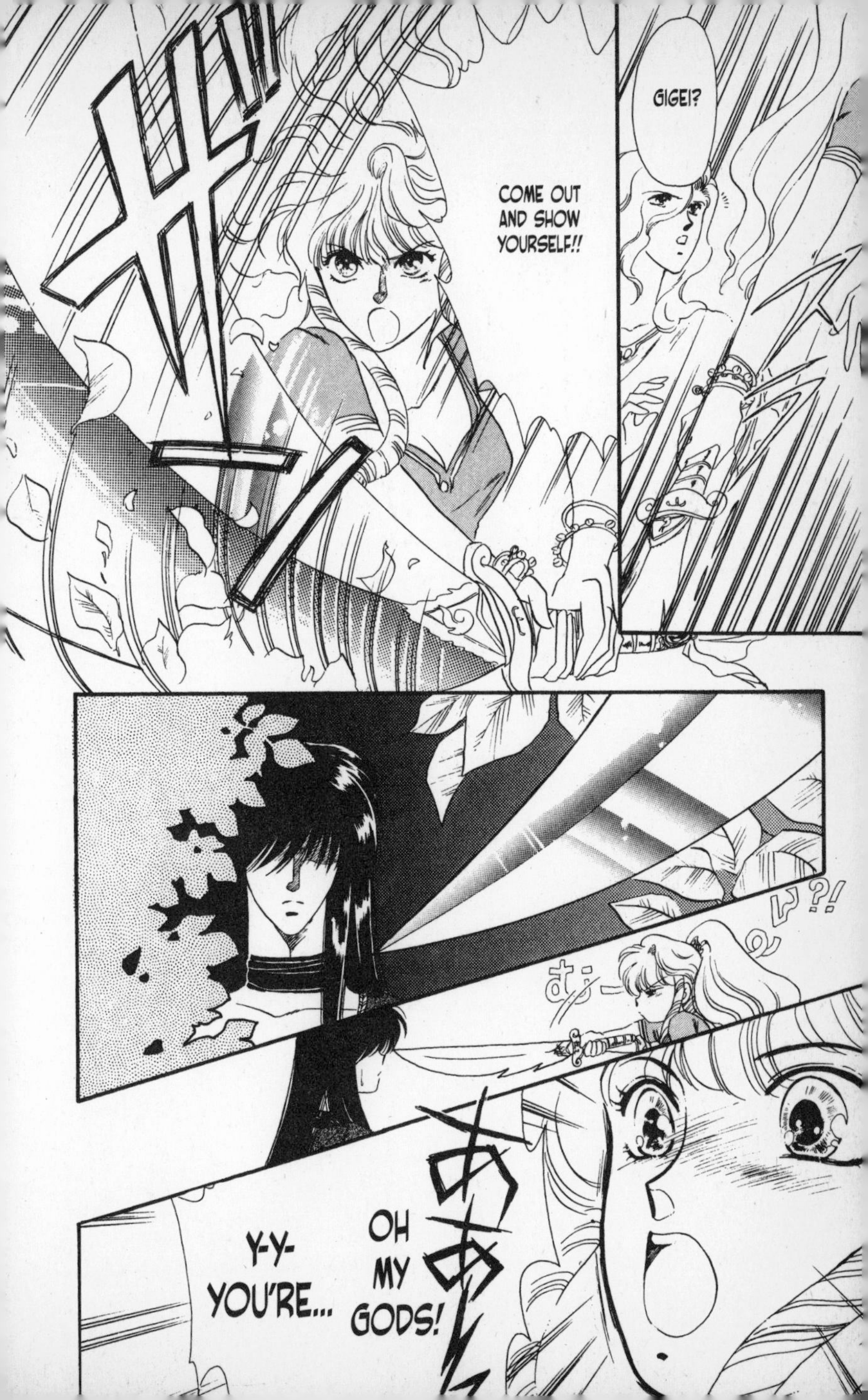
GIGEI?
COME OUT AND SHOW YOURSELF!!
OH MY GODS!
Y-Y- YOU'RE...

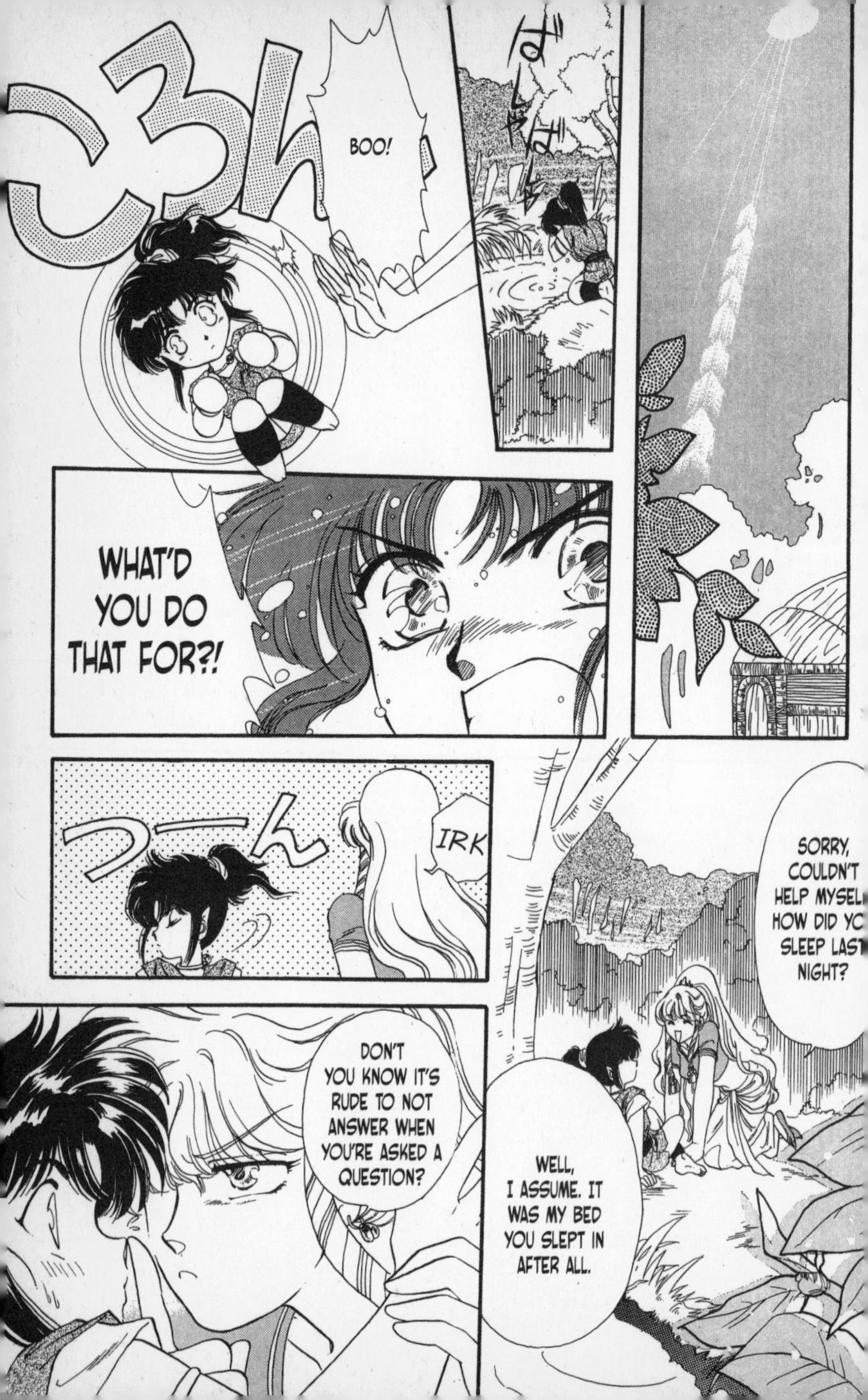
ばしゃばしゃ
ころん
BOO!
WHAT'D YOU DO THAT FOR?!
SORRY, COULDN'T HELP MYSEL HOW DID YO SLEEP LAST NIGHT?
WELL, I ASSUME. IT WAS MY BED YOU SLEPT IN AFTER ALL.
IRK
つーん
DON'T YOU KNOW IT'S RUDE TO NOT ANSWER WHEN YOU'RE ASKED A QUESTION?

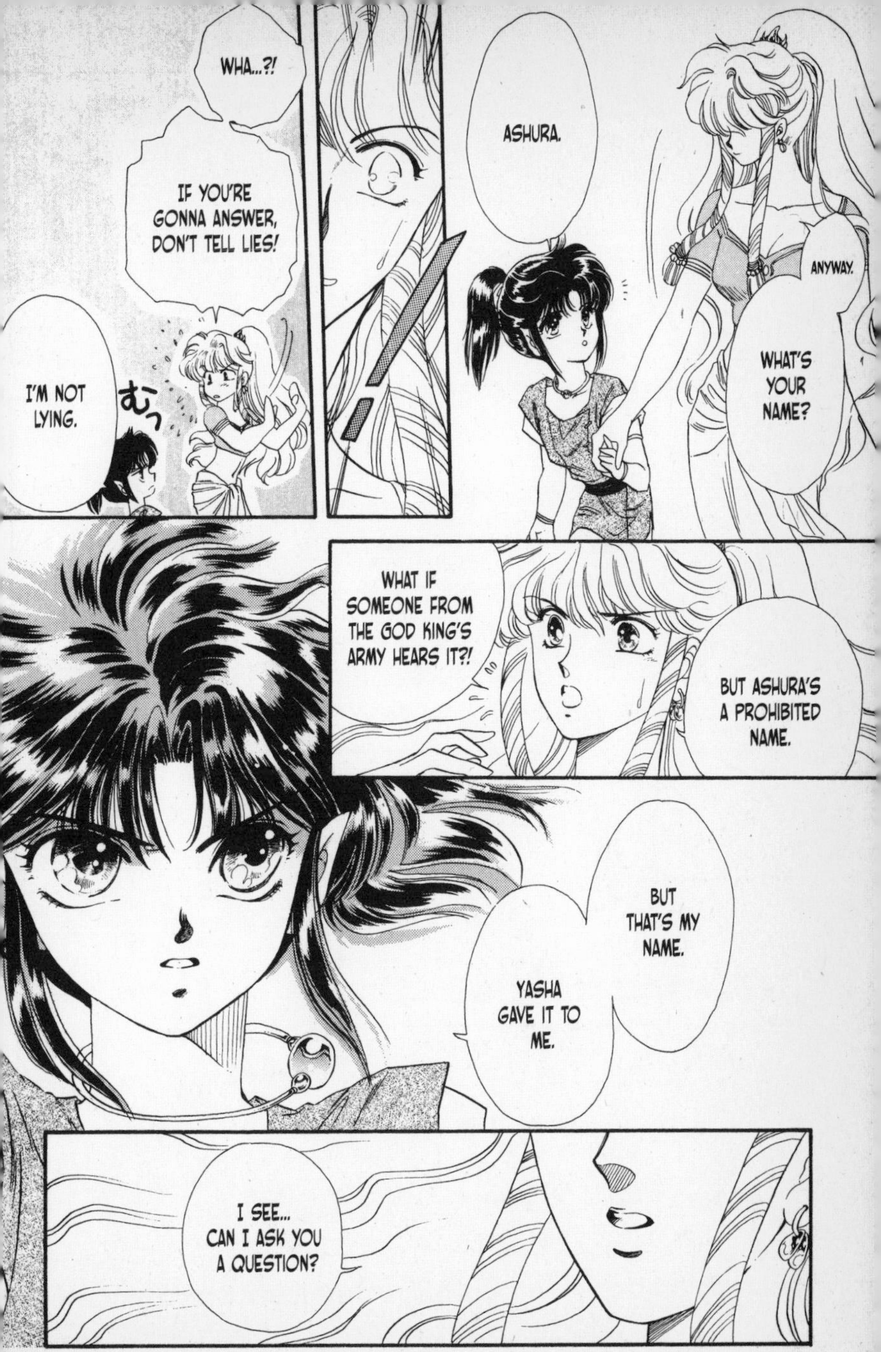
ANYWAY.
WHAT'S YOUR NAME?
ASHURA.
WHA...?!
IF YOU'RE GONNA ANSWER, DON'T TELL LIES!
むっ
I'M NOT LYING.
BUT ASHURA'S A PROHIBITED NAME.
WHAT IF SOMEONE FROM THE GOD KING'S ARMY HEARS IT?!
BUT THAT'S MY NAME.
YASHA GAVE IT TO ME.
I SEE... CAN I ASK YOU A QUESTION?

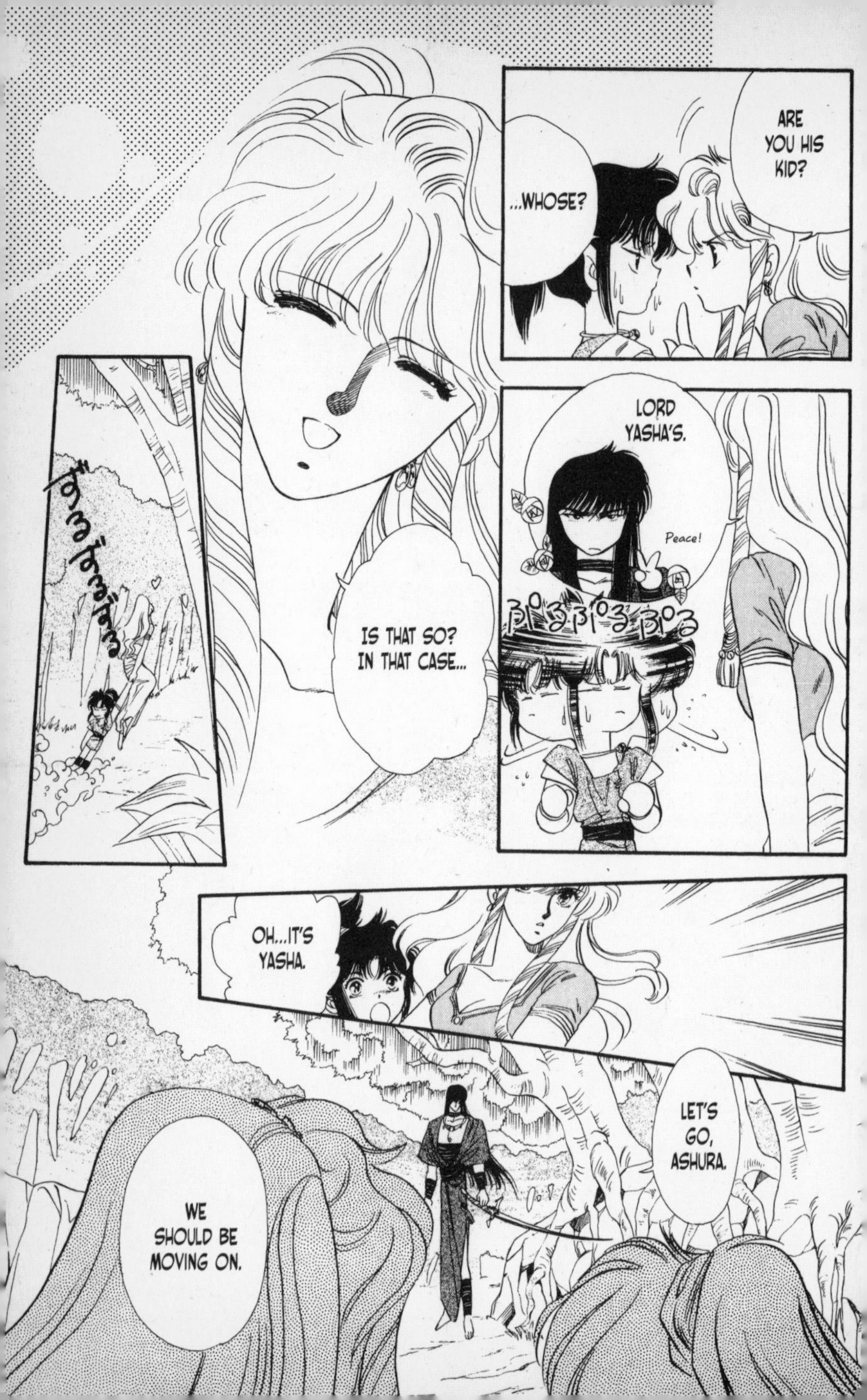
ARE YOU HIS KID?
...WHOSE?
LORD YASHA'S.
Peace!
IS THAT SO? IN THAT CASE...
OH...IT'S YASHA.
LET'S GO, ASHURA.
WE SHOULD BE MOVING ON.

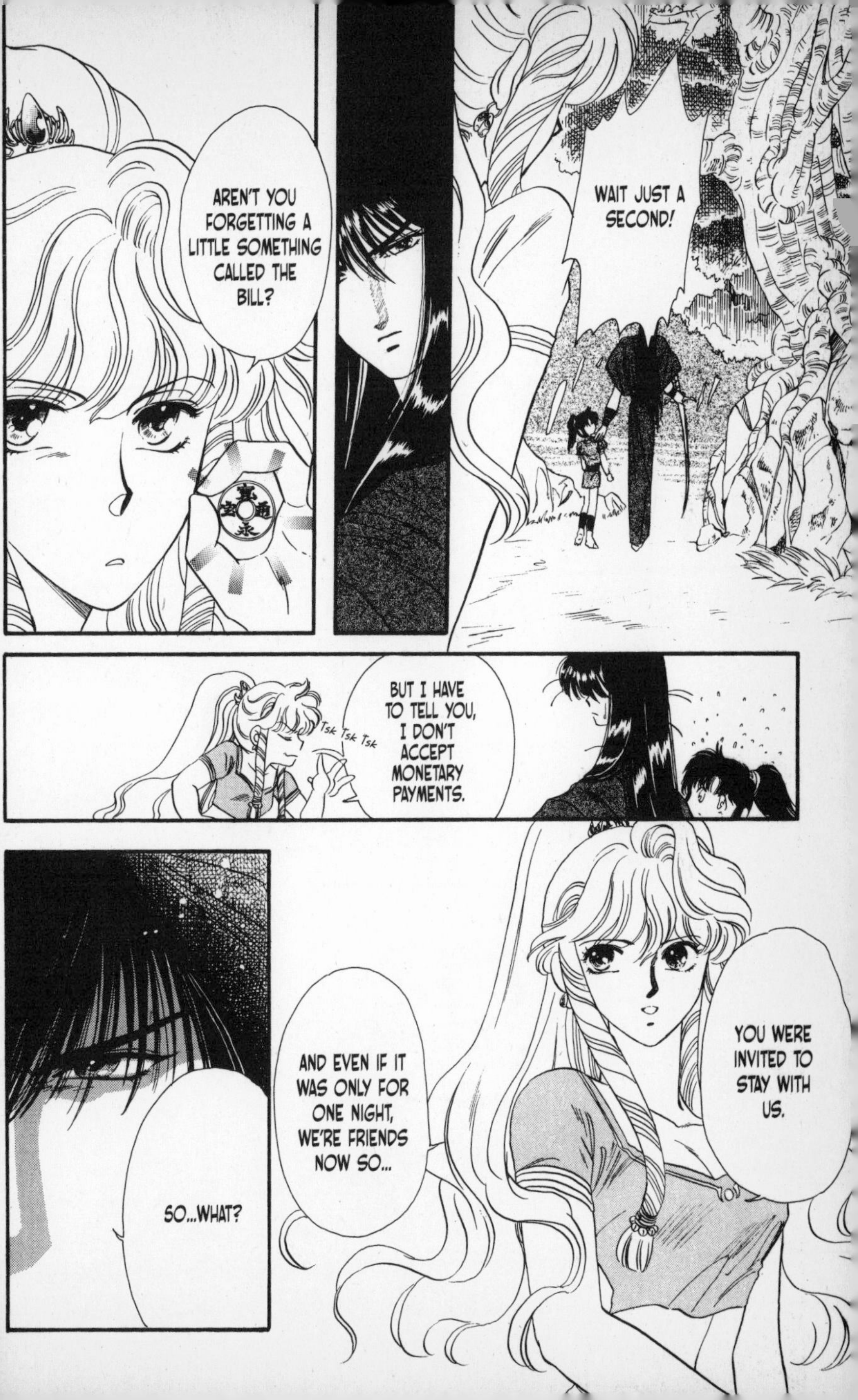
WAIT JUST A SECOND!
AREN'T YOU FORGETTING A LITTLE SOMETHING CALLED THE BILL?
BUT I HAVE TO TELL YOU, I DON'T ACCEPT MONETARY PAYMENTS.
Tsk Tsk Tsk
YOU WERE INVITED TO STAY WITH US.
AND EVEN IF IT WAS ONLY FOR ONE NIGHT, WE'RE FRIENDS NOW SO...
SO...WHAT?

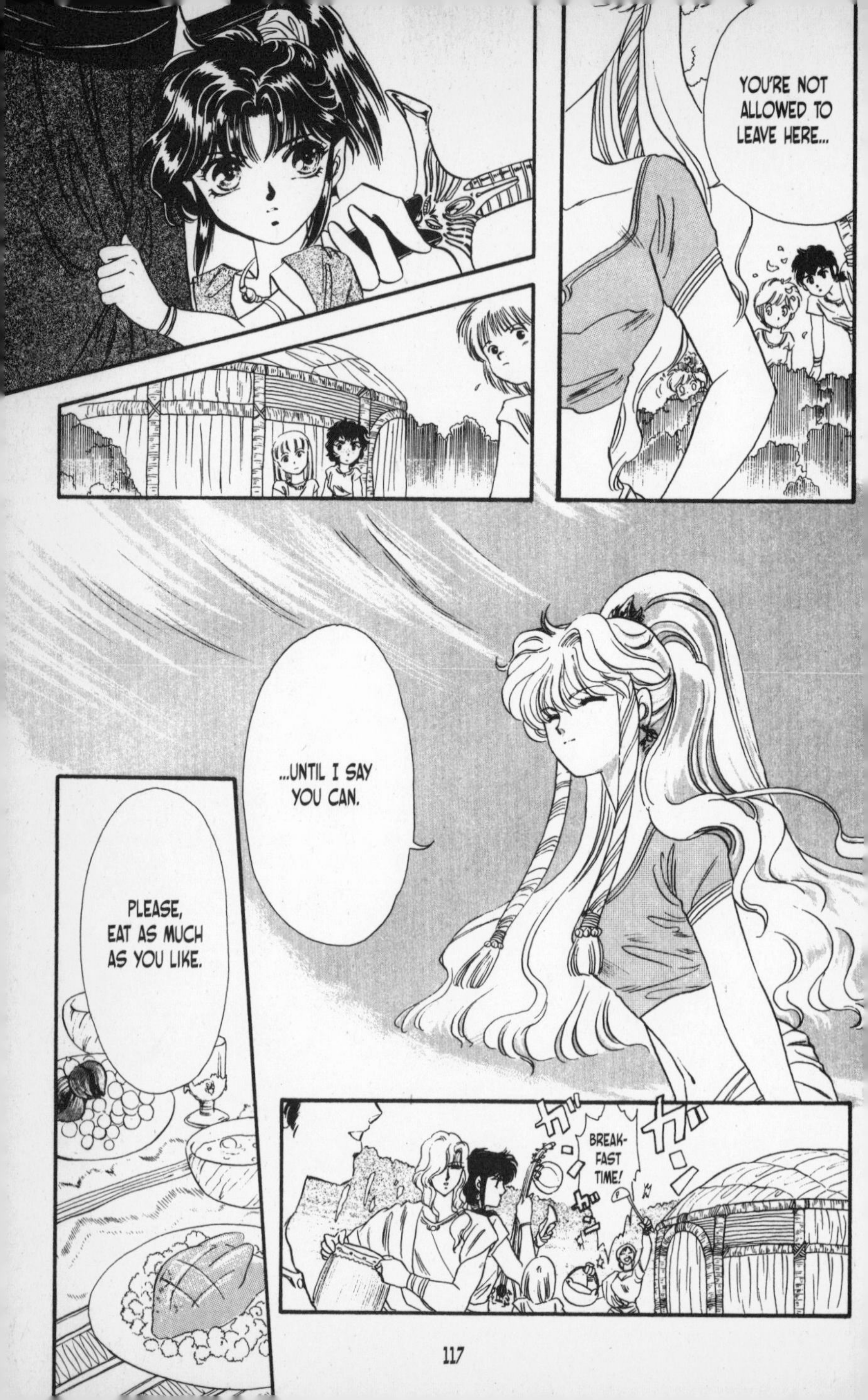
YOU'RE NOT ALLOWED TO LEAVE HERE...
...UNTIL I SAY YOU CAN.
BREAK-FAST TIME!
PLEASE, EAT AS MUCH AS YOU LIKE.

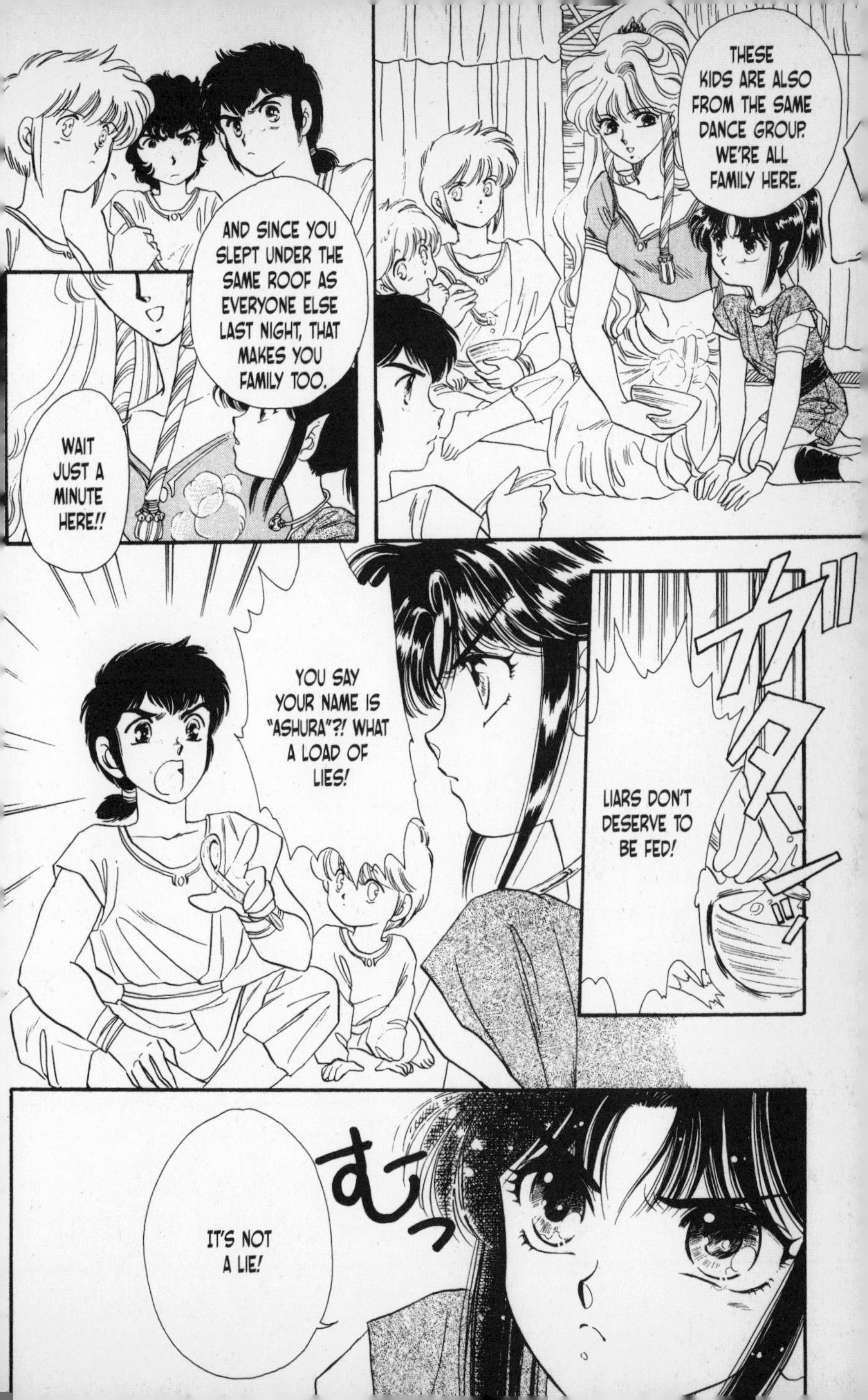
THESE KIDS ARE ALSO FROM THE SAME DANCE GROUP. WE'RE ALL FAMILY HERE.
AND SINCE YOU SLEPT UNDER THE SAME ROOF AS EVERYONE ELSE LAST NIGHT, THAT MAKES YOU FAMILY TOO.
WAIT JUST A MINUTE HERE!!
YOU SAY YOUR NAME IS "ASHURA"?! WHAT A LOAD OF LIES!
ガタ
LIARS DON'T DESERVE TO BE FED!
むっ
IT'S NOT A LIE!

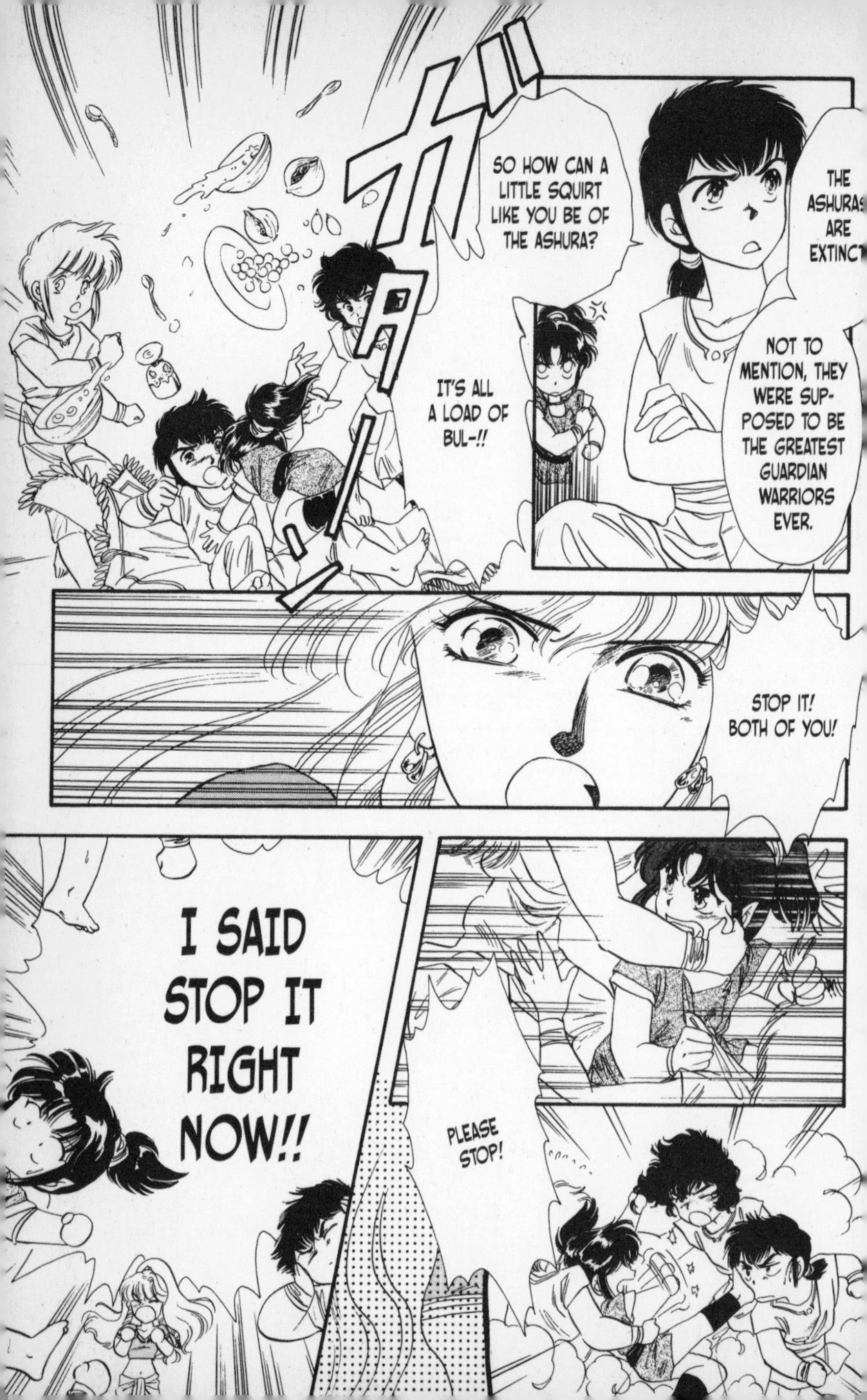
THE ASHURAS ARE EXTINCT
NOT TO MENTION, THEY WERE SUP-POSED TO BE THE GREATEST GUARDIAN WARRIORS EVER.
SO HOW CAN A LITTLE SQUIRT LIKE YOU BE OF THE ASHURA?
IT'S ALL A LOAD OF BUL-!!
STOP IT! BOTH OF YOU!
PLEASE STOP!
I SAID STOP IT RIGHT NOW!!

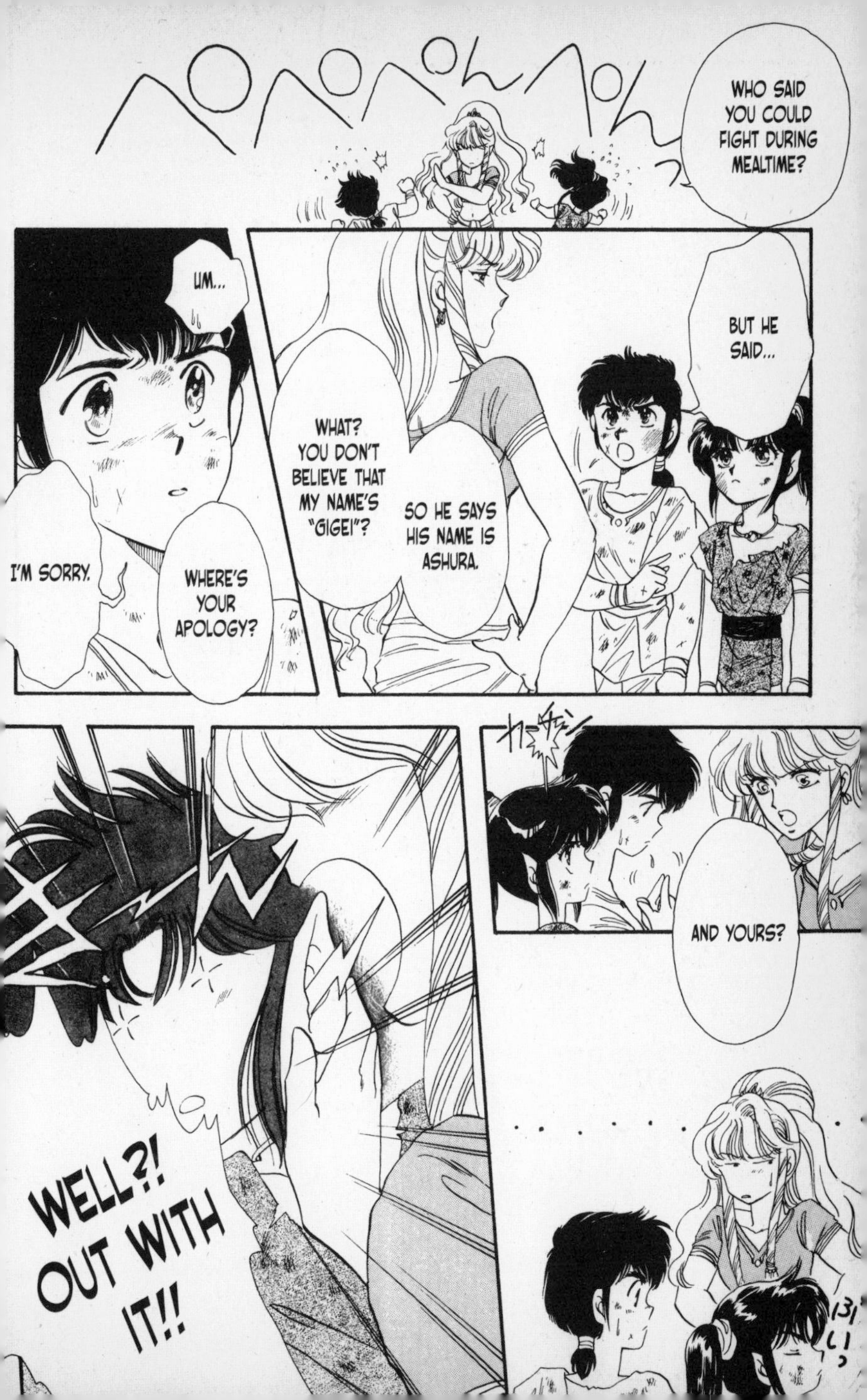
WHO SAID YOU COULD FIGHT DURING MEALTIME?
BUT HE SAID...
SO HE SAYS HIS NAME IS ASHURA.
WHAT? YOU DON'T BELIEVE THAT MY NAME'S "GIGEI"?
UM...
WHERE'S YOUR APOLOGY?
I'M SORRY.
AND YOURS?
WELL?! OUT WITH IT!!
. . . . . .

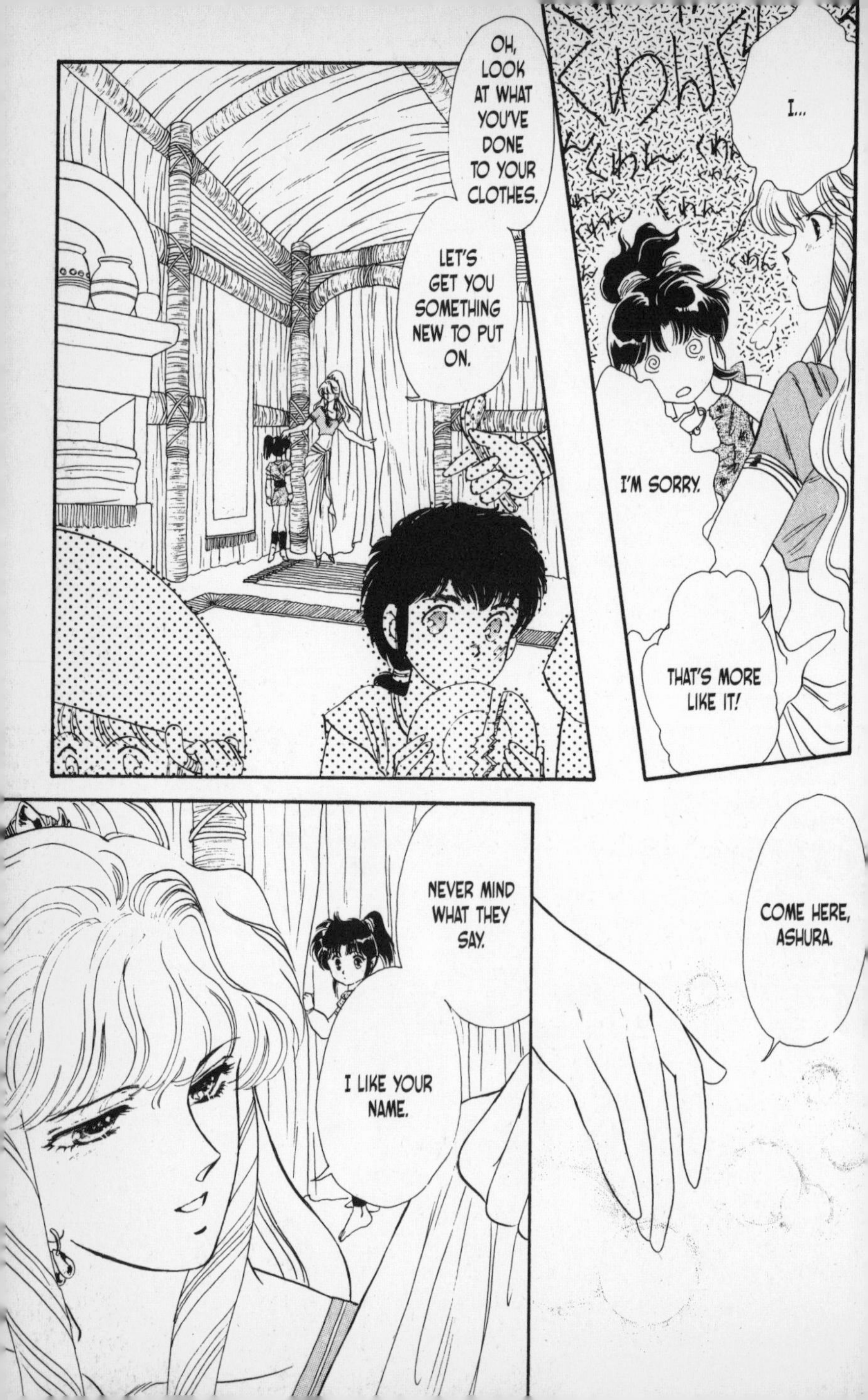
I...
I'M SORRY.
THAT'S MORE LIKE IT!
OH, LOOK AT WHAT YOU'VE DONE TO YOUR CLOTHES.
LET'S GET YOU SOMETHING NEW TO PUT ON.
COME HERE, ASHURA.
NEVER MIND WHAT THEY SAY.
I LIKE YOUR NAME.

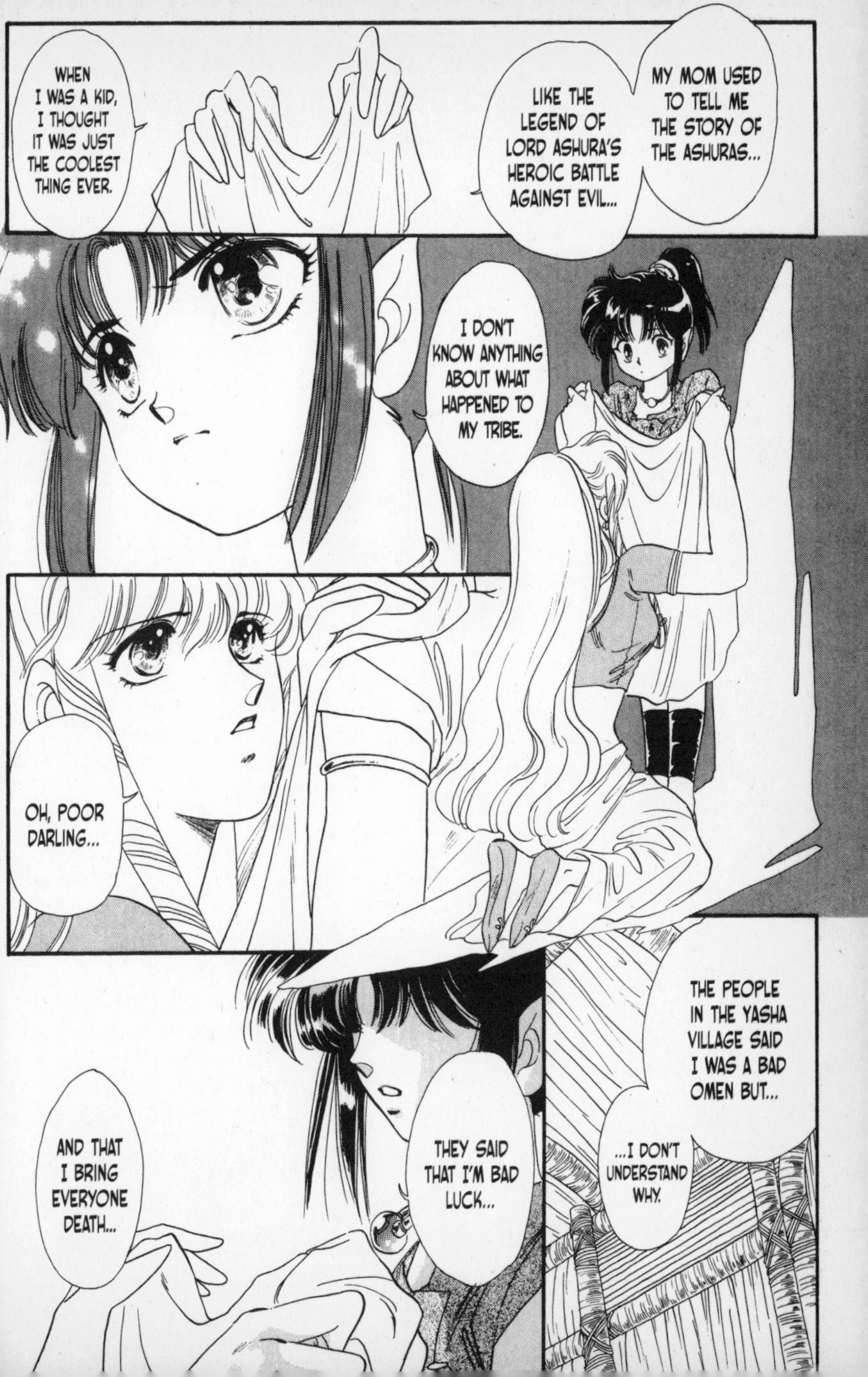
MY MOM USED TO TELL ME THE STORY OF THE ASHURAS...
LIKE THE LEGEND OF LORD ASHURA'S HEROIC BATTLE AGAINST EVIL...
WHEN I WAS A KID, I THOUGHT IT WAS JUST THE COOLEST THING EVER.
I DON'T KNOW ANYTHING ABOUT WHAT HAPPENED TO MY TRIBE.
OH, POOR DARLING...
THE PEOPLE IN THE YASHA VILLAGE SAID I WAS A BAD OMEN BUT...
...I DON'T UNDERSTAND WHY.
THEY SAID THAT I'M BAD LUCK...
AND THAT I BRING EVERYONE DEATH...

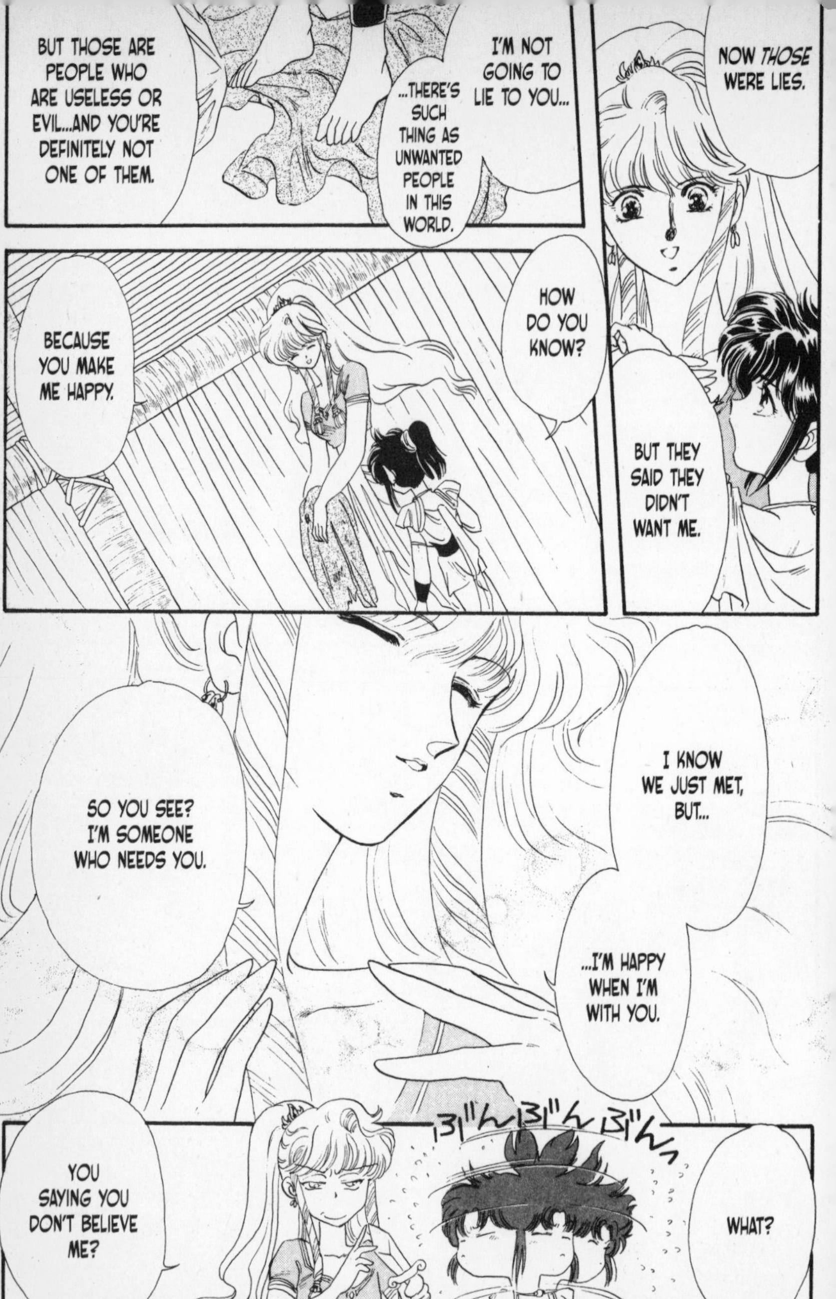
NOW *THOSE* WERE LIES.
BUT THEY SAID THEY DIDN'T WANT ME.
I'M NOT GOING TO LIE TO YOU...
...THERE'S SUCH THING AS UNWANTED PEOPLE IN THIS WORLD.
BUT THOSE ARE PEOPLE WHO ARE USELESS OR EVIL...AND YOU'RE DEFINITELY NOT ONE OF THEM.
HOW DO YOU KNOW?
BECAUSE YOU MAKE ME HAPPY.
I KNOW WE JUST MET, BUT...
...I'M HAPPY WHEN I'M WITH YOU.
SO YOU SEE? I'M SOMEONE WHO NEEDS YOU.
WHAT?
ぶんぶんぶん
YOU SAYING YOU DON'T BELIEVE ME?

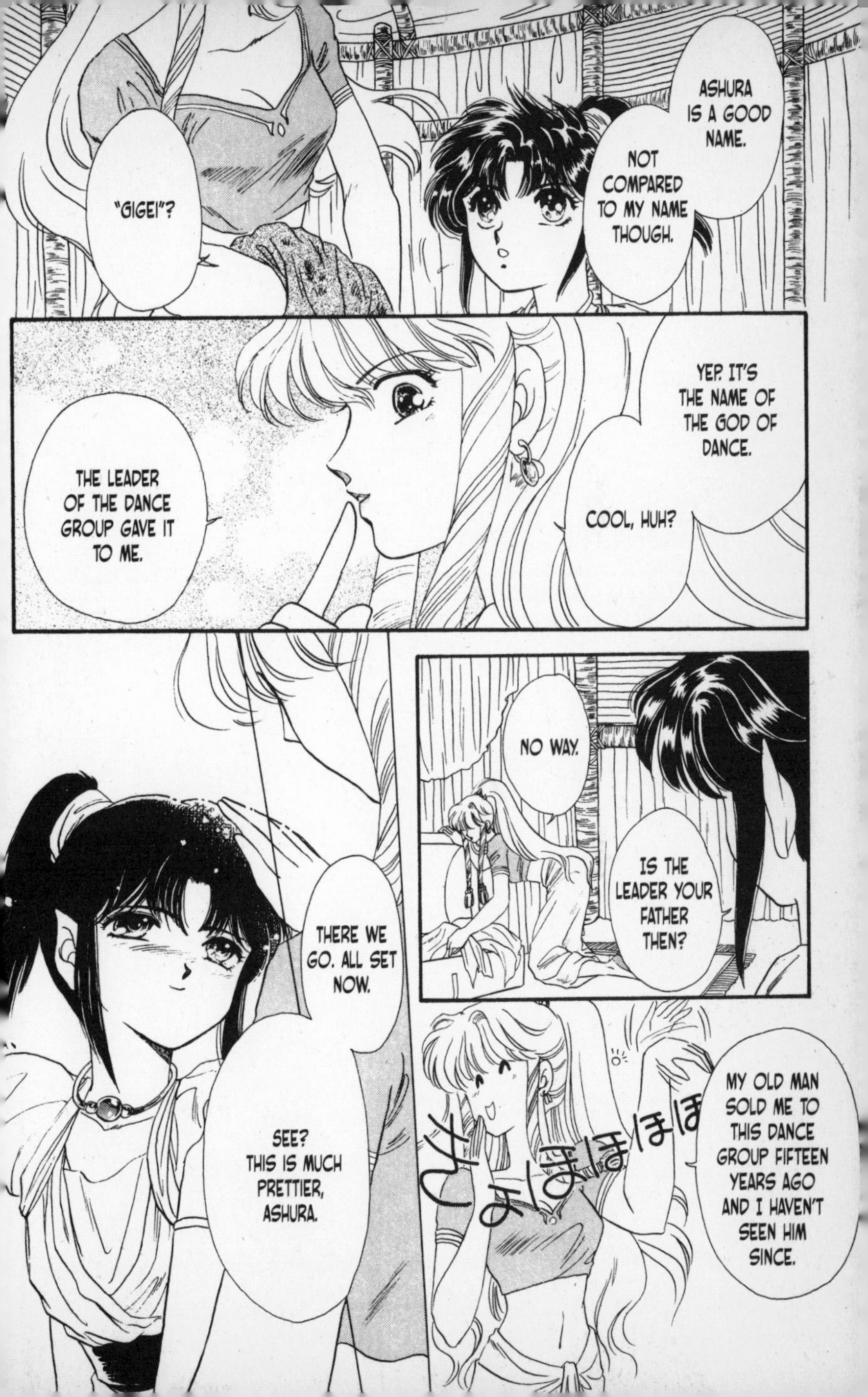
ASHURA IS A GOOD NAME.
NOT COMPARED TO MY NAME THOUGH.
"GIGEI"?
YEP. IT'S THE NAME OF THE GOD OF DANCE.
COOL, HUH?
THE LEADER OF THE DANCE GROUP GAVE IT TO ME.
IS THE LEADER YOUR FATHER THEN?
NO WAY.
MY OLD MAN SOLD ME TO THIS DANCE GROUP FIFTEEN YEARS AGO AND I HAVEN'T SEEN HIM SINCE.
きょほほほほ
THERE WE GO. ALL SET NOW.
SEE? THIS IS MUCH PRETTIER, ASHURA.

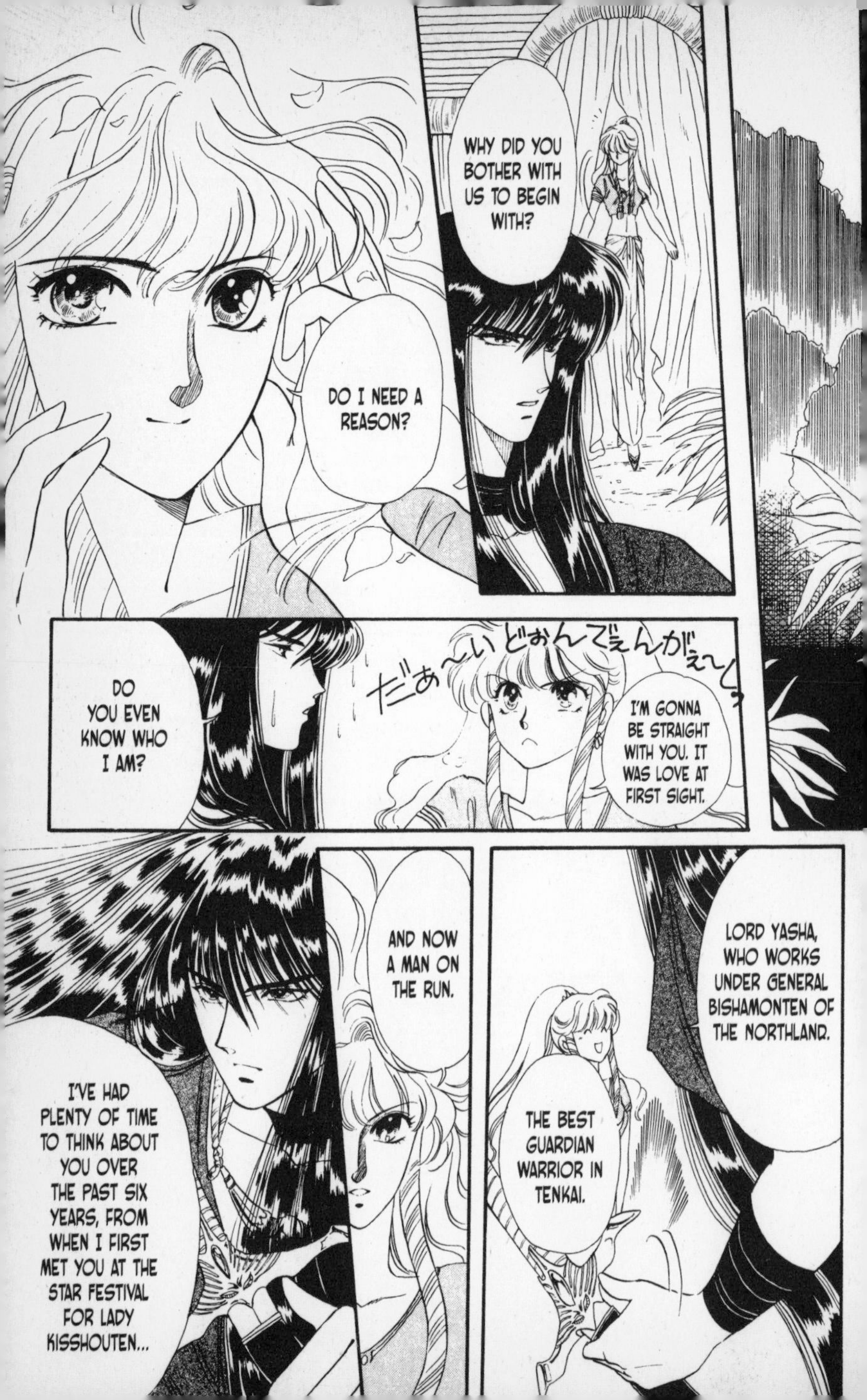
WHY DID YOU BOTHER WITH US TO BEGIN WITH?
DO I NEED A REASON?
だぁ〜いどぉんでぇんがぇ〜
I'M GONNA BE STRAIGHT WITH YOU. IT WAS LOVE AT FIRST SIGHT.
DO YOU EVEN KNOW WHO I AM?
LORD YASHA, WHO WORKS UNDER GENERAL BISHAMONTEN OF THE NORTHLAND.
THE BEST GUARDIAN WARRIOR IN TENKAI.
AND NOW A MAN ON THE RUN.
I'VE HAD PLENTY OF TIME TO THINK ABOUT YOU OVER THE PAST SIX YEARS, FROM WHEN I FIRST MET YOU AT THE STAR FESTIVAL FOR LADY KISSHOUTEN...

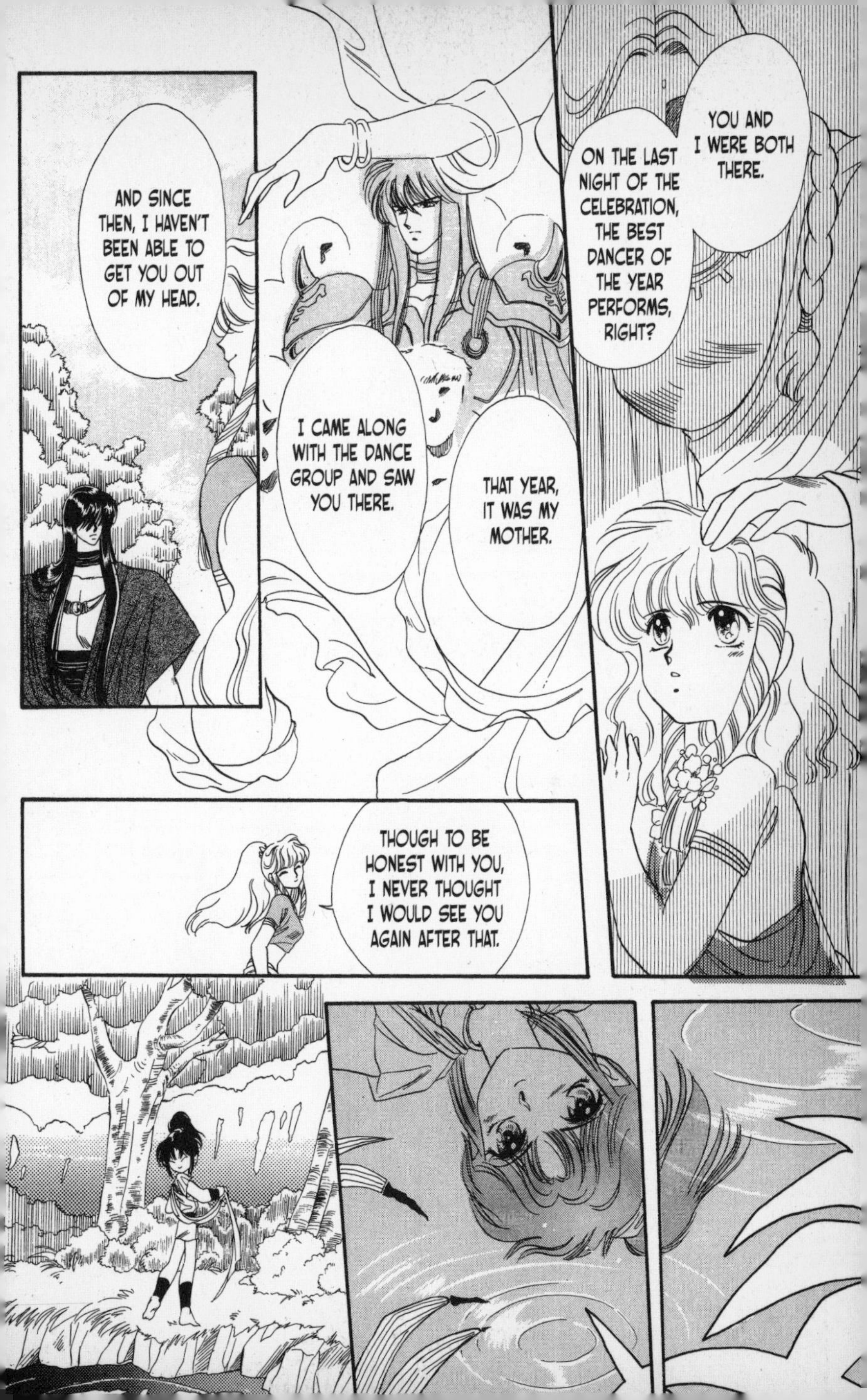
YOU AND I WERE BOTH THERE.
ON THE LAST NIGHT OF THE CELEBRATION, THE BEST DANCER OF THE YEAR PERFORMS, RIGHT?
THAT YEAR, IT WAS MY MOTHER.
I CAME ALONG WITH THE DANCE GROUP AND SAW YOU THERE.
AND SINCE THEN, I HAVEN'T BEEN ABLE TO GET YOU OUT OF MY HEAD.
THOUGH TO BE HONEST WITH YOU, I NEVER THOUGHT I WOULD SEE YOU AGAIN AFTER THAT.

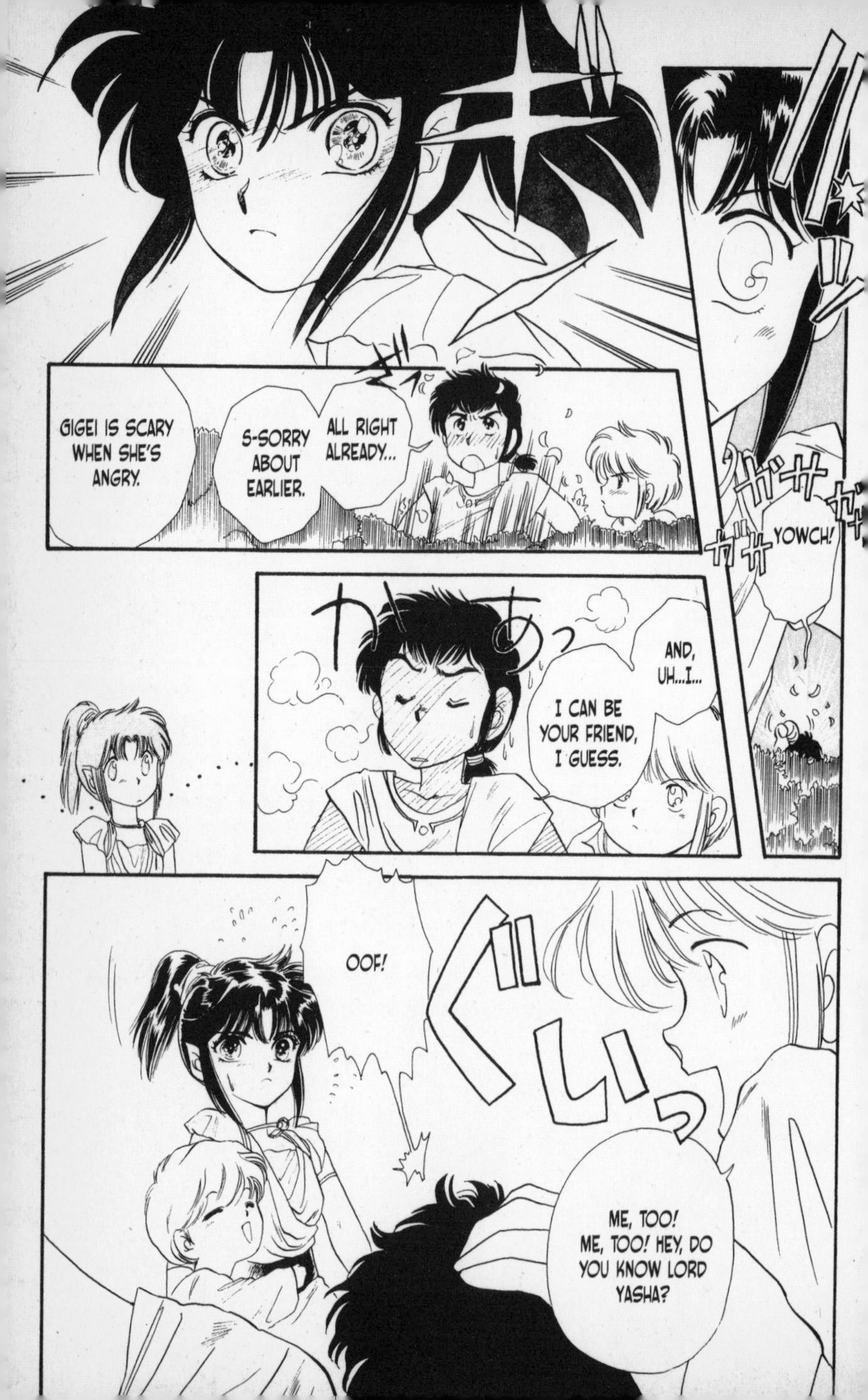
YOWCH!
ALL RIGHT ALREADY...
S-SORRY ABOUT EARLIER.
GIGEI IS SCARY WHEN SHE'S ANGRY.
AND, UH...I...
I CAN BE YOUR FRIEND, I GUESS.
OOF!
ME, TOO! ME, TOO! HEY, DO YOU KNOW LORD YASHA?

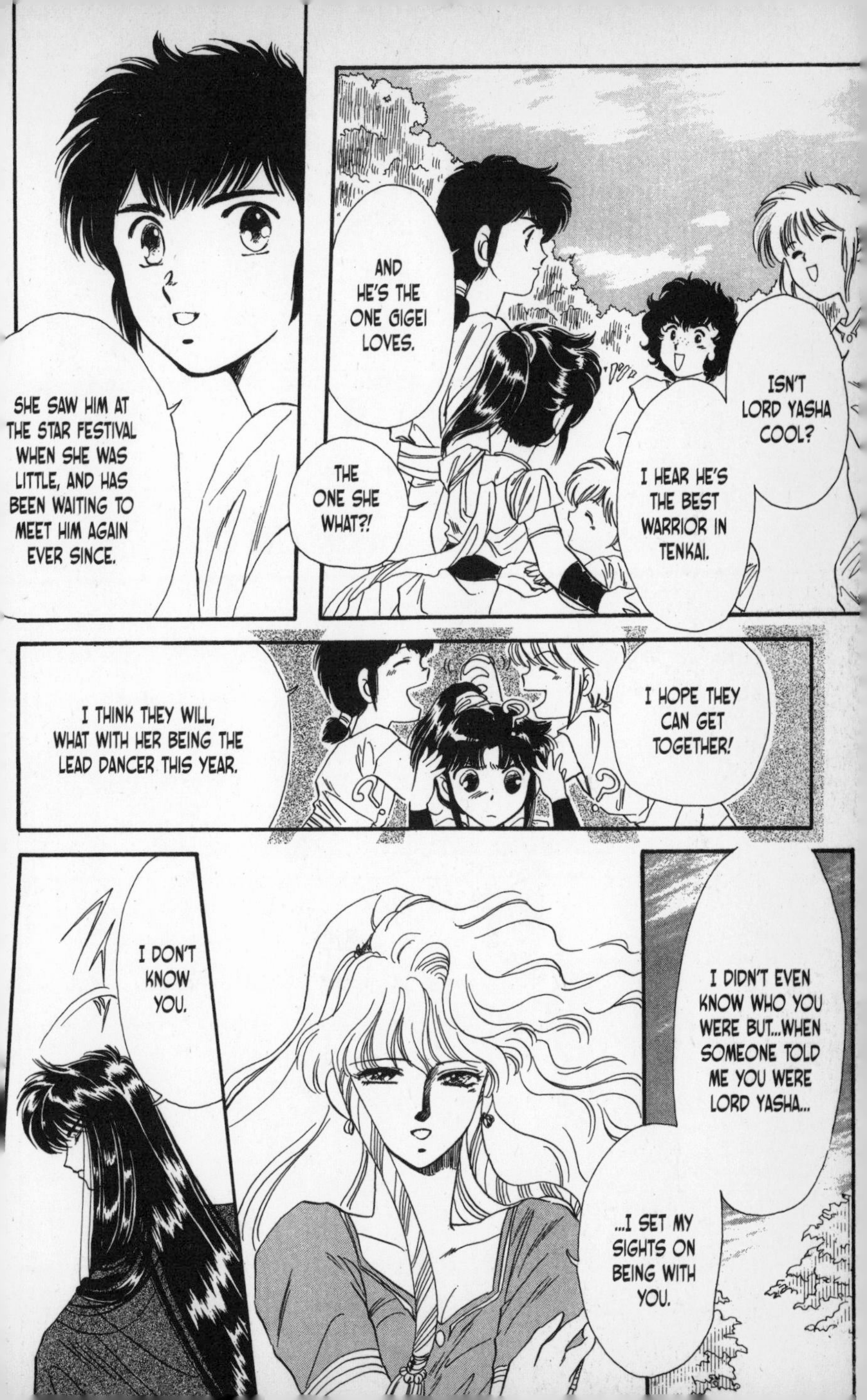
ISN'T LORD YASHA COOL?
I HEAR HE'S THE BEST WARRIOR IN TENKAI.
AND HE'S THE ONE GIGEI LOVES.
THE ONE SHE WHAT?!
SHE SAW HIM AT THE STAR FESTIVAL WHEN SHE WAS LITTLE, AND HAS BEEN WAITING TO MEET HIM AGAIN EVER SINCE.
I HOPE THEY CAN GET TOGETHER!
I THINK THEY WILL, WHAT WITH HER BEING THE LEAD DANCER THIS YEAR.
I DIDN'T EVEN KNOW WHO YOU WERE BUT...WHEN SOMEONE TOLD ME YOU WERE LORD YASHA...
...I SET MY SIGHTS ON BEING WITH YOU.
I DON'T KNOW YOU.

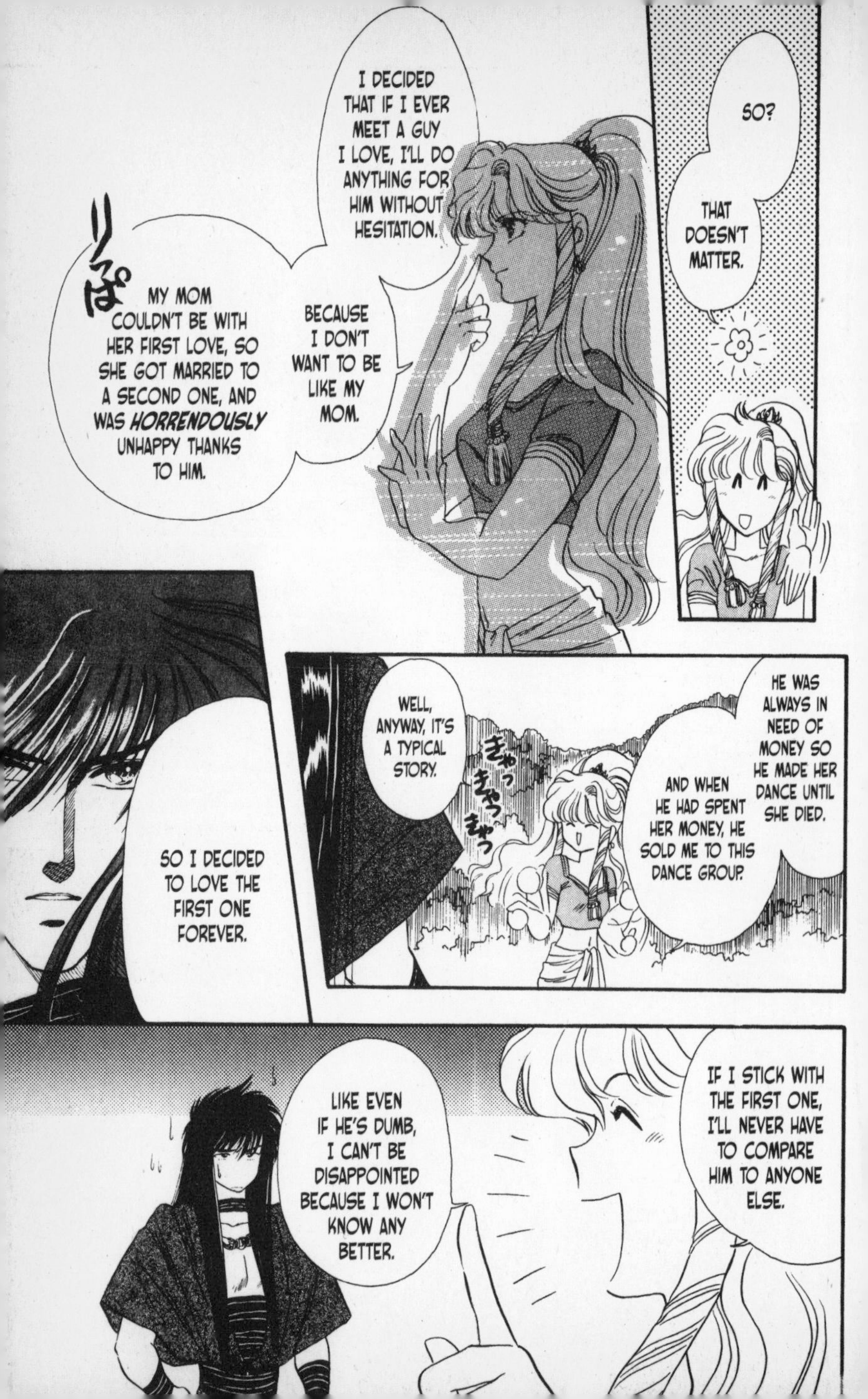
SO?
THAT DOESN'T MATTER.
I DECIDED THAT IF I EVER MEET A GUY I LOVE, I'LL DO ANYTHING FOR HIM WITHOUT HESITATION.
BECAUSE I DON'T WANT TO BE LIKE MY MOM.
りっぱ
MY MOM COULDN'T BE WITH HER FIRST LOVE, SO SHE GOT MARRIED TO A SECOND ONE, AND WAS *HORRENDOUSLY* UNHAPPY THANKS TO HIM.
HE WAS ALWAYS IN NEED OF MONEY SO HE MADE HER DANCE UNTIL SHE DIED.
AND WHEN HE HAD SPENT HER MONEY, HE SOLD ME TO THIS DANCE GROUP.
きゃっ きゃっ きゃっ
WELL, ANYWAY, IT'S A TYPICAL STORY.
SO I DECIDED TO LOVE THE FIRST ONE FOREVER.
IF I STICK WITH THE FIRST ONE, I'LL NEVER HAVE TO COMPARE HIM TO ANYONE ELSE.
LIKE EVEN IF HE'S DUMB, I CAN'T BE DISAPPOINTED BECAUSE I WON'T KNOW ANY BETTER.

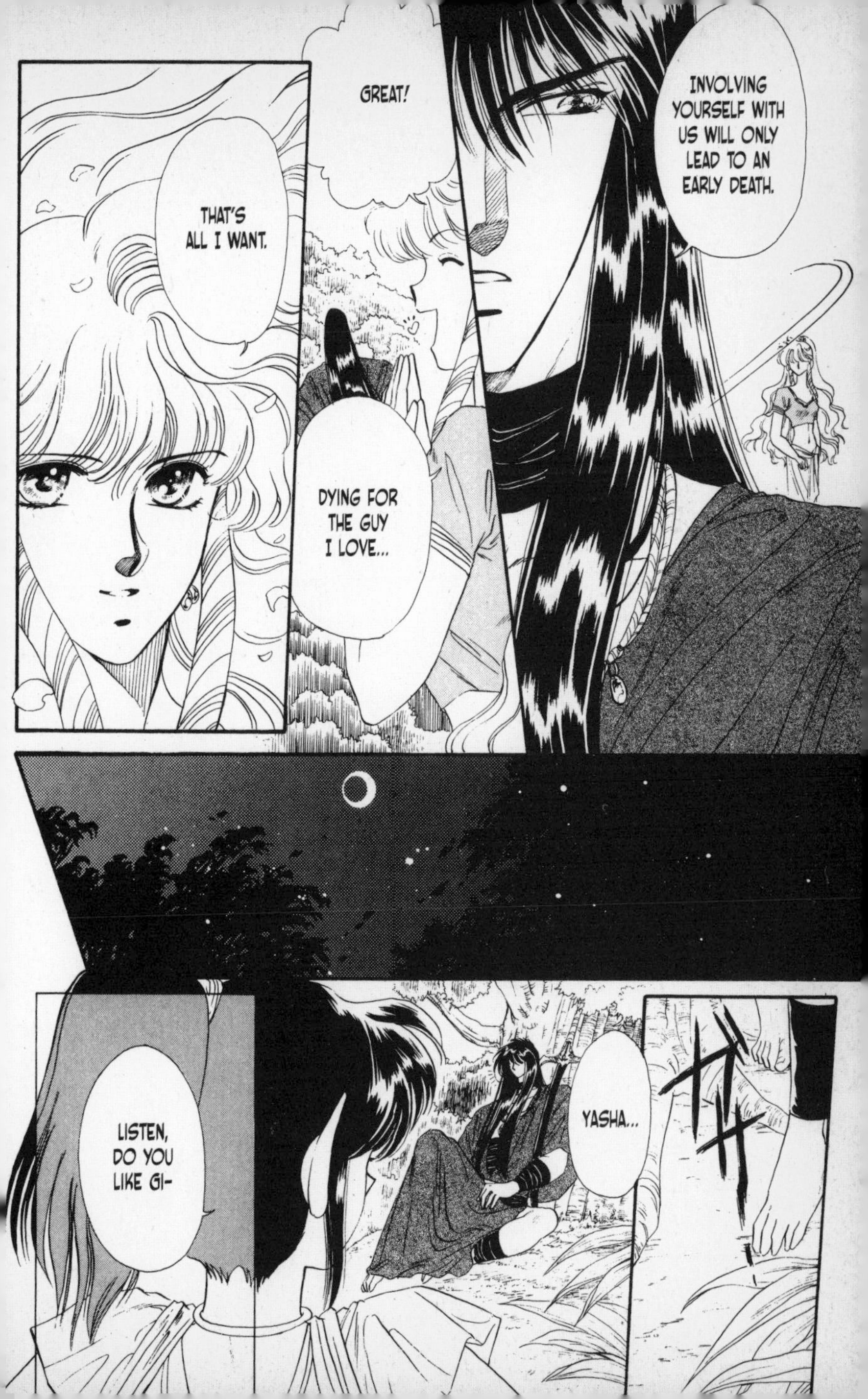
INVOLVING YOURSELF WITH US WILL ONLY LEAD TO AN EARLY DEATH.
GREAT!
DYING FOR THE GUY I LOVE...
THAT'S ALL I WANT.
YASHA...
LISTEN, DO YOU LIKE GI-

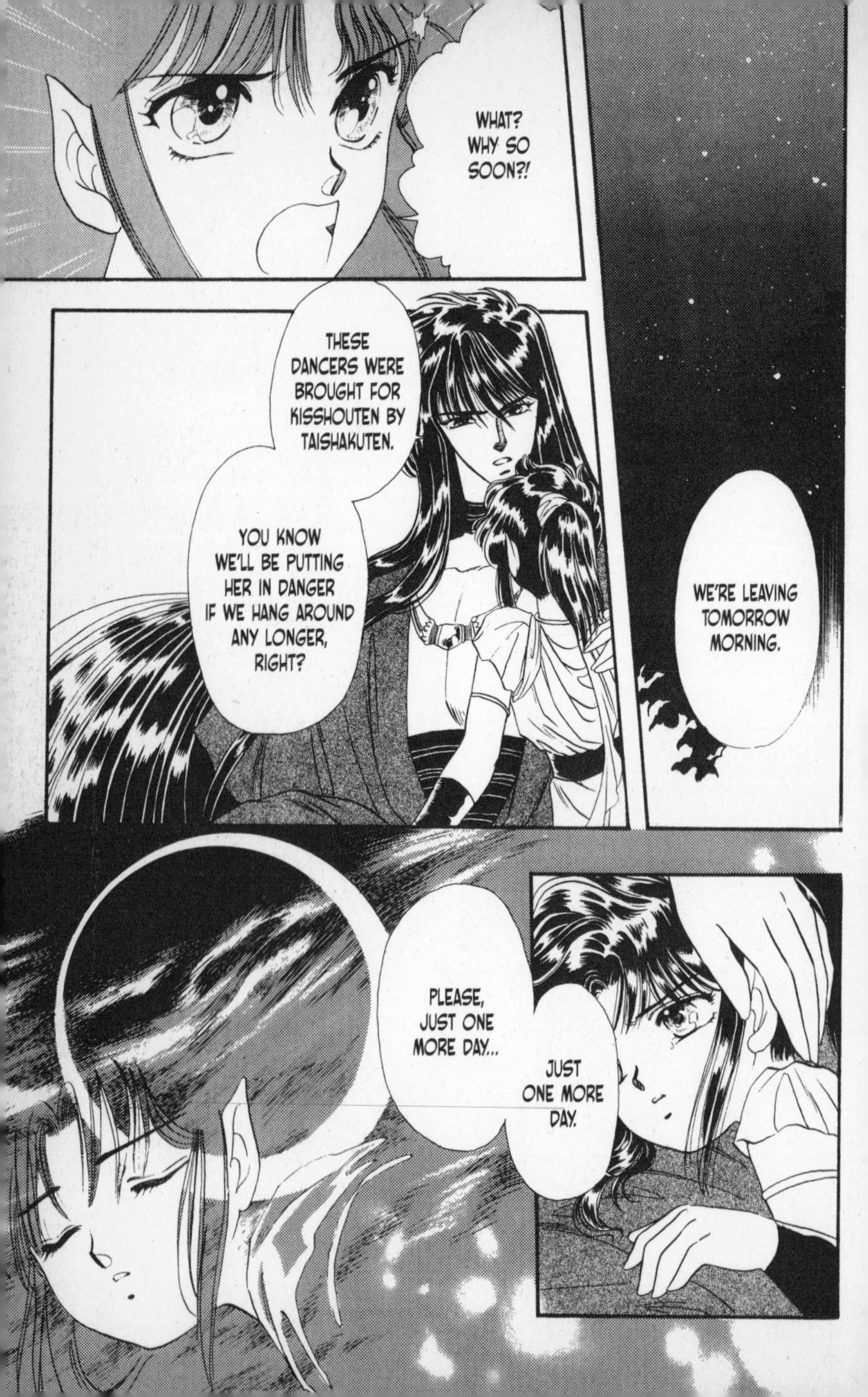
WE'RE LEAVING TOMORROW MORNING.
WHAT? WHY SO SOON?!
THESE DANCERS WERE BROUGHT FOR KISSHOUTEN BY TAISHAKUTEN.
YOU KNOW WE'LL BE PUTTING HER IN DANGER IF WE HANG AROUND ANY LONGER, RIGHT?
PLEASE, JUST ONE MORE DAY...
JUST ONE MORE DAY.

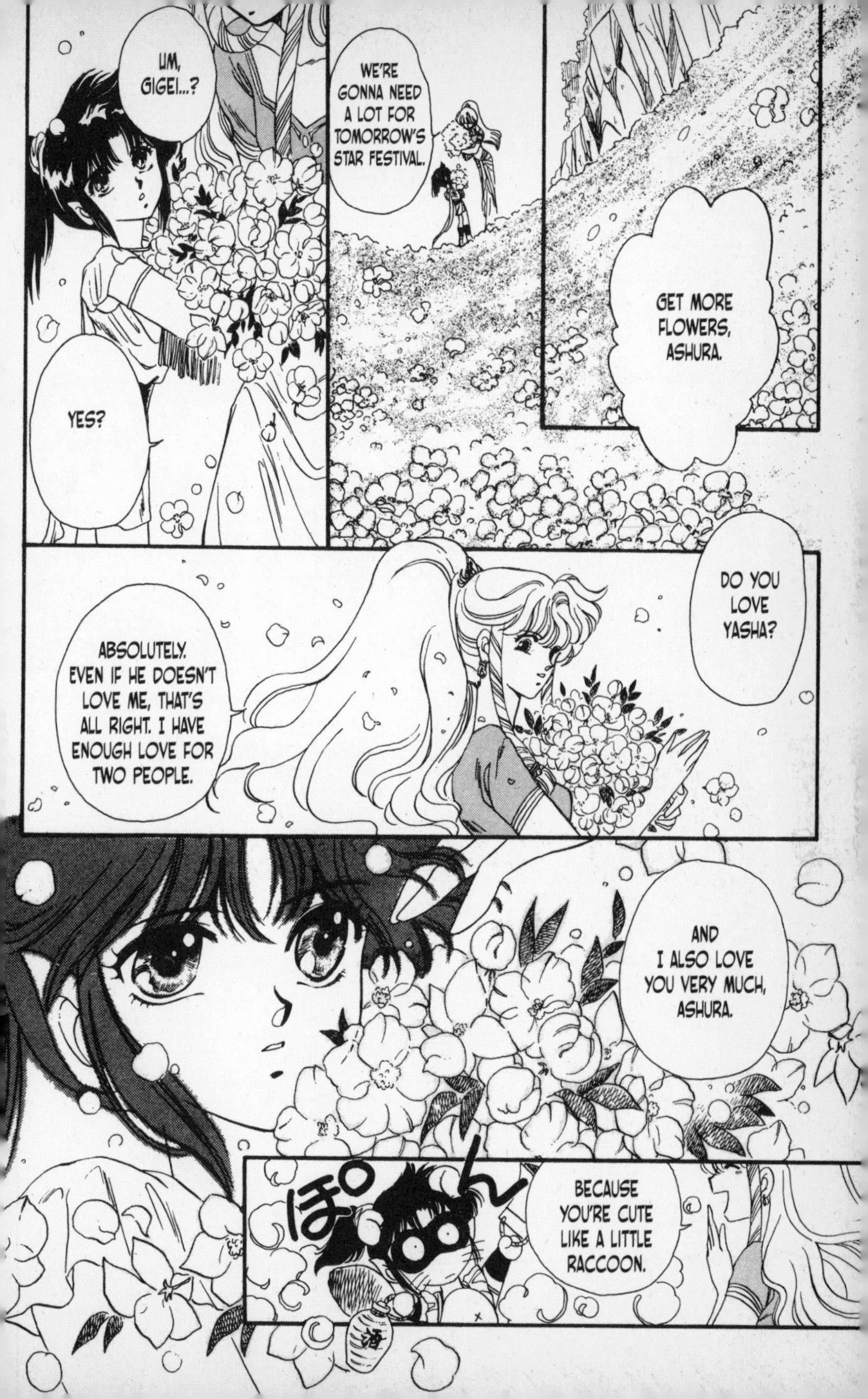
GET MORE FLOWERS, ASHURA.
WE'RE GONNA NEED A LOT FOR TOMORROW'S STAR FESTIVAL.
UM, GIGEI...?
YES?
DO YOU LOVE YASHA?
ABSOLUTELY. EVEN IF HE DOESN'T LOVE ME, THAT'S ALL RIGHT. I HAVE ENOUGH LOVE FOR TWO PEOPLE.
AND I ALSO LOVE YOU VERY MUCH, ASHURA.
BECAUSE YOU'RE CUTE LIKE A LITTLE RACCOON.
ぽん
酒

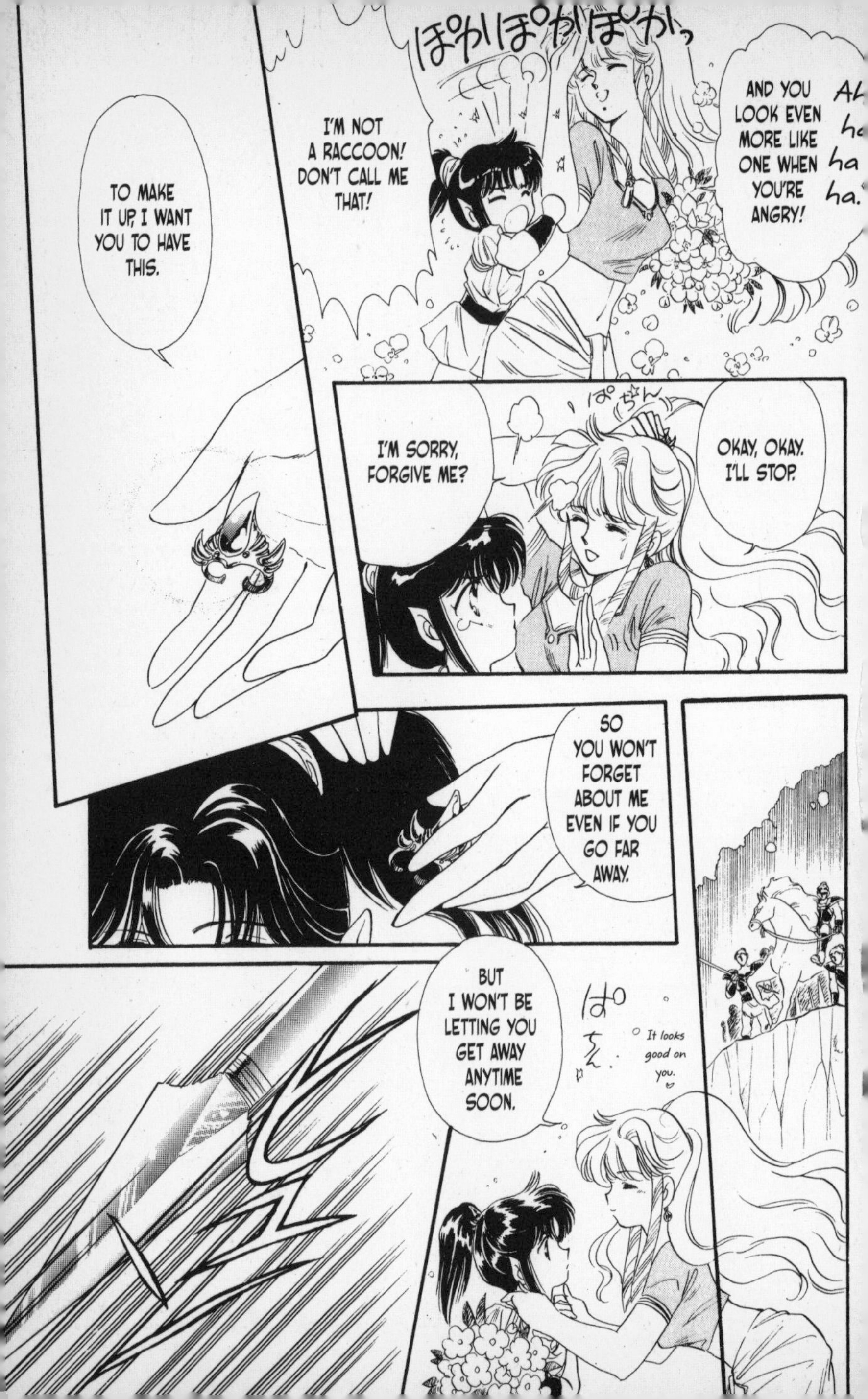
ぽかぽかぽかっ
AND YOU LOOK EVEN MORE LIKE ONE WHEN YOU'RE ANGRY!
Ah ha ha ha.
I'M NOT A RACCOON! DON'T CALL ME THAT!
OKAY, OKAY. I'LL STOP.
ぱちん
I'M SORRY, FORGIVE ME?
TO MAKE IT UP, I WANT YOU TO HAVE THIS.
SO YOU WON'T FORGET ABOUT ME EVEN IF YOU GO FAR AWAY.
It looks good on you.
ぱちん
BUT I WON'T BE LETTING YOU GET AWAY ANYTIME SOON.

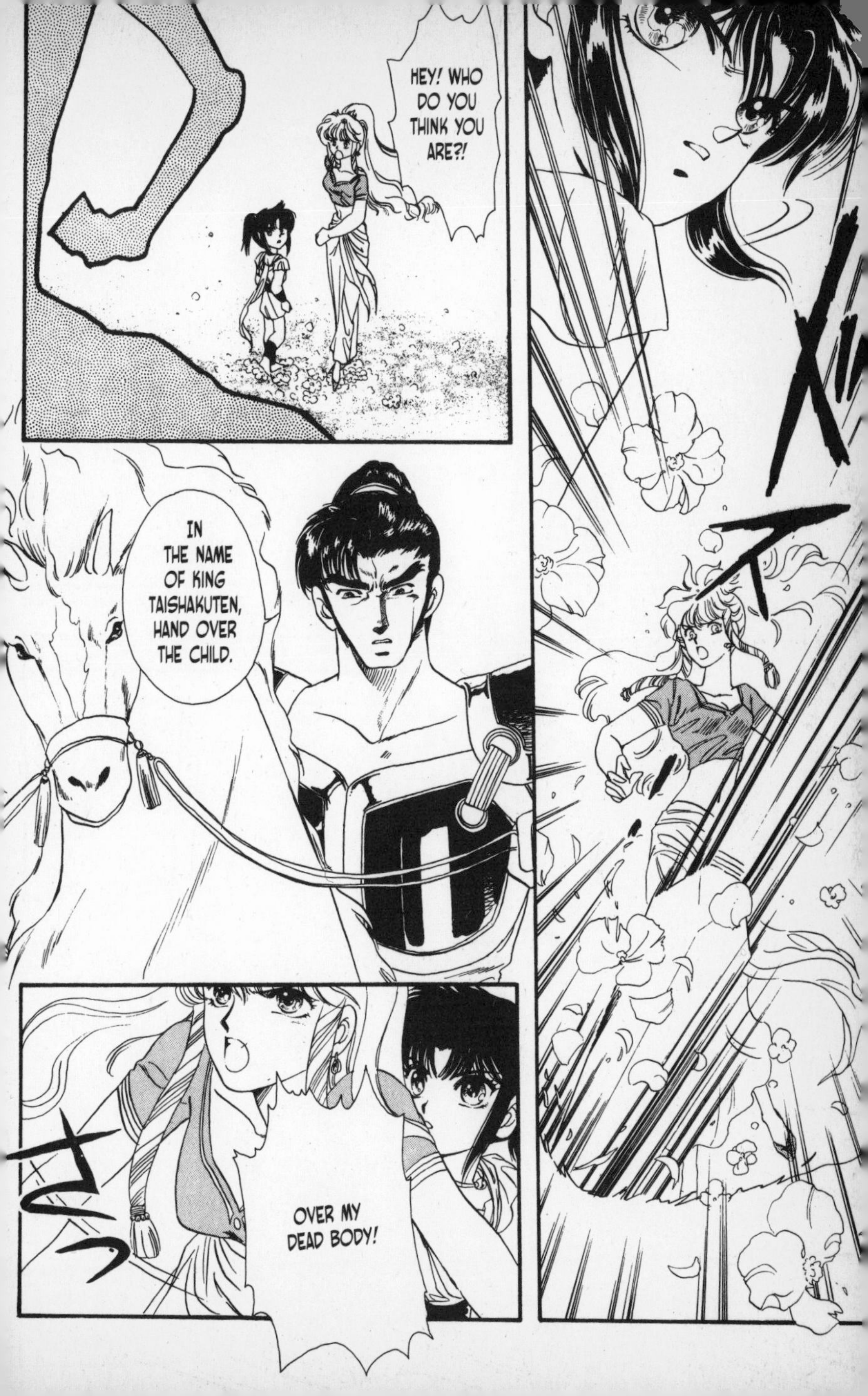
HEY! WHO DO YOU THINK YOU ARE?!
IN THE NAME OF KING TAISHAKUTEN, HAND OVER THE CHILD.
OVER MY DEAD BODY!

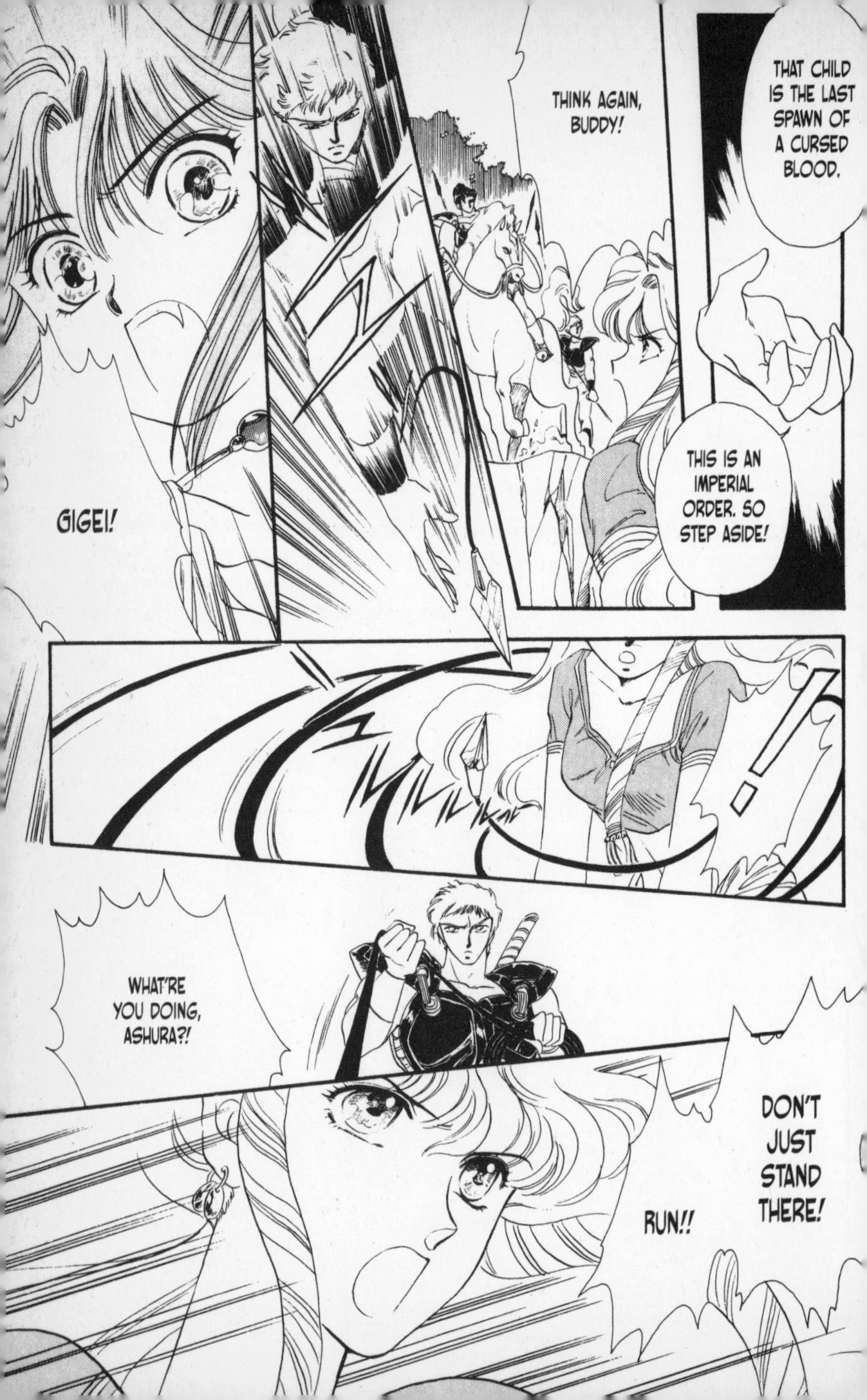
THAT CHILD IS THE LAST SPAWN OF A CURSED BLOOD.
THIS IS AN IMPERIAL ORDER. SO STEP ASIDE!
THINK AGAIN, BUDDY!
GIGEI!
!
WHAT'RE YOU DOING, ASHURA?!
DON'T JUST STAND THERE!
RUN!!

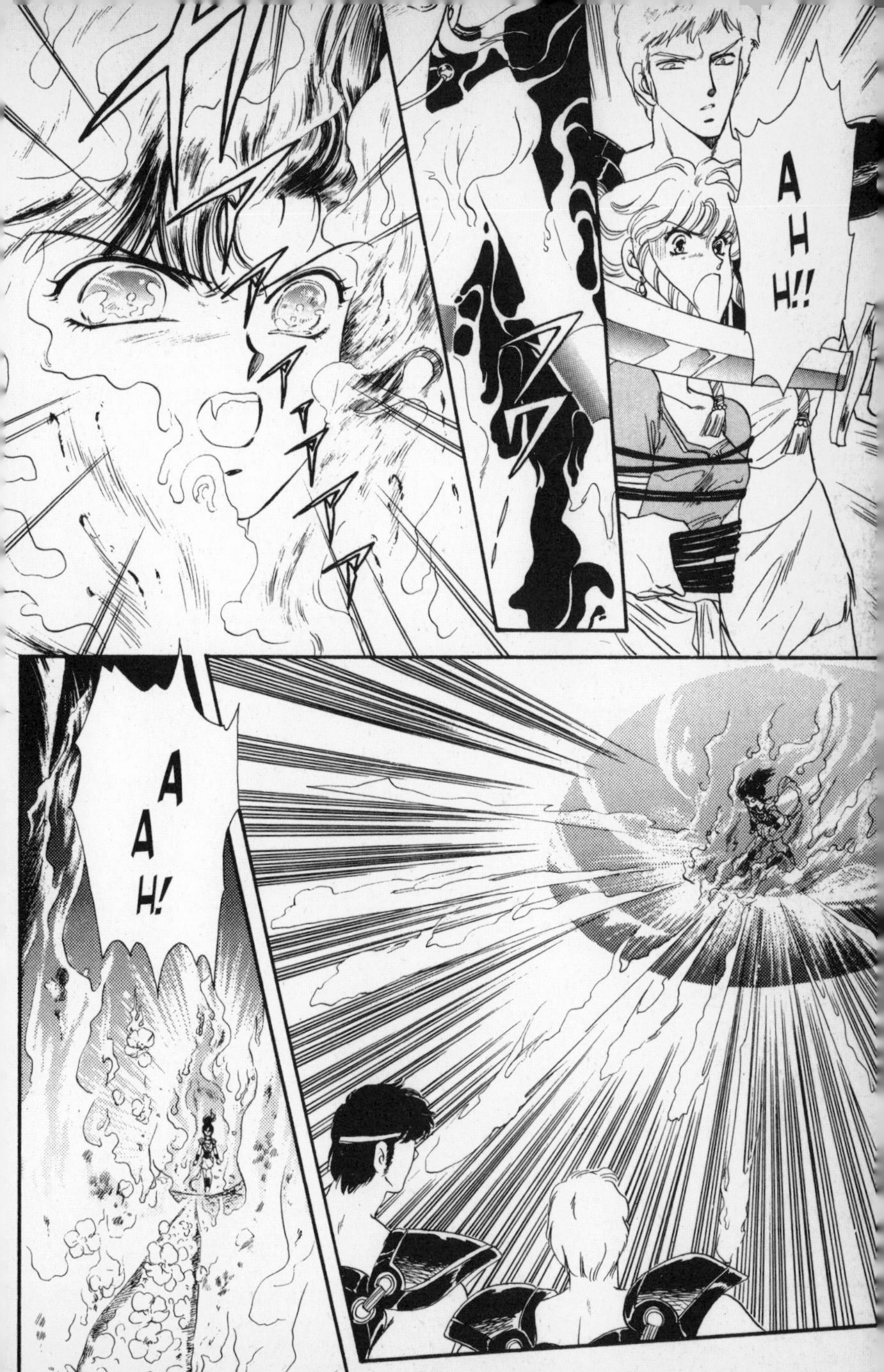
AHH!!
AAH!

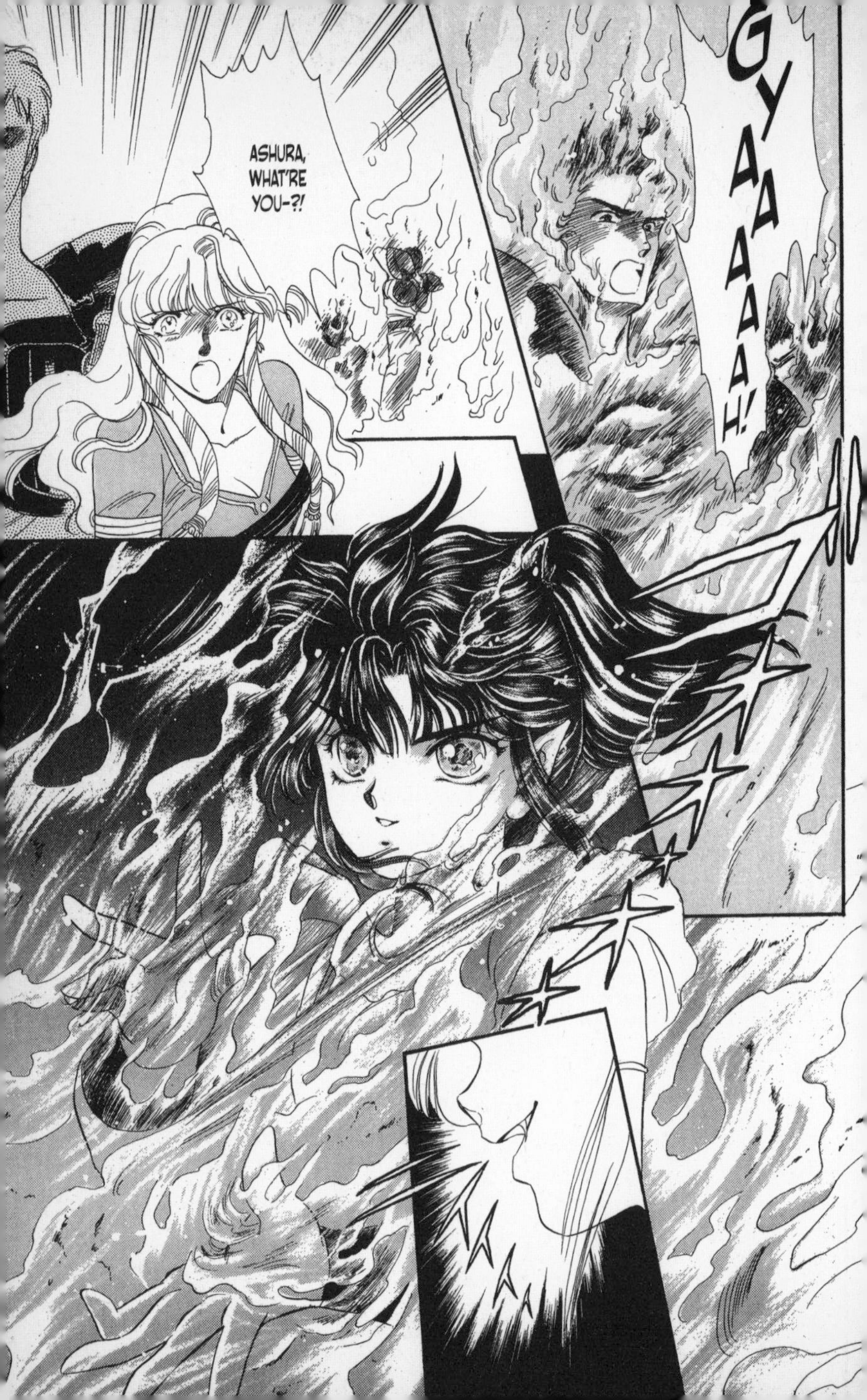
GYAAAAAH!
ASHURA, WHAT'RE YOU-?!

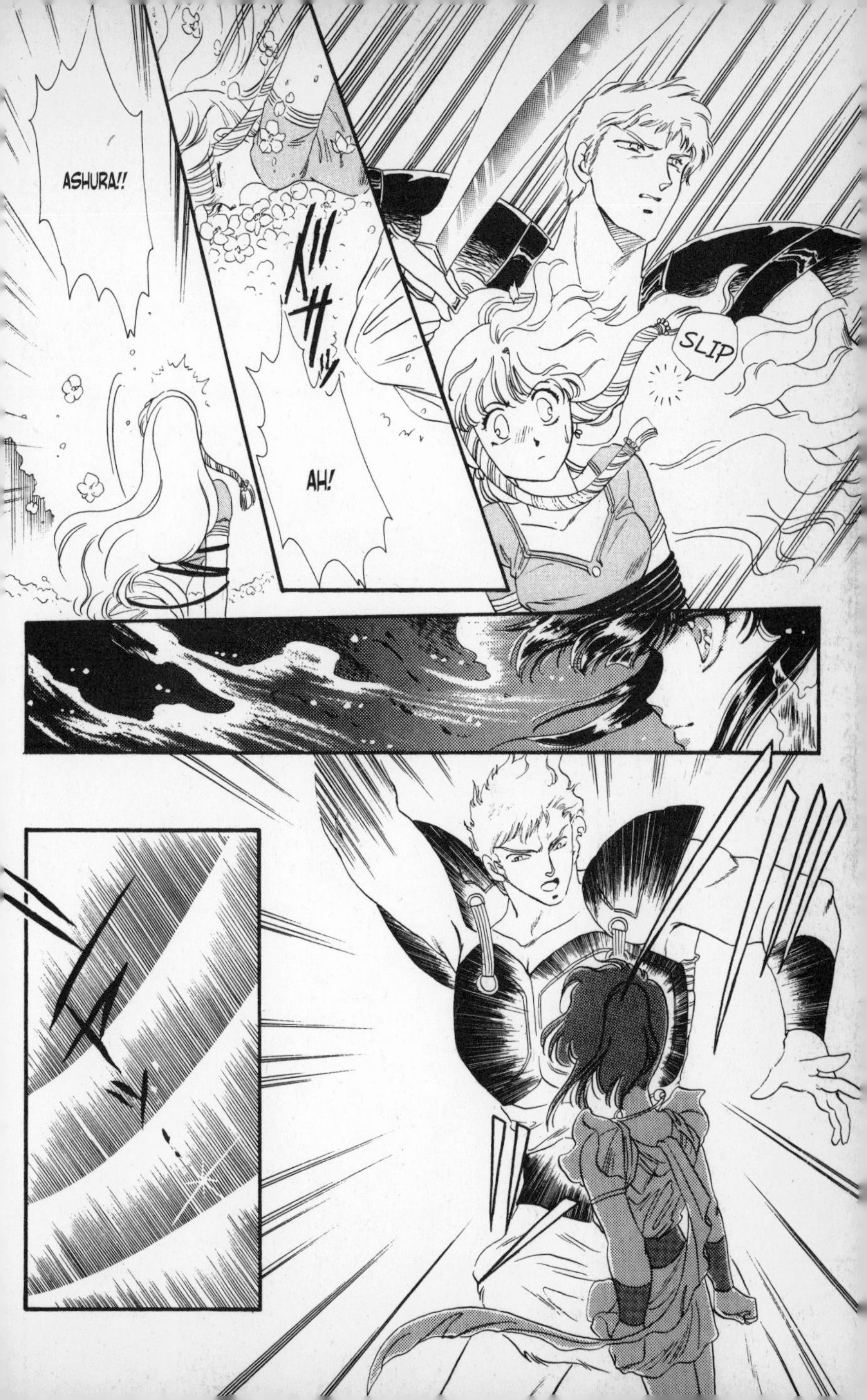
SLIP
AH!
ASHURA!!

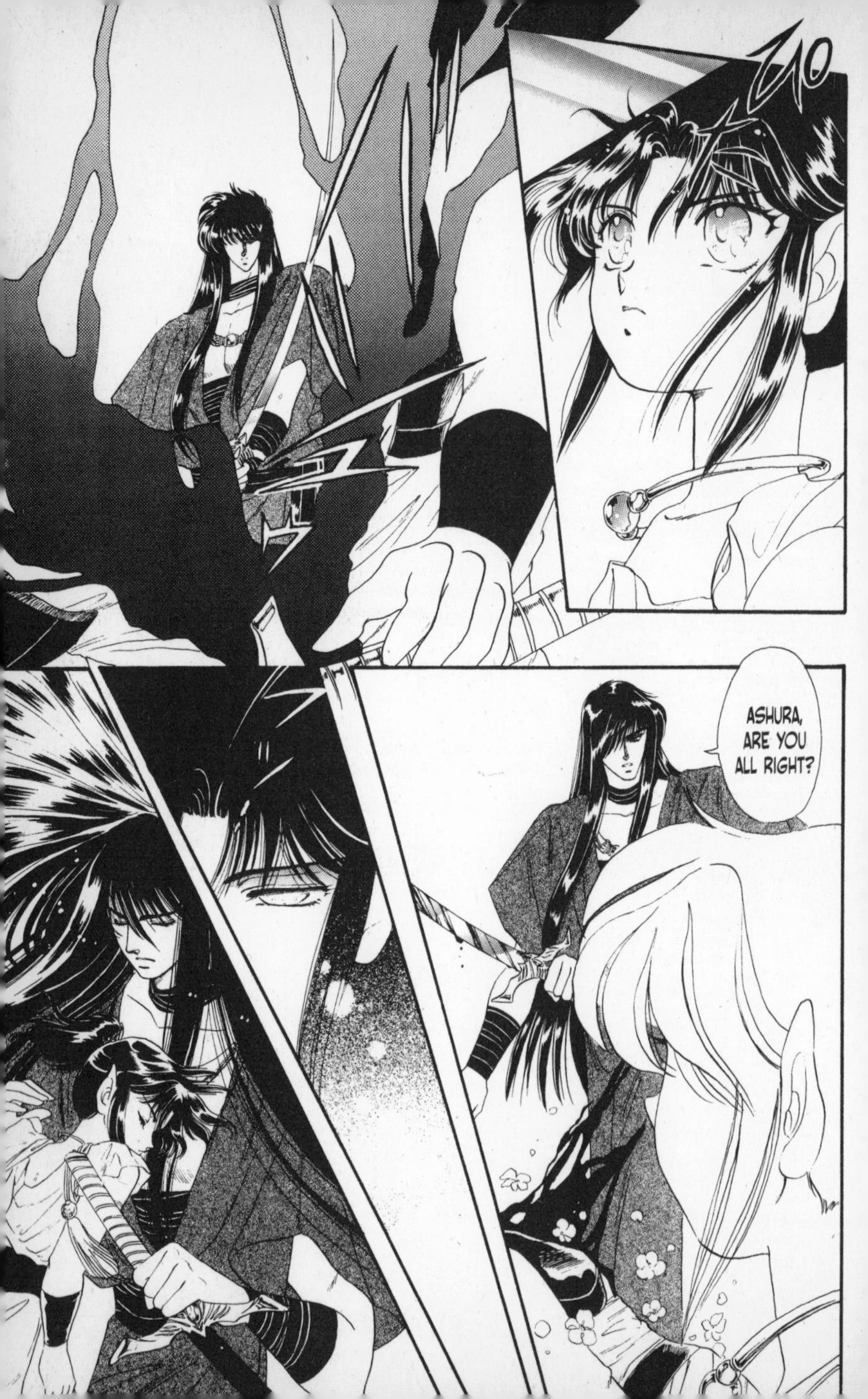
ZAO
ASHURA, ARE YOU ALL RIGHT?

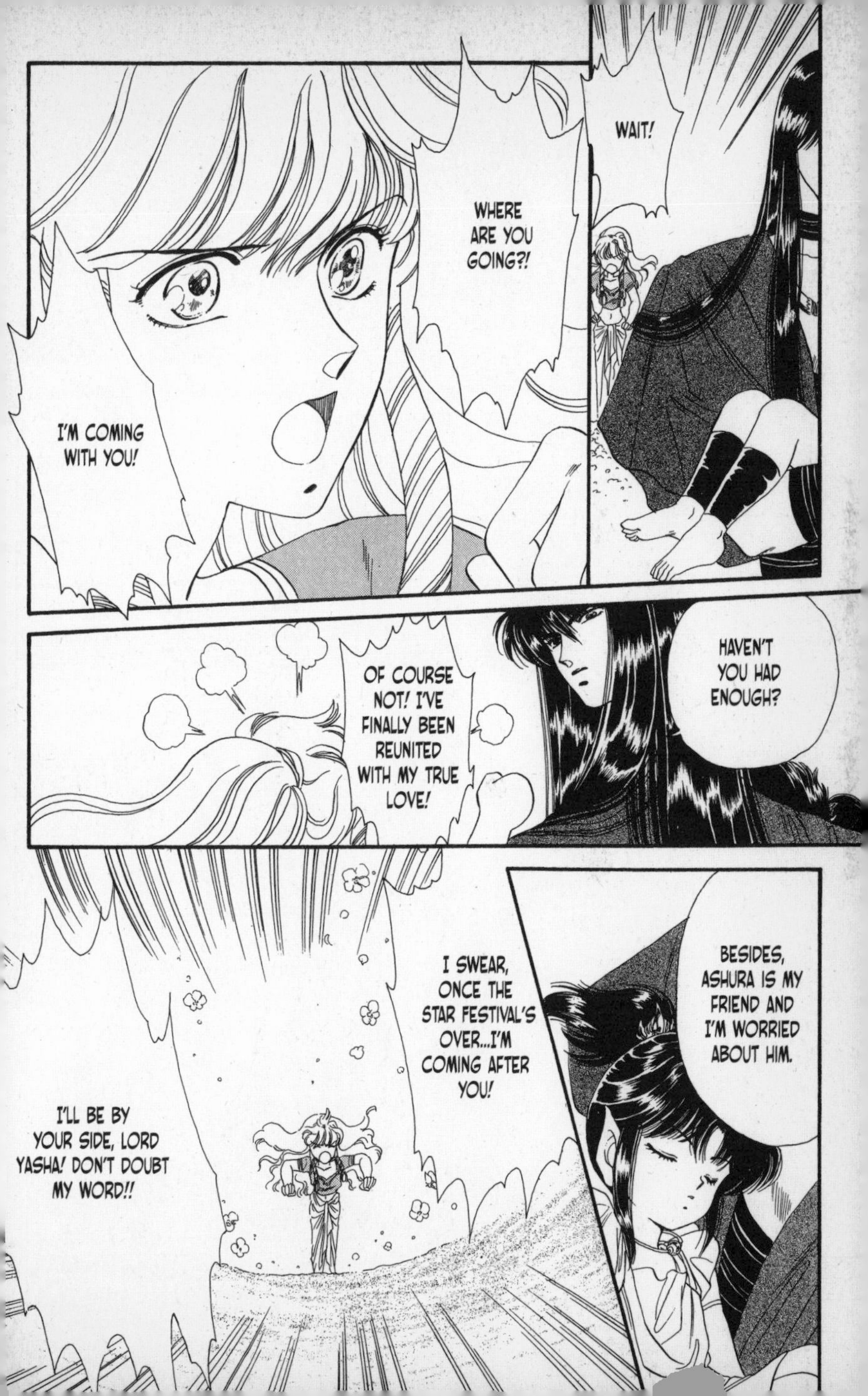
WAIT!
WHERE ARE YOU GOING?!
I'M COMING WITH YOU!
HAVEN'T YOU HAD ENOUGH?
OF COURSE NOT! I'VE FINALLY BEEN REUNITED WITH MY TRUE LOVE!
BESIDES, ASHURA IS MY FRIEND AND I'M WORRIED ABOUT HIM.
I SWEAR, ONCE THE STAR FESTIVAL'S OVER...I'M COMING AFTER YOU!
I'LL BE BY YOUR SIDE, LORD YASHA! DON'T DOUBT MY WORD!!

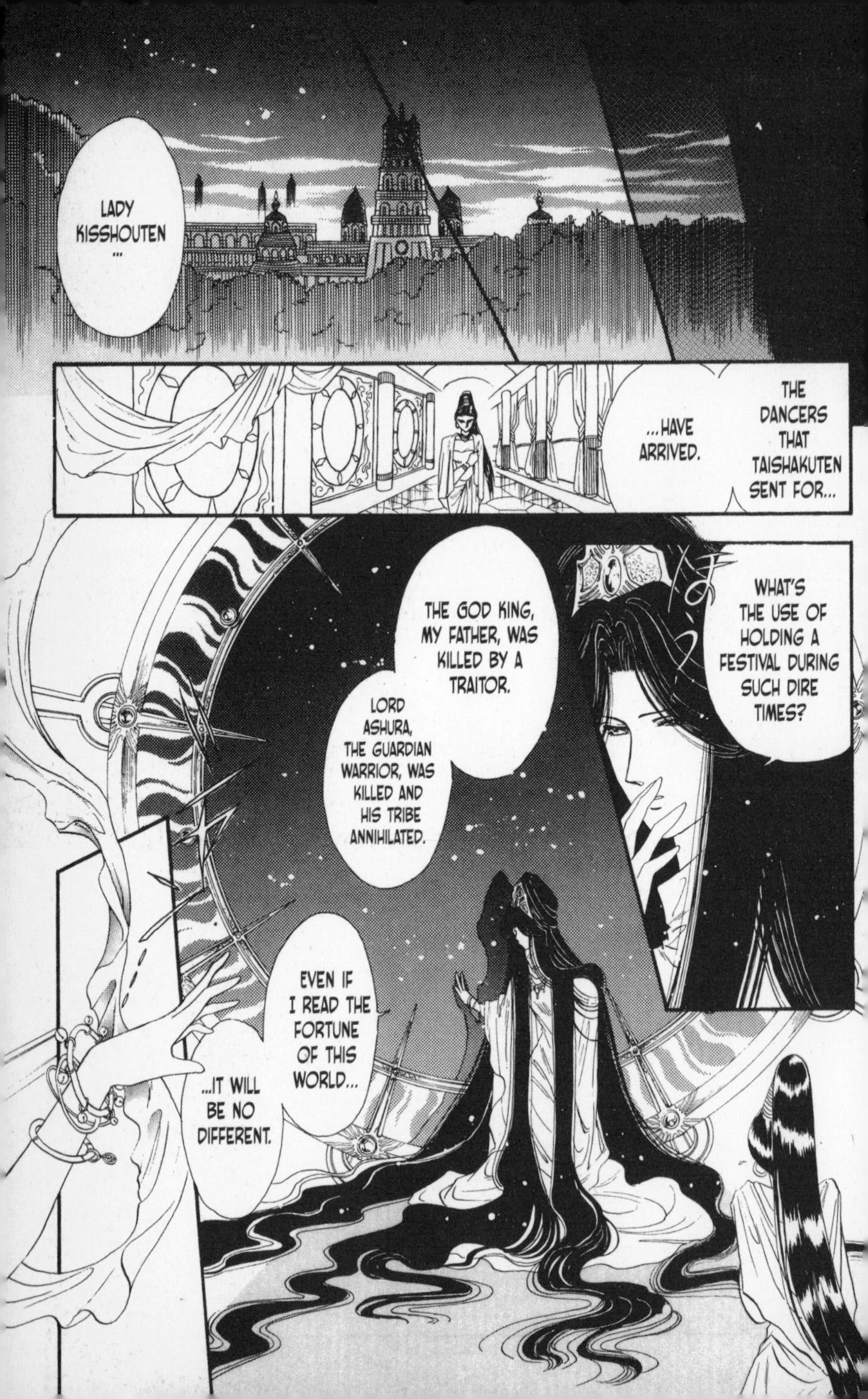
LADY KISSHOUTEN ...
THE DANCERS THAT TAISHAKUTEN SENT FOR...
...HAVE ARRIVED.
WHAT'S THE USE OF HOLDING A FESTIVAL DURING SUCH DIRE TIMES?
THE GOD KING, MY FATHER, WAS KILLED BY A TRAITOR.
LORD ASHURA, THE GUARDIAN WARRIOR, WAS KILLED AND HIS TRIBE ANNIHILATED.
EVEN IF I READ THE FORTUNE OF THIS WORLD...
...IT WILL BE NO DIFFERENT.

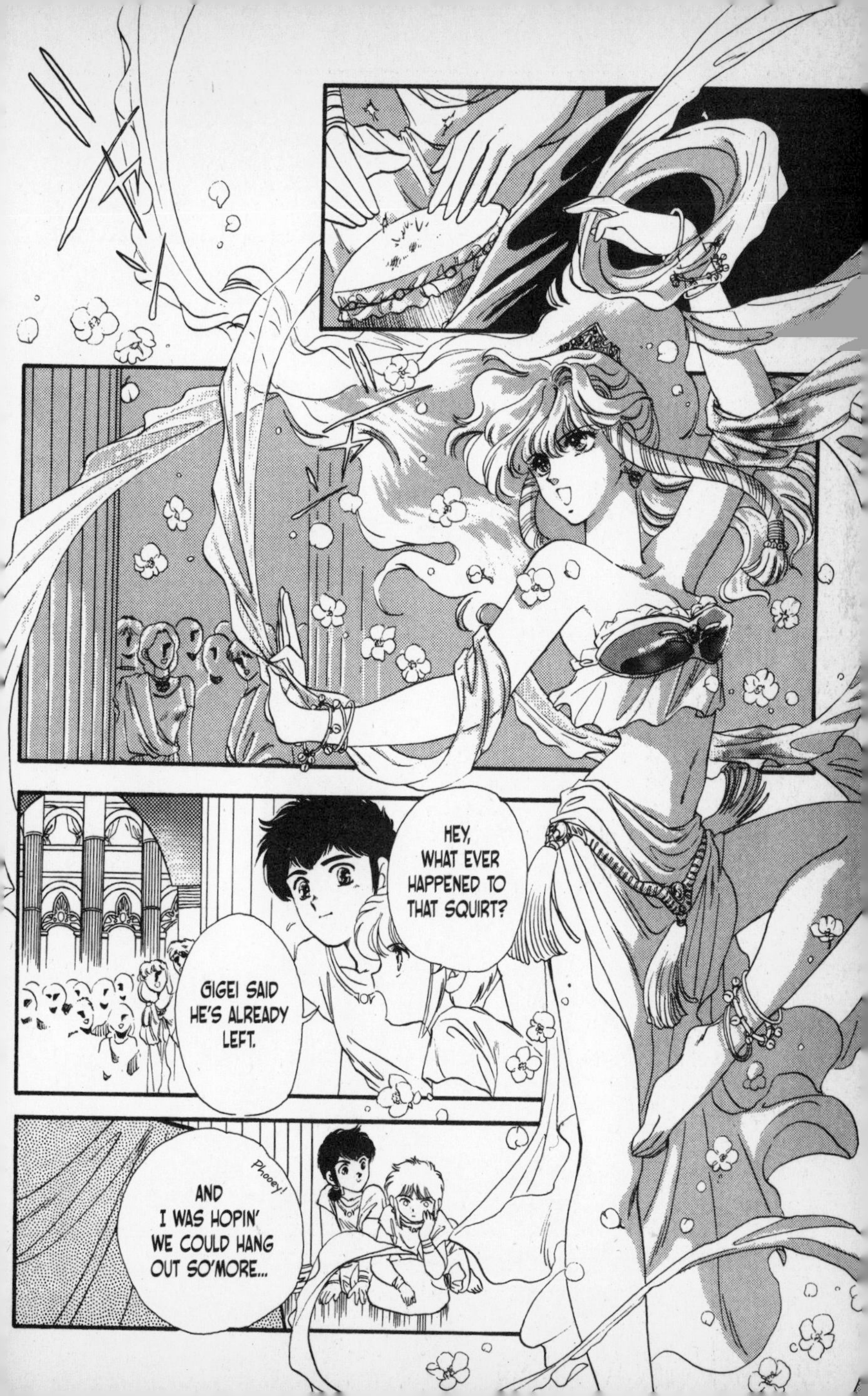
HEY, WHAT EVER HAPPENED TO THAT SQUIRT?
GIGEI SAID HE'S ALREADY LEFT.
Phooey!
AND I WAS HOPIN' WE COULD HANG OUT SO'MORE...

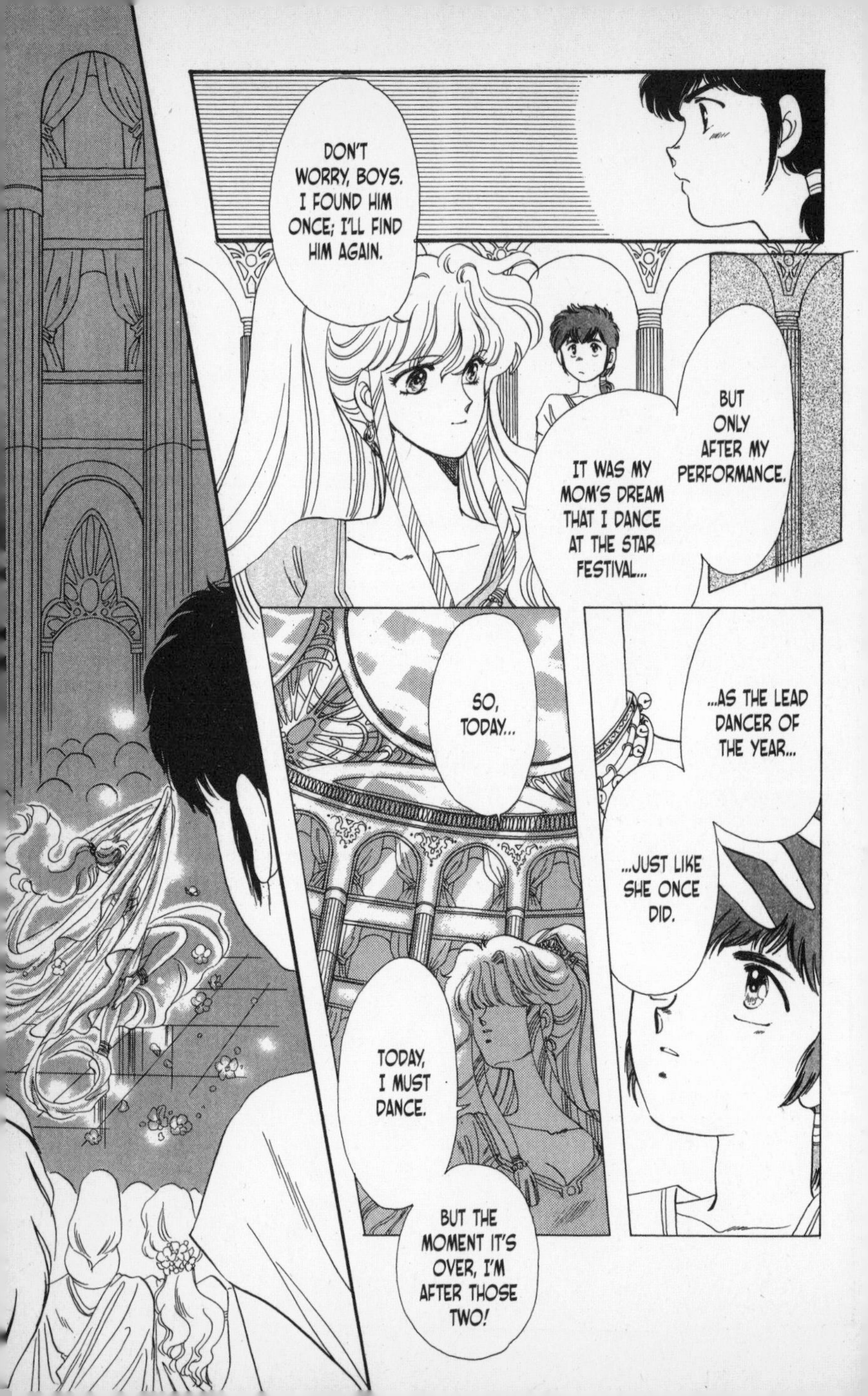
DON'T WORRY, BOYS. I FOUND HIM ONCE; I'LL FIND HIM AGAIN.
BUT ONLY AFTER MY PERFORMANCE.
IT WAS MY MOM'S DREAM THAT I DANCE AT THE STAR FESTIVAL...
...AS THE LEAD DANCER OF THE YEAR...
...JUST LIKE SHE ONCE DID.
SO, TODAY...
TODAY, I MUST DANCE.
BUT THE MOMENT IT'S OVER, I'M AFTER THOSE TWO!

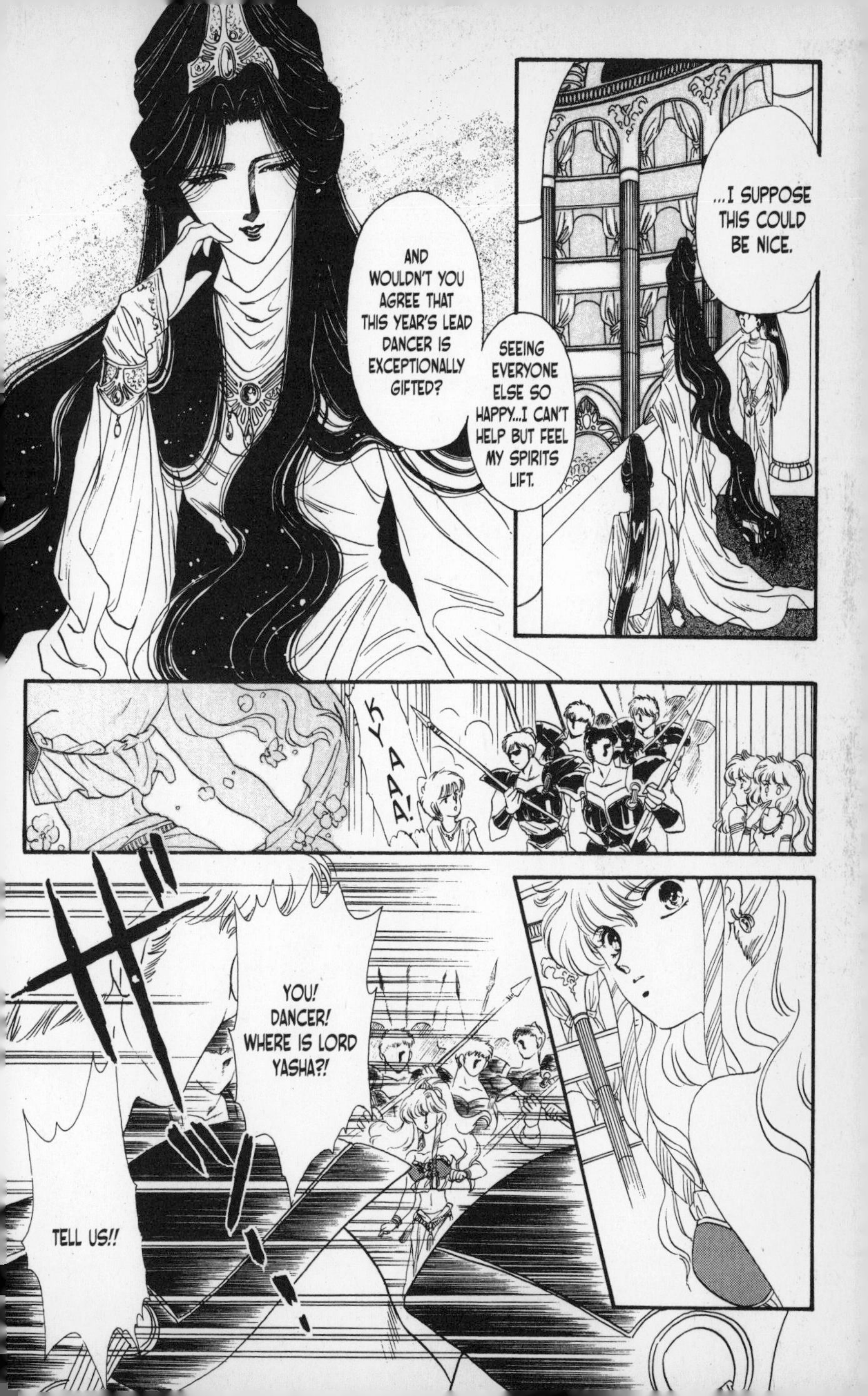
...I SUPPOSE THIS COULD BE NICE.
SEEING EVERYONE ELSE SO HAPPY...I CAN'T HELP BUT FEEL MY SPIRITS LIFT.
AND WOULDN'T YOU AGREE THAT THIS YEAR'S LEAD DANCER IS EXCEPTIONALLY GIFTED?
KYAAA!
YOU! DANCER! WHERE IS LORD YASHA?!
TELL US!!

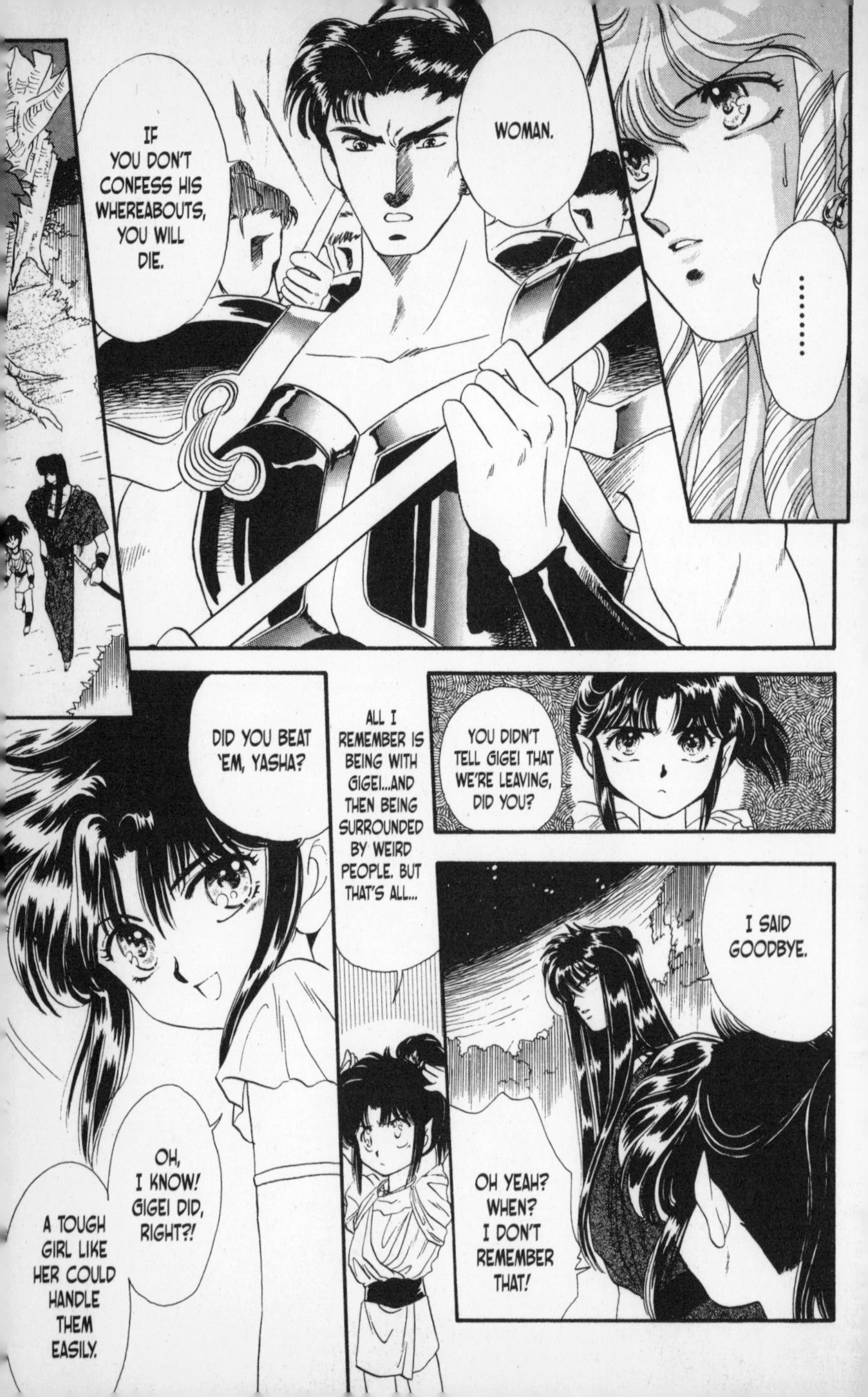
......
WOMAN.
IF YOU DON'T CONFESS HIS WHEREABOUTS, YOU WILL DIE.
YOU DIDN'T TELL GIGEI THAT WE'RE LEAVING, DID YOU?
I SAID GOODBYE.
OH YEAH? WHEN? I DON'T REMEMBER THAT!
DID YOU BEAT 'EM, YASHA?
ALL I REMEMBER IS BEING WITH GIGEI...AND THEN BEING SURROUNDED BY WEIRD PEOPLE. BUT THAT'S ALL...
OH, I KNOW! GIGEI DID, RIGHT?!
A TOUGH GIRL LIKE HER COULD HANDLE THEM EASILY.

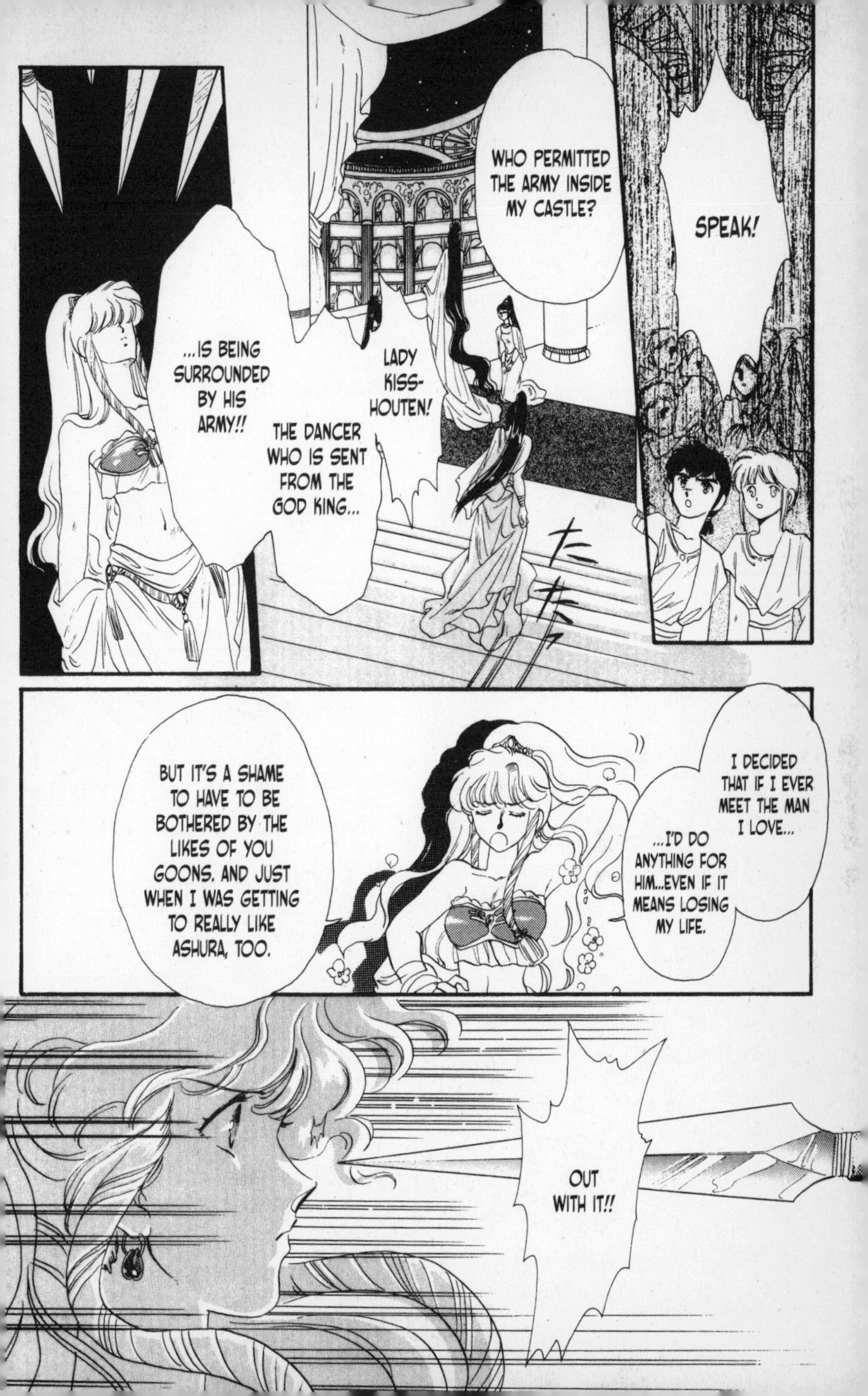
WHO PERMITTED THE ARMY INSIDE MY CASTLE?
SPEAK!
LADY KISS-HOUTEN!
THE DANCER WHO IS SENT FROM THE GOD KING...
...IS BEING SURROUNDED BY HIS ARMY!!
I DECIDED THAT IF I EVER MEET THE MAN I LOVE...
...I'D DO ANYTHING FOR HIM...EVEN IF IT MEANS LOSING MY LIFE.
BUT IT'S A SHAME TO HAVE TO BE BOTHERED BY THE LIKES OF YOU GOONS. AND JUST WHEN I WAS GETTING TO REALLY LIKE ASHURA, TOO.
OUT WITH IT!!

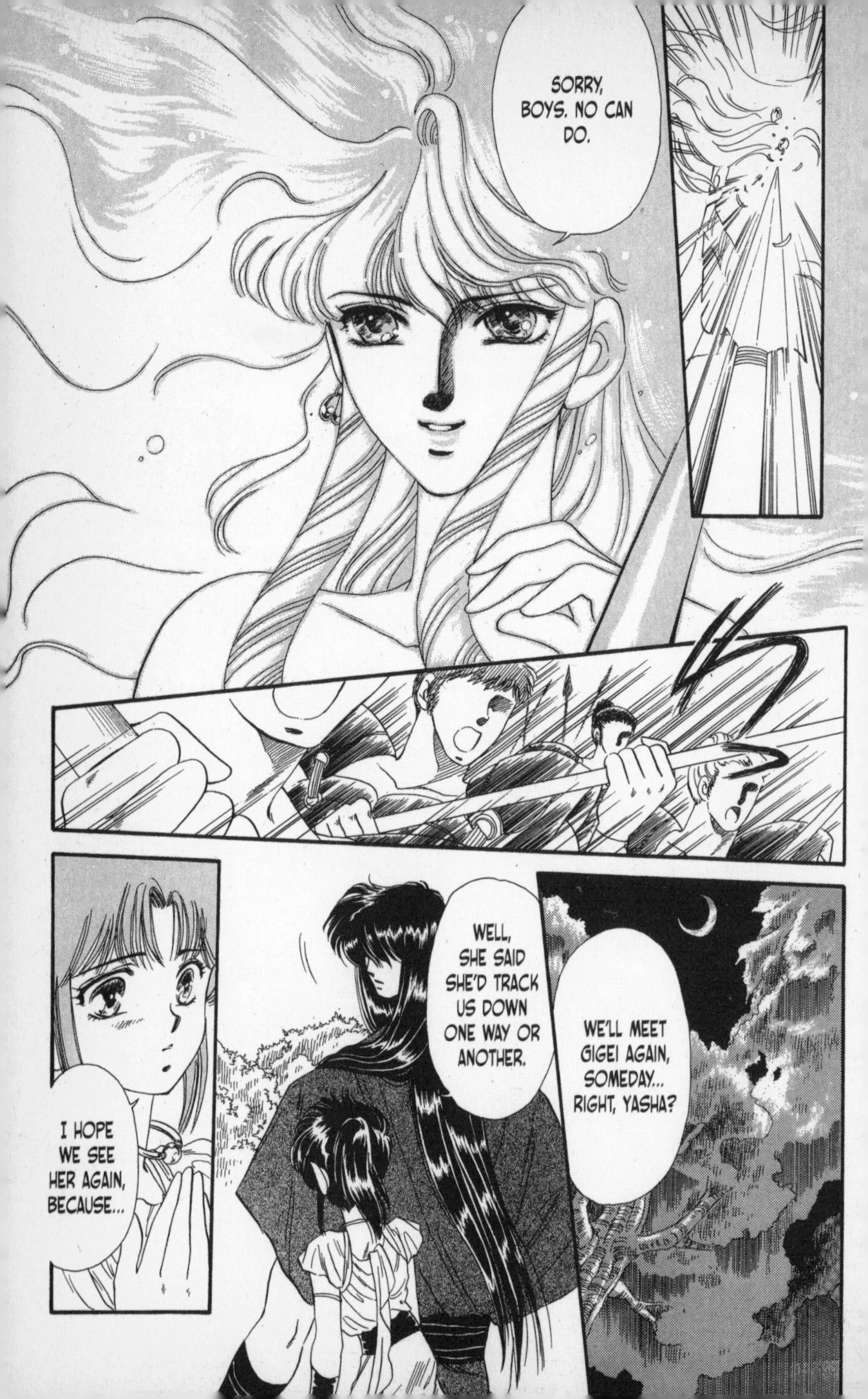
SORRY, BOYS. NO CAN DO.
WE'LL MEET GIGEI AGAIN, SOMEDAY... RIGHT, YASHA?
WELL, SHE SAID SHE'D TRACK US DOWN ONE WAY OR ANOTHER.
I HOPE WE SEE HER AGAIN, BECAUSE...

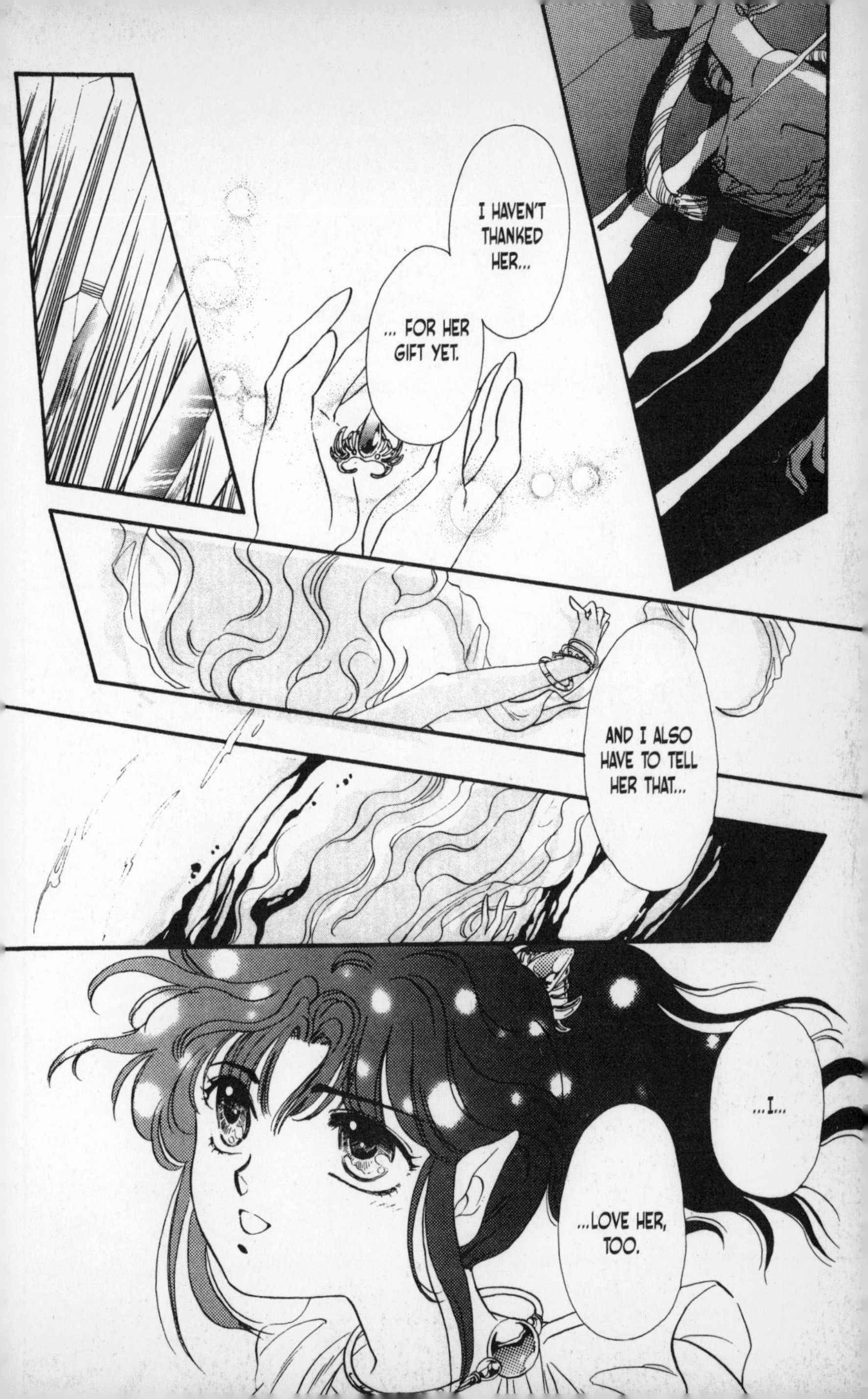
I HAVEN'T THANKED HER...
... FOR HER GIFT YET.
AND I ALSO HAVE TO TELL HER THAT...
...I...
...LOVE HER, TOO.

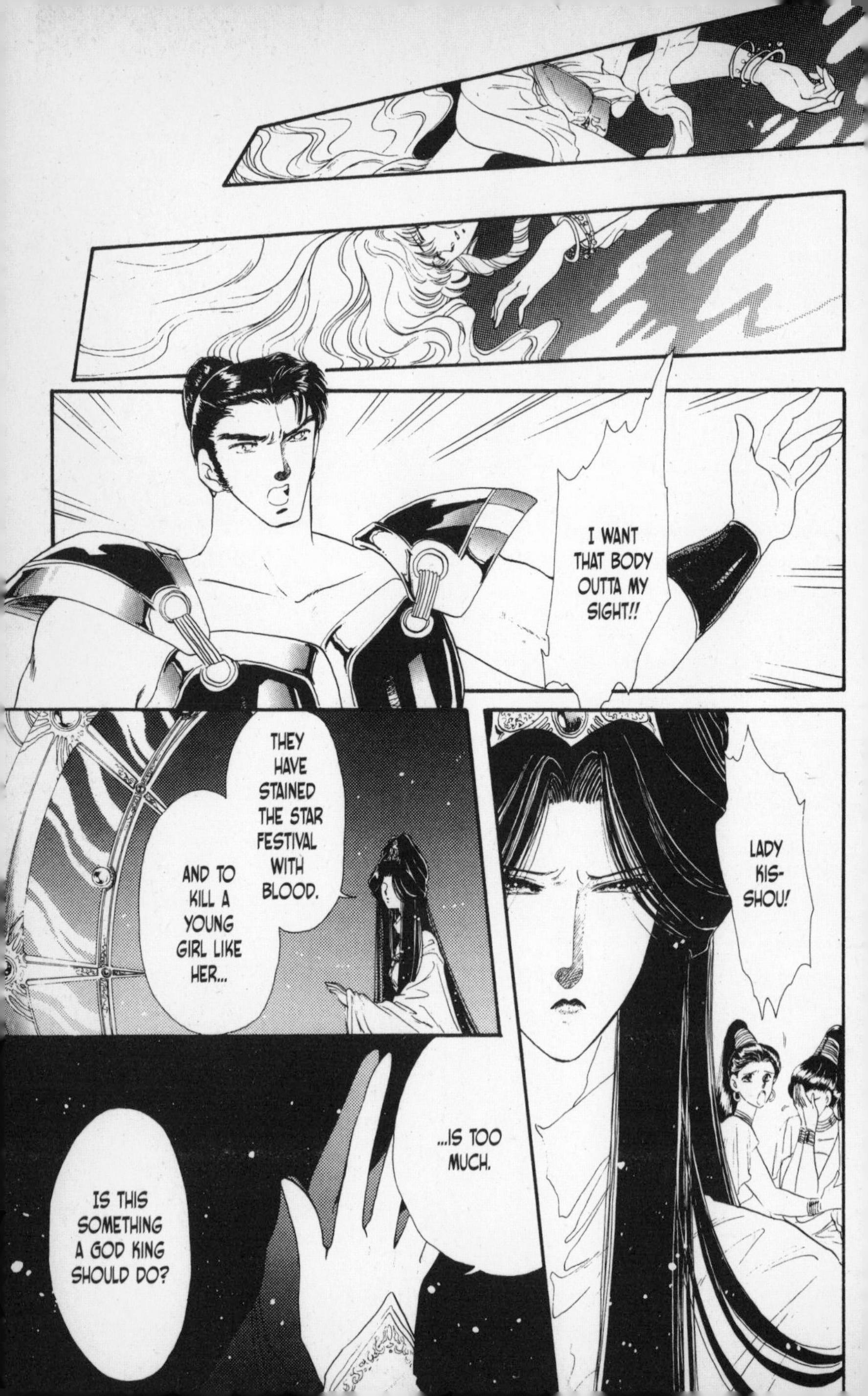
I WANT THAT BODY OUTTA MY SIGHT!!
LADY KIS-SHOU!
THEY HAVE STAINED THE STAR FESTIVAL WITH BLOOD.
AND TO KILL A YOUNG GIRL LIKE HER...
...IS TOO MUCH.
IS THIS SOMETHING A GOD KING SHOULD DO?

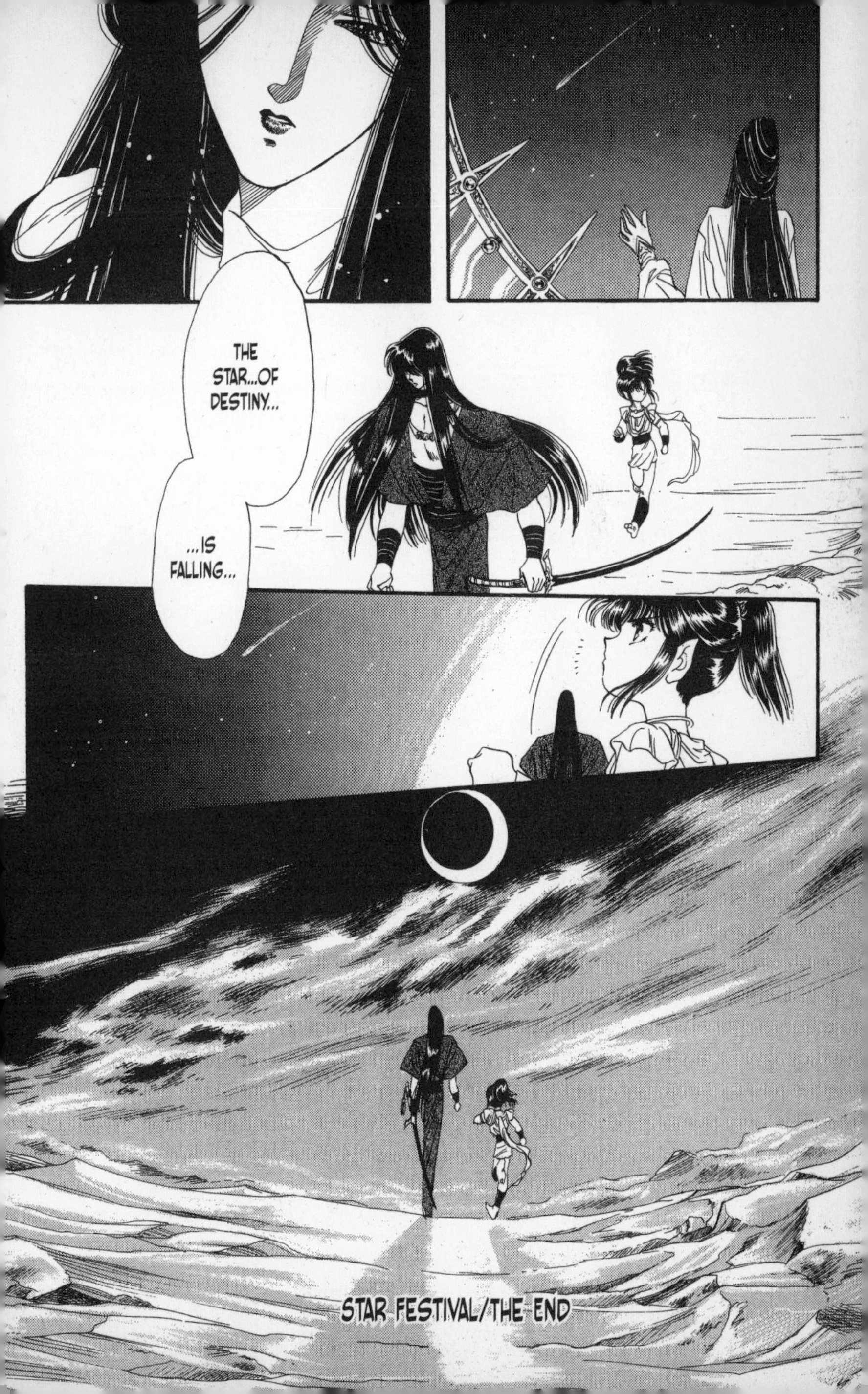
THE STAR...OF DESTINY...
...IS FALLING...
STAR FESTIVAL/THE END

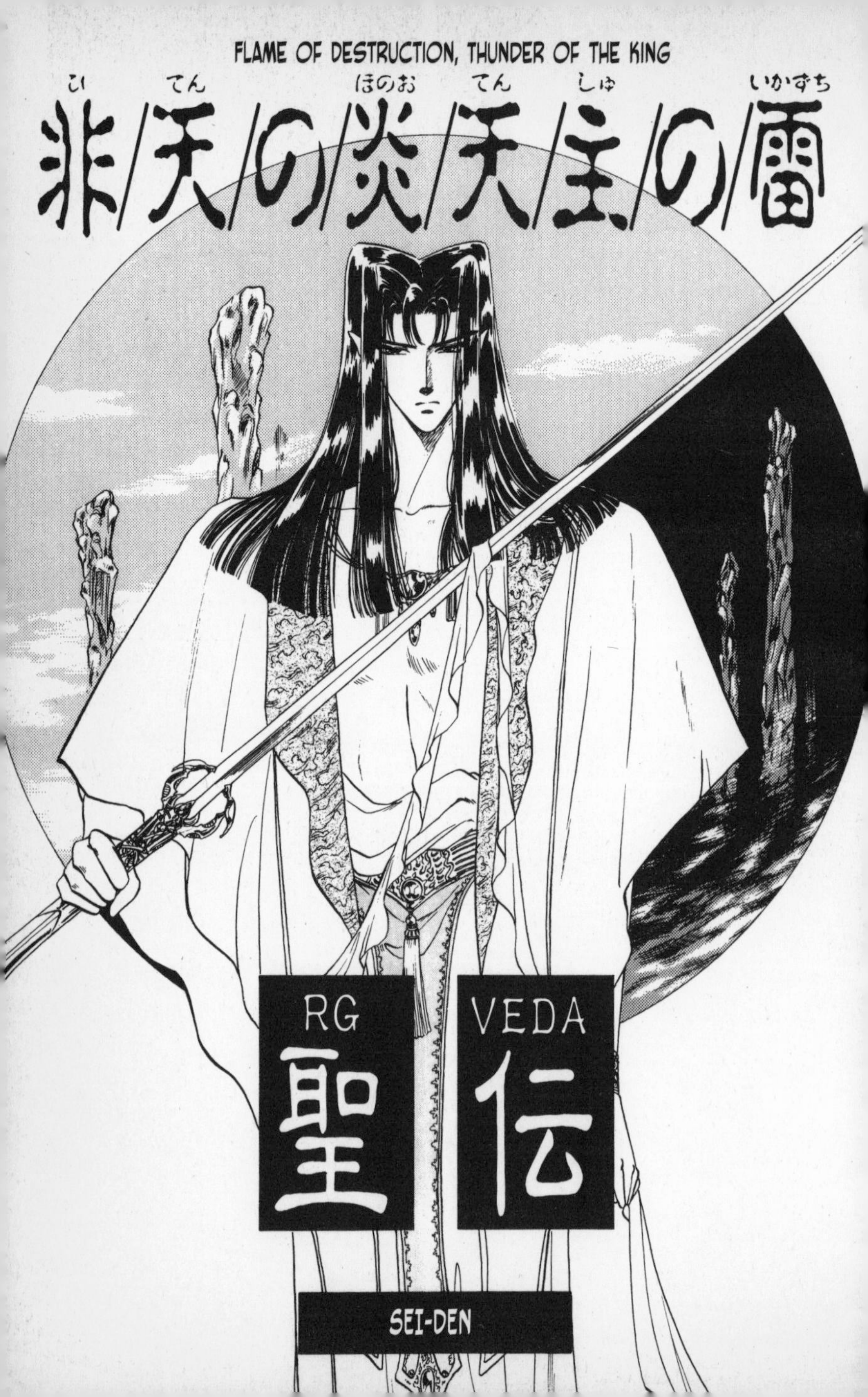
FLAME OF DESTRUCTION, THUNDER OF THE KING
非天の炎天主の雷
こてん ほのお てんしゅ いかずち
RG VEDA
聖伝
SEI-DEN

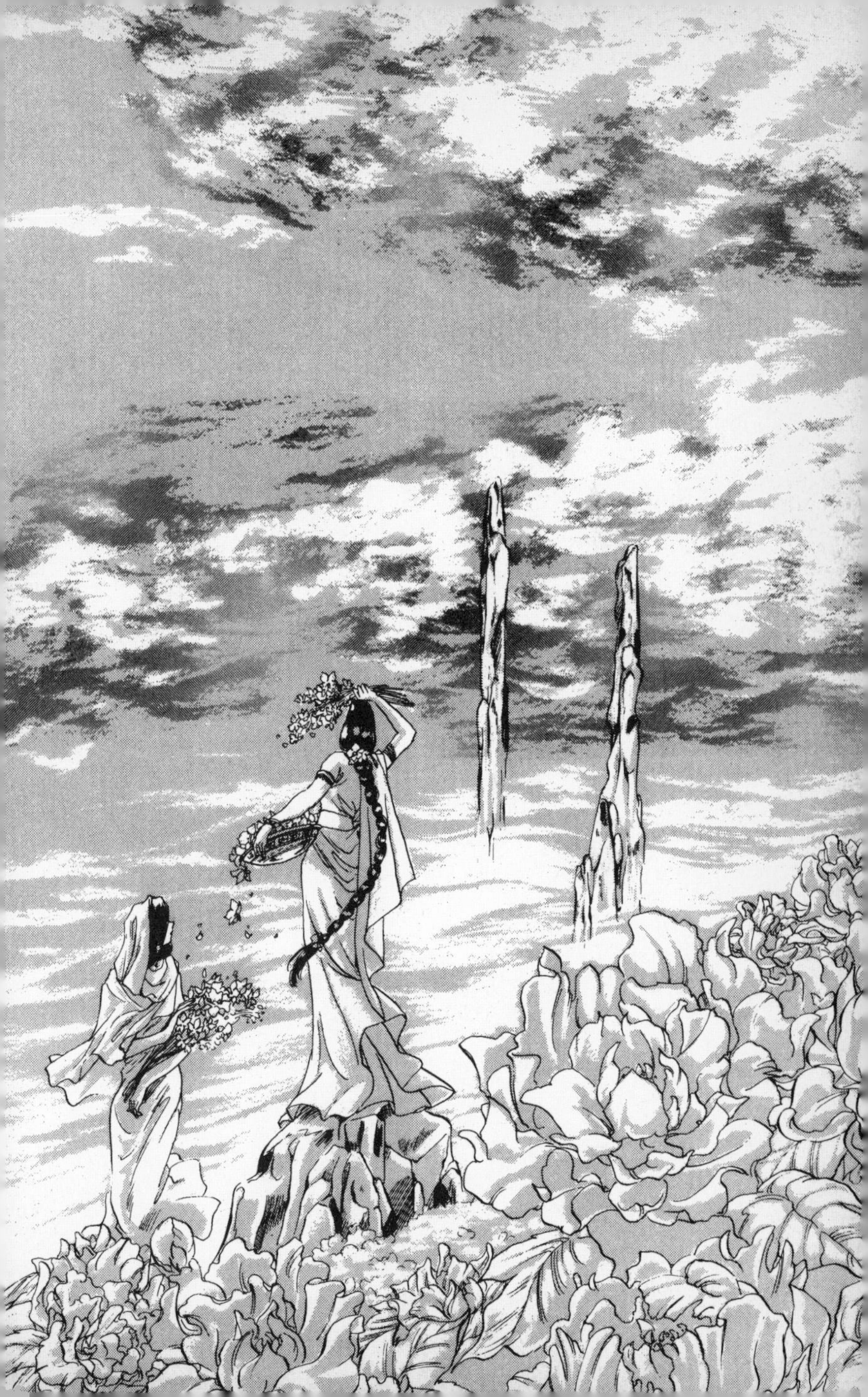

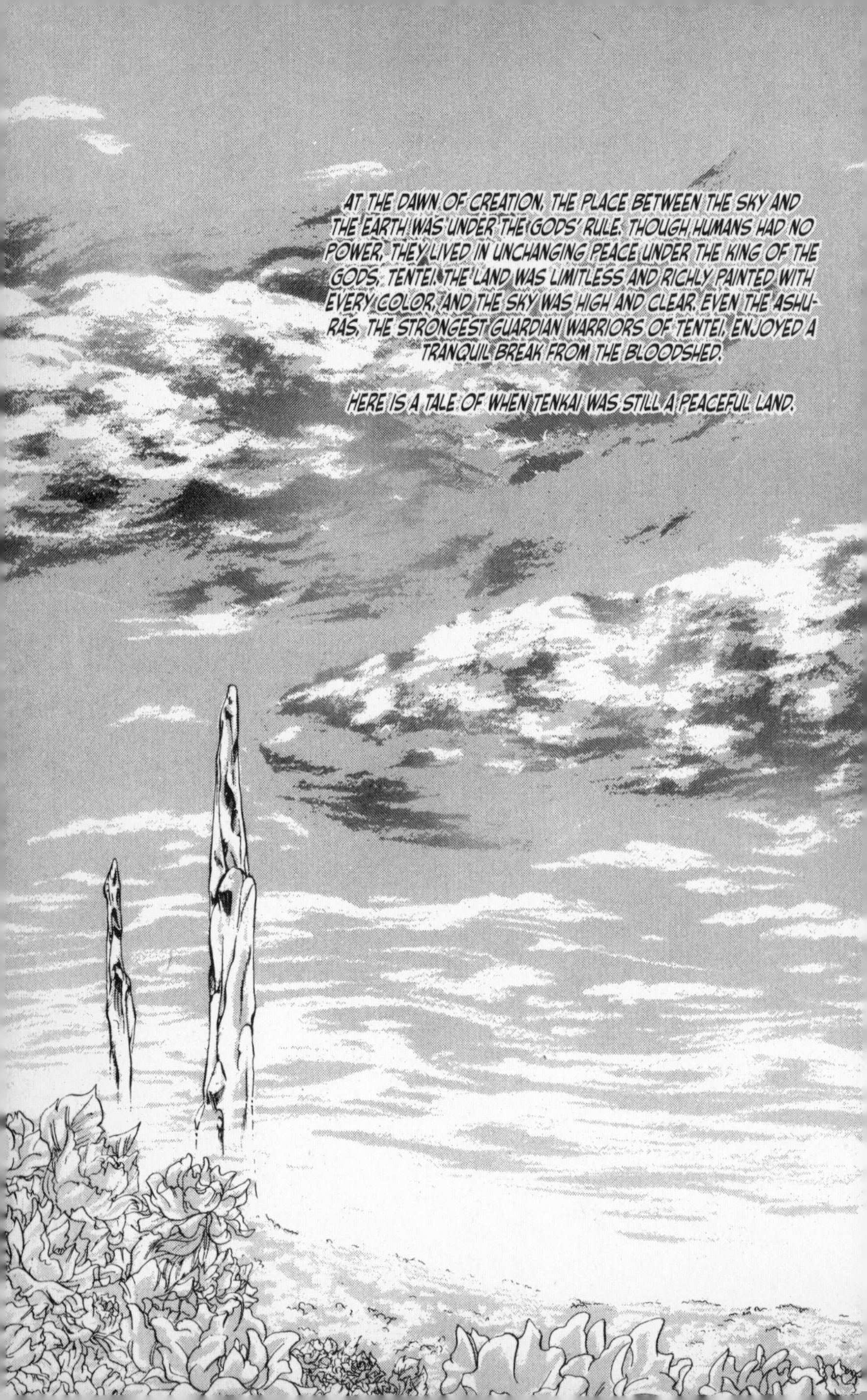
AT THE DAWN OF CREATION, THE PLACE BETWEEN THE SKY AND THE EARTH WAS UNDER THE GODS' RULE. THOUGH HUMANS HAD NO POWER, THEY LIVED IN UNCHANGING PEACE UNDER THE KING OF THE GODS, TENTEI. THE LAND WAS LIMITLESS AND RICHLY PAINTED WITH EVERY COLOR, AND THE SKY WAS HIGH AND CLEAR. EVEN THE ASHURAS, THE STRONGEST GUARDIAN WARRIORS OF TENTEI, ENJOYED A TRANQUIL BREAK FROM THE BLOODSHED.
HERE IS A TALE OF WHEN TENKAI WAS STILL A PEACEFUL LAND.

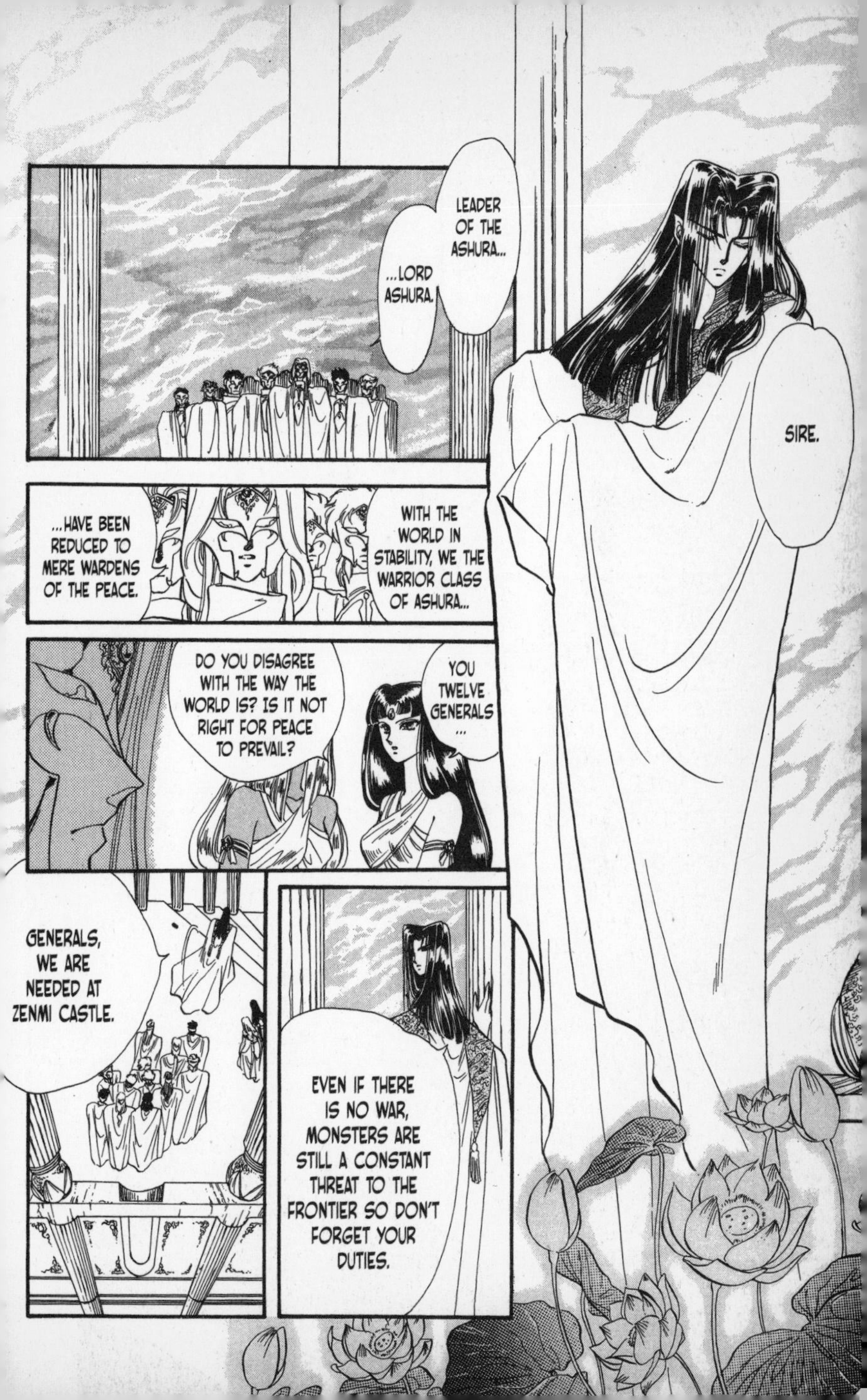
LEADER OF THE ASHURA...
...LORD ASHURA.
SIRE.
WITH THE WORLD IN STABILITY, WE THE WARRIOR CLASS OF ASHURA...
...HAVE BEEN REDUCED TO MERE WARDENS OF THE PEACE.
YOU TWELVE GENERALS ...
DO YOU DISAGREE WITH THE WAY THE WORLD IS? IS IT NOT RIGHT FOR PEACE TO PREVAIL?
EVEN IF THERE IS NO WAR, MONSTERS ARE STILL A CONSTANT THREAT TO THE FRONTIER SO DON'T FORGET YOUR DUTIES.
GENERALS, WE ARE NEEDED AT ZENMI CASTLE.

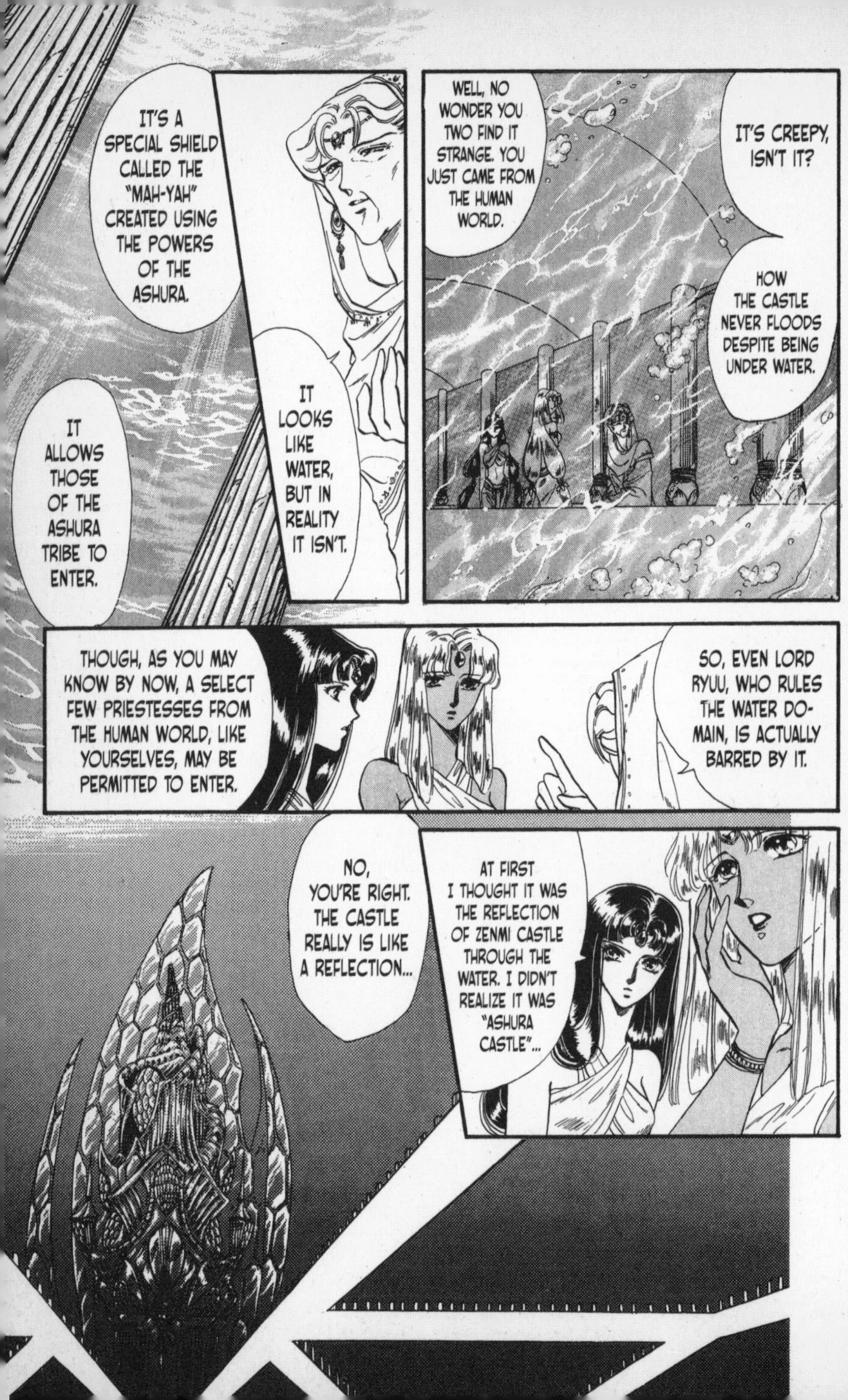
IT'S CREEPY, ISN'T IT?
HOW THE CASTLE NEVER FLOODS DESPITE BEING UNDER WATER.
WELL, NO WONDER YOU TWO FIND IT STRANGE. YOU JUST CAME FROM THE HUMAN WORLD.
IT'S A SPECIAL SHIELD CALLED THE "MAH-YAH" CREATED USING THE POWERS OF THE ASHURA.
IT LOOKS LIKE WATER, BUT IN REALITY IT ISN'T.
IT ALLOWS THOSE OF THE ASHURA TRIBE TO ENTER.
SO, EVEN LORD RYUU, WHO RULES THE WATER DO-MAIN, IS ACTUALLY BARRED BY IT.
THOUGH, AS YOU MAY KNOW BY NOW, A SELECT FEW PRIESTESSES FROM THE HUMAN WORLD, LIKE YOURSELVES, MAY BE PERMITTED TO ENTER.
AT FIRST I THOUGHT IT WAS THE REFLECTION OF ZENMI CASTLE THROUGH THE WATER. I DIDN'T REALIZE IT WAS "ASHURA CASTLE"...
NO, YOU'RE RIGHT. THE CASTLE REALLY IS LIKE A REFLECTION...

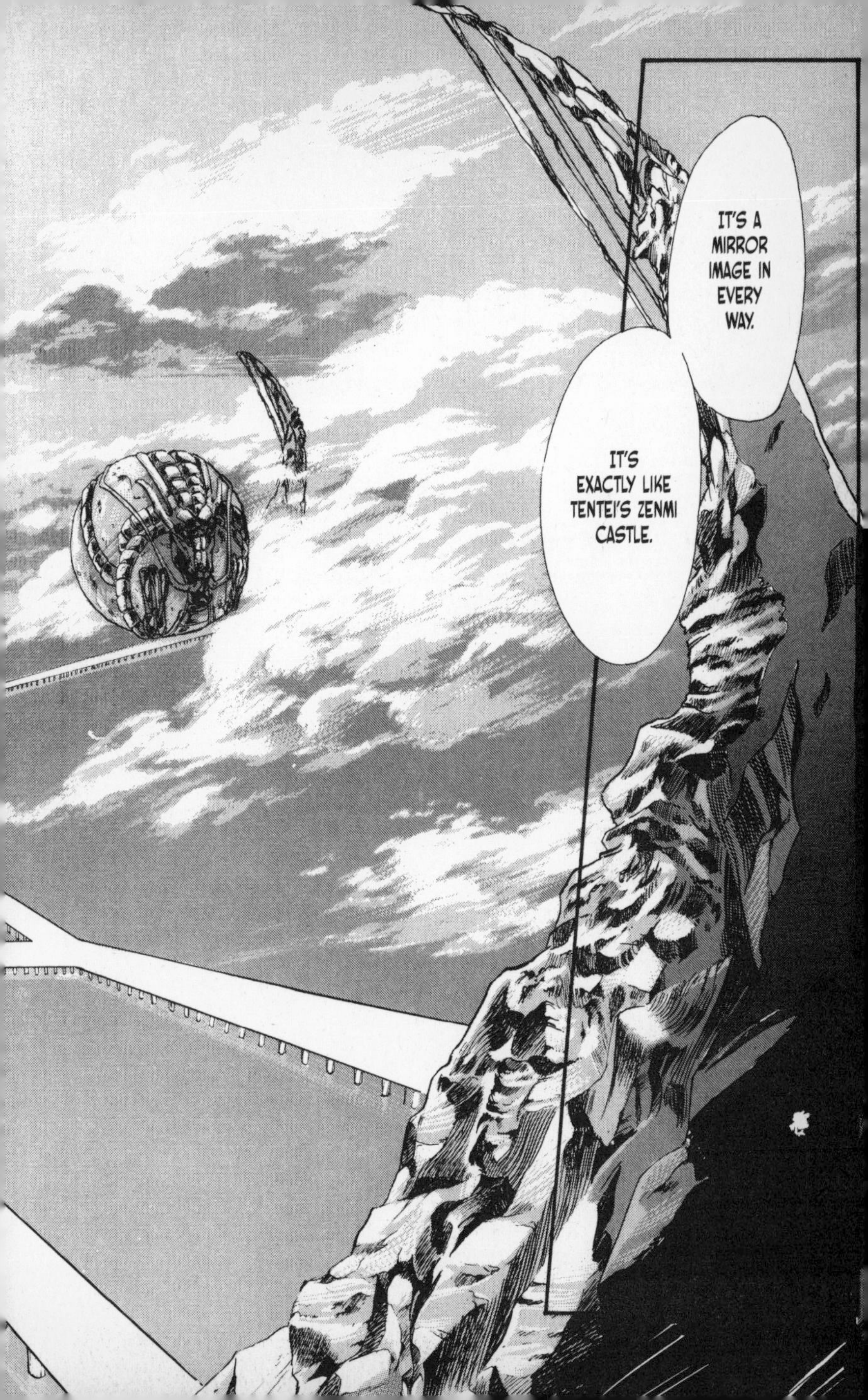
IT'S A MIRROR IMAGE IN EVERY WAY.
IT'S EXACTLY LIKE TENTEI'S ZENMI CASTLE.

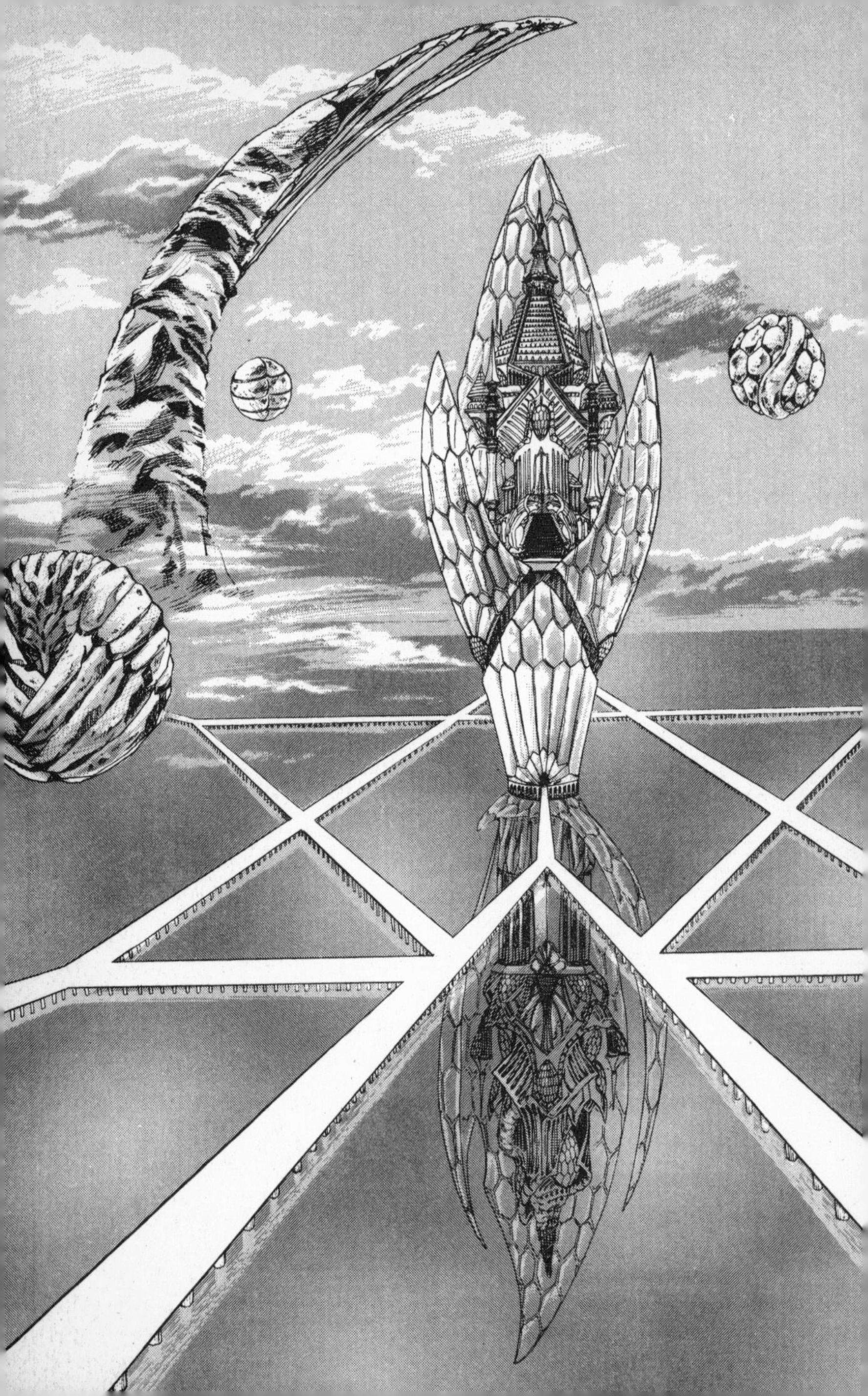

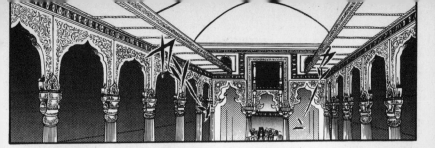

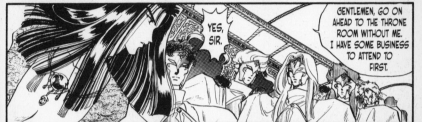

YES, SIR.

GENTLEMEN, GO ON AHEAD TO THE THRONE ROOM WITHOUT ME. I HAVE SOME BUSINESS TO ATTEND TO FIRST.

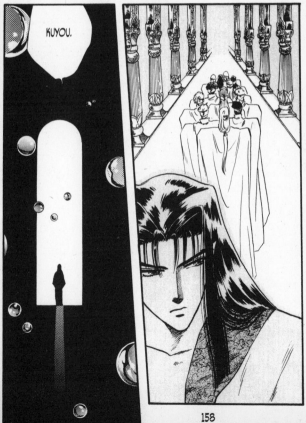

KUYOU.

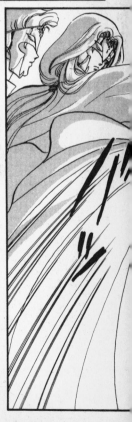

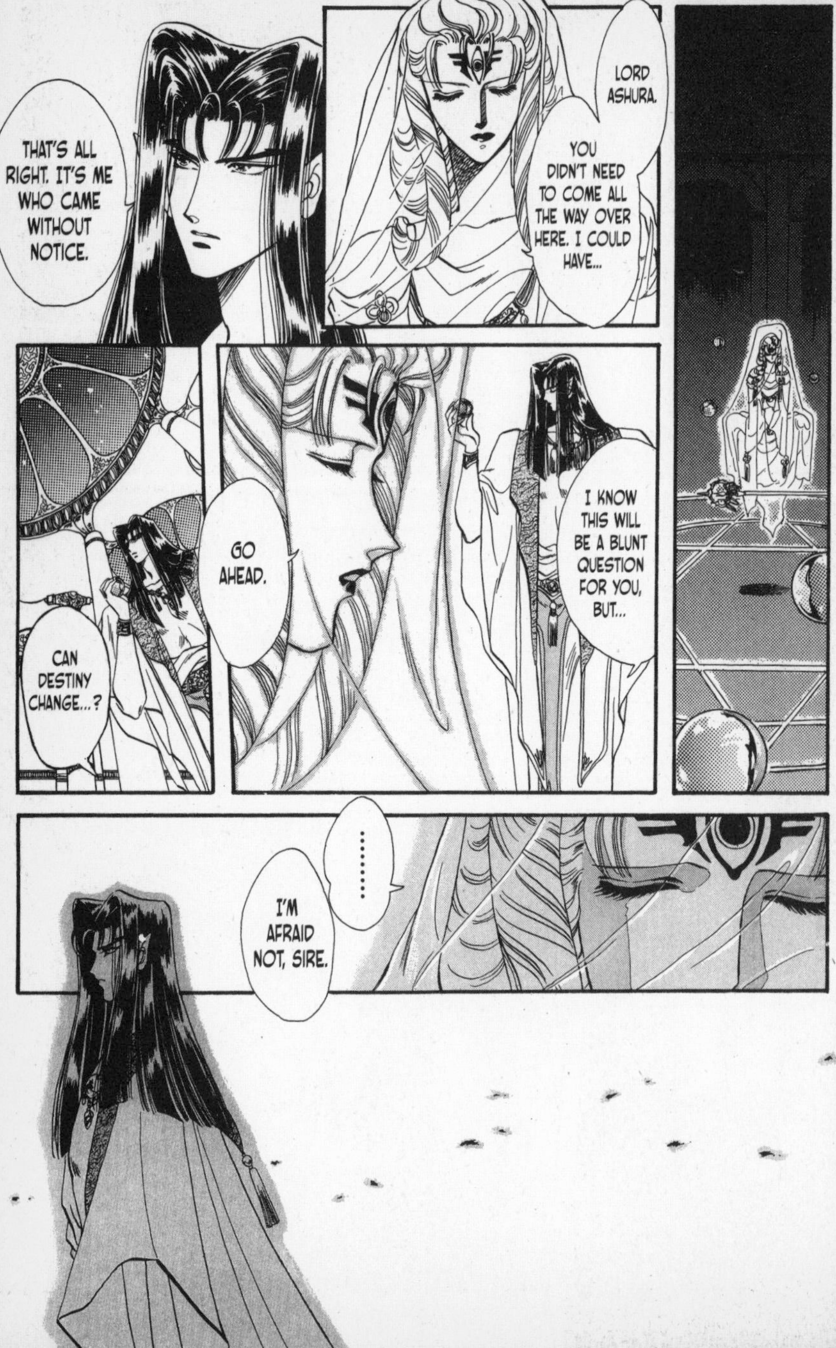
LORD ASHURA.
YOU DIDN'T NEED TO COME ALL THE WAY OVER HERE. I COULD HAVE...
THAT'S ALL RIGHT. IT'S ME WHO CAME WITHOUT NOTICE.
I KNOW THIS WILL BE A BLUNT QUESTION FOR YOU, BUT...
GO AHEAD.
CAN DESTINY CHANGE...?
....
I'M AFRAID NOT, SIRE.

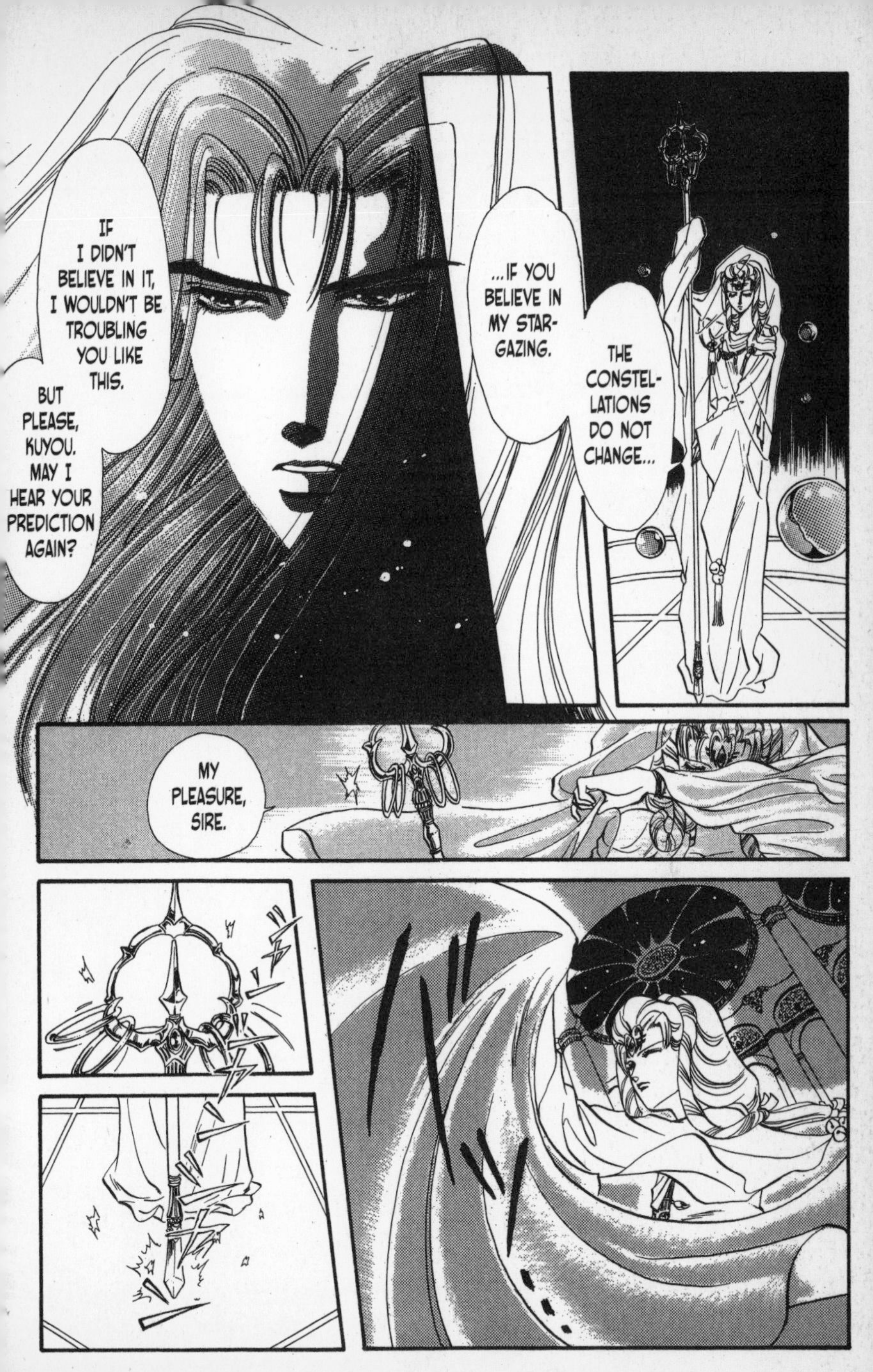
THE CONSTEL-LATIONS DO NOT CHANGE...
...IF YOU BELIEVE IN MY STAR-GAZING.
IF I DIDN'T BELIEVE IN IT, I WOULDN'T BE TROUBLING YOU LIKE THIS.
BUT PLEASE, KUYOU. MAY I HEAR YOUR PREDICTION AGAIN?
MY PLEASURE, SIRE.

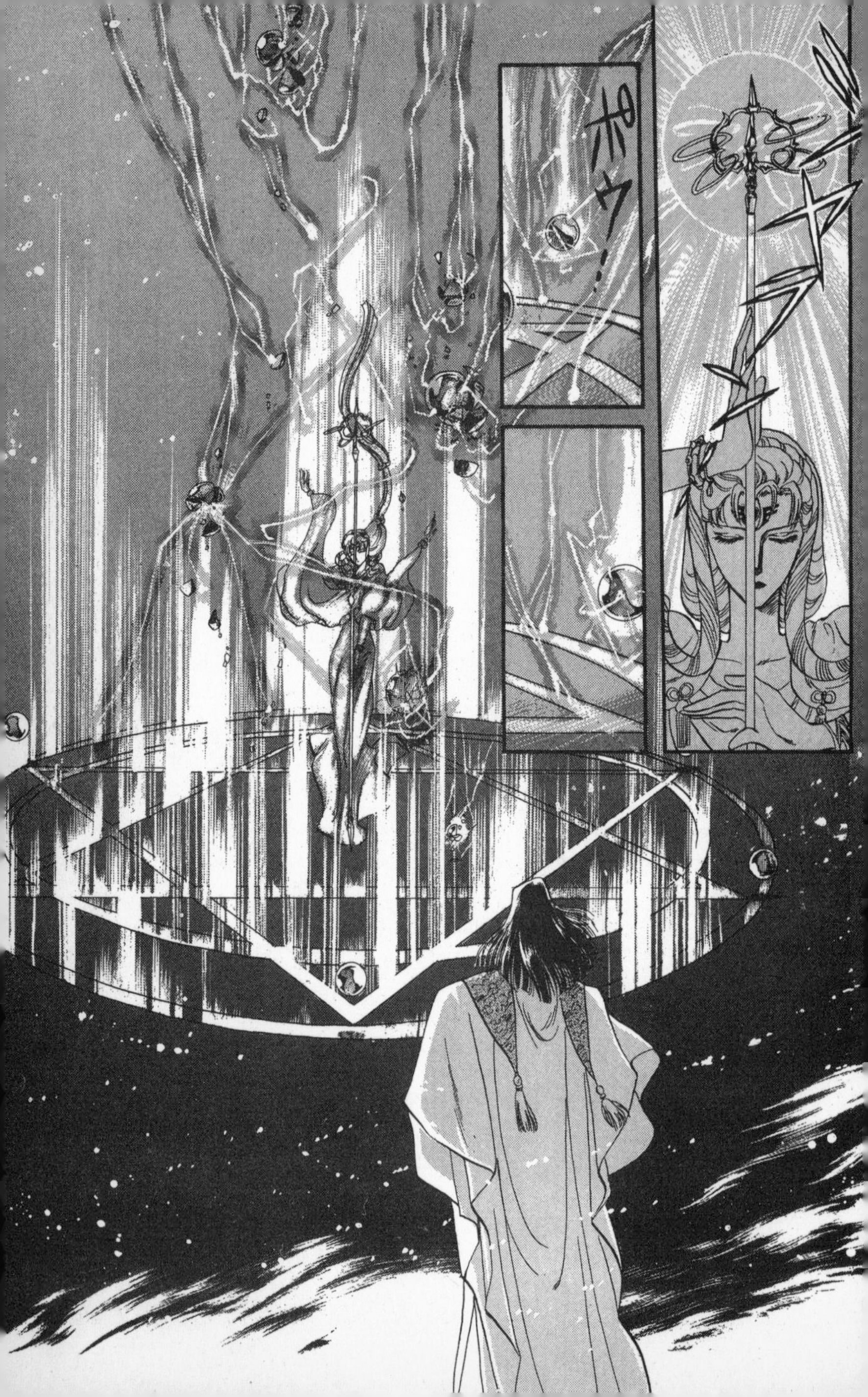
シャラン
ポウ…

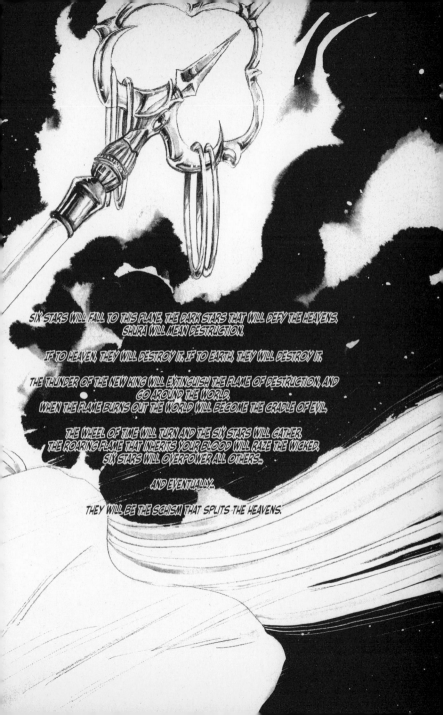

SIX STARS WILL FALL TO THIS PLANE, THE DARK STARS THAT WILL DEFY THE HEAVENS.
SHURA WILL MEAN DESTRUCTION.

IF TO HEAVEN, THEY WILL DESTROY IT, IF TO EARTH, THEY WILL DESTROY IT.

THE THUNDER OF THE NEW KING WILL EXTINGUISH THE FLAME OF DESTRUCTION, AND
GO AROUND THE WORLD.
WHEN THE FLAME BURNS OUT THE WORLD WILL BECOME THE CRADLE OF EVIL.

THE WHEEL OF TIME WILL TURN AND THE SIX STARS WILL GATHER.
THE ROARING FLAME THAT INHERITS YOUR BLOOD WILL RAZE THE WICKED.
SIX STARS WILL OVERPOWER ALL OTHERS...

AND EVENTUALLY...

THEY WILL BE THE SCHISM THAT SPLITS THE HEAVENS.

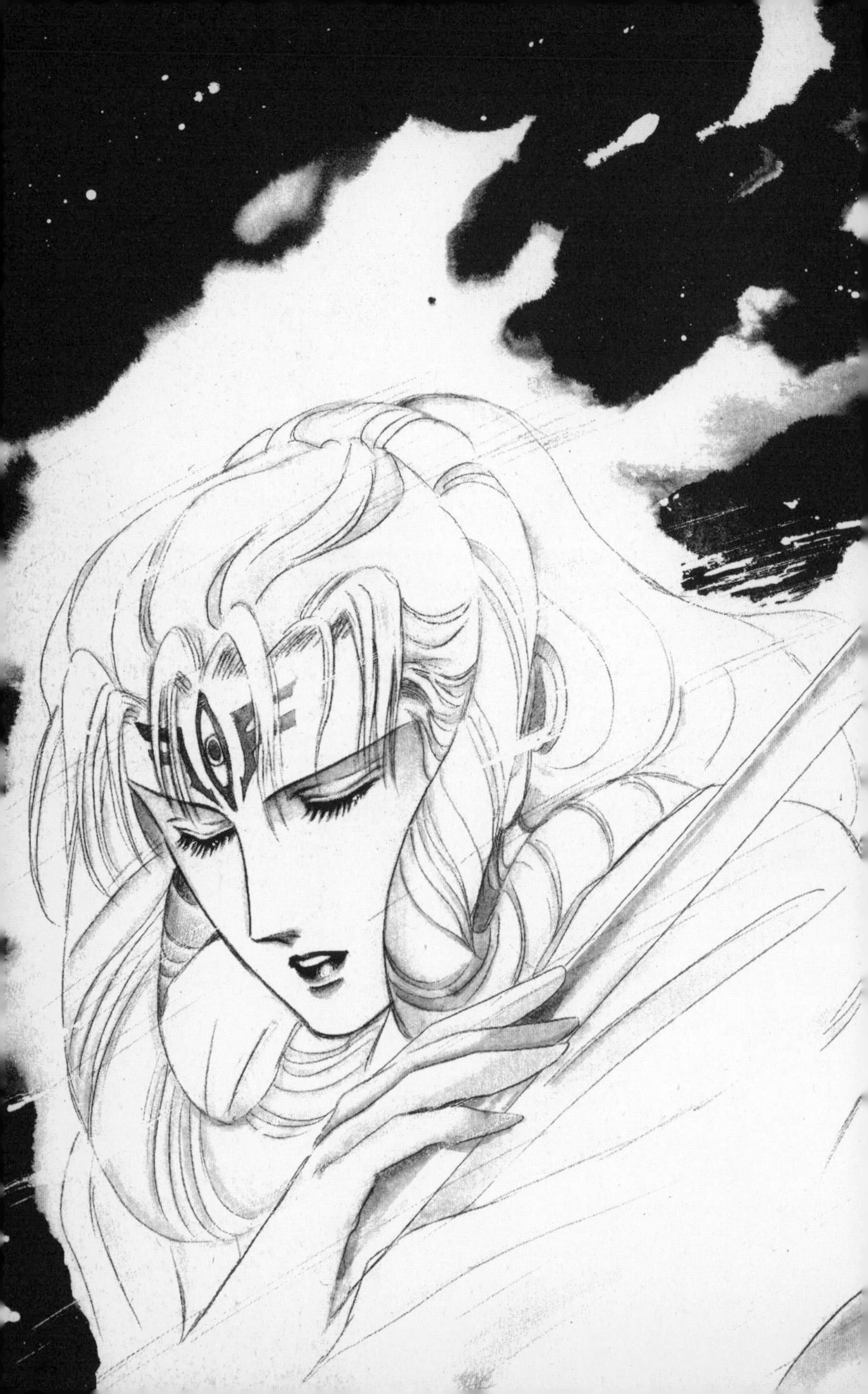

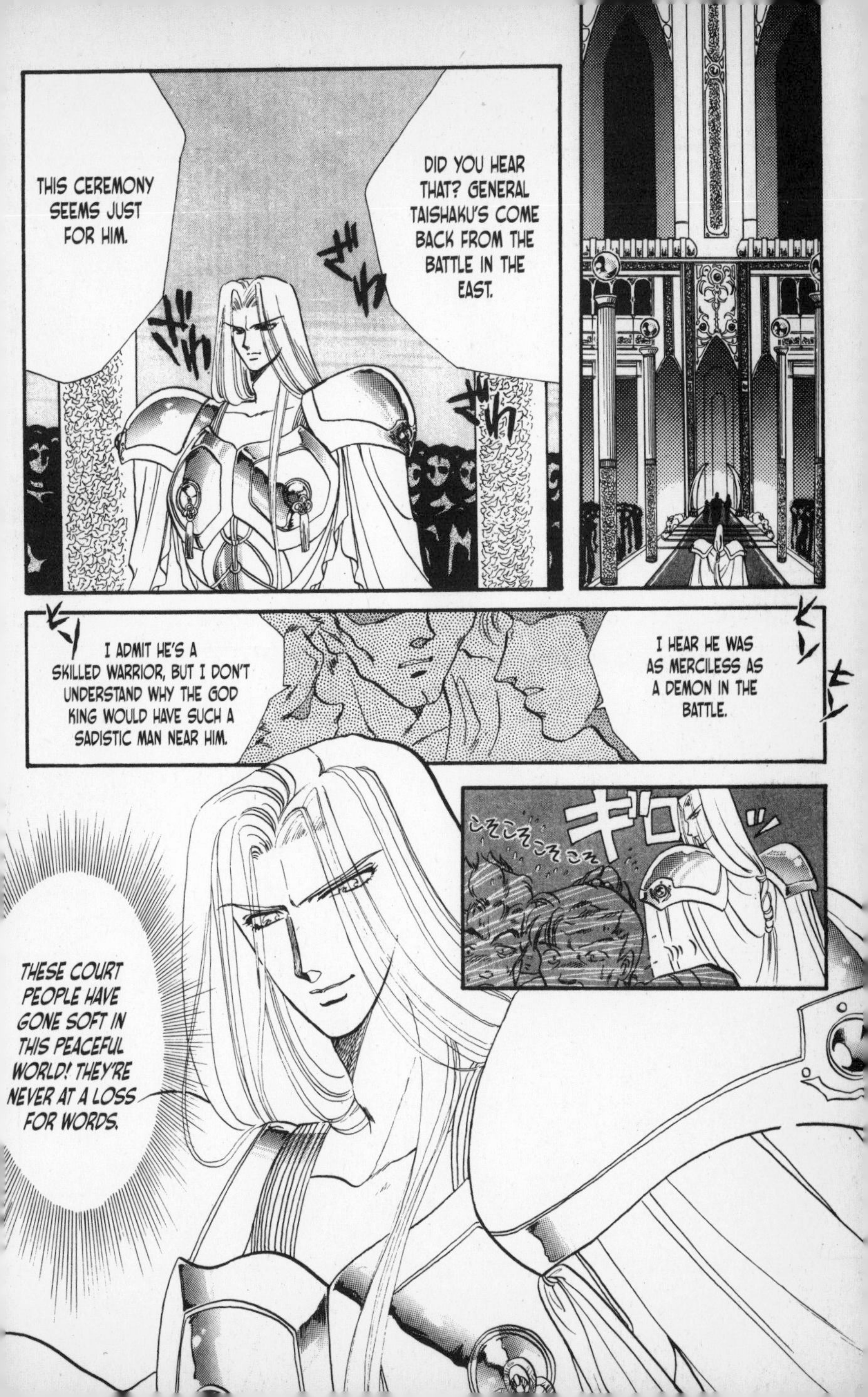
DID YOU HEAR THAT? GENERAL TAISHAKU'S COME BACK FROM THE BATTLE IN THE EAST.
ざわ
ざわ
ざわ
THIS CEREMONY SEEMS JUST FOR HIM.
I HEAR HE WAS AS MERCILESS AS A DEMON IN THE BATTLE.
I ADMIT HE'S A SKILLED WARRIOR, BUT I DON'T UNDERSTAND WHY THE GOD KING WOULD HAVE SUCH A SADISTIC MAN NEAR HIM.
ギロッ
こそこそこそこそ
THESE COURT PEOPLE HAVE GONE SOFT IN THIS PEACEFUL WORLD! THEY'RE NEVER AT A LOSS FOR WORDS.

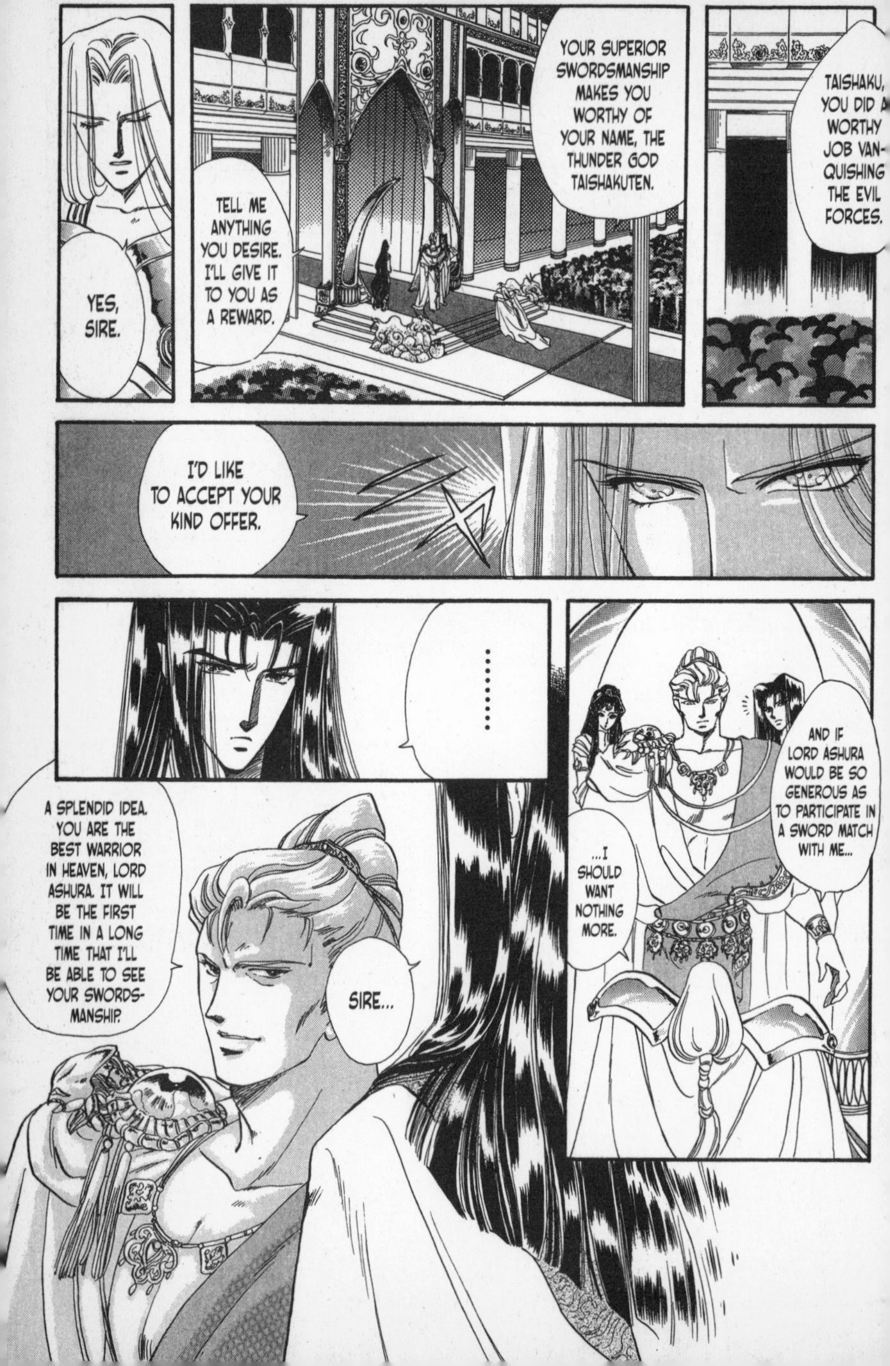
TAISHAKU, YOU DID A WORTHY JOB VANQUISHING THE EVIL FORCES.
YOUR SUPERIOR SWORDSMANSHIP MAKES YOU WORTHY OF YOUR NAME, THE THUNDER GOD TAISHAKUTEN.
TELL ME ANYTHING YOU DESIRE. I'LL GIVE IT TO YOU AS A REWARD.
YES, SIRE.
I'D LIKE TO ACCEPT YOUR KIND OFFER.
AND IF LORD ASHURA WOULD BE SO GENEROUS AS TO PARTICIPATE IN A SWORD MATCH WITH ME...
...I SHOULD WANT NOTHING MORE.
......
A SPLENDID IDEA. YOU ARE THE BEST WARRIOR IN HEAVEN, LORD ASHURA. IT WILL BE THE FIRST TIME IN A LONG TIME THAT I'LL BE ABLE TO SEE YOUR SWORDSMANSHIP.
SIRE...

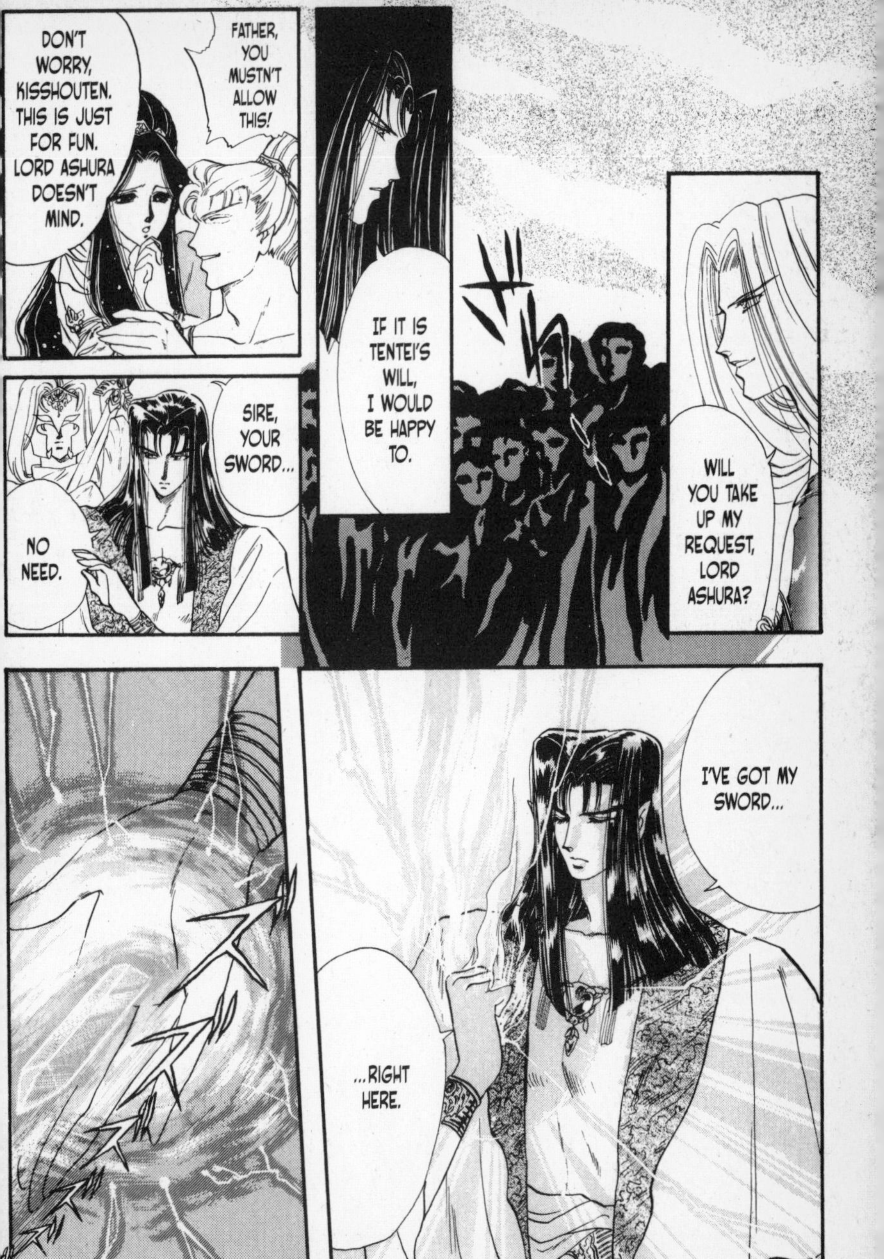
WILL YOU TAKE UP MY REQUEST, LORD ASHURA?
IF IT IS TENTEI'S WILL, I WOULD BE HAPPY TO.
FATHER, YOU MUSTN'T ALLOW THIS!
DON'T WORRY, KISSHOUTEN. THIS IS JUST FOR FUN. LORD ASHURA DOESN'T MIND.
SIRE, YOUR SWORD...
NO NEED.
I'VE GOT MY SWORD...
...RIGHT HERE.

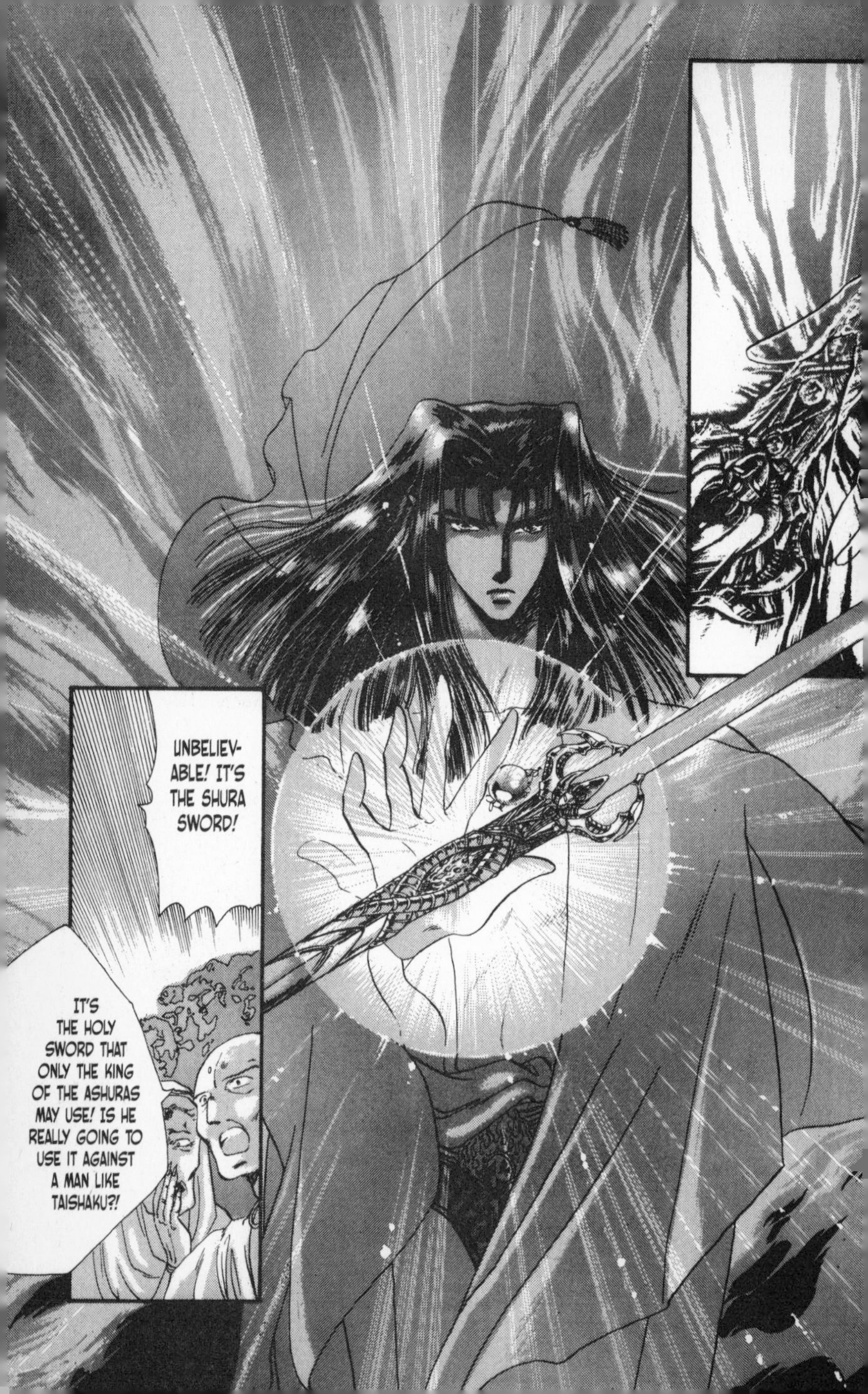
UNBELIEV-ABLE! IT'S THE SHURA SWORD!
IT'S THE HOLY SWORD THAT ONLY THE KING OF THE ASHURAS MAY USE! IS HE REALLY GOING TO USE IT AGAINST A MAN LIKE TAISHAKU?!

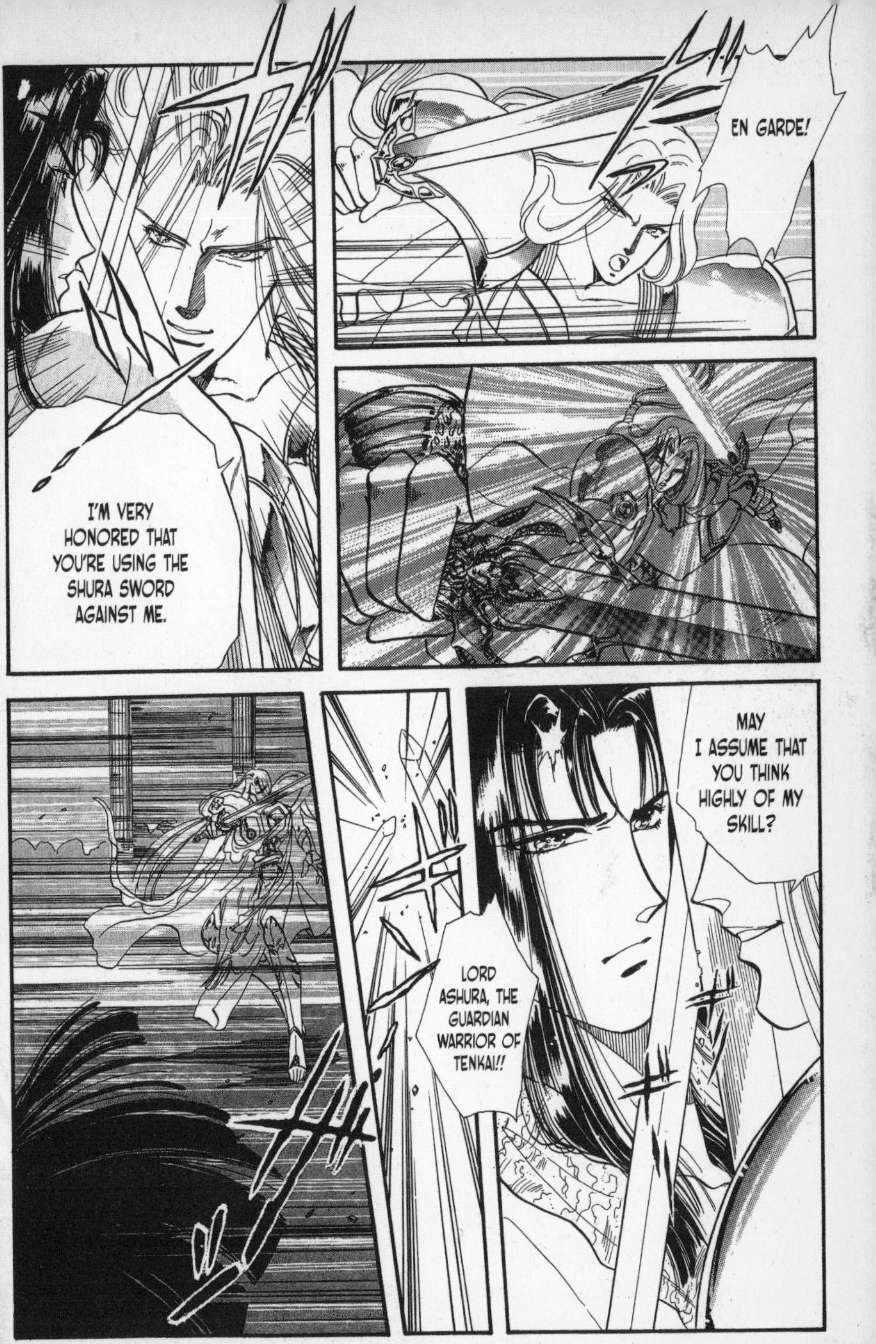
EN GARDE!
I'M VERY HONORED THAT YOU'RE USING THE SHURA SWORD AGAINST ME.
MAY I ASSUME THAT YOU THINK HIGHLY OF MY SKILL?
LORD ASHURA, THE GUARDIAN WARRIOR OF TENKAI!!

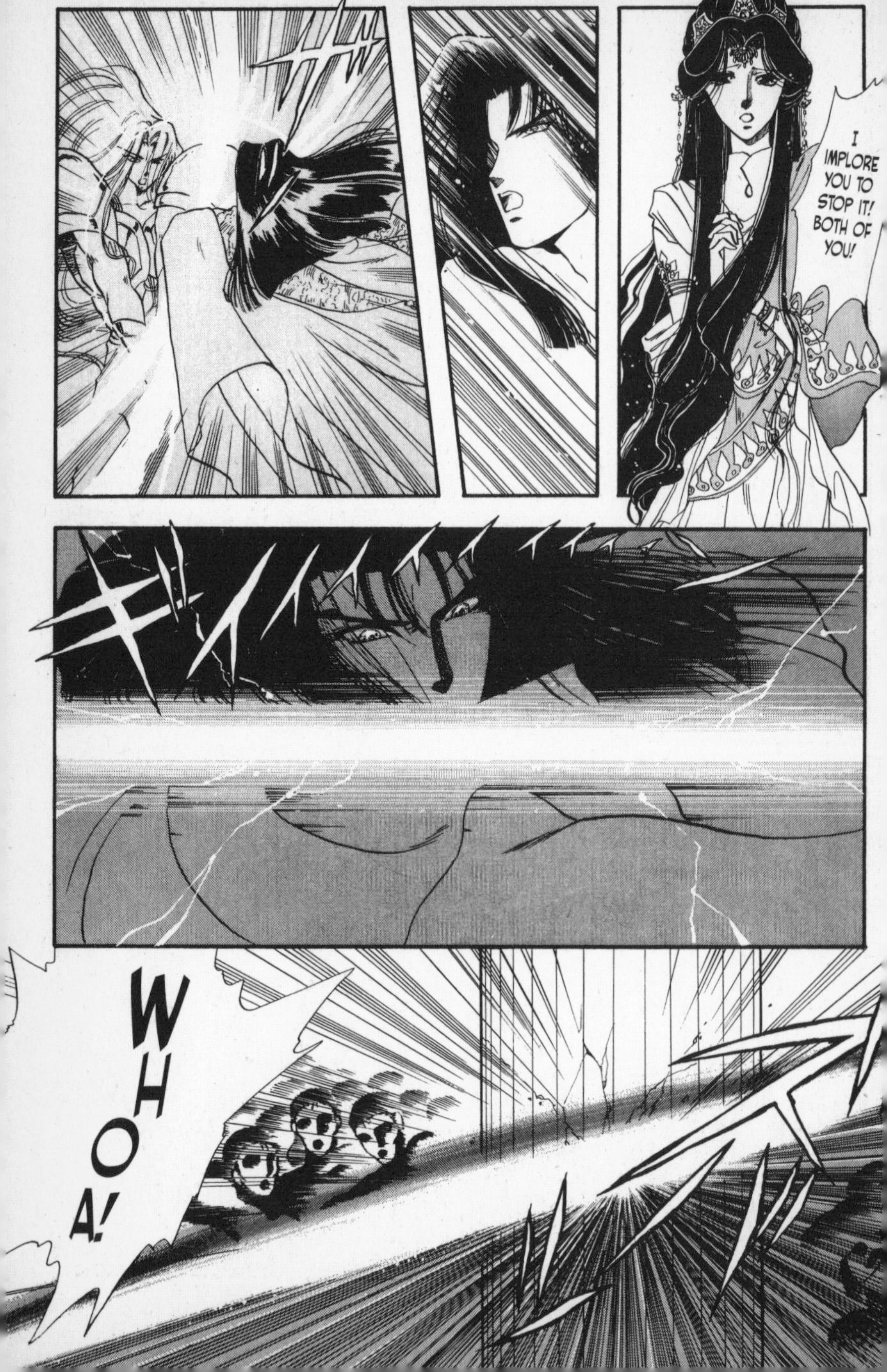
I IMPLORE YOU TO STOP IT! BOTH OF YOU!
WHOA!

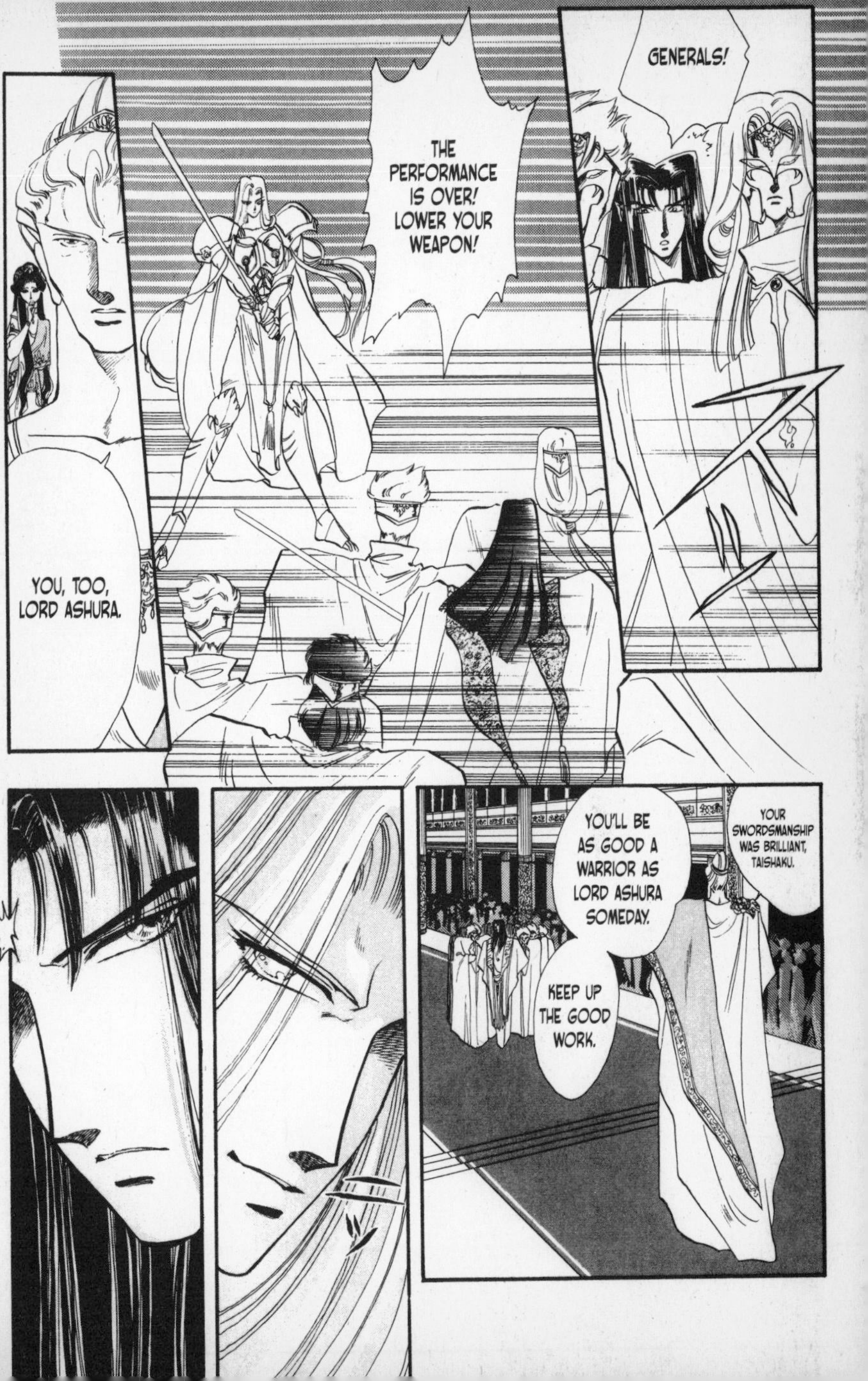
GENERALS!
THE PERFORMANCE IS OVER! LOWER YOUR WEAPON!
YOU, TOO, LORD ASHURA.
YOUR SWORDSMANSHIP WAS BRILLIANT, TAISHAKU.
YOU'LL BE AS GOOD A WARRIOR AS LORD ASHURA SOMEDAY.
KEEP UP THE GOOD WORK.

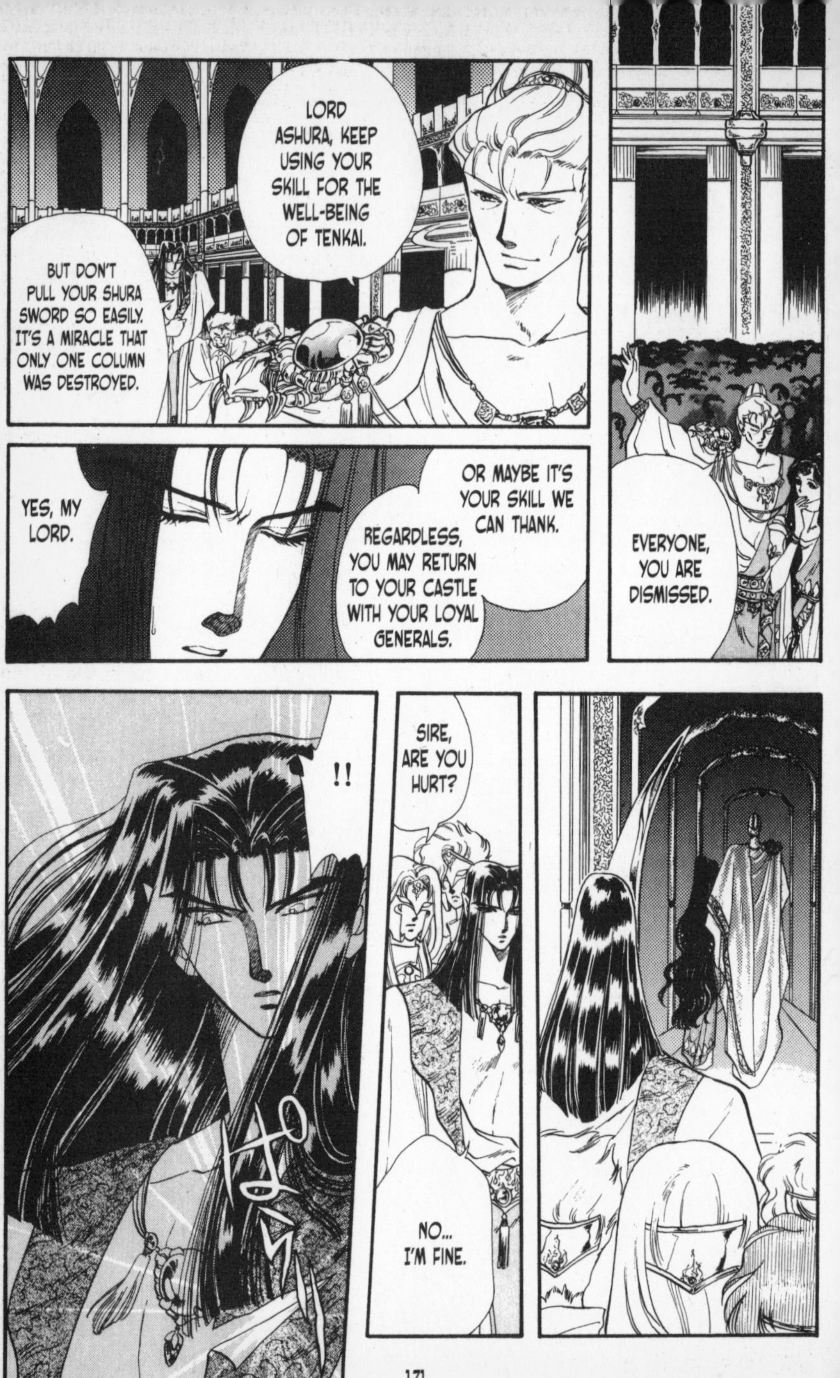

EVERYONE, YOU ARE DISMISSED.
LORD ASHURA, KEEP USING YOUR SKILL FOR THE WELL-BEING OF TENKAI.
BUT DON'T PULL YOUR SHURA SWORD SO EASILY. IT'S A MIRACLE THAT ONLY ONE COLUMN WAS DESTROYED.
OR MAYBE IT'S YOUR SKILL WE CAN THANK.
REGARDLESS, YOU MAY RETURN TO YOUR CASTLE WITH YOUR LOYAL GENERALS.
YES, MY LORD.
SIRE, ARE YOU HURT?
NO... I'M FINE.
!!

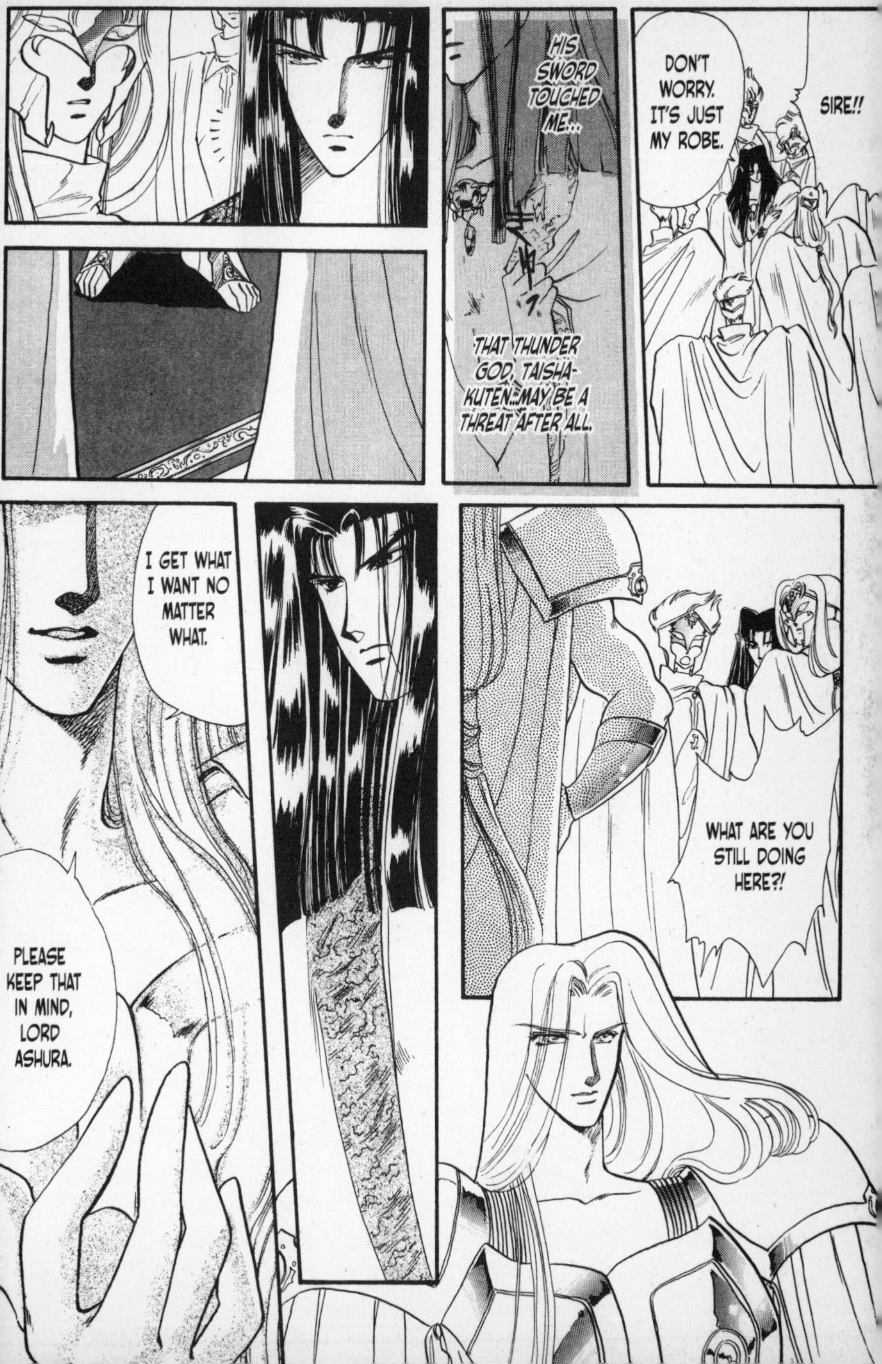
SIRE!!
DON'T WORRY. IT'S JUST MY ROBE.
HIS SWORD TOUCHED ME...
THAT THUNDER GOD, TAISHA-KUTEN... MAY BE A THREAT AFTER ALL.
WHAT ARE YOU STILL DOING HERE?!
I GET WHAT I WANT NO MATTER WHAT.
PLEASE KEEP THAT IN MIND, LORD ASHURA.

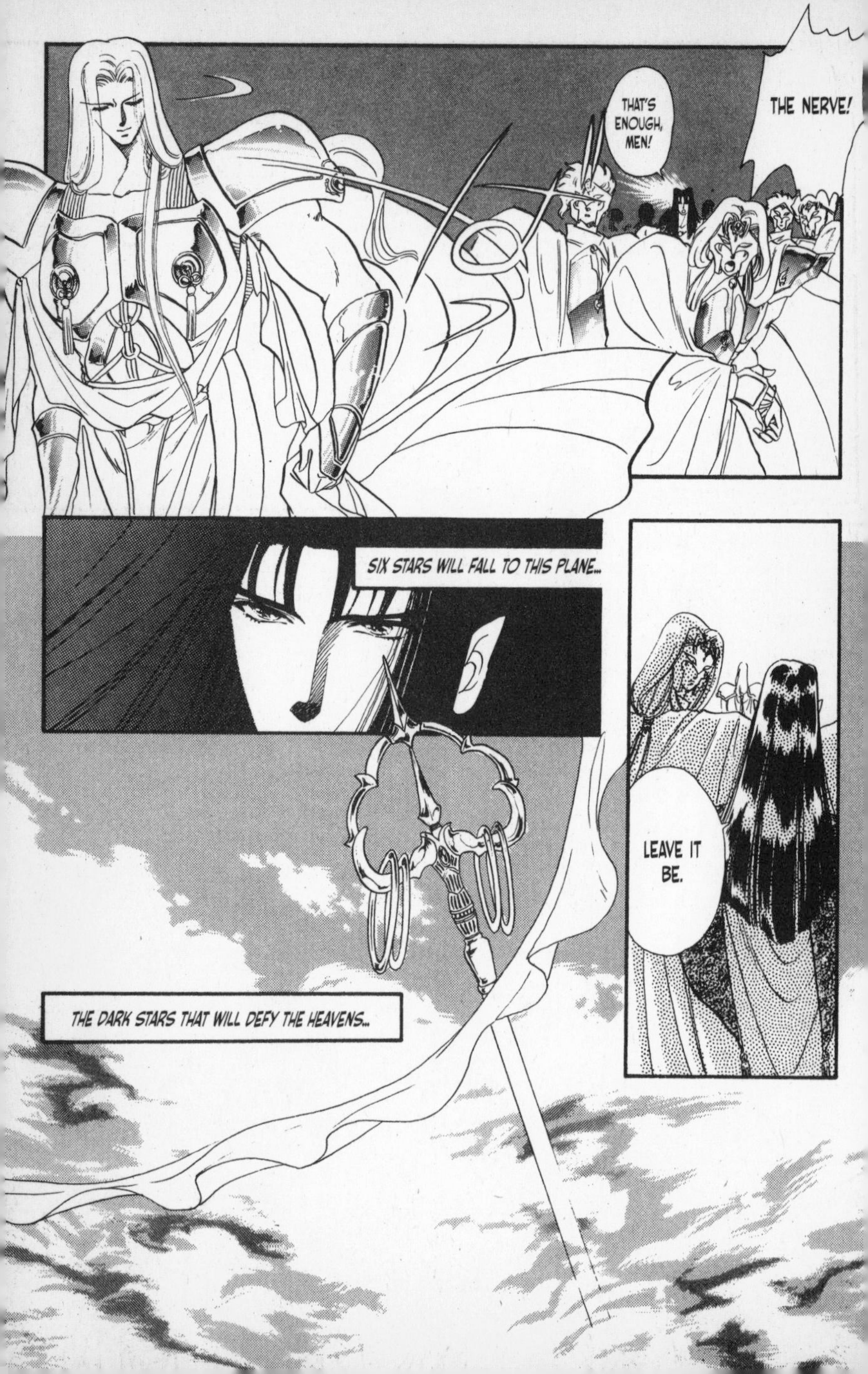
THE NERVE!
THAT'S ENOUGH, MEN!
LEAVE IT BE.
SIX STARS WILL FALL TO THIS PLANE...
THE DARK STARS THAT WILL DEFY THE HEAVENS...

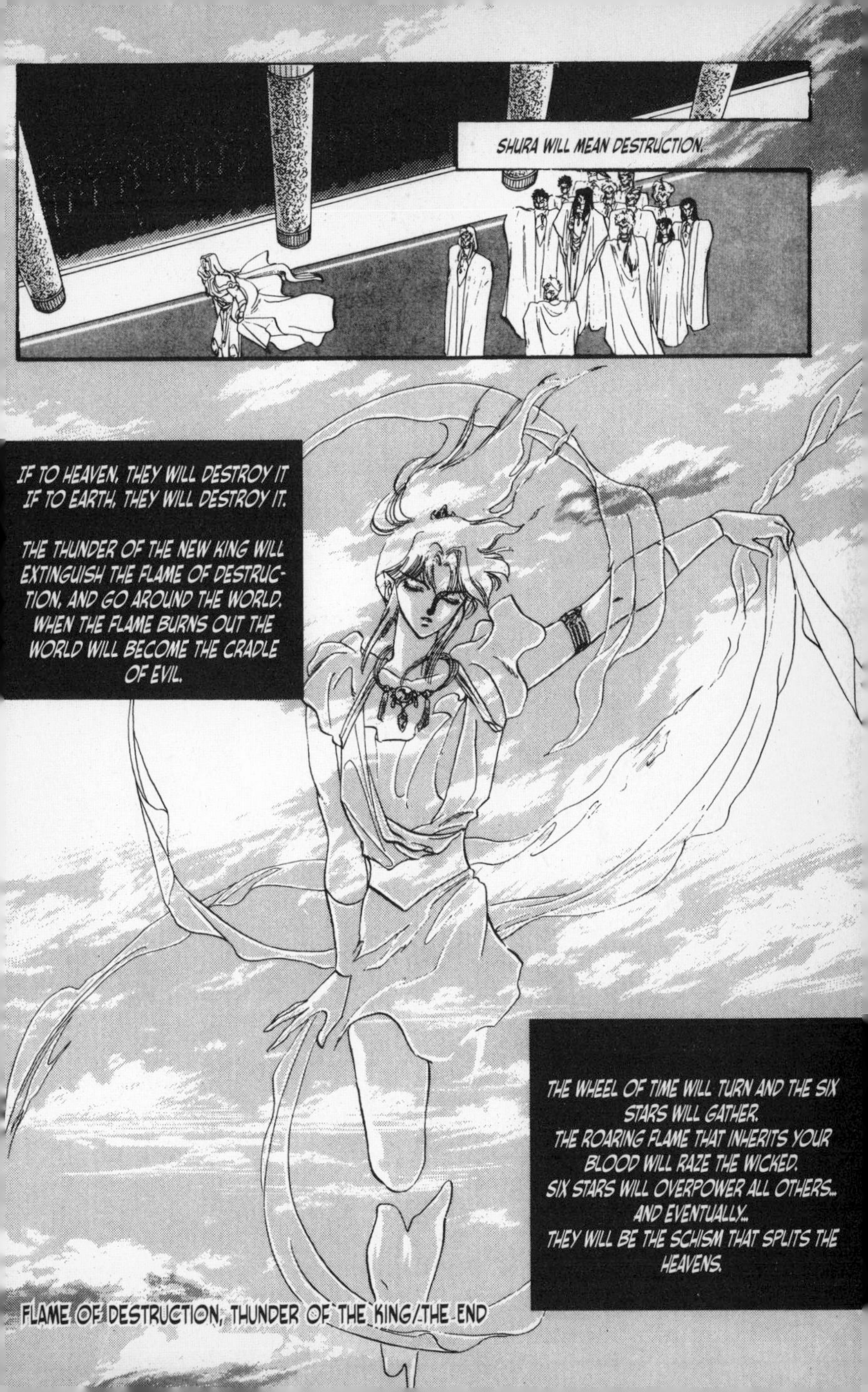
SHURA WILL MEAN DESTRUCTION.
IF TO HEAVEN, THEY WILL DESTROY IT
IF TO EARTH, THEY WILL DESTROY IT.
THE THUNDER OF THE NEW KING WILL EXTINGUISH THE FLAME OF DESTRUCTION, AND GO AROUND THE WORLD. WHEN THE FLAME BURNS OUT THE WORLD WILL BECOME THE CRADLE OF EVIL.
THE WHEEL OF TIME WILL TURN AND THE SIX STARS WILL GATHER.
THE ROARING FLAME THAT INHERITS YOUR BLOOD WILL RAZE THE WICKED.
SIX STARS WILL OVERPOWER ALL OTHERS...
AND EVENTUALLY...
THEY WILL BE THE SCHISM THAT SPLITS THE HEAVENS.
FLAME OF DESTRUCTION, THUNDER OF THE KING/THE END

聖

SEI-

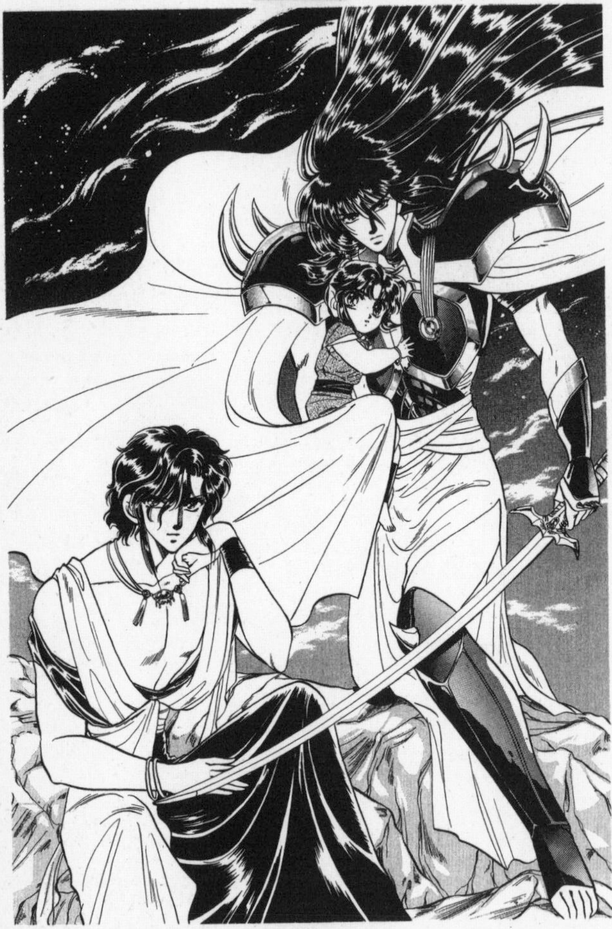

伝

DEN

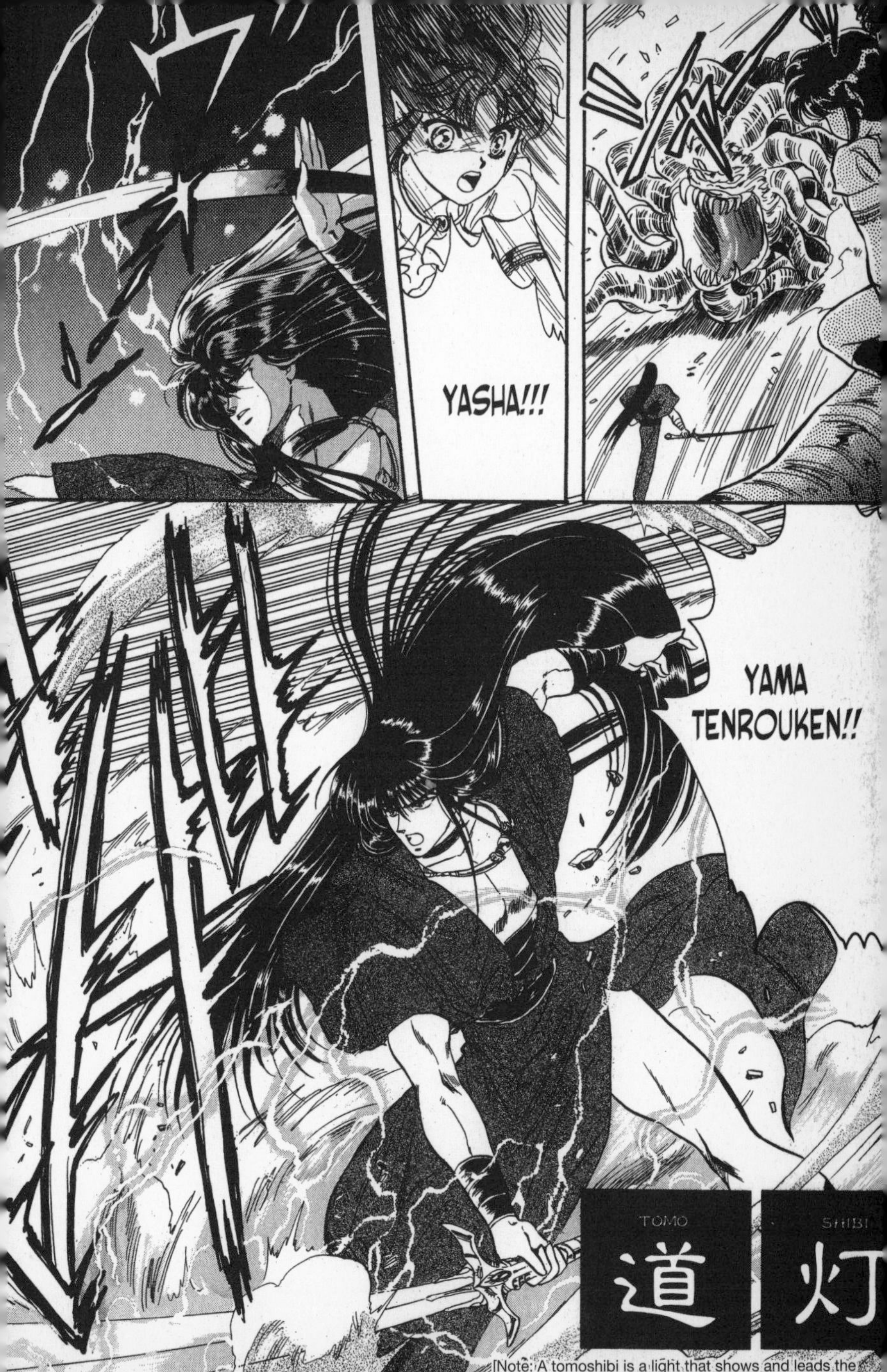
YASHA!!!
YAMA
TENROUKEN!!
TOMO
SHIBI
道灯

[Note: A tomoshibi is a light that shows and leads the way for travelers]

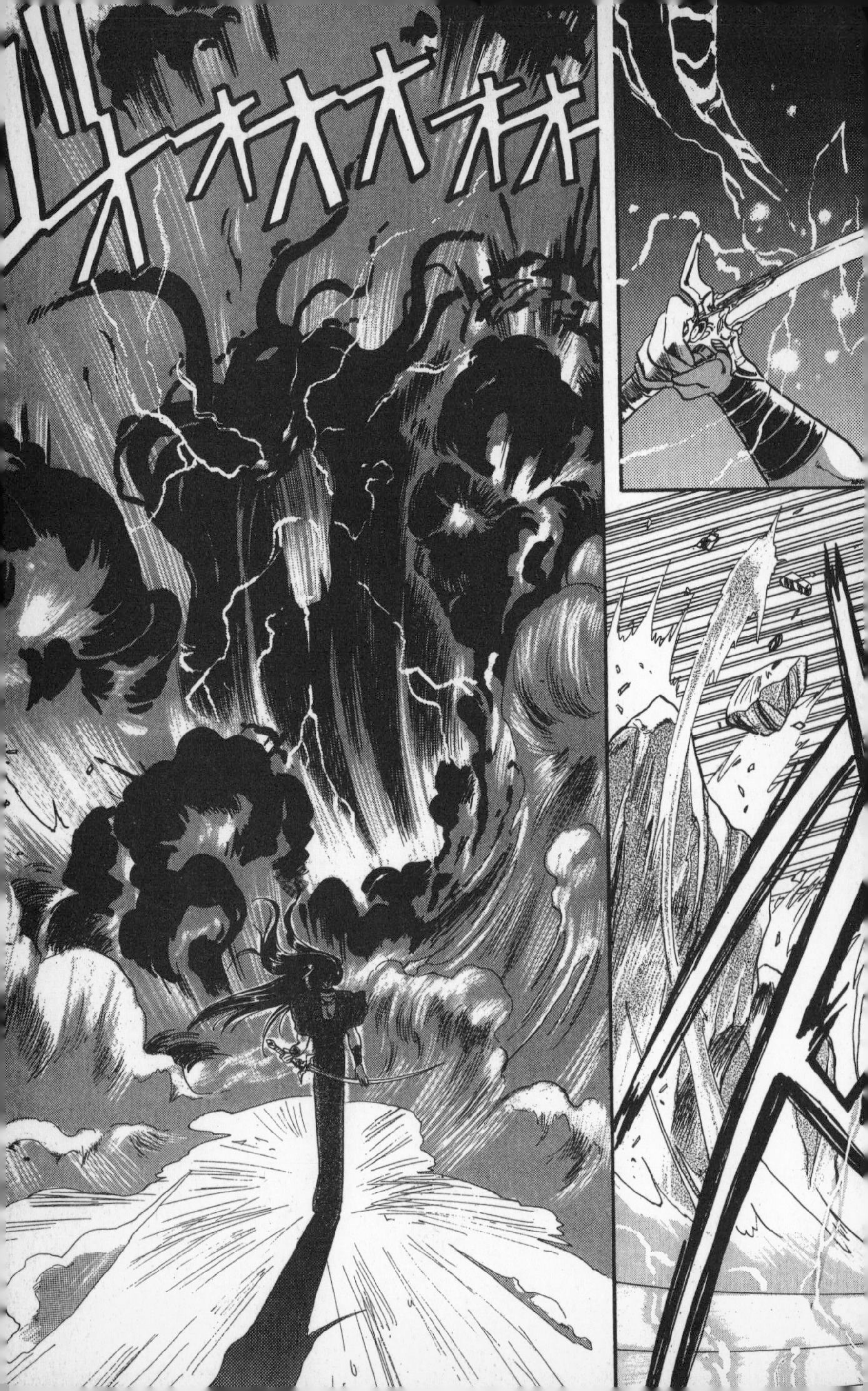
オオオオオオ

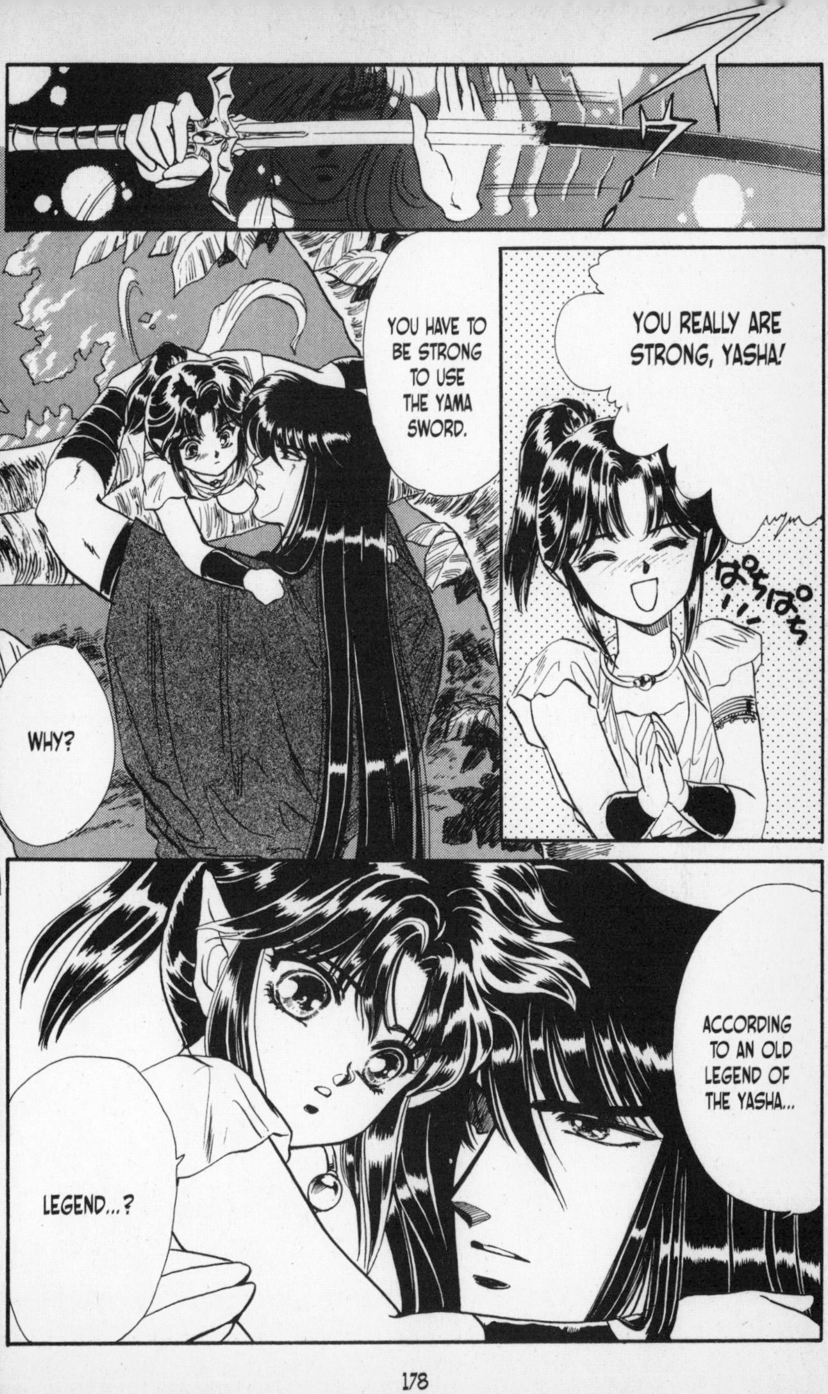
YOU REALLY ARE STRONG, YASHA!
ぱちぱち
YOU HAVE TO BE STRONG TO USE THE YAMA SWORD.
WHY?
ACCORDING TO AN OLD LEGEND OF THE YASHA...
LEGEND...?

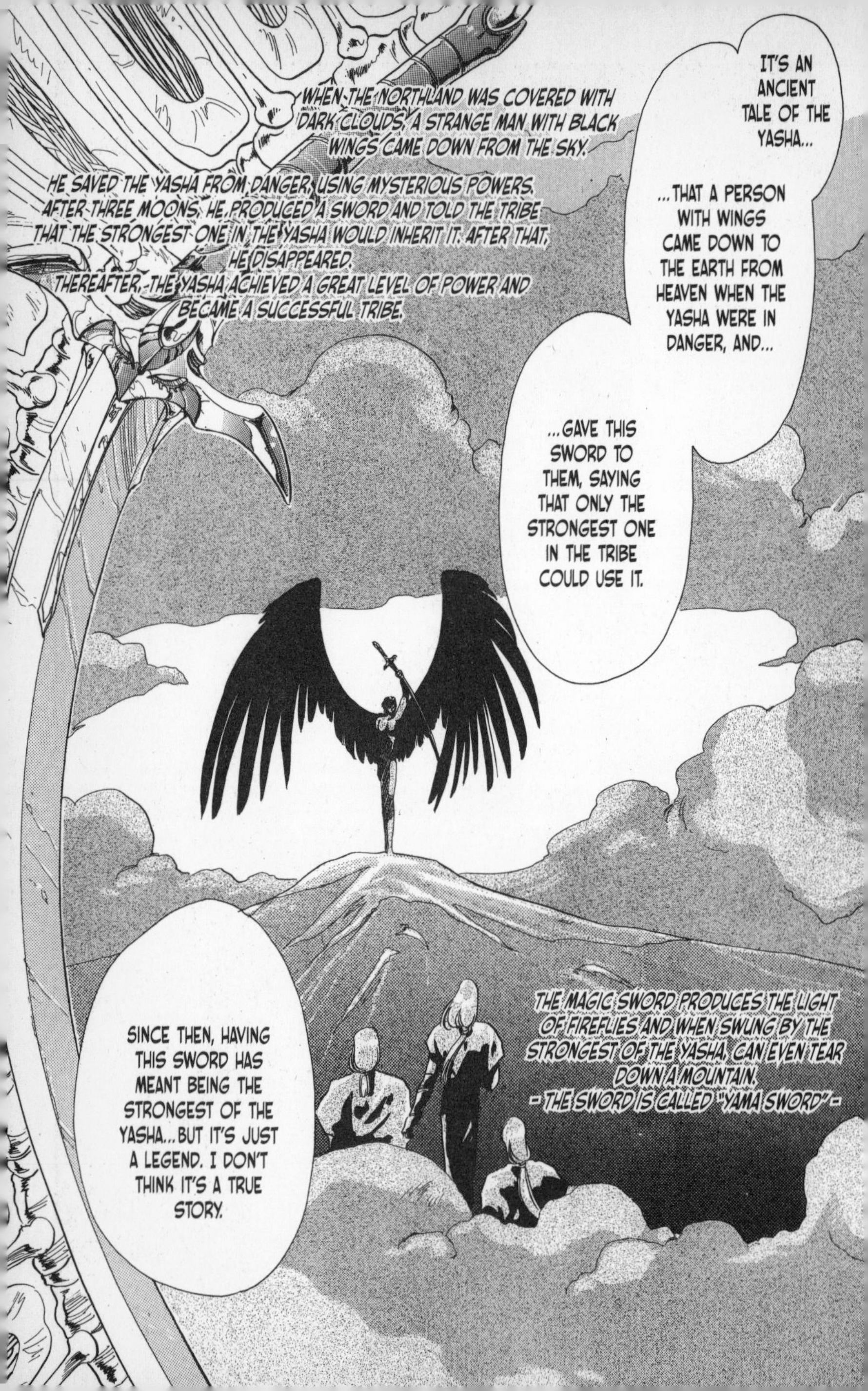
IT'S AN ANCIENT TALE OF THE YASHA...
...THAT A PERSON WITH WINGS CAME DOWN TO THE EARTH FROM HEAVEN WHEN THE YASHA WERE IN DANGER, AND...
...GAVE THIS SWORD TO THEM, SAYING THAT ONLY THE STRONGEST ONE IN THE TRIBE COULD USE IT.
WHEN THE NORTHLAND WAS COVERED WITH DARK CLOUDS, A STRANGE MAN WITH BLACK WINGS CAME DOWN FROM THE SKY.
HE SAVED THE YASHA FROM DANGER, USING MYSTERIOUS POWERS. AFTER THREE MOONS, HE PRODUCED A SWORD AND TOLD THE TRIBE THAT THE STRONGEST ONE IN THE YASHA WOULD INHERIT IT. AFTER THAT, HE DISAPPEARED.
THEREAFTER, THE YASHA ACHIEVED A GREAT LEVEL OF POWER AND BECAME A SUCCESSFUL TRIBE.
THE MAGIC SWORD PRODUCES THE LIGHT OF FIREFLIES AND WHEN SWUNG BY THE STRONGEST OF THE YASHA, CAN EVEN TEAR DOWN A MOUNTAIN.
- THE SWORD IS CALLED "YAMA SWORD" -
SINCE THEN, HAVING THIS SWORD HAS MEANT BEING THE STRONGEST OF THE YASHA...BUT IT'S JUST A LEGEND. I DON'T THINK IT'S A TRUE STORY.

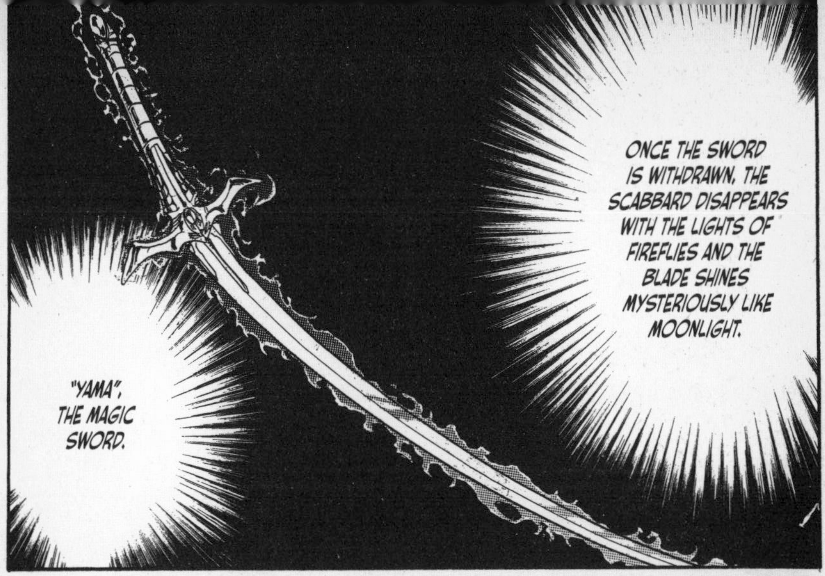
ONCE THE SWORD IS WITHDRAWN, THE SCABBARD DISAPPEARS WITH THE LIGHTS OF FIREFLIES AND THE BLADE SHINES MYSTERIOUSLY LIKE MOONLIGHT.
"YAMA", THE MAGIC SWORD.

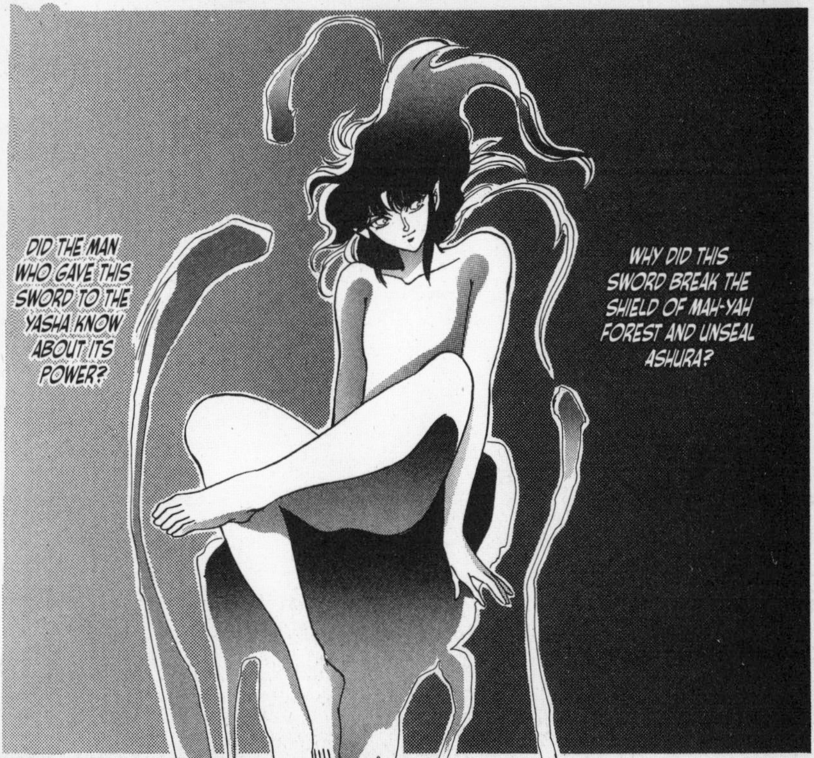
WHY DID THIS SWORD BREAK THE SHIELD OF MAH-YAH FOREST AND UNSEAL ASHURA?
DID THE MAN WHO GAVE THIS SWORD TO THE YASHA KNOW ABOUT ITS POWER?

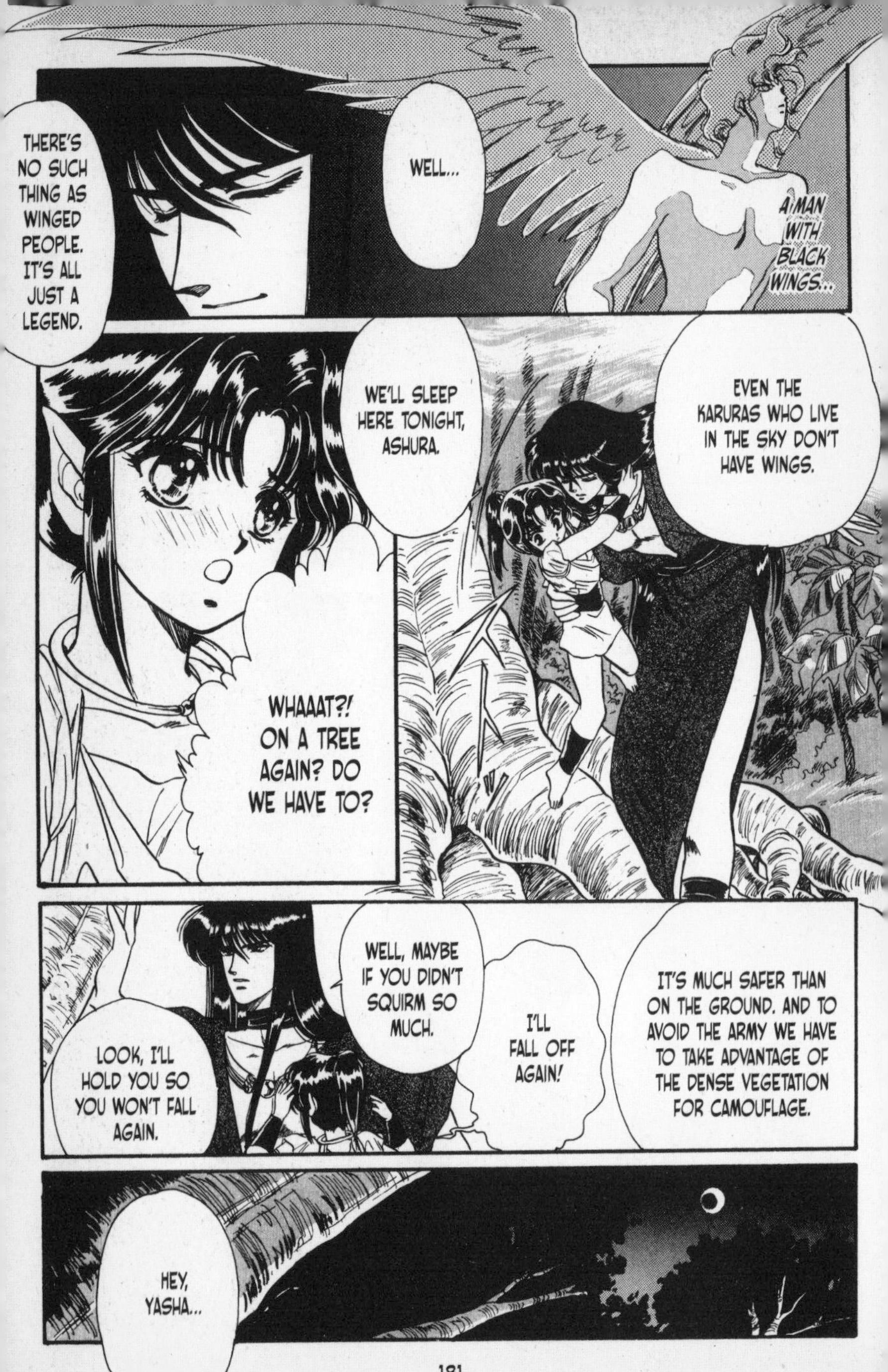
A MAN WITH BLACK WINGS...
WELL...
THERE'S NO SUCH THING AS WINGED PEOPLE. IT'S ALL JUST A LEGEND.
EVEN THE KARURAS WHO LIVE IN THE SKY DON'T HAVE WINGS.
WE'LL SLEEP HERE TONIGHT, ASHURA.
WHAAAT?! ON A TREE AGAIN? DO WE HAVE TO?
IT'S MUCH SAFER THAN ON THE GROUND. AND TO AVOID THE ARMY WE HAVE TO TAKE ADVANTAGE OF THE DENSE VEGETATION FOR CAMOUFLAGE.
I'LL FALL OFF AGAIN!
WELL, MAYBE IF YOU DIDN'T SQUIRM SO MUCH.
LOOK, I'LL HOLD YOU SO YOU WON'T FALL AGAIN.
HEY, YASHA...

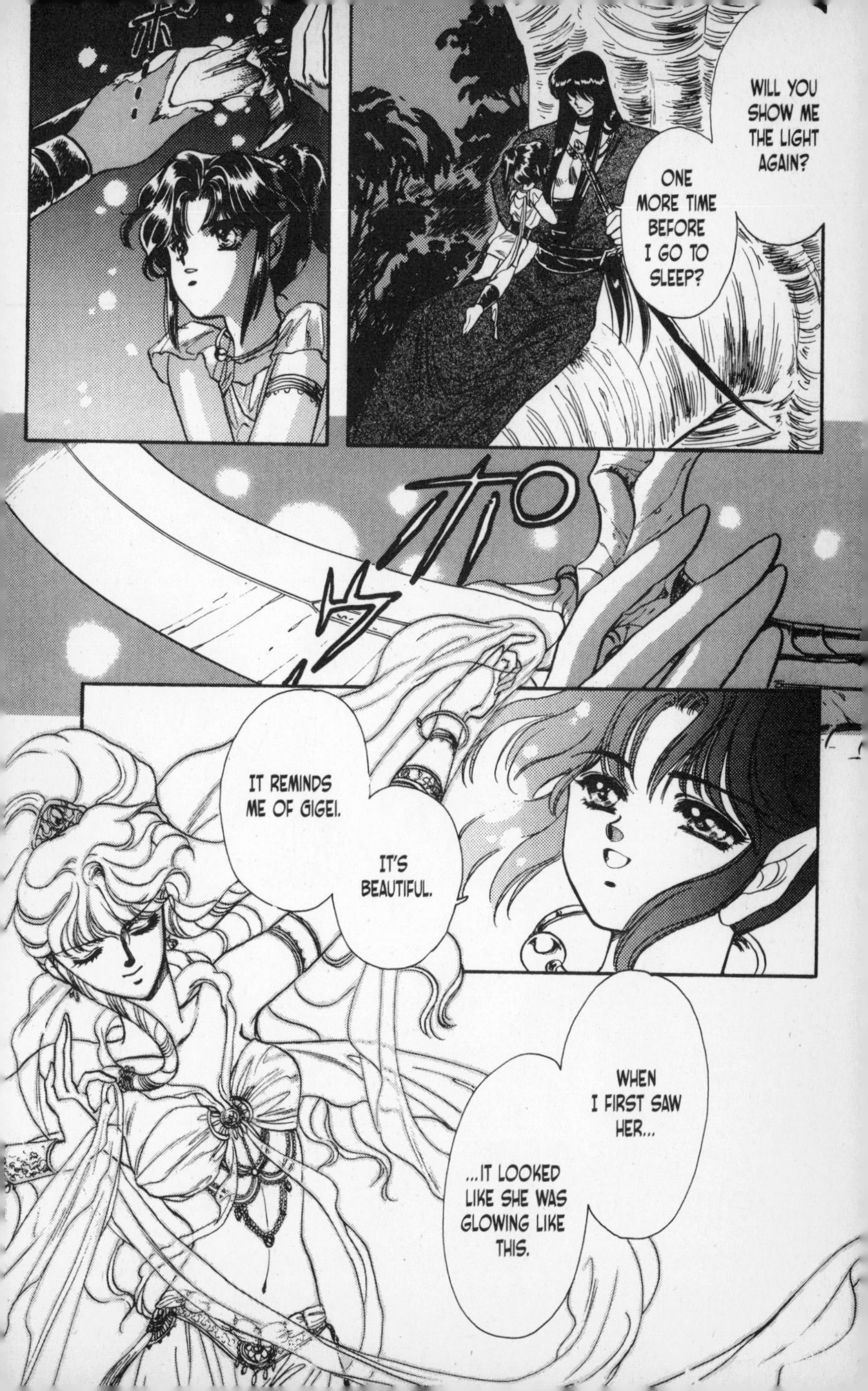
WILL YOU SHOW ME THE LIGHT AGAIN?
ONE MORE TIME BEFORE I GO TO SLEEP?
IT REMINDS ME OF GIGEI.
IT'S BEAUTIFUL.
WHEN I FIRST SAW HER...
...IT LOOKED LIKE SHE WAS GLOWING LIKE THIS.

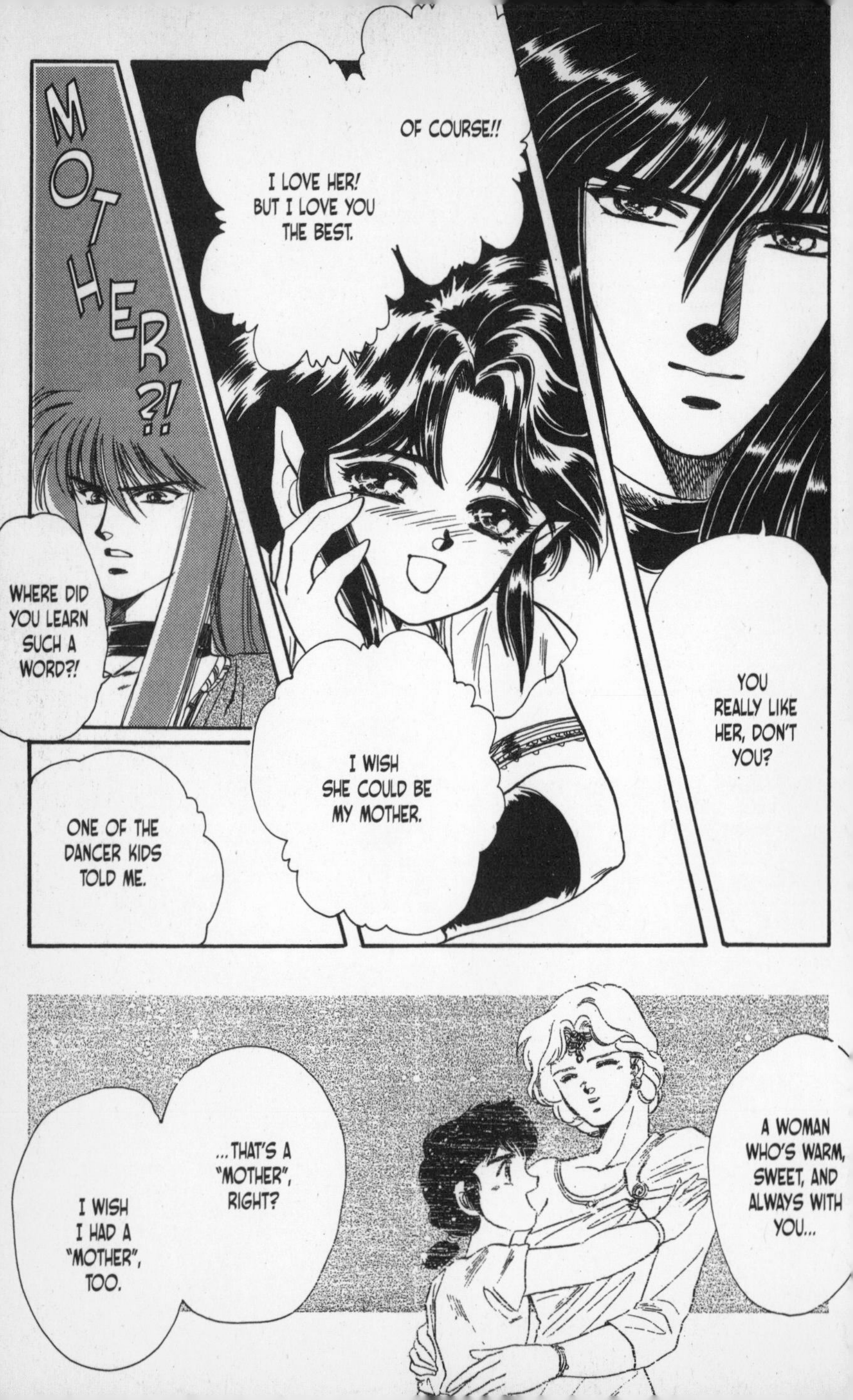
YOU REALLY LIKE HER, DON'T YOU?
OF COURSE!! I LOVE HER! BUT I LOVE YOU THE BEST.
I WISH SHE COULD BE MY MOTHER.
MOTHER?!
WHERE DID YOU LEARN SUCH A WORD?!
ONE OF THE DANCER KIDS TOLD ME.
A WOMAN WHO'S WARM, SWEET, AND ALWAYS WITH YOU...
...THAT'S A "MOTHER", RIGHT?
I WISH I HAD A "MOTHER", TOO.

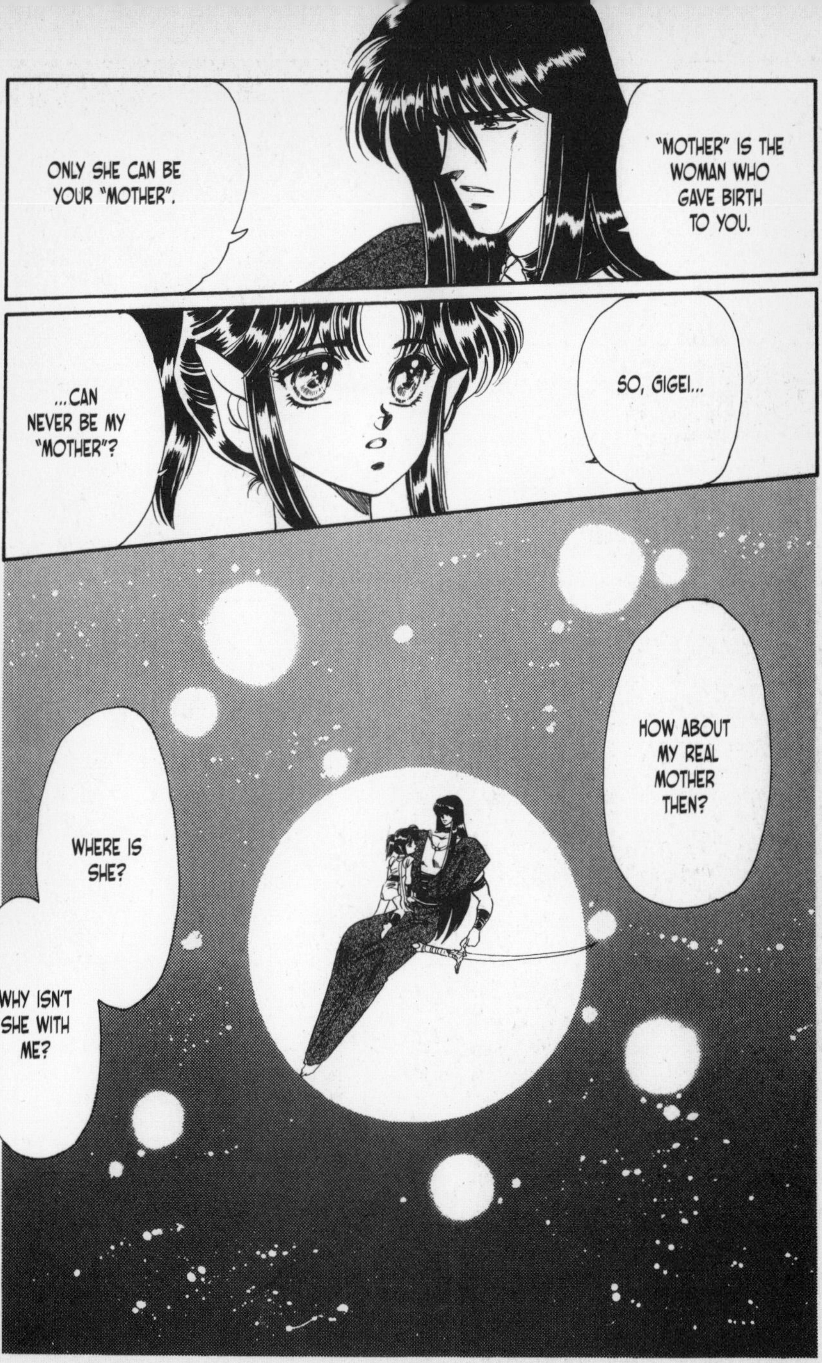
"MOTHER" IS THE WOMAN WHO GAVE BIRTH TO YOU.
ONLY SHE CAN BE YOUR "MOTHER".
SO, GIGEI...
...CAN NEVER BE MY "MOTHER"?
HOW ABOUT MY REAL MOTHER THEN?
WHERE IS SHE?
WHY ISN'T SHE WITH ME?

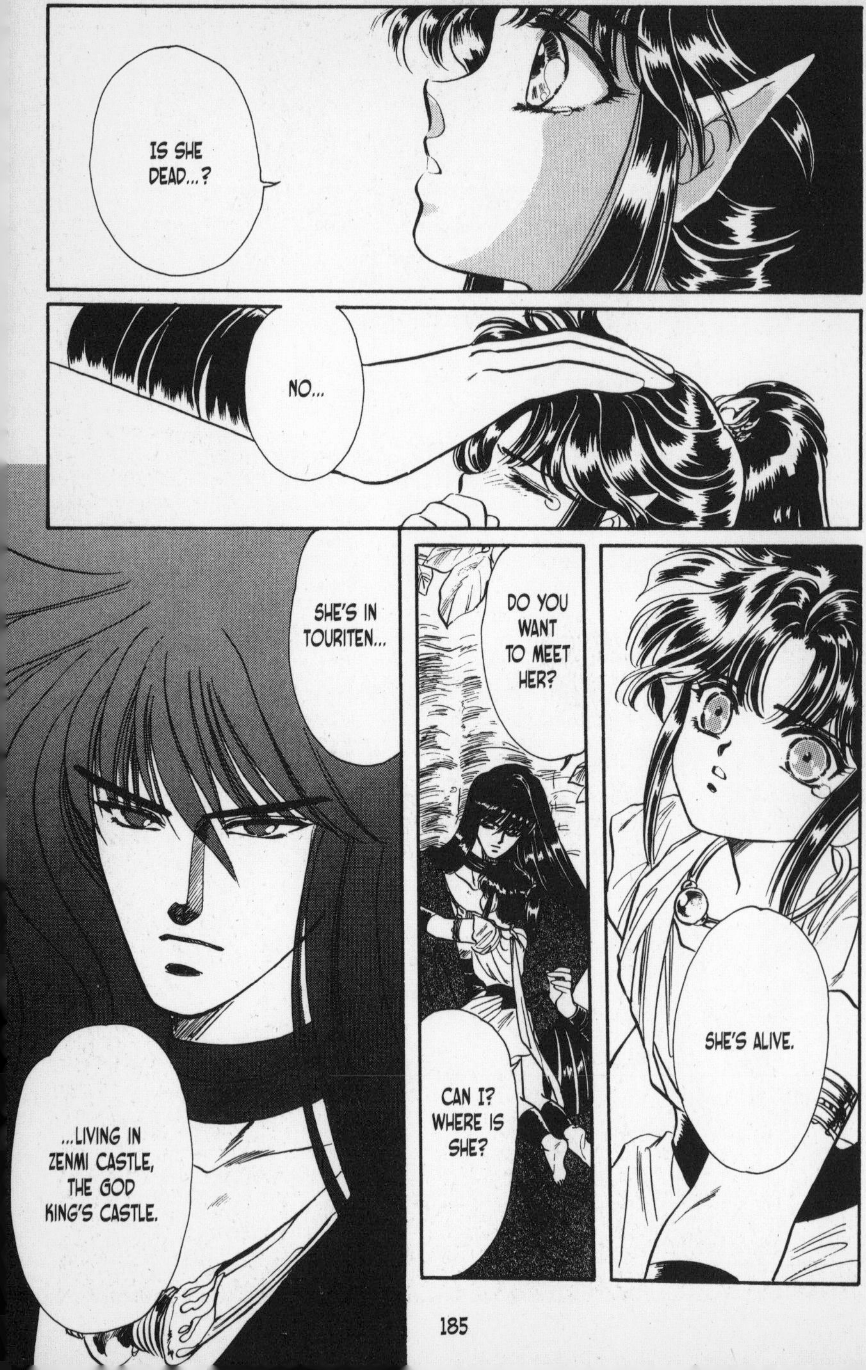
IS SHE DEAD...?
NO...
SHE'S ALIVE.
DO YOU WANT TO MEET HER?
CAN I? WHERE IS SHE?
SHE'S IN TOURITEN...
...LIVING IN ZENMI CASTLE, THE GOD KING'S CASTLE.

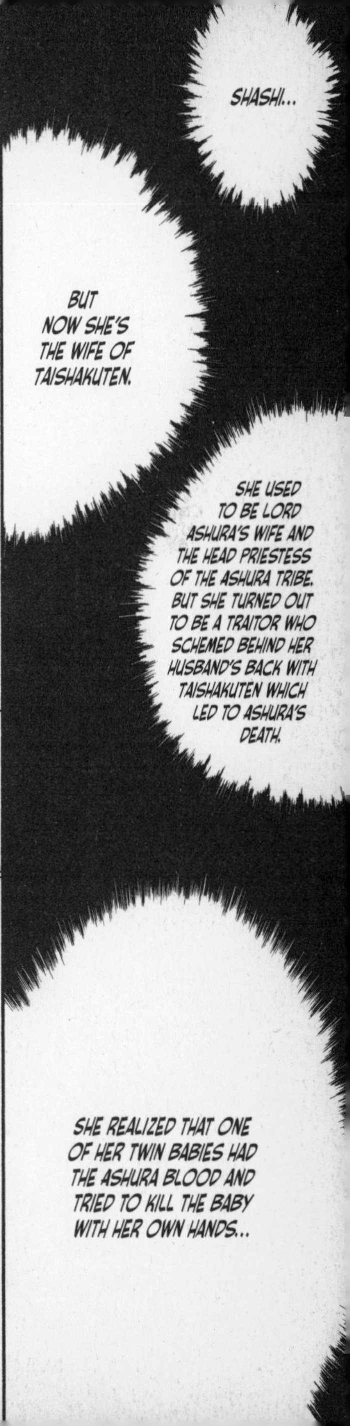
SHASHI...
BUT NOW SHE'S THE WIFE OF TAISHAKUTEN.
SHE USED TO BE LORD ASHURA'S WIFE AND THE HEAD PRIESTESS OF THE ASHURA TRIBE. BUT SHE TURNED OUT TO BE A TRAITOR WHO SCHEMED BEHIND HER HUSBAND'S BACK WITH TAISHAKUTEN WHICH LED TO ASHURA'S DEATH.
SHE REALIZED THAT ONE OF HER TWIN BABIES HAD THE ASHURA BLOOD AND TRIED TO KILL THE BABY WITH HER OWN HANDS...

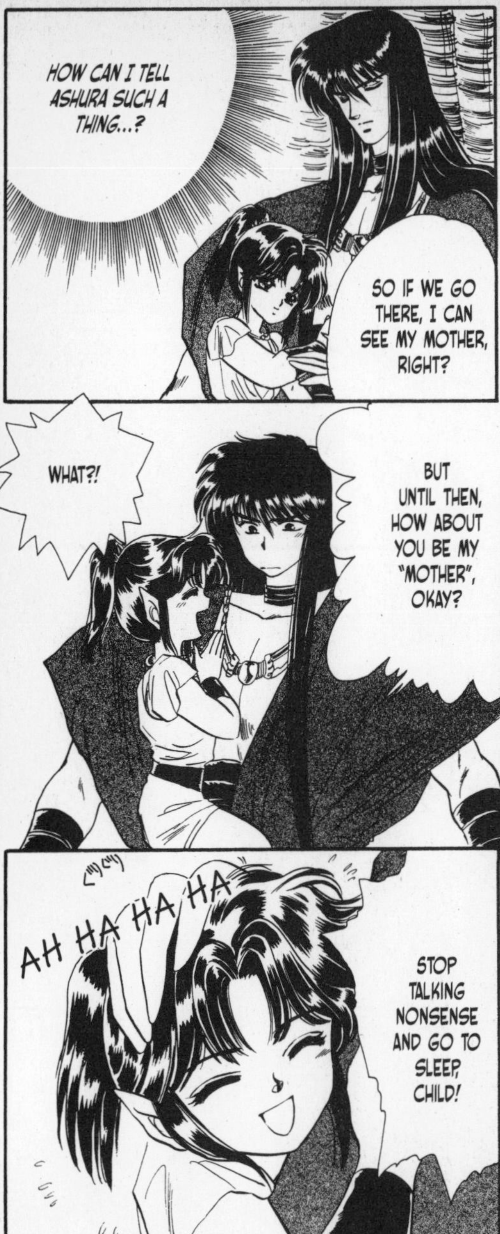
HOW CAN I TELL ASHURA SUCH A THING...?
SO IF WE GO THERE, I CAN SEE MY MOTHER, RIGHT?
BUT UNTIL THEN, HOW ABOUT YOU BE MY "MOTHER", OKAY?
WHAT?!
STOP TALKING NONSENSE AND GO TO SLEEP, CHILD!
AH HA HA HA

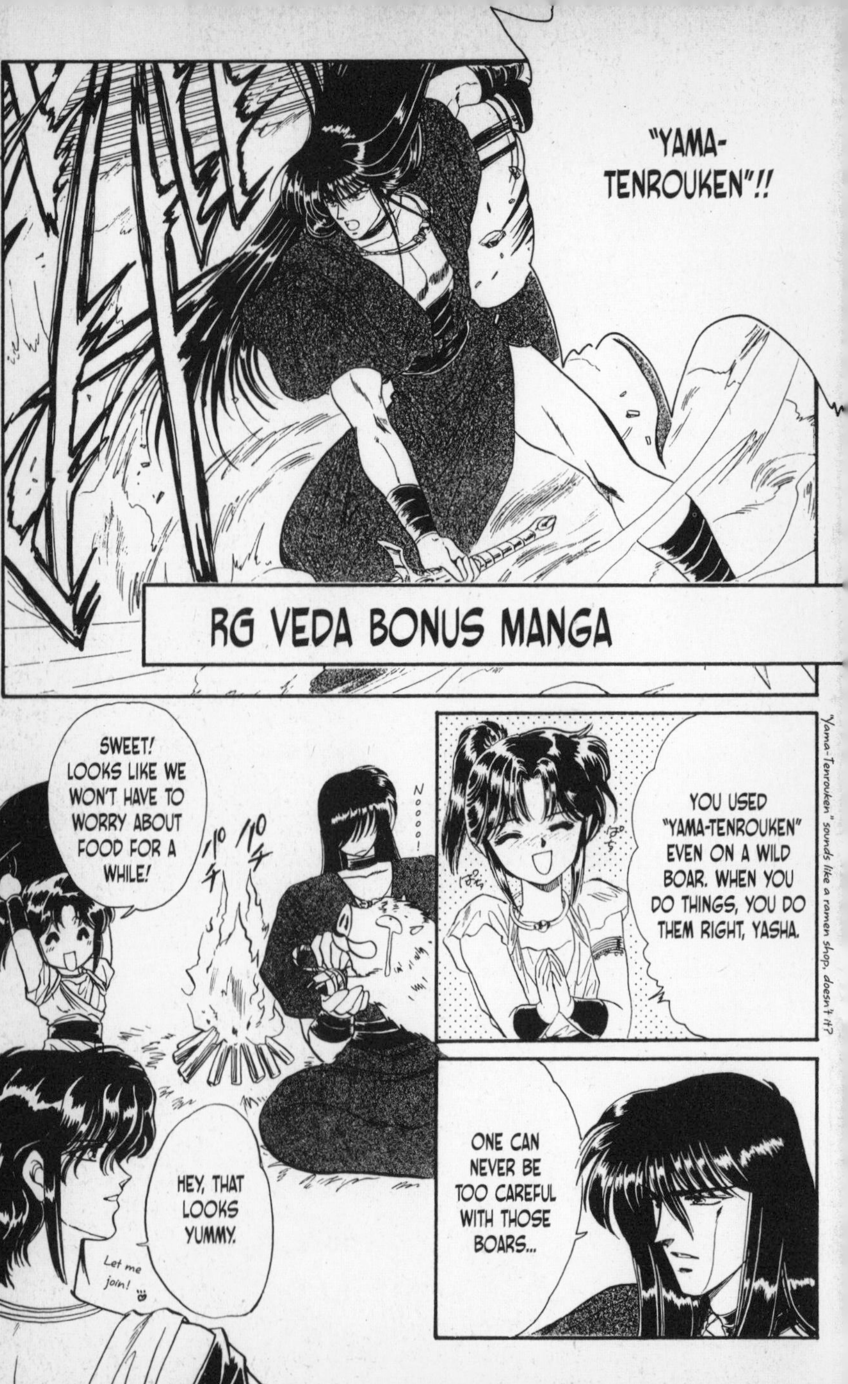
"YAMA-TENROUKEN"!!
RG VEDA BONUS MANGA
YOU USED "YAMA-TENROUKEN" EVEN ON A WILD BOAR. WHEN YOU DO THINGS, YOU DO THEM RIGHT, YASHA.
ONE CAN NEVER BE TOO CAREFUL WITH THOSE BOARS...
SWEET! LOOKS LIKE WE WON'T HAVE TO WORRY ABOUT FOOD FOR A WHILE!
パチ パチ
Noooo!
HEY, THAT LOOKS YUMMY.
Let me join!

"Here's your order!!" Wow, our ramen delivery boy is so energetic.

"Yama-Tenrouken" sounds like a ramen shop, doesn't it?

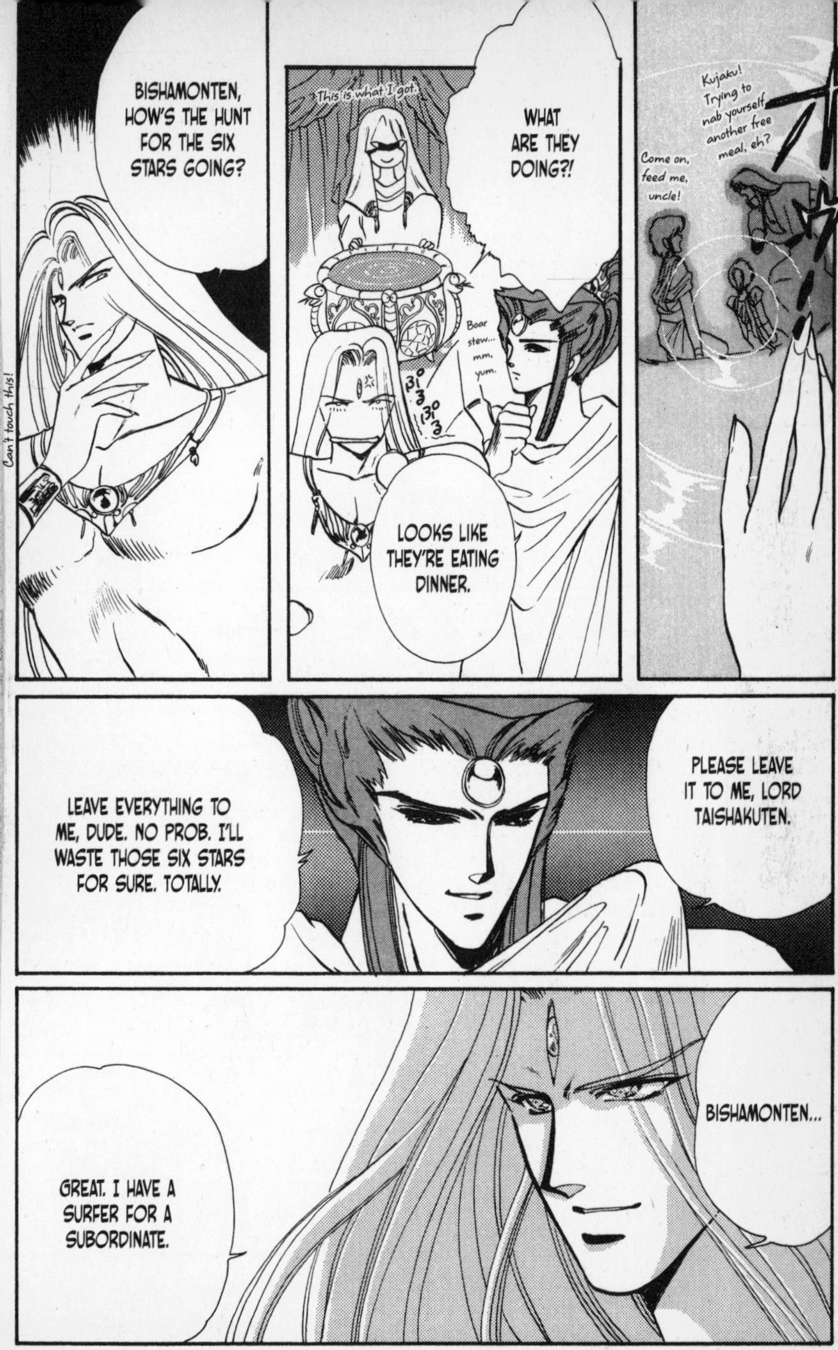
Kujaku! Trying to nab yourself another free meal, eh?
Come on, feed me, uncle!
WHAT ARE THEY DOING?!
This is what I got.
Boar stew... mm, yum.
LOOKS LIKE THEY'RE EATING DINNER.
BISHAMONTEN, HOW'S THE HUNT FOR THE SIX STARS GOING?
Can't touch this!
PLEASE LEAVE IT TO ME, LORD TAISHAKUTEN.
LEAVE EVERYTHING TO ME, DUDE. NO PROB. I'LL WASTE THOSE SIX STARS FOR SURE. TOTALLY.
BISHAMONTEN...
GREAT. I HAVE A SURFER FOR A SUBORDINATE.

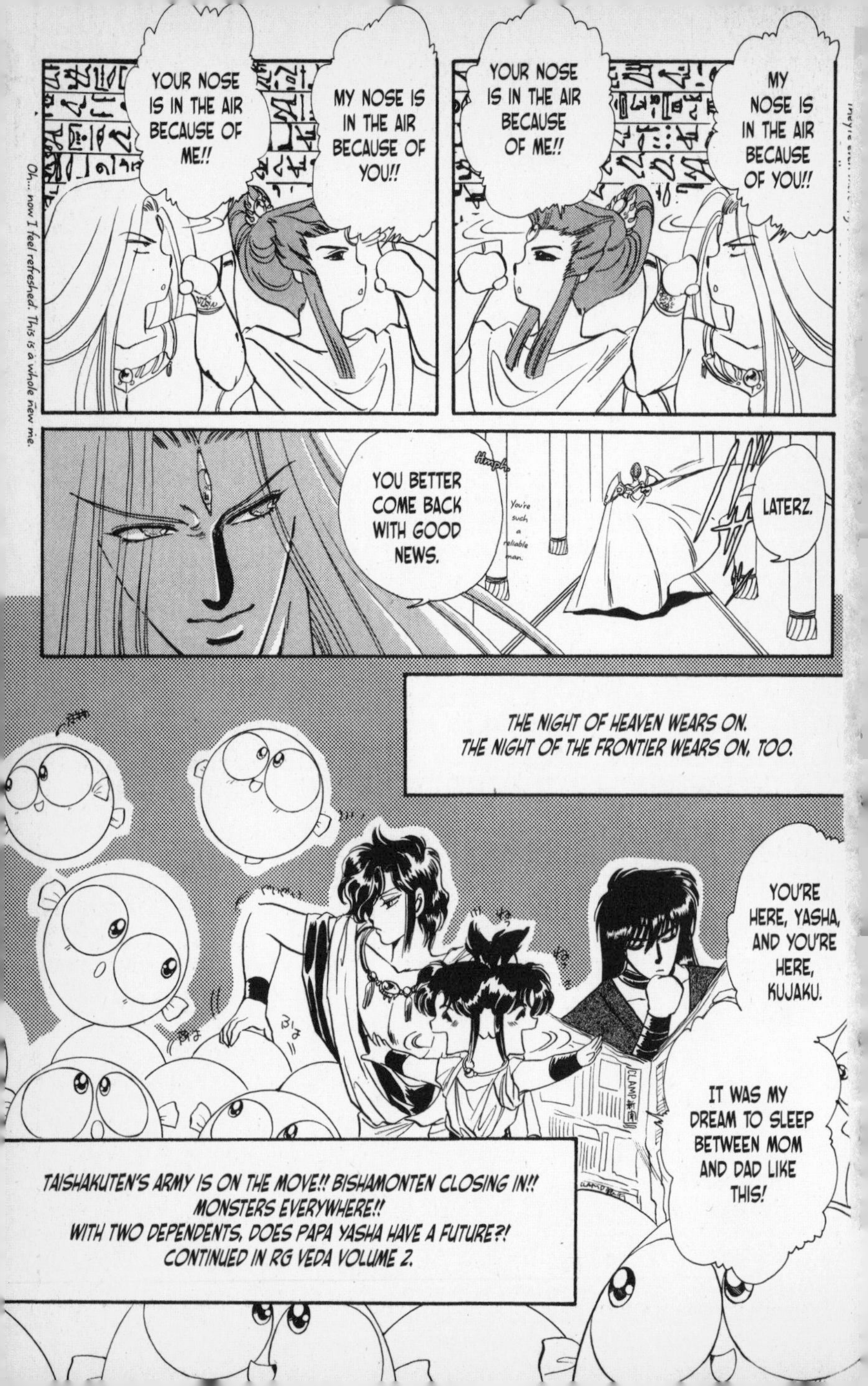
MY NOSE IS IN THE AIR BECAUSE OF YOU!!
YOUR NOSE IS IN THE AIR BECAUSE OF ME!!
MY NOSE IS IN THE AIR BECAUSE OF YOU!!
YOUR NOSE IS IN THE AIR BECAUSE OF ME!!
Oh... now I feel refreshed. This is a whole new me.
LATERZ.
You're such a reliable man.
Hmph.
YOU BETTER COME BACK WITH GOOD NEWS.
THE NIGHT OF HEAVEN WEARS ON.
THE NIGHT OF THE FRONTIER WEARS ON, TOO.
YOU'RE HERE, YASHA, AND YOU'RE HERE, KUJAKU.
IT WAS MY DREAM TO SLEEP BETWEEN MOM AND DAD LIKE THIS!
CLAMP
TAISHAKUTEN'S ARMY IS ON THE MOVE!! BISHAMONTEN CLOSING IN!!
MONSTERS EVERYWHERE!!
WITH TWO DEPENDENTS, DOES PAPA YASHA HAVE A FUTURE?!
CONTINUED IN RG VEDA VOLUME 2.

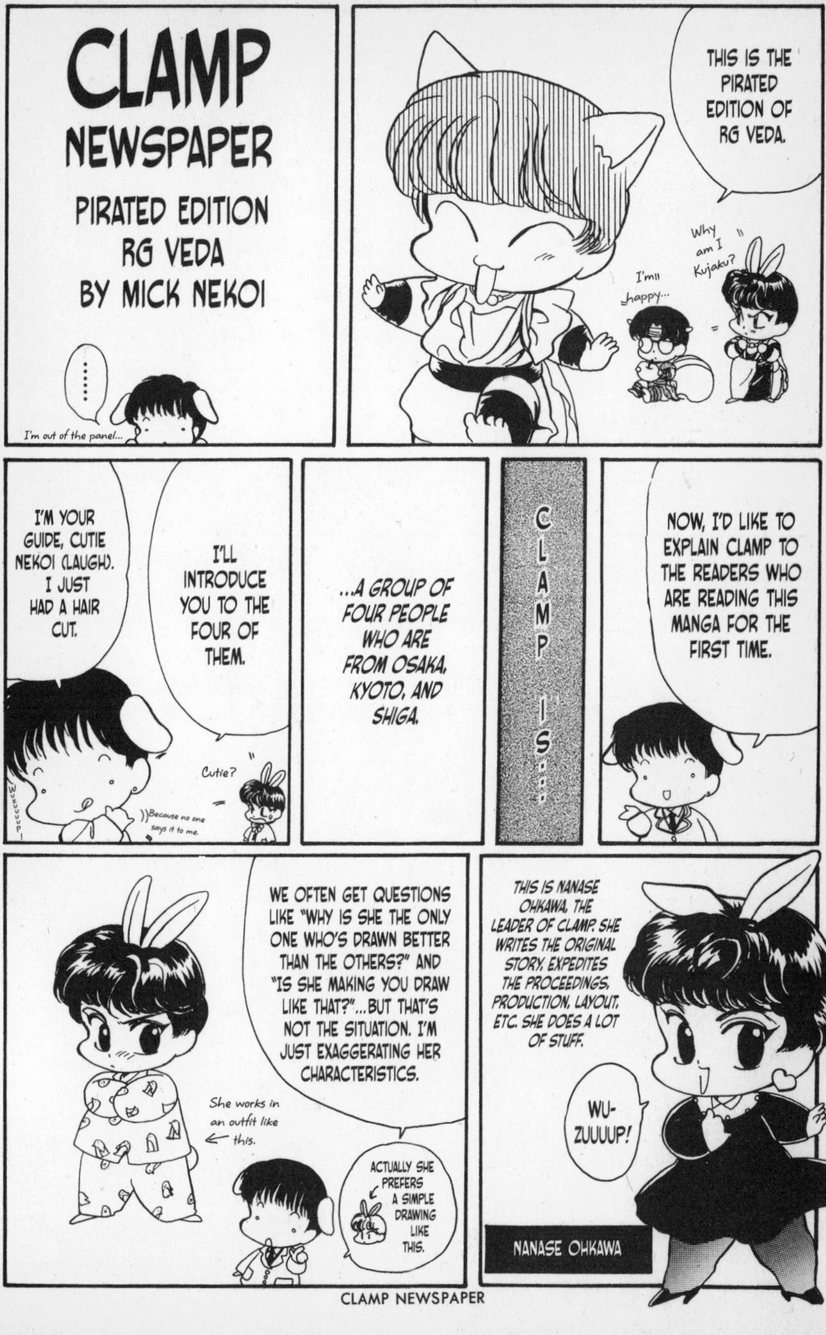
THIS IS THE PIRATED EDITION OF RG VEDA.
Why am I Kujaku?
I'm happy...
CLAMP NEWSPAPER
PIRATED EDITION RG VEDA BY MICK NEKOI
......
I'm out of the panel...
NOW, I'D LIKE TO EXPLAIN CLAMP TO THE READERS WHO ARE READING THIS MANGA FOR THE FIRST TIME.
CLAMP IS...
...A GROUP OF FOUR PEOPLE WHO ARE FROM OSAKA, KYOTO, AND SHIGA.
I'LL INTRODUCE YOU TO THE FOUR OF THEM.
I'M YOUR GUIDE, CUTIE NEKOI (LAUGH). I JUST HAD A HAIR CUT.
Cutie?
Because no one says it to me.
WUZUUUP!
THIS IS NANASE OHKAWA, THE LEADER OF CLAMP. SHE WRITES THE ORIGINAL STORY, EXPEDITES THE PROCEEDINGS, PRODUCTION, LAYOUT, ETC. SHE DOES A LOT OF STUFF.
WU-ZUUUUP!
NANASE OHKAWA
WE OFTEN GET QUESTIONS LIKE "WHY IS SHE THE ONLY ONE WHO'S DRAWN BETTER THAN THE OTHERS?" AND "IS SHE MAKING YOU DRAW LIKE THAT?"...BUT THAT'S NOT THE SITUATION. I'M JUST EXAGGERATING HER CHARACTERISTICS.
She works in an outfit like this.
ACTUALLY SHE PREFERS A SIMPLE DRAWING LIKE THIS.

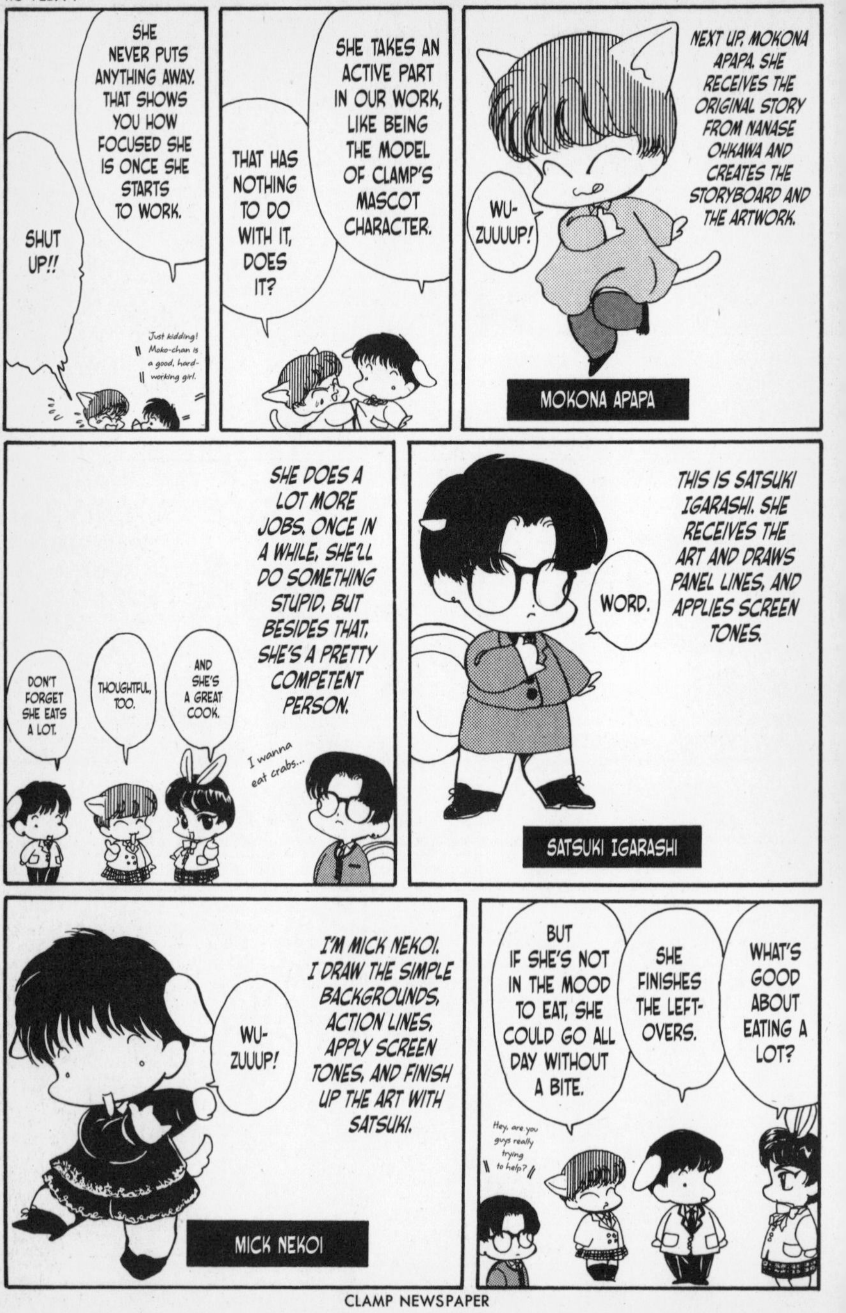
NEXT UP, MOKONA APAPA. SHE RECEIVES THE ORIGINAL STORY FROM NANASE OHKAWA AND CREATES THE STORYBOARD AND THE ARTWORK.
WU-ZUUUUP!
MOKONA APAPA
SHE TAKES AN ACTIVE PART IN OUR WORK, LIKE BEING THE MODEL OF CLAMP'S MASCOT CHARACTER.
THAT HAS NOTHING TO DO WITH IT, DOES IT?
SHE NEVER PUTS ANYTHING AWAY. THAT SHOWS YOU HOW FOCUSED SHE IS ONCE SHE STARTS TO WORK.
SHUT UP!!
Just kidding! Moko-chan is a good, hard-working girl.
THIS IS SATSUKI IGARASHI. SHE RECEIVES THE ART AND DRAWS PANEL LINES, AND APPLIES SCREEN TONES.
WORD.
SATSUKI IGARASHI
SHE DOES A LOT MORE JOBS. ONCE IN A WHILE, SHE'LL DO SOMETHING STUPID, BUT BESIDES THAT, SHE'S A PRETTY COMPETENT PERSON.
I wanna eat crabs...
AND SHE'S A GREAT COOK.
THOUGHTFUL, TOO.
DON'T FORGET SHE EATS A LOT.
WHAT'S GOOD ABOUT EATING A LOT?
SHE FINISHES THE LEFT-OVERS.
BUT IF SHE'S NOT IN THE MOOD TO EAT, SHE COULD GO ALL DAY WITHOUT A BITE.
Hey, are you guys really trying to help?
I'M MICK NEKOI. I DRAW THE SIMPLE BACKGROUNDS, ACTION LINES, APPLY SCREEN TONES, AND FINISH UP THE ART WITH SATSUKI.
WU-ZUUUP!
MICK NEKOI

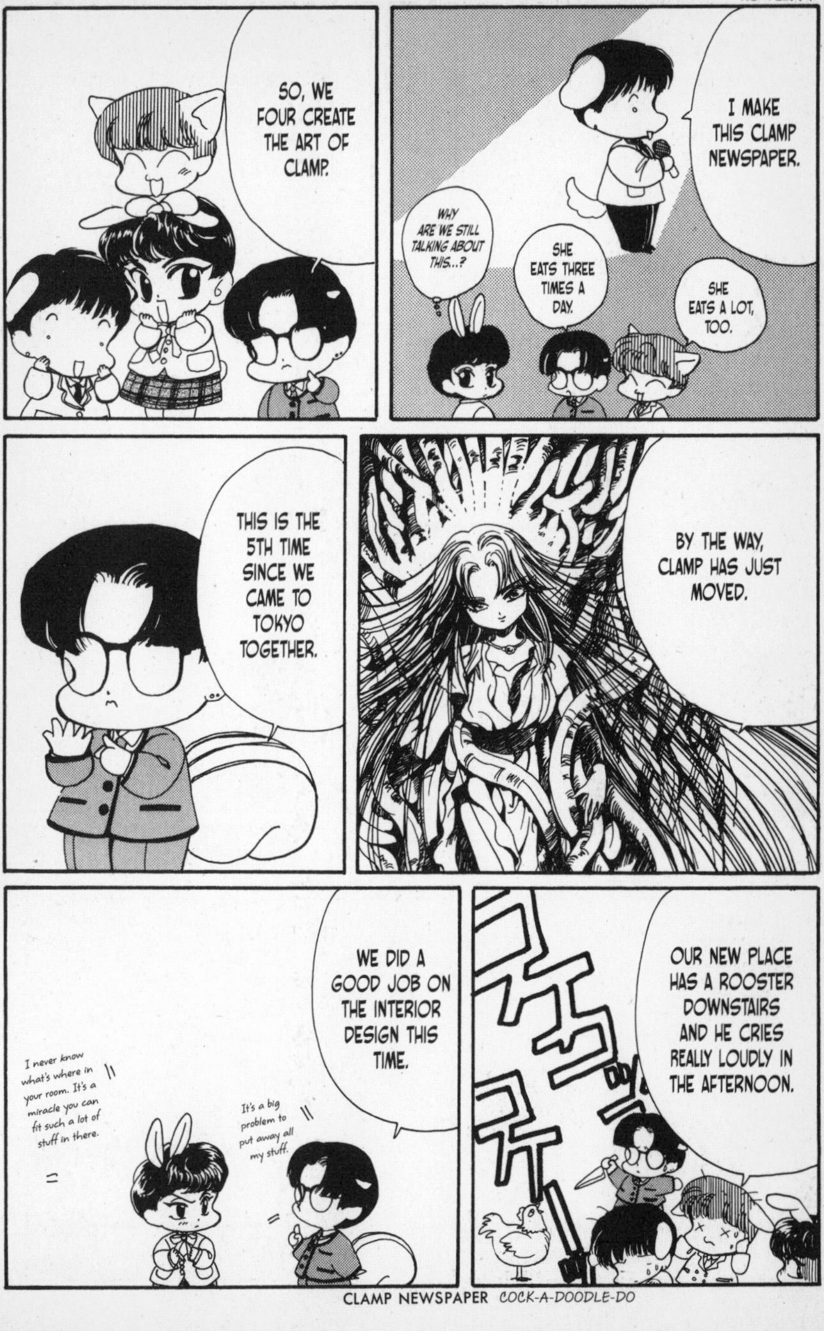
I MAKE THIS CLAMP NEWSPAPER.
WHY ARE WE STILL TALKING ABOUT THIS...?
SHE EATS THREE TIMES A DAY.
SHE EATS A LOT, TOO.
SO, WE FOUR CREATE THE ART OF CLAMP.
BY THE WAY, CLAMP HAS JUST MOVED.
THIS IS THE 5TH TIME SINCE WE CAME TO TOKYO TOGETHER.
OUR NEW PLACE HAS A ROOSTER DOWNSTAIRS AND HE CRIES REALLY LOUDLY IN THE AFTERNOON.
WE DID A GOOD JOB ON THE INTERIOR DESIGN THIS TIME.
It's a big problem to put away all my stuff.
I never know what's where in your room. It's a miracle you can fit such a lot of stuff in there.

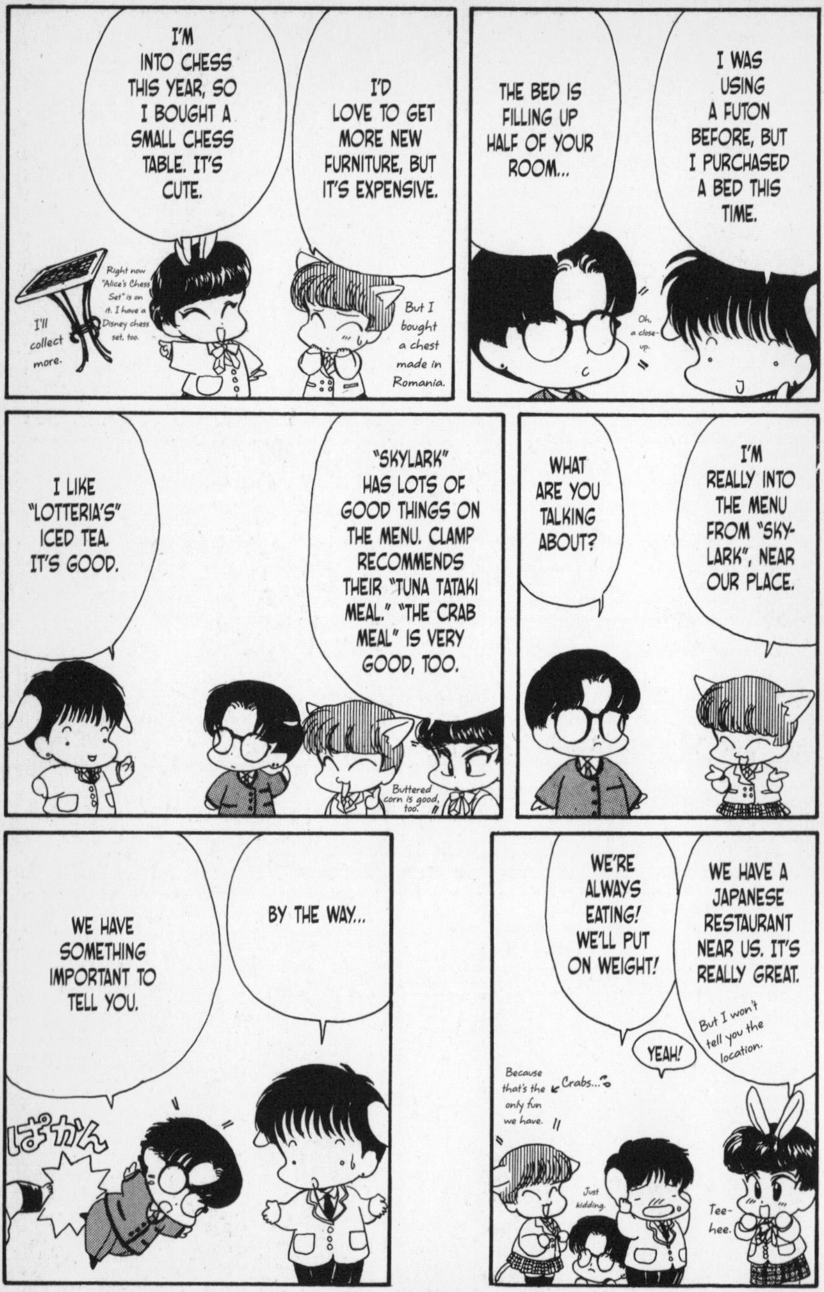
I WAS USING A FUTON BEFORE, BUT I PURCHASED A BED THIS TIME.
THE BED IS FILLING UP HALF OF YOUR ROOM...
Oh, a close-up.
I'D LOVE TO GET MORE NEW FURNITURE, BUT IT'S EXPENSIVE.
But I bought a chest made in Romania.
I'M INTO CHESS THIS YEAR, SO I BOUGHT A SMALL CHESS TABLE. IT'S CUTE.
Right now "Alice's Chess Set" is on it. I have a Disney chess set, too.
I'll collect more.
I'M REALLY INTO THE MENU FROM "SKY-LARK", NEAR OUR PLACE.
WHAT ARE YOU TALKING ABOUT?
"SKYLARK" HAS LOTS OF GOOD THINGS ON THE MENU. CLAMP RECOMMENDS THEIR "TUNA TATAKI MEAL." "THE CRAB MEAL" IS VERY GOOD, TOO.
Buttered corn is good, too.
I LIKE "LOTTERIA'S" ICED TEA. IT'S GOOD.
WE HAVE A JAPANESE RESTAURANT NEAR US. IT'S REALLY GREAT.
But I won't tell you the location.
WE'RE ALWAYS EATING! WE'LL PUT ON WEIGHT!
YEAH!
Crabs...
Because that's the only fun we have.
Just kidding.
Tee-hee.
BY THE WAY...
WE HAVE SOMETHING IMPORTANT TO TELL YOU.
ぱかん

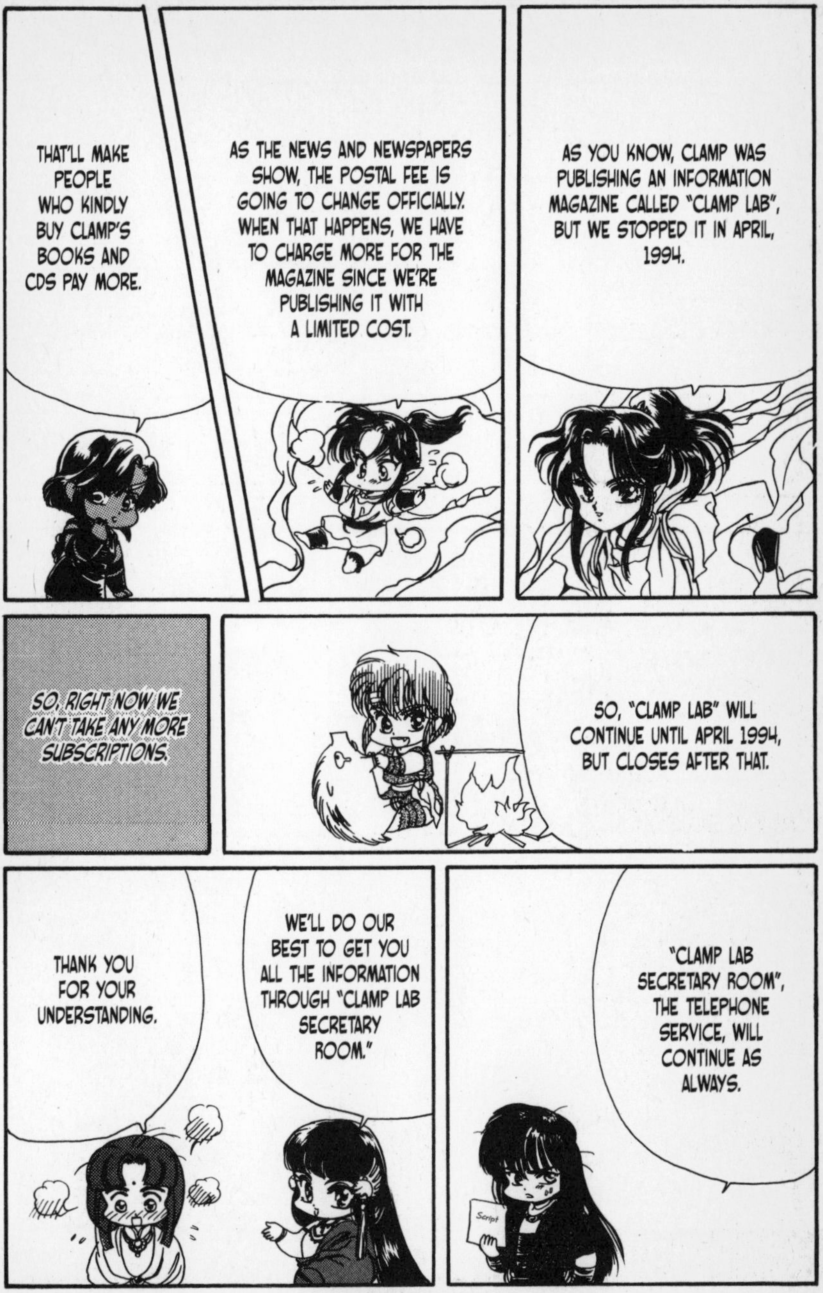
AS YOU KNOW, CLAMP WAS PUBLISHING AN INFORMATION MAGAZINE CALLED "CLAMP LAB", BUT WE STOPPED IT IN APRIL, 1994.
AS THE NEWS AND NEWSPAPERS SHOW, THE POSTAL FEE IS GOING TO CHANGE OFFICIALLY. WHEN THAT HAPPENS, WE HAVE TO CHARGE MORE FOR THE MAGAZINE SINCE WE'RE PUBLISHING IT WITH A LIMITED COST.
THAT'LL MAKE PEOPLE WHO KINDLY BUY CLAMP'S BOOKS AND CDS PAY MORE.
SO, "CLAMP LAB" WILL CONTINUE UNTIL APRIL 1994, BUT CLOSES AFTER THAT.
SO, RIGHT NOW WE CAN'T TAKE ANY MORE SUBSCRIPTIONS.
"CLAMP LAB SECRETARY ROOM", THE TELEPHONE SERVICE, WILL CONTINUE AS ALWAYS.
Script
WE'LL DO OUR BEST TO GET YOU ALL THE INFORMATION THROUGH "CLAMP LAB SECRETARY ROOM."
THANK YOU FOR YOUR UNDERSTANDING.

● "The Resurrection of Ashura" was published in "Wings" 9-11 edition in 1989, "Star Festival" was published in "South" Volume 3, "Flame of Destruction, Thunder of the King" was published in "South" Volume 4, and "Tomoshibi" was created just for this book.

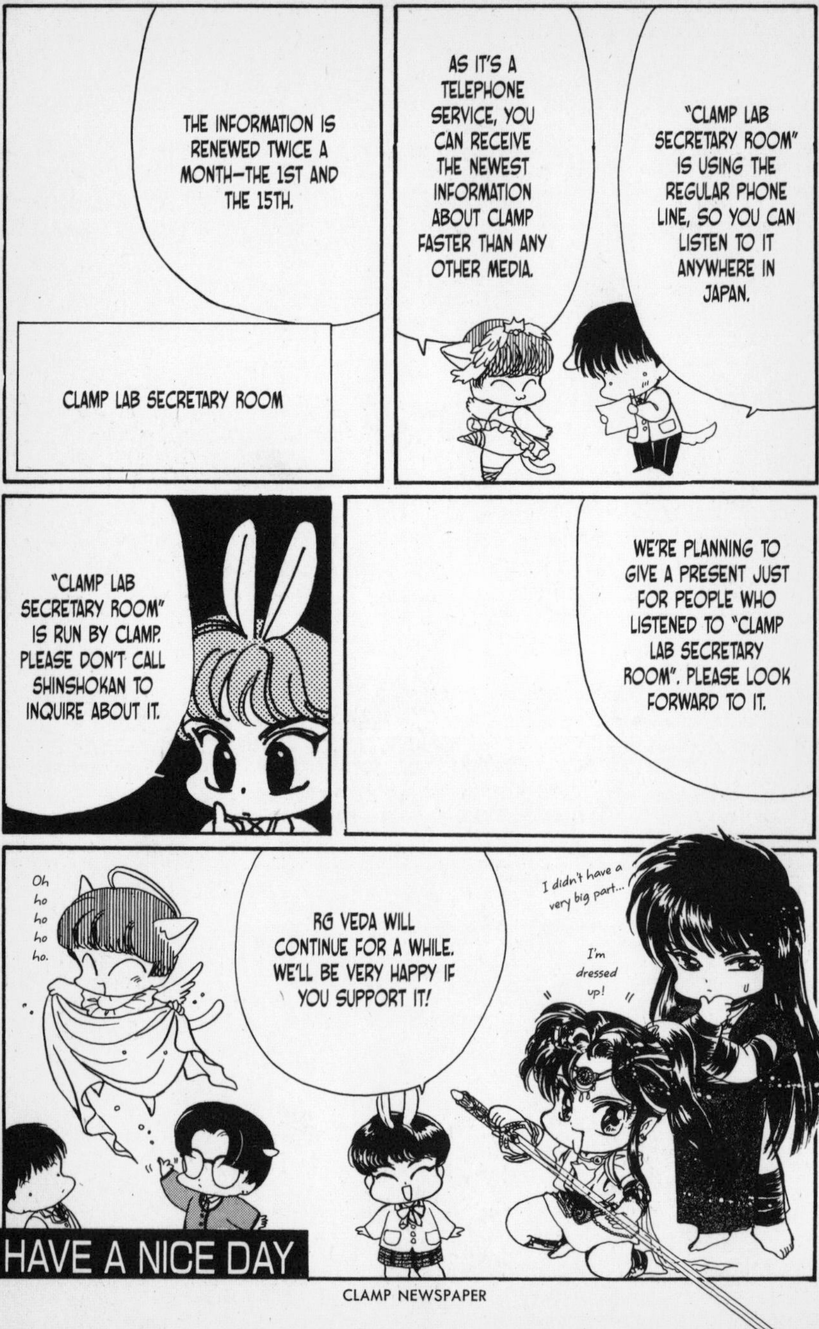
"CLAMP LAB SECRETARY ROOM" IS USING THE REGULAR PHONE LINE, SO YOU CAN LISTEN TO IT ANYWHERE IN JAPAN.
AS IT'S A TELEPHONE SERVICE, YOU CAN RECEIVE THE NEWEST INFORMATION ABOUT CLAMP FASTER THAN ANY OTHER MEDIA.
THE INFORMATION IS RENEWED TWICE A MONTH—THE 1ST AND THE 15TH.
CLAMP LAB SECRETARY ROOM
WE'RE PLANNING TO GIVE A PRESENT JUST FOR PEOPLE WHO LISTENED TO "CLAMP LAB SECRETARY ROOM". PLEASE LOOK FORWARD TO IT.
"CLAMP LAB SECRETARY ROOM" IS RUN BY CLAMP. PLEASE DON'T CALL SHINSHOKAN TO INQUIRE ABOUT IT.
I didn't have a very big part...
I'm dressed up!
RG VEDA WILL CONTINUE FOR A WHILE. WE'LL BE VERY HAPPY IF YOU SUPPORT IT!
Oh ho ho ho ho.
HAVE A NICE DAY

NEXT TIME IN RG VEDA

SOUMA AND RYUU-OU JOIN YASHA AND ASHURA'S JOURNEY. LED BY KUJAKU'S ADVICE, THEY GO TO KUSUMAPURA, THE DESTROYED CITY IN THE WEST-END OF HEAVEN, IN SEARCH OF THE SHURA SWORD-- THE KEY TO FINDING THE SIX STARS!

COMING SOON!

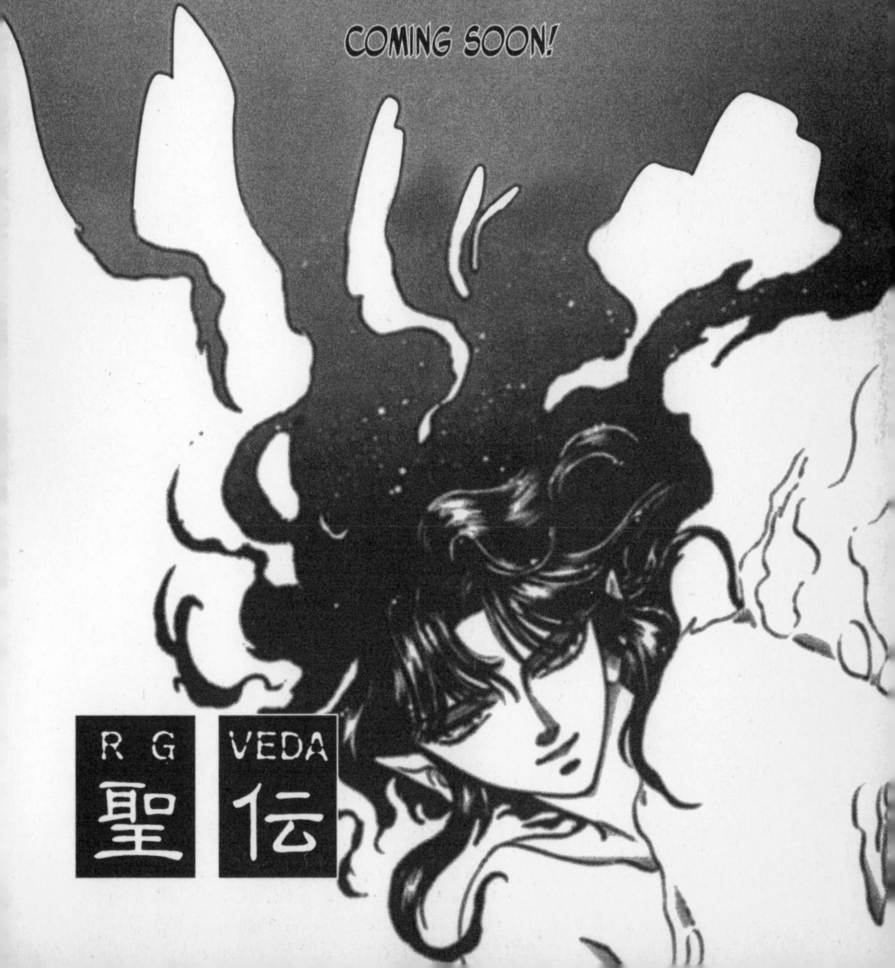
R G VEDA
聖伝

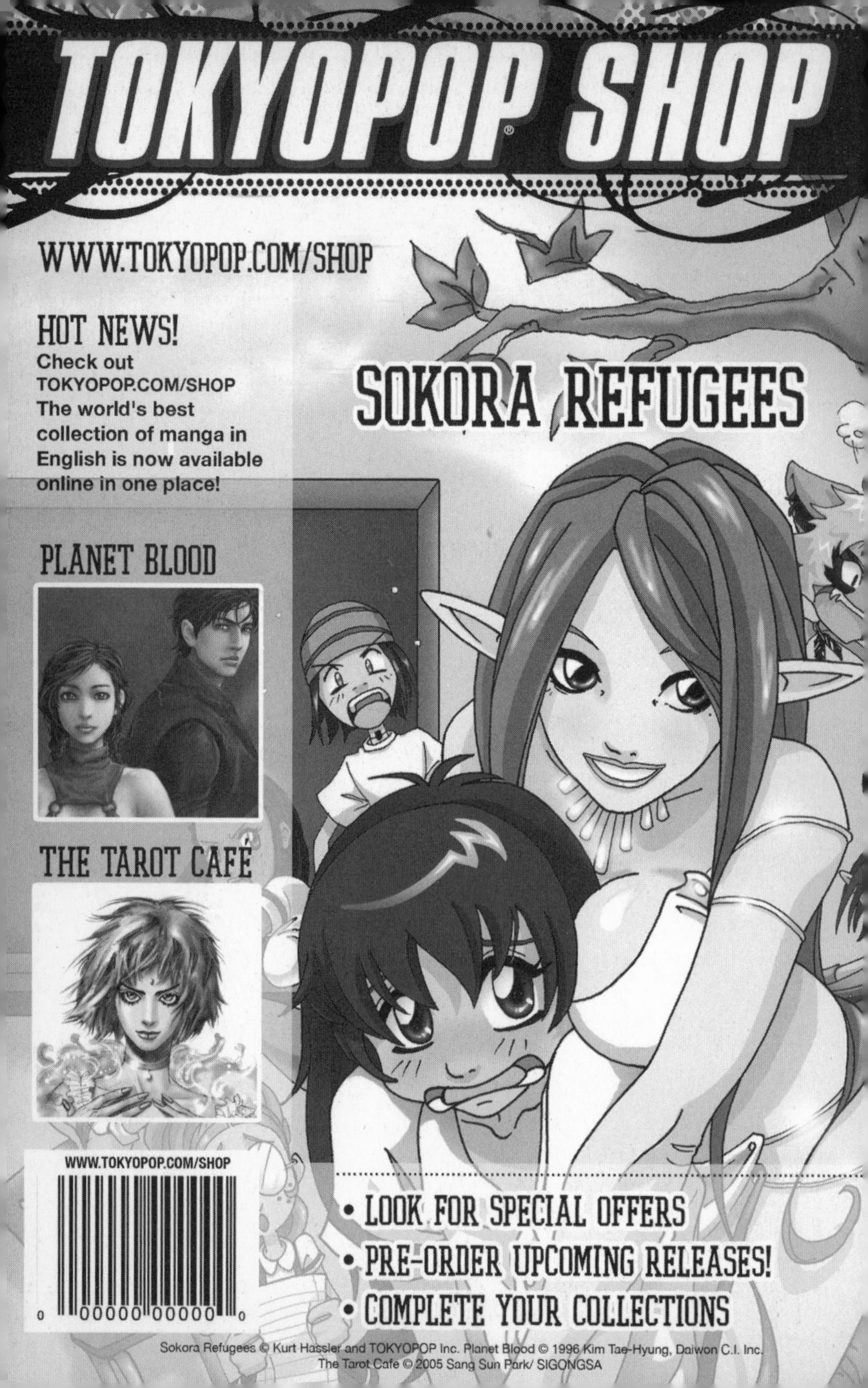
TOKYOPOP® SHOP
WWW.TOKYOPOP.COM/SHOP
HOT NEWS!
Check out TOKYOPOP.COM/SHOP The world's best collection of manga in English is now available online in one place!
SOKORA REFUGEES
PLANET BLOOD
THE TAROT CAFÉ
WWW.TOKYOPOP.COM/SHOP
0 00000 00000 0
• LOOK FOR SPECIAL OFFERS
• PRE-ORDER UPCOMING RELEASES!
• COMPLETE YOUR COLLECTIONS
Sokora Refugees © Kurt Hassler and TOKYOPOP Inc. Planet Blood © 1996 Kim Tae-Hyung, Daiwon C.I. Inc.
The Tarot Cafe © 2005 Sang Sun Park/ SIGONGSA

VAN VON HUNTER™

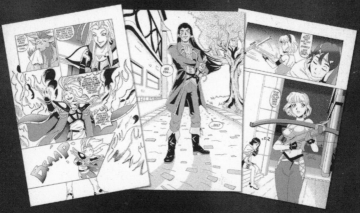

In the dark ages long ago, in a war-torn land where tranquility and harmony once blossomed, tyranny ruled with a flaming fist! At last, a hero arose to defeat the evildoers and returned hope to the people and peace to the countryside. Now...the sinister forces are back with a vengeance, and in their hour of direst-est need, the commoners once again seek a champion to right wrongs and triumph over villainy! Unfortunately, they could only get the mighty warrior Van Von Hunter, Hunter of Evil...Stuff!

Together with his loyal, memory-challenged sidekick, Van Von Hunter is on a never-ending quest to smite the bad guys—and believe us, they're real bad!

Preview the manga at:

www.TOKYOPOP.com/vanvonhunter
www.VanVonHunter.com

T TEEN AGE 13+

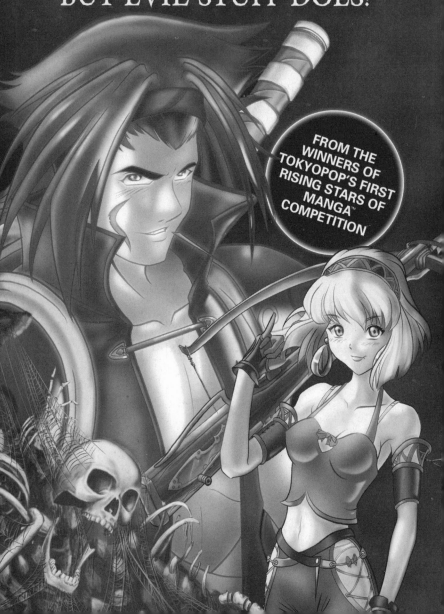

IN DREAM WORLD: FOLLOW YOUR DREAMS... BUT BEWARE OF THE NIGHTMARES!

Nightmares are bad enough when you are asleep, but in In Dream World, nightmares are real monsters! Drake, Hanee and Kyle battle these night terrors with special "In Dream Cards," magical cards that have unusual and devastating powers. Those who wield the cards gain the power of the elements, and our heroes must master the cards before they are put into a permanent state of sleep!

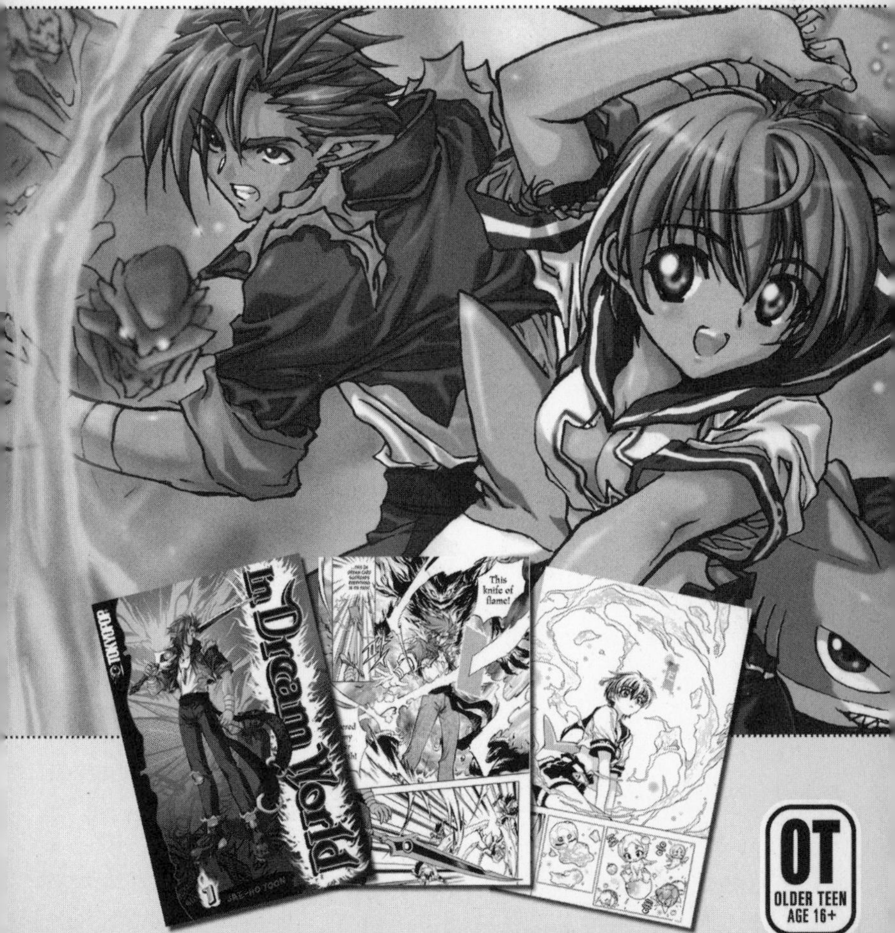
TOKYOPOP
In Dream World
JAE-HO YOON
This knife of flame!

OT
OLDER TEEN AGE 16+

For more information visit: **www.TOKYOPOP.com**

EDITORS' PICKS
TOKYOPOP MANGA SUPPLEMENT

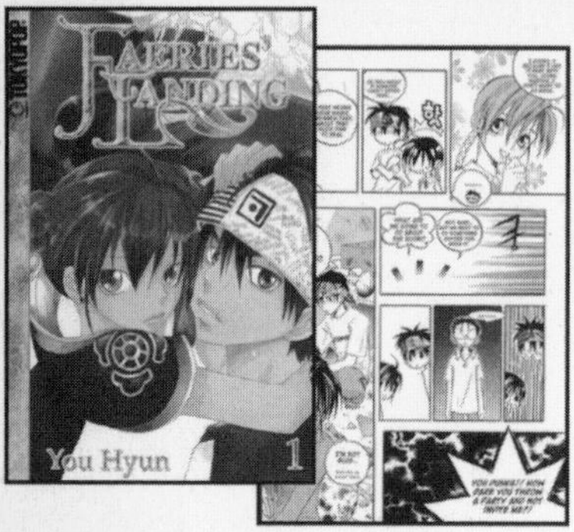

Faeries' Landing
You Hyun
1

BY YOU HYUN

FAERIES' LANDING

Following the misadventures of teenager Ryang Jegal and Fanta, a faerie who has fallen from the heavens straight into South Korea, *Faeries' Landing* is both a spoof of modern-day teen romance and a lighthearted fantasy epic. Imagine if Shakespeare's *A Midsummer Night's Dream* had come from the pen of Joss Whedon after about a dozen shots of espresso, and you have an idea of what to expect from You Hyun's funny little farce. Bursting with sharp wit, hip attitude and vibrant art, *Faeries' Landing* is guaranteed to get you giggling.

~Tim Beedle, Editor

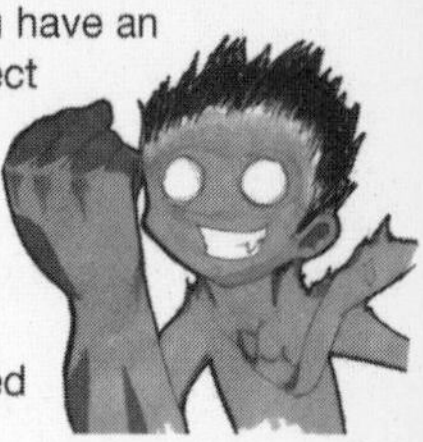

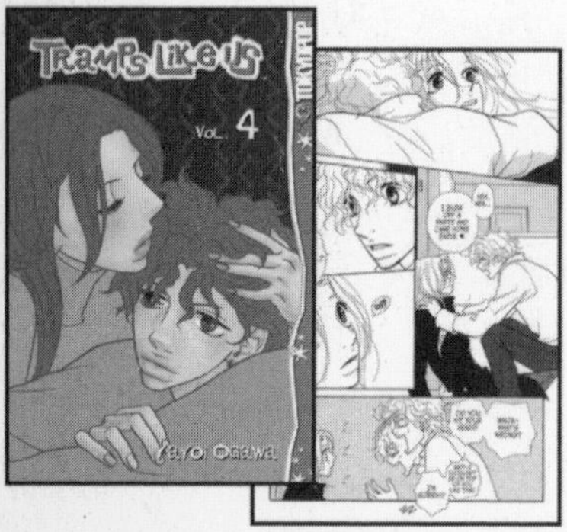

Tramps Like Us
Vol. 4
Yayoi Ogawa

BY YAYOI OGAWA

TRAMPS LIKE US

Yayoi Ogawa's *Tramps Like Us*—known as *Kimi wa Pet* in Japan—is the touching and humorous story of Sumire, a woman whose striking looks and drive for success alienate her from her friends and co-workers...until she takes in Momo, a cute homeless boy, as her "pet." As sketchy as the situation sounds, it turns out to be the sanest thing in Sumire's hectic life. In his quiet way, Momo teaches Sumire how to care for another being while also caring for herself...in other words, how to love. And there ain't nothin' wrong with that.

~Carol Fox, Editor

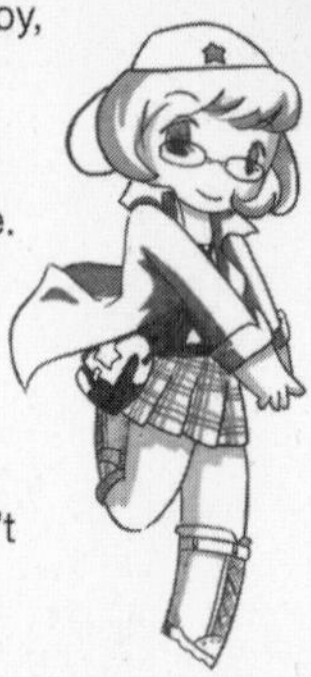

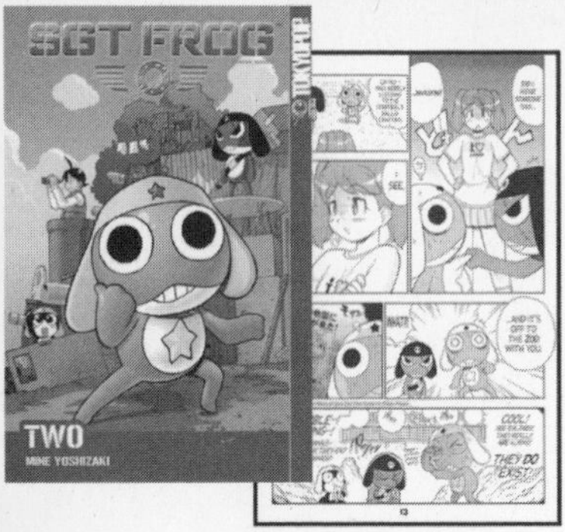
SGT FROG
TWO
MINE YOSHIZAKI

BY MINE YOSHIZAKI

SGT FROG

Sgt. Frog is so absurdly comical, it has me in stitches every time I edit it. Mine Yoshizaki's clever sci-fi spoof showcases the hijinks of Sergeant Keroro, a cuddly looking alien, diabolically determined to oppress our planet! While some E.T.s phone home, this otherworldly menace has your number! Abandoned on Earth, Keroro takes refuge in the Hinata home, whose residents quickly take advantage of his stellar cleaning skills. But between scrubbing, vacuuming and an unhealthy obsession with Gundam models, Keroro still finds time to plot the subjugation of humankind!

~ Paul Morrissey, Editor

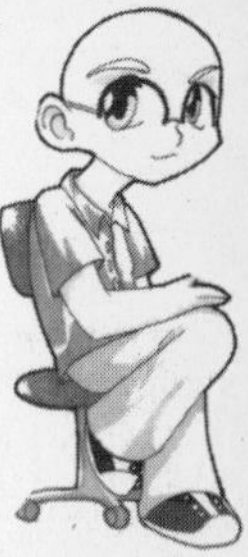

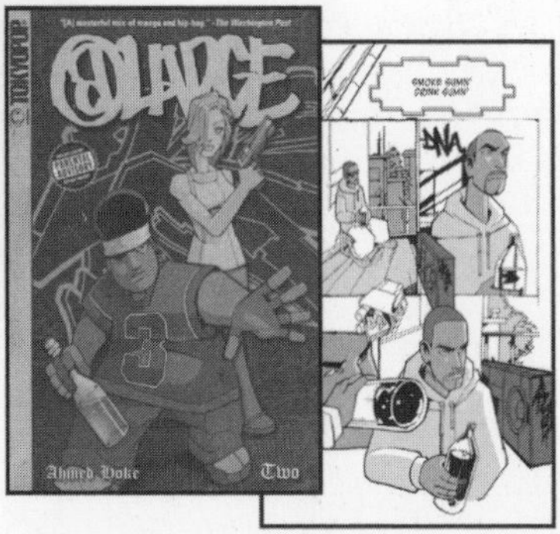
Ahmed Hoke
Two

BY AHMED HOKE

@LARGE

Ahmed Hoke's revolutionary hip-hop manga is a groundbreaking graphic novel. While at first glace this series may seem like a dramatic departure from traditional manga styles, on a deeper level one will find a rich, lyrical world full of wildly imaginative characters, intense action and heartfelt human emotions. This is a truly unique manga series that needs to be read by everyone—whether they are fans of hip-hop or not.

~Rob Valois, Editor

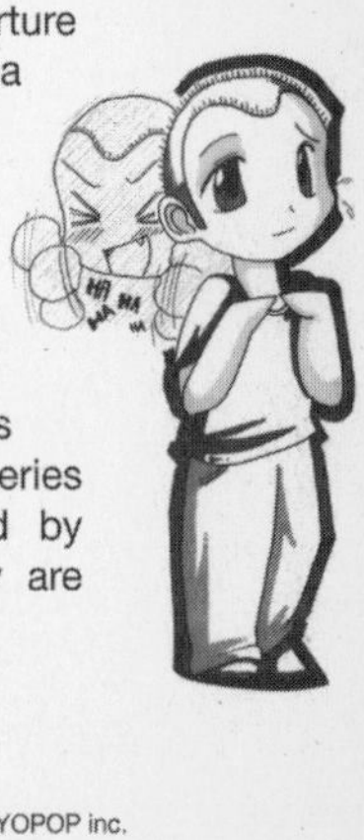

SHOWCASE TOKYOPOP MANGA SUPPLEMENT

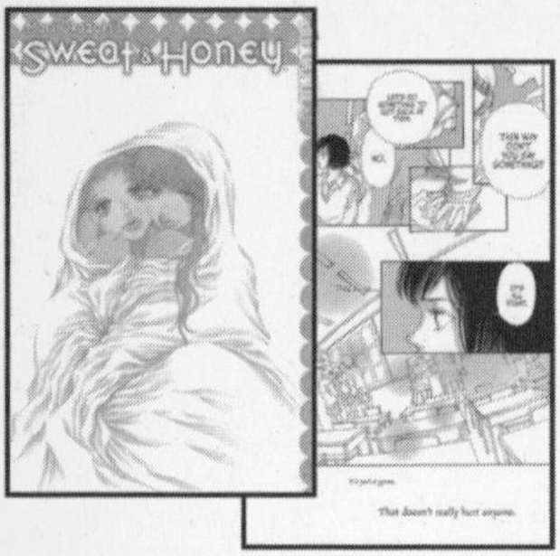
Sweat & Honey

PASSION FRUIT

BY MARI OKAZAKI

Passion Fruit is a unique, unforgettable collection of stylish stories that touch upon our most private inhibitions and examine our deepest desires. This uncompromising blend of realism and raw emotion focuses on women exploring the vulnerability and frailty of the human condition. With uninhibited authenticity and pathos, passion proves to be stranger than fiction.

OT OLDER TEEN AGE 16+

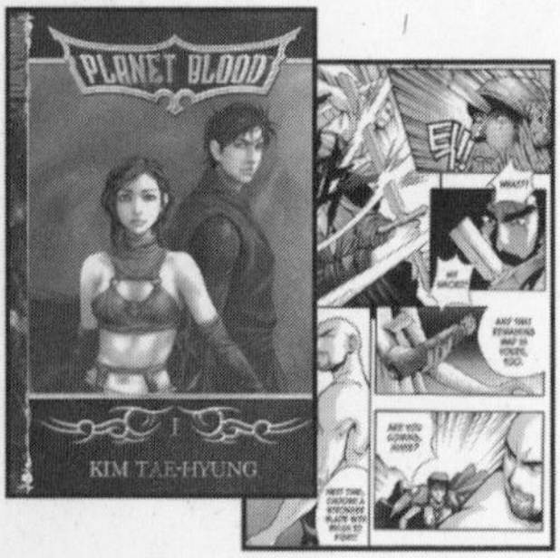
PLANET BLOOD
1
KIM TAE-HYUNG

PLANET BLOOD

BY TAE-HYUNG KIM

Universal Century 0091. The Mars and Moon colonies fight for repatriation rights over the newly restored Earth. Amidst the bloody battle, one soldier, is rendered unconscious—only to awaken in an entirely different world enmeshed in an entirely different war...

T TEEN AGE 13+

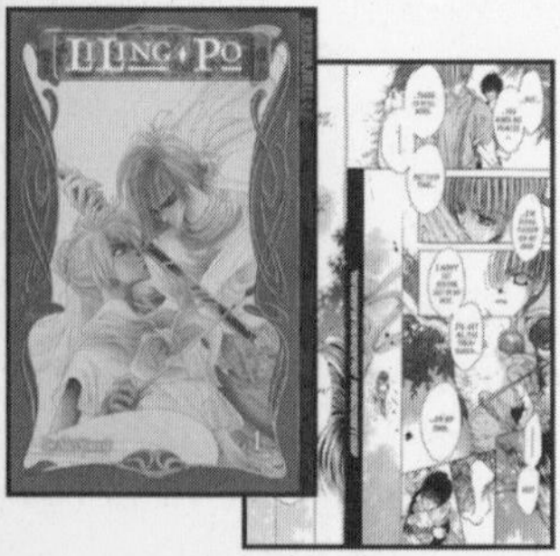
LILING-PO

LILING-PO

BY AKO YUTENJI

Master thief Liling-Po has finally been captured! However, the government offers a chance for Liling-Po to redeem himself. All he has to do is "retrieve" some special items—eight mystic treasures that are fabled to grant their owners any wish!

T TEEN AGE 13+

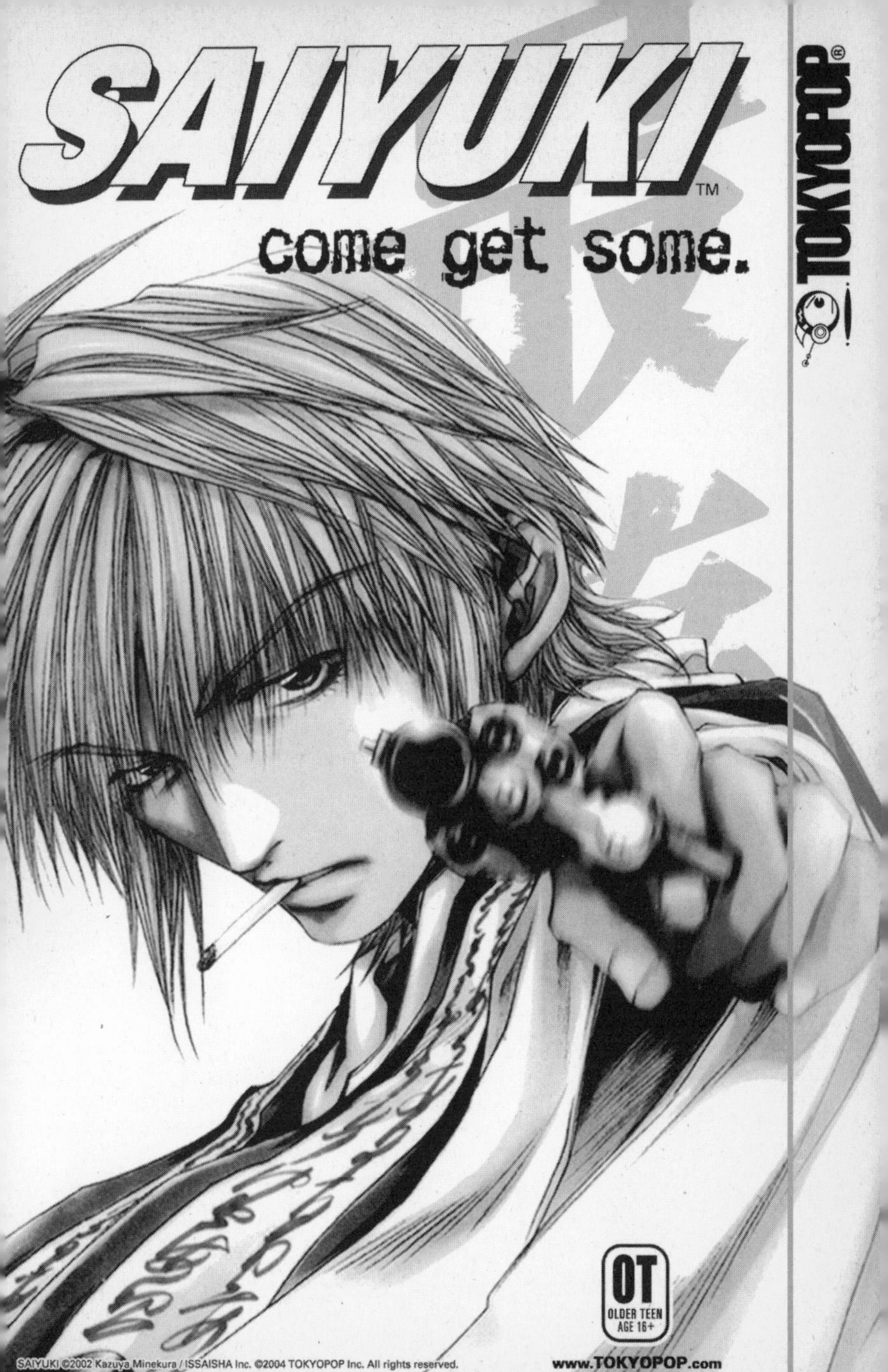
SAIYUKI™
come get some.
TOKYOPOP®
OT
OLDER TEEN
AGE 16+

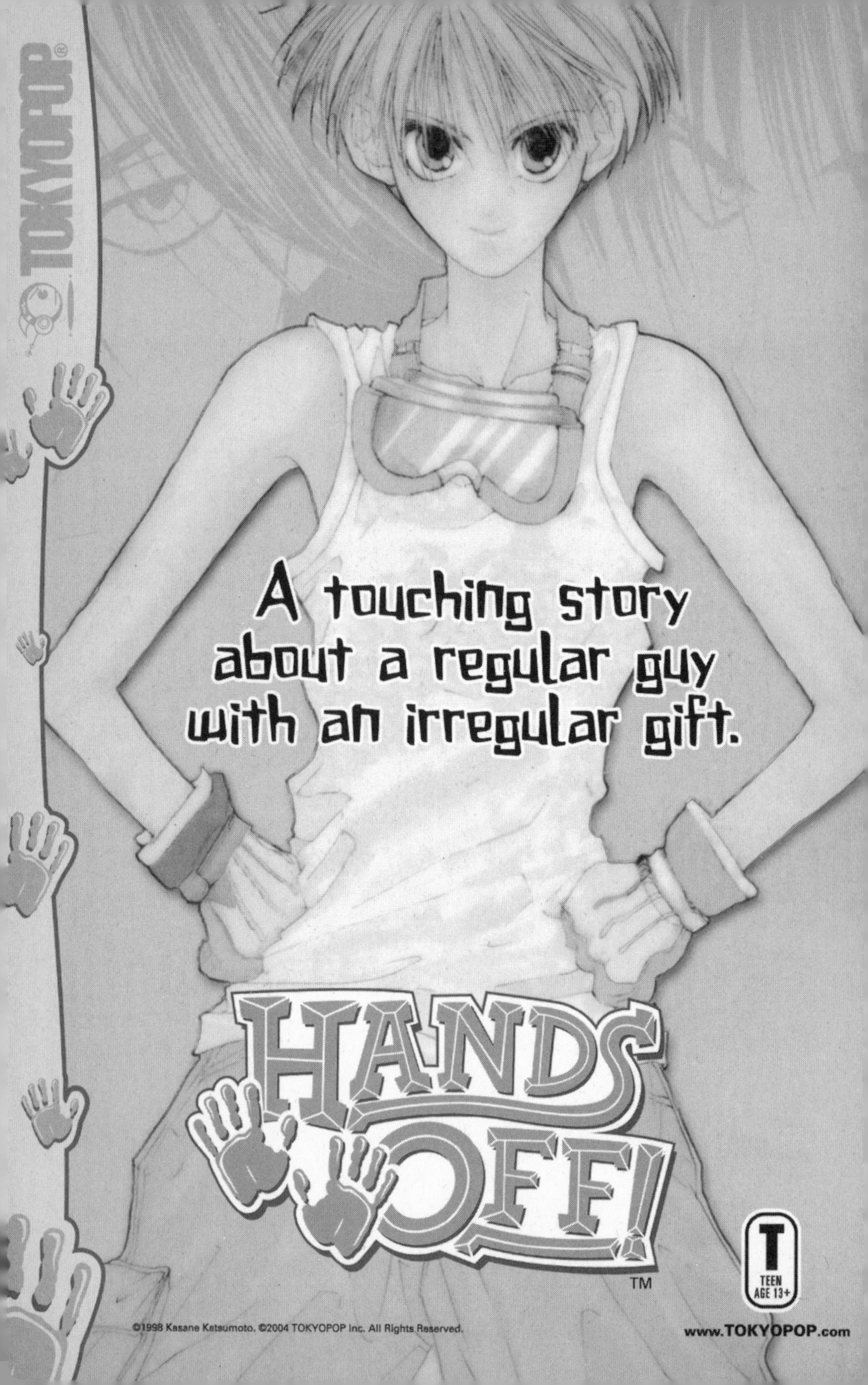
TOKYOPOP®
A touching story
about a regular guy
with an irregular gift.
HANDS OFF!
TM
T
TEEN
AGE 13+
www.TOKYOPOP.com

STOP!

This is the back of the book.
You wouldn't want to spoil a great ending!

This book is printed "manga-style," in the authentic Japanese right-to-left format. Since none of the artwork has been flipped or altered, readers get to experience the story just as the creator intended. You've been asking for it, so TOKYOPOP® delivered: authentic, hot-off-the-press, and far more fun!

DIRECTIONS

1
2
3
4
5
6
7
8
9
10

If this is your first time reading manga-style, here's a quick guide to help you understand how it works.

It's easy... just start in the top right panel and follow the numbers. Have fun, and look for more 100% authentic manga from TOKYOPOP®!

100% AUTHENTIC MANGA
品質第一公式商品

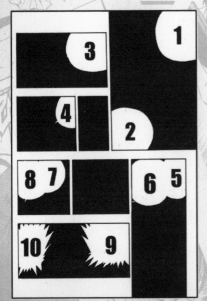

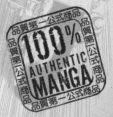